Why People Get Lost

Why People Get Lost
The psychology and neuroscience of spatial cognition

Paul A. Dudchenko, PhD
Senior Lecturer
Department of Psychology
University of Stirling

OXFORD
UNIVERSITY PRESS

OXFORD
UNIVERSITY PRESS

Great Clarendon Street, Oxford OX2 6DP

Oxford University Press is a department of the University of Oxford.
It furthers the University's objective of excellence in research, scholarship,
and education by publishing worldwide in

Oxford New York

Athens Auckland Bangkok Bogotá Buenos Aires Cape-Town
Chennai Dar es Salaam Delhi Florence Hong Kong Istanbul Karachi
Kolkata Kuala Lumpur Madrid Melbourne Mexico City Mumbai Nairobi
Paris São Paulo Shanghai Singapore Taipei Tokyo Toronto Warsaw

with associated companies in Berlin Ibadan

Oxford is a registered trade mark of Oxford University Press
in the UK and in certain other countries

Published in the United States
by Oxford University Press Inc., New York

British Library Cataloguing in Publication Data

Data available

Library of Congress Cataloguing in Publication Data

Data available

Typeset in Minion by Glyph International., Bangalore, India
Printed in Great Britain
on acid-free paper by
MPG Books Group, Bodmin and King's Lynn

ISBN 978–0–19–921086–2

10 9 8 7 6 5 4 3 2 1

For Molly and Sam

Acknowledgements

The opportunity to write this book has arisen with the support of several institutions and individuals. First, from a personal and professional standpoint, I like to acknowledge the support of my wife, Dr Emma R. Wood. Her critical reading of what follows has been invaluable in improving this text. On a personal level, her willingness to hold down the fort at home with our young children has given me the time to concentrate on this endeavour. From an institutional perspective, I'd like to thank the University of Stirling for providing the sabbatical leave during which much of the research and writing for this book took place. I'd also like to thank the Biotechnology and Biological Sciences Research Council (United Kingdom) for their support of my research over the past several years. Their support has enabled me to attract talented researchers to my laboratory, including Dr Larissa E. Zinyuk and Dr James A. Ainge. I'd also like to acknowledge the outstanding students who I've had the privilege of working with, including Dr Matthijs van der Meer, Dr Stephen Huang, and David Bett. Finally, I'd like to thank my academic mentors over the years: Professor Martin Sarter, who introduced me to science; Professor Jeffrey S. Taube, who introduced me to electrophysiology and the fascinating phenomenon of head direction neurons; and Professor Howard Eichenbaum, who introduced me to the wonders of the hippocampus.

Preface

I work at a small university in the United Kingdom, and for a period of several years I commuted to and from it by train. On my way home from work in the evening, I occasionally had a very powerful sense that the train was going in the wrong direction—not homeward, but back towards the university. This sense of disorientation usually occurred when I drifted off while reading a document or book. From an intellectual standpoint I knew that the train hadn't changed directions. However, I had a compelling 'gut' sense that the train was heading the wrong way. As I will describe in this book, such a sense of disorientation, and even the specific experience of disorientation on a moving train, is not uncommon.

My work at the university is on the relationship between the brain and the ability to find one's way around an environment. It turns out that a great deal is known about how space—in the sense of one's spatial location and one's direction in an environment—is represented in the mammalian brain. My goal in writing this book is to summarize this large and growing body of knowledge. The reader I envisioned would be a student joining my laboratory. I wished to take them from the beginnings of the psychology and neuroscience of spatial cognition, to a complete review of what is currently known. Such a treatment would assume no specialized knowledge of spatial learning or neuroscience, but would still be of interest for those with a background in the field.

Beyond reviewing what we know about spatial cognition, I also wish to build a tentative link between our experience of getting lost and what we know about the neuroscience of spatial orientation. Doubtless, this link will be incomplete, as our knowledge of the brain is incomplete. But I believe that we can start to speculate about how our brain misleads us, and we can certainly reflect on one of the universal experiences of mankind: getting lost.

Contents

1 On being lost *1*

2 A history of 'maze' psychology *9*

3 Contemporary studies of spatial cognition *31*

4 Human navigation *65*

5 Spatial cognition in children *93*

6 The hippocampus as a cognitive map *115*

7 Place cells and brain imaging *153*

8 The neural basis for a sense of direction: head direction neurons *191*

9 Alzheimer's disease, the parietal lobe, and topographical disorientation *221*

10 Why we get lost *251*

References *257*

Index *295*

Chapter 1

On being lost

In 1900, the famous Scottish mountaineer William W. Naismith set out to walk up a mountain in the Scottish highlands.[1] Although Scottish mountains are not high in absolute elevation, they are subject to extreme weather and sudden, disorienting mists. Naismith was not well equipped for the walk, and did not have a map or compass. He also started late in the day—5 p.m.—and brought only two small sandwiches. Naismith climbed for about 2 ½ hours and reached what he took to be the summit of Ben More, the mountain he had intended to climb.

Then a mist descended. The tops of adjacent peaks—useful orientation landmarks when visible—became shrouded in the cloud. Naismith descended from the mountaintop in the direction that he thought would take him back home. However, as he reached the base of the mountain he realized that something was amiss. 'By-and-by the air cleared sufficiently to show me that I was in a strange country . . . Oh for a map and compass!'

Instead of returning in the direction of his lodgings, he had come down the other side of the mountain. It was raining heavily. 'I was wet through, dead beat and painfully hungry', Naismith recounts. He sat down to rest and noticed a streak of red in the sky. In June, in northern Scotland, the sun does not set until nearly midnight. Naismith realized that he was facing the wrong direction, and, perhaps equally galling, that the only sure way of return was to re-climb the mountain and descend it in the correct direction. At 1.30 a.m., 6 hours after first reaching the summit of the mountain, he reached it a second time. This time, however, he descended in the correct direction, and reached the lodge where he had begun his walk at 4 a.m.

Naismith became disoriented because the visual landmarks he might have used to orient himself—adjacent peaks, the setting sun, and the village

---

[1] William Naismith is known for his method of estimating how long it takes to walk a given distance, known as Naismith's rule: assuming the walker is fit, one can walk 3 miles in 1 hour, with an additional hour for every 2,000 ft. of uphill climbing. The account of Naismith's disorientation on Ben More is based on that found in *The Munroist's Companion*, by Robin N. Campbell.

below—were obscured by a thick mist. Without these landmarks, he presumably thought he was maintaining the correct direction, but his directional sense was quite evidently unreliable.

A second account of being lost highlights the difficulty of losing sight of a distinctive landmark—the sun—and trying to find one's way in a deep forest. Primo Levi, an Italian chemist, was held in a German prison camp near Auschwitz during World War II. His experience in the camp is described in *If This Is a Man*, and in a second book, *The Truce*, he describes his indirect return to Italy following the liberation of the prison camp by the Russians. At one point, Levi is housed by the Russians in Starye Dorogi, a small village in current-day Belarus. The village was surrounded by deep forests, and the first time Levi explored these woods on his own he became lost:

> . . . I learnt to my cost, with surprise and fear, that the risk of 'losing oneself in a wood' existed not only in fairy tales. I had been walking for about an hour, orienting myself as best I could by the sun, which was visible occasionally, where the branches were less thick; but then the sky clouded over, threatening rain, and when I wanted to return I realized that I had lost the north. Moss on the tree trunks? It covered them on all sides. I set out in what seemed the correct direction; but after a long and painful walk through the brambles and undergrowth I found myself in as unrecognizable a spot as that from which I had started.

Levi continued walking for hours and worried that he would remain lost in the deep forest and perish. As it began to get dark, and the mosquitoes increased their activity, he tried to head north by keeping the brighter bit of sky to his left.

> . . . I continued in the prolonged twilight of the northern summer, until it was almost night, a prey now to utter panic, to the age-old fear of the dark, the forest and the unknown. Despite my weariness, I felt a violent impulse to rush headlong in any direction, and to continue running so long as my strength and breath lasted.

Eventually, Levi heard a train whistle coming from what he thought was the wrong direction. He realized that he, not the train, was heading the wrong way. Levi followed the sound of the train until he reached the train tracks, and then followed the tracks until he returned to the village.

Levi's eloquent description of his ordeal highlights the descent from a rationale attempt to find one's way to a sense of panic. He describes having a 'violent impulse' to run in any direction. This panic was also experienced by a lost hunter in Canada. He was hunting for partridges, and was drawn more deeply into the woods until he became quite disoriented. He tried to head in the direction in which he thought he would encounter a familiar road, but as the hours passed his apprehension increased: 'I fought off several waves of overwhelming panic—every tree looked familiar, every stone, every clearing—but it wasn't'.

Eventually, the hunter emerged from the woods very near the point at which he had entered them.[2]

Of course, this sense of getting 'turned around' isn't limited to misty mountain tops or deep woods. In an entertaining and anecdote-filled book entitled *Inner Navigation*, Erik Jonsson, a Swedish engineer and navigation enthusiast, describes his own experience of disorientation in Paris. He had travelled to Paris from Sweden, and taken the subway to his hotel. At his hotel:

> ... I looked out of my window [and] I saw the old city gate called Porte Saint-Martin in what I felt was north despite the fact that the map showed it was in the south. My sense of direction must have been confused during the underground ride, so that when I emerged into the street at the [subway] station, my 'automatic pilot' jumped to the wrong conclusion and made me feel that north was south. (p. 17)

Indeed, the French psychologist Alfred Binet, developer of one of the first I.Q. tests, describes several observations of what he termed 'Reverse illusions of orientation' (1894). Binet relates the experience of a colleague at the Collége de France:

> I have often felt a complete change of direction on the railroad or in a carriage. It has been generally on waking from a more or less profound sleep, or after some degree of drowsiness, that I have had this illusion. For example, being asleep in the car, I was at a given moment awakened by the arrival of the train at the station, and by the noise of the depot. Then sleep began to seize me. The departure of the train caused an awakening more or less complete, and it then seemed to me that the direction of the journey was absolutely changed. I remember very clearly having under these conditions a moment of very disagreeable anxiety, of real pain. It was only after some moments that, after thoroughly waking, I recognized my error, by comparing the relative situations of the different objects. (p. 343)

Binet also describes his personal experience of an 'illusion of direction' in the Louvre Museum. He frequented the museum, and often lost his sense of direction as he travelled from room to room. On one occasion, he chanced upon an open window that provided a view of the Seine River below. Binet writes: 'I saw the Seine rolling before me from left to right; but it seemed quite wrong, for in the position in which I found myself the Seine ought, as I thought, to roll in the opposite direction: the landscape seemed to be turned around'.

As these examples illustrate, and as the reader's own experience will likely confirm, an occasional sense of spatial disorientation is a universal occurrence.

---

[2] The anxiety and panic associated with getting lost doubtless increases the danger of the situation. Thus, the advice given by the search and rescue expert Gordon Snow is to: 'stop, sit down, and gather your thoughts'. Running in an unknown direction, Snow writes, serves no purpose.

But why do we get turned around? One account can again be found in Jonnson's *Inner Navigation*:

> . . .humans must have a 'direction sense' that we are not aware of. Our minds have a directional reference frame that we rely on to orient ourselves. It is the mainstay of our spatial system. We know in which direction to go, but if we are asked how we know, we would have no answer. It is automatic. When something goes wrong so that it works against us, it becomes a terrible nuisance; when it works right, it is a tremendous asset. And it does work right most of the time—astonishingly so. (p. 19)

But do humans (and other mammals) really have an internal sense of direction? If so, where is it? How does it develop? Are there brain disorders that specifically interfere with spatial abilities? These are the questions I will address in subsequent chapters.

Before doing so, I will define what we mean by being 'lost', and its converse–spatial orientation. Being lost means being unable to find one's way. In neurological studies, this inability to way-find in a large-scale space is sometimes referred to as *topographical disorientation*. Under normal circumstances, we spend our days in quite familiar surroundings: our homes, our places of work, our neighbourhoods. Having experienced these environments repeatedly, and having travelled between them extensively, we find our way with little apparent effort. Indeed, our routines for travelling from one location to another can become so automatic that we find ourselves unintentionally driving to work on a Sunday morning having started for the grocery store.

As a digression, I'll mention that there are instances where brain damage may interfere with navigation even in the most familiar of environments. For example, Paterson and Zangwill (1945) describe a British patient who was struck in the head by a mortar fragment. The fragment damaged a portion of the right-hand side of the brain, and initially the patient displayed some difficulties in recognition memory and a tendency to neglect the environment to his left. In addition to these problems, he was unable to recognize rooms in the hospital where he stayed, or even his home when taken there from the hospital. He also mistook a salient landmark in his hometown of Edinburgh, Arthur's Seat (an extinct volcano near the cite centre), for another location. For this patient, the ability to recognize familiar landmarks and use these as orientation cues was severely disrupted.

But what if we find ourselves someplace unfamiliar? If I were to leave my office now, drive a few hours north into the Scottish highlands, leave my car and begin climbing a hill, I could quickly get to a location that I'd never visited before—an unfamiliar surrounding. Would I be lost? Probably not. On my return journey to the car I would likely recognize landmarks that were encountered on my outward trip—a large, upturned boulder, a lone

Scots pine, a gurgling burn (small stream)—and use these landmarks to guide my navigation.

So, being someplace unfamiliar doesn't necessarily mean we can't find our way. How then, do we get lost? As the anecdotes above suggest, disorientation may occur when visual landmarks are unavailable.[3] For Naismith, distinctive mountain peaks and valleys were obscured by a thick mist. For Primo Levi, the homogeneity of a forest provided no distinctive information regarding which direction he was heading. In the absence of distinctive landmarks, we must rely on how well we are able to monitor the distances and directions we've travelled. As will be evident in a subsequent chapter, our capacity for doing so is quite limited. A related case would be navigating in the presence of relatively novel landmarks. If, on my trip to an unfamiliar patch of the Scottish highlands I didn't make an effort to attend to the stimuli I encountered as I walked (and my incidental attention is weak or directed elsewhere), it's quite possible that these would no longer be sufficient to guide my return route. In other situations our direction sense may become 'turned around'—as suggested by the experiences of Erik Jonsson and Alfred Binet's colleague. This type of disorientation suggests that we possess an internal mechanism for orienting in our environment. This mechanism may work seamlessly in most situations, but may become detached from reality when we interrupt our contact with our environment by sleeping, or by attending to one aspect of the environment (for example, a newspaper we might be reading) while being passively transported on a train or bus. Spatial orientation thus appears to require:

(1) a recognition of one's surrounding;

(2) an ability to use familiar landmarks to decide which way we need to turn; or

(3) a maintenance of orientation by keeping track of previous experience. A failure of any of these may get us lost.

Of course, there are many ways in which we can plot our course, or *navigate* from one location to another. Only the foolhardy would enter the Scottish mountains in the mist without a compass and map. If the sun or the North Star is out, we can estimate direction in the absence of a compass. We can use the alignment of the sand dunes in the desert, the sastrugi (small snow drifts) on

---

[3] A fictional account of getting lost in a Russian snowstorm is found in Leo Tolstoy's short story *The Snow Storm*. In it, the narrator spends a long night in a horse-drawn sledge, being driven in circles, and experiences vivid dreams as he drifts in and out of an exhausted sleep.

the polar ice caps, or the prevailing winds in Polynesia to estimate direction. But these are *acquired* strategies for wayfinding. We're not born with the knowledge of how to use a map and compass—we must learn this. Indeed, as O'Keefe and Nadel (1978) suggest, and as the reader's experience may confirm, identifying where one is on a map can require a considerable amount of deduction. 'If I am here', one may reason, 'then the next road on my left should be High Street'. Such a hypothetico-deductive strategy may allow us to match our three-dimensional views with the two-dimensional representation provided by a map.

The concern of the current work, however, is not with the range of navigational strategies one might learn, but rather with our native ability to find our way in the world, and the neural bases for this ability. This innate ability is likely to be shared, and perhaps exceeded, by other mammals, and thus the findings from animals such as rats, hamsters, and monkeys speak to our human capacities. As I shall describe, recordings from individual neurons within the mammalian brain have revealed surprisingly specific types of encoding for spatial information. Also, experiments using rats and hamsters have suggested that it is possible to keep track of where one has come from by knowing the distance and direction in which one has moved. For example, in complete darkness, rats can leave a nest, wander about an environment until they encounter food, and then run straight back to the nest. Such 'homing' behaviour, independent of external landmarks, and thus presumably dependent on an internal integration of distance and directions travelled, is referred to as *path integration*.

When we consider how we find our way—what psychologists refer to as spatial cognition—we need to make clear what our reference point is. If we are talking about the location of things relative to ourselves, we are considering *egocentric* space. For example, as I write these words, my coffee mug is to my left. If I were to walk around to the other side of my desk and not move my coffee mug, it would be to my right. Egocentric space is the 'left—right' and 'front—back' space we use when specifying locations relative to our bodies. If our reference point were absolute space—where we are located relative to other objects in our surroundings—we would be talking about *allocentric* space. If I had a Global Positioning System on my desk, I could obtain the coordinates for my absolute, or allocentric, position on this planet.

Finally, in describing what is known about spatial cognition and the brain, I have made certain assumptions about the world which, as a disclaimer, I lay bare to the reader now. First, I assume that absolute space exists, and that the outside world isn't simply a construct of our minds. This is a specific case of a general positivism that I hold: there is a reality, and it is knowable. Second, the absolute space that surrounds us is represented, to an extent, in our brains. This representation, I will argue, is prone to an accumulating error when we travel in an ambiguous environment or are inattentive. If uncorrected, we become lost.

Chapter 2

A history of 'maze' psychology

As part of my teaching at the university, I offer a small course on the history of psychology. My motivation for offering this course is both personal—it was one of my favourites as an undergraduate—and practical; students were wary of the difficulty of my previous course, 'Biological bases of animal spatial cognition', and did not enrol in it in large numbers.

The truth is, however, that both topics are intertwined: the history of psychology is, in part, a history of how rats find their way in mazes. Psychologists at the beginning of the 20th century attempted to answer basic questions of how the learning process occurs by using these small animals, with the underlying assumption that the basic processes of learning and memory can be more easily controlled and studied in experimental animals. This is a *reductionist* approach—an attempt to answer a question by using the simpler example of a phenomenon. As we'll see, however, learning and spatial cognition in rodents is by no means simple, but this work has yielded a great deal of information on the brain and spatial behaviour. Many mazes are essentially spatial tasks: a rat running a maze is a mammal navigating to a spatially defined goal. Understanding how a rat remembers where a food reward is in a maze may help us understand how we remember where we've parked our car in a crowded parking lot.

So what follows has a historical flavour. I first consider behaviourism and the earliest studies of maze-running with rats. Next, I describe the studies of spatial learning done by Edward Chase Tolman and his students. I conclude with a description of Tolman's influential 'cognitive map' view.

The rise of behaviourism

The tension within the field of psychology, as it established itself as a discipline, centred around the question of what, exactly, was the correct approach and subject matter for psychological investigation. Was psychology—the study of the mind—a hard science like chemistry or physics, or was it something else? Wilhelm Wundt, credited with establishing the first psychology laboratory in Leipszig, Germany, in 1879, had a very broad view of psychology. For him, it included not just how the human mind processed stimuli from the outside world, but also topics like social or ethnic psychology, and the study of animals and children (Hothersall 2004).

Wundt's true legacy to psychology, perhaps, lies is the astonishing number of Ph.D. students he supervized: 186. One of these in particular, Edward Titchener, was to take psychology in a decidedly, and exclusively, human direction. Titchener was a brilliant student, and a powerful personality. For him, psychology was the study of the contents of human experience. These could be broken down into three categories: sensations, images, and feelings. Titchener's technique was to have trained 'subjects' reflect on their perceptions of stimuli. This was termed introspection.

The problem with introspection, however, was that it was subjective and difficult to replicate. Whose introspections were valid, and whose were not? How did one laboratory replicate the findings of another? Was Titchener always right?

A young man by the name of John B. Watson was to lead the charge against introspection. Watson was from North Carolina, and grew up poor. He worked his way through college, and, at the University of Chicago, conducted elegant studies on the spatial behaviour of rats in mazes. Watson believed that if psychology was to advance, it must adopt the methods of the hard sciences. It could not languish in the subjective assessment of the contents of experience that introspection provided. In his call to arms entitled 'Psychology as the behaviorist views it' (1913) Watson wrote:

> I do not wish unduly to criticize psychology. It has failed signally, I believe, during the fifty-odd years of its existence as an experimental discipline to make its place in the world as an undisputed natural science. Psychology, as it is generally thought of, has something esoteric in its methods. If you fail to reproduce my findings, it is not due to some fault in your apparatus or in the control of your stimulus, but it is due to the fact that your introspection is untrained. The attack is made upon the observer and not upon the experimental setting. In physics and in chemistry the attack is made upon the experimental conditions. The apparatus was not sensitive enough, impure chemicals were used, etc. In these sciences a better technique will give reproducible results. Psychology is otherwise. If you can't observe 3–9 states of clearness in attention, your introspection is poor.

As an alternative Watson proposed the objective approach of *behaviorism*:

> Psychology as the behaviorist views it is a purely objective experimental branch of natural science. Its theoretical goal is the prediction and control of behavior. Introspection forms no essential part of its methods, nor is the scientific value of its data dependent upon the readiness with which they lend themselves to interpretation in terms of consciousness. The behaviorist, in his efforts to get a unitary scheme of animal response, recognizes no dividing line between man and brute. The behavior of

man, with all of its refinement and complexity, forms only a part of the behaviorist's total scheme of investigation.

Thus, an early concern of psychology was behaviour, and one of the early applications of this concern was the behaviour of rats in mazes. As we'll see, many maze problems are inherently spatial—that is, the rat on the maze has to find its way from a start location to a goal location. Determining how rats navigate through mazes tells us not just about the nature of animal intelligence, but also about spatial navigation. Admittedly, rats aren't people, and it may be that the way in which they find their way through environments is qualitatively different from how we might navigate. But rats are mammals, as are humans, and our nervous systems are organized in fundamentally similar ways. Thus, the assumption underlying behaviourism, and implicit in contemporary studies with animal models, is that the *basic* principles of learning, memory, and perception are similar in animals and humans. In addition, some of the basic notions of spatial cognition—such as a cognitive map—have their origins in maze studies.

The first studies of spatial cognition

In 1901 Willard Small, an honorary fellow at Clark University, published a paper entitled 'Experimental study of the mental processes of the rat'. In it, he described the first use of a maze for the study of rodent learning. The maze was based on the Hampton Court Maze, and took advantage of the rats' 'instinctive fondness for following out devious ways' (p. 229). (As I have observed, the Hampton Court Maze is no small challenge (see box).)

The Hampton Court Maze

On a rainy December day, I travelled to the Hampton Palace to attempt its famous Maze. The Maze is located in the extensive gardens of the palace, and is believed to have been built in the late 17th century. It is largely unchanged since its construction, and is one of the only remaining original features of this section of the garden.

The maze comprises hedges that are a good bit taller than the author (see Figs 2.1 and 2.2), and the maze's overall shape, if viewed from above, is triangular. One enters the maze near the tip of the triangle, and the task is to get to an open area in the maze centre.

It's not easy. I timed myself for each 'run' (although I walked), and on the first run I felt that little was learned of the correct route. The way out of the maze is the same way as the route in, and I returned to the start, again entering a number of

The Hampton Court Maze *(Continued)*

blind alleys and repeating loops, to the start. On seven consecutive efforts these were my times:

Trial 1: 3:49 (minutes:seconds)
Trial 2: 3:55
Trial 3: 4:09
Trial 4: 4:25
Trial 5: 2:53*
Trial 6: 2:48
Trial 7: 2:57

From trial 5 on, I had learned the successful route through the maze, and my times reflect how long it takes a healthy 40-year-old to walk the distance of the route. But how did I finally 'get' the route? Although I'd like to say that I'd developed an overall, flexible representation of the environment, it never really felt that way. Rather, I began to recognize choice points within the maze, and recalled which choice (left or right) was correct. At other points in the maze, I'd use local views, for example a flowering tree visible at the end of one particular alleyway, or an asymmetry in the hedge itself.

* Trial 5 was the first run on which I didn't enter any blind alleys.

Fig. 2.1 Photo of the alleyways within the Hampton Court maze.

Fig. 2.2 Overhead view of the Hampton Court maze.

In Small's study, the rats' task was to enter the maze from the side, and make their way through the maze to its centre, where food was found (see Fig. 2.3). Small watched the rats as they ran through the maze, and was blunt in describing the performance of his initial two white rats:

> ... the two rats ran about the maze, most of the time in a circuit immediately around the center ... fagging back and forth, digging at the base of the wall and biting at the wires—the depth of stupidity, one would say. (p. 214)

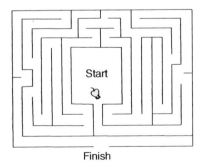

Fig. 2.3 Schematic of Willard Small's maze for studying the mental processes of the rat. This was first use of a maze (for rats, at least) in psychology, and was based on the Hampton Court maze.

In their initial exploration of the maze, the rats exhibited 'the general appearance of *lostness*', with a number of repeated mistakes and retracing of their paths. Eventually, by apparent accident, they found the centre of the maze and reached the food. However, with experience in the maze, the rats began to eliminate their entries into dead ends, and to increase the speed and certainty of their movement through the maze. Thus, whereas the rats' first 'run' through the maze took 13 minutes and contained 13 errors, the 9th test took 1 minute and contained only 2 errors.

What strategy did the rats use to solve the maze? Small tested blind rats on this same maze and found that they were also accurate. This result suggests that being able to see the maze isn't necessary for it to be learned. Another possibility was that the rats could smell the food in the centre of the maze or an odour trail left by a previous rat. Small argues against this by stating that although the rats appeared sensitive to odours on the maze, they did not appear to follow odour trails, and did not appear to use olfaction cues to decide which alleyways to enter. Rather, he suggests that they associate the 'motor image of turning in one direction' with finding food, and the motor image of turning in the other direction with not finding food. These associations became habitual as the rats had more experience on the maze.

This is referred to as motor–kinaesthetic memory. It is, perhaps, akin to our response when driving a car with a 'stick—shift' (manual) transmission. We make the motor response of shifting gears smoothly without a great deal of conscious effort.

The maze studies of John Watson

In a monograph published in 1907, John Watson provided a fuller examination of how rats find their way through mazes. Watson believed that this comparative research would allow a better functional comparison of the sensory processes of animals and humans. Further, the behavioural approach could be applied to the study of animal minds and 'human defective minds or the minds of children' (p. 2). In support of this equivalence between species, Watson cites A.J. Kinnaman's (1902) finding that Rhesus monkeys solved a monkey-sized version of Small's Hampton Court maze in a manner similar to rodents.

Watson used a maze that was essentially the same as Small's, but slightly smaller, and with walls that the rats could not see through. Food—a saucer of bread soaked in milk—was placed in the centre of the maze, and the rats' task was to find their way from the maze entrance to the food. The total distance from the entrance to the food was 40 feet.

Watson started with normal rats. Initially they explored the entire maze, and entered all of the blind alleyways. Watson tracked their learning by recording the average time that it took the rats to traverse the maze and find the food. On the first trial, the rats took an average of 29.01 minutes. On the second, they cut this to 10.59 minutes. By the 19th trial on the maze, their average time was below a minute, and by about the 40th trial, the rats' performance reached a plateau of around 30 seconds. With a larger group of 19 rats, a similar pattern of improvement across trials was observed. Put simply, the rats learned to find the food quickly, and ultimately made few, if any, errors.

Next, Watson and his colleague Dr. Carr tried to identify which sensory processes were necessary for learning and performing the maze. Rats tested on the maze in the dark were as good, if not slightly better, than those tested with the lights on. Indeed, rats could learn the maze without difficulty even if they were only run on it in the dark. Only one rat from those whose records are provided appeared to have difficulty in the dark.

To remove *any* possibility that the rats might use vision (for example, their eyes might adjust to the darkness to a much greater extent than ours), Watson surgically blinded a small number of rats. The blind rats performed well, as is evident from their individual records:

> Rat 1, 1st trial . . . [the rat] ran the first half of the maze absolutely without error. He then turned and retraced his way to the entrance, again without error. He turned at the entrance, got his cue, and went to the food-box without error. Total time: 2:35 min. (p. 57)

As I will describe later, this 'getting the cue' likely refers to the rat's recognition of its location within the maze. After a few additional trials, the blind rats eliminated all errors and ran through the maze as quickly as rats with normal vision.

Watson then tested rats on the maze either without a sense of smell, without a full sense of hearing, without their vibrissae (whiskers), or with their feet anaesthetized. In each condition, the rats ran the maze normally. Watson concluded that the rats solved the maze by using an internal kinaesthetic series of responses—that is, a more or less automatic sequence of motor movements.

In a subsequent study, Carr and Watson (1908) showed, in a clever and convincing way, that well-trained rats used such a motor–kinaesthetic strategy. They trained rats on a variant of the Hampton Court maze until they ran it accurately. They then shortened the maze by removing a section of it, much as one would shorten a dining room table by removing it centre leaf (Fig. 2.4). The shortened maze was identical to the full-size maze, in terms of the turns that were necessary to solve it, but the alleyways in one dimension were shorter. Carr and Watson reasoned that if the rats used their perception of the walls and corners of the maze to find their way, they would have no problem on this

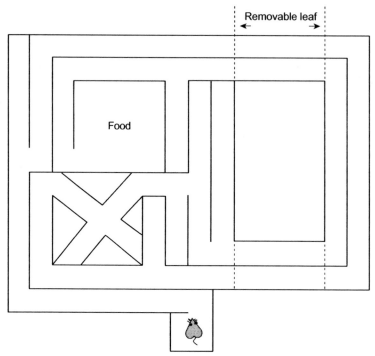

Fig. 2.4 The Carr and Watson (1908) maze had a removable leaf in the centre. Rats were initially trained on the maze until they ran it accurately, and they were then tested with the centre leaf removed. On this shortened maze, rats ran into the walls of the shortened alleyways with some force. This suggests that the rats did not solve the maze based on vision, but based on a well-learned series of motor (kinaesthetic) responses.

shorter variant of the problem. If, however, they used an internal, kinaesthetic strategy to solve the maze, they would end up bumping into the walls of the shorter maze, because they would be executing a series of automatic motor responses learned on the full-sized maze.

On the shortened maze the rats were terrible. One rat ran into the wall at the end of the first shortened alleyway with her full force, and 'was badly staggered'. On the second day of testing, this same rat again ran into the wall 'with sufficient force to land her whole body against the wall' (p. 39). This pattern of behaviour suggested that the rats had indeed used a kinaesthetic strategy to solve this particular maze problem.

Although this evidence is clear, there was one additional finding in the Watson 1907 work which suggests that, in addition to executing a series of motor responses, the rats possessed a sense of direction. Once the maze task was well learned, Watson rotated the entire apparatus by 180°. This rotation changed the relationship of the maze with other cues in the testing room, although the maze itself was unchanged. Thus, the same kinaesthetic series of responses—the same left and right turns in the alleyways—would bring the rat to the food. Surprisingly, the rats performed quite poorly following this manipulation:

> Rat 1. 1st trial [following the 180° rotation of the maze]. Absolutely lost. Ran into all the cul-de-sacs. Back home, etc. It was like learning the maze for the first time. Time: 2.31 min. (p. 87)

Moreover, rats were not disturbed if the maze was simply moved within the room (by 8 feet) without changing its direction. In a subsequent study, Carr (1917) also observed that rotation of a well-learned maze produced a disturbance in the rats' ability to run the maze without error. Based on these findings, Watson suggested that:

> . . . the rat has some non-human modality of sensation which, whatever it may be, is thrown out of gear temporarily by altering the customary relation [of the maze] to the cardinal points of the compass ('sense orientation'). We have reason to suspect that such a 'sense of orientation' functions in many orders of animals. . . . Something possibly may come in the way of control over this 'sense', even if further investigation proves that the human organism is not supplied with it. (p. 92)

In the light of the discovery in the 1990s of neurons within the rodent brain that encode the direction that the animal faces (Chapter 8), this conclusion is prescient. It suggests that rats possess a representation of their direction in the testing room, and that when they are placed on the maze, their 'kinaesthetic series' of responses becomes linked to this sense of direction. Put differently, when rats enter a room with a maze repeatedly, they may learn how the maze is oriented within the room. A mismatch between the rat's sense of orientation within the room and the position of the maze (for example, when the maze has been rotated by 180°) disrupts performance. Although this sense of direction isn't relevant for the actual solving of the maze, it is automatic, and difficult for the rat to ignore.

Others early studies suggesting a direction sense

Additional evidence for a directional sense in rats is mentioned in Karl Spence Lashley's classic work *Brain Mechanisms of Intelligence* (1929). Lashley (1890–1958) was a major figure in psychology, and particularly in physiological psychology, in the first half of the 20th century. He received his Ph.D. in zoology at Johns Hopkins in 1914, and collaborated with Watson there. He moved to the University of Minnesota and then to the Institute of Juvenile Research, Chicago, where he conducted a series of careful experiments attempting to assess where in the cortex memory resided.

In these experiments, Lashley would train rats to run from the beginning of a maze to its end to find a food reward. The mazes varied in complexity, and Lashley's Maze III (Fig. 2.5) was one of the more difficult versions. After learning the maze, Lashley surgically removed or disconnected different portions of the rat cortex. The rats were then retested for their memory of the maze. The idea behind this work was that if the memory (later referred to as the *engram*) for the maze solution was stored in a specific portion of the cortex, removal of that portion should remove the memory. What Lashley observed, however, was that it didn't matter so much what portion of the cortex was removed, but rather how much was removed. These were Lashley's notions of *equipotentiality* and *mass action*, respectively. That is, all regions of the cortex had a relatively equal potential to subserve memory, and there was a positive correlation

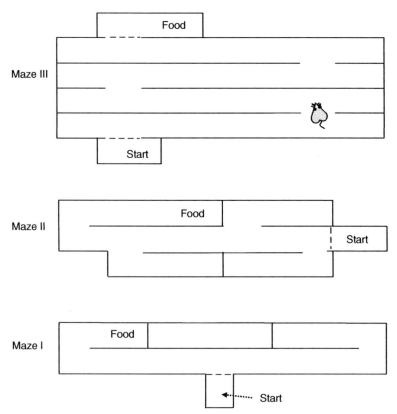

Fig. 2.5 Karl Spence Lashley developed these mazes to assess where in the brain memories—engrams—were stored.

between the amount of cortex removed and the number of errors the rats made on the maze.

As an aside, modern views of memory storage differ from those of Lashley's. Eric Kandel, in his autobiography entitled *In Search of Memory*, makes the point that Lashley wasn't correct: there are specific brain regions that *are* critical for memory storage, but they lie beneath the cortex. In addition, maze tasks may not be the most clear-cut way of assessing memory, as they can be solved in a number of ways—as, indeed, the Watson and Carr experiments described earlier suggest.

But to return to the *Brain Mechanisms of Intelligence*, Lashley described in it an attempt to figure how normal, non-lesioned animals solved Maze III. He took the wire mesh lid off of the top of maze, and blocked the rat's first entrance into the maze. What he found was that some rats ran directly to the food box from the start box across the tops of the maze partitions. Lashley argues that:

> . . . the behavior of the 5 [rats] that followed the direct course to the food strongly suggested that they were perfectly oriented with respect to its direction, although they had never before reached it save by the indirect path of the maze. (p.137)

Thus, in this maze, rats appeared to know that the food was in a specific direction relative to the start box. Given the opportunity, they took a form of a short cut—running across the maze partition tops—to get directly to the food.

A more systematic exploration of a directional sense is found in a series of experiments by Dashiell (1930). He started with the observation that when rats run through a maze with a number of blind alleyways they make more mistakes in some directions than others. Specifically, rats tend not to enter blind alleyways leading in the direction opposite to the food goal at the end of the maze. Instead, the mistakes are entries to blind alleyways in a similar direction to the food goal. For Dashiell, this suggests that the rats may possess an overall sense of which direction the food lies.

To test this, the author created a maze in which a number of different routes led to the maze exit (and food; see Fig. 2.6). What Dashiell observed was that rats would tend to take different routes to the food, but generally these all headed in the correct direction. Thus:

> It is at least imaginable that an animal might carry about with it some direction-indicator that would serve as an orienting device with reference to the cardinal directions, in a way analogous to the function of an electric compass. (p. 39)

Additional manipulations, and an earlier study by Leuba and Fain (1929), suggested that the rats established their directional orientation from the point at which they entered the maze.

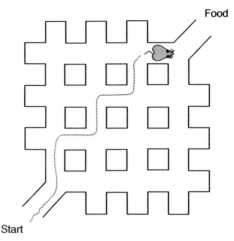

Fig. 2.6 Dashiell (1930) used this maze to show that rats tended to head in the direction of the food at the end of the maze. For Dashiell, this was evidence that rats possess an internal direction sense.

Though the results from Dashiell's studies are suggestive, and the conclusion that rats establish their orientation based on where they enter the maze is likely correct, the results may have another explanation. It could be that rats, with training, tended to head in as straight a route as possible through the maze when leaving the start box. If the rats start by facing the correct direction, they'd simply have to maintain this as they run through the maze. Even this interpretation, however, assumes that the rat can maintain its orientation over a number of deviations.

To summarize, the findings of Lashley and Dashiell provide a hint that as rats run through a maze they develop an overall sense of the direction of the food goal. In the studies of Tolman, to which I turn next, this idea is made explicit.

Edward Chase Tolman's 'Studies in spatial learning'

In the 1940s, a series of experiments by Edward Chase Tolman provided a different, more cognitive view of the rat on the maze. Tolman began graduate school at Harvard in 1911, and there, in a course taught by Robert Yerkes, was influenced by Watson's behaviourism. After graduating from Harvard, Tolman worked for 3 years at Northwestern University, from which he was dismissed in part because of his poor teaching. In his autobiography, he suggests that part of the reason for his dismissal may have been his pacifist leanings during the world war. Eventually, he obtained an instructorship at the University of

California at Berkeley, and, finding that the west coast of the United States suited him, remained there for the rest of his career.

In a series of nine papers entitled 'Studies in spatial learning', Tolman and his students chipped away at the stimulus–response view of learning. His studies were to provide evidence that the rats, in running mazes, didn't simply learn a series of responses. Rather, the rats had *cognitions* about where they were going. From a broader context, this was the beginning of the shift in psychology from strict behaviourism, itself a product of a break from introspectionism, to cognitivism. Of course, there was more behaviourism to come in the form of B.F. Skinner's deeply influential neo-behaviourism, but Tolman's views would gain traction with the support from neuroscience experiments in the 1970s (Olton 1992).

The experiment described in the first of the 'Studies' is a classic in the field of psychology, and is perhaps one of the best-known findings from the Tolman lab. The question Tolman, Ritchie, and Kalish (1946a) asked is whether rats, in running an indirect route to a goal location that contained food, developed an *expectation* that food was in a specific location. They trained rats for 4 days to run on their maze (Fig. 2.7, left), beginning at the base of the maze (A), running through B, through a higher-walled alley at C, then making three turns (D, E, and F) before getting to the goal where the food reward was located.

From a stimulus–response perspective, this maze problem could be solved by learning a sequence of responses: run straight, turn left, turn right, turn left, and then run straight again. However, Tolman and his colleagues hypothesized that rats, in running the maze, learn that the food was in a certain direction relative to the beginning of the maze. They believed that, given the opportunity, the rats would take a short cut that led in the direction of the food. To test this, after the initial 4 days of training, the rats were tested on what has been termed the 'sun-burst' maze (Fig. 2.7, right). Here the previously trained path was blocked and 18 alternative alleys were provided. The most frequently chosen path was the alley that led directly to the food. The rats demonstrated, in essence, an expectation of the food's location. This internal representation allowed the rats to make a spatial inference of the most direct route to the goal.

The second of Tolman's 'Studies' sparked off a debate that wasn't settled until the 1950s. In this study (Tolman, Ritchie, and Kalish 1946b), the authors tried to find out what exactly rats learn when they run to one arm of a plus-shaped maze (see Fig. 2.8). If the rat always starts on one arm of the maze, and always finds food at the end of another specified arm (for example, food 1), there are two possible strategies it might learn. First, the rat might use a response strategy—that is, the rat may simply make a left turn at the intersection of the

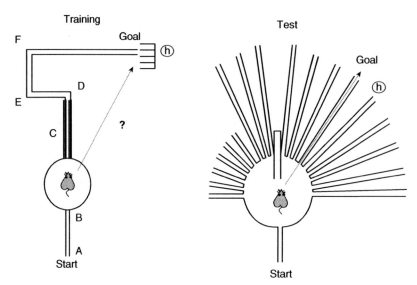

Fig. 2.7 The sun-burst maze of Edward Chase Tolman and colleagues. *Left*: Rats were trained to run from the start of the maze, through a high-walled alleyway (C), to a goal where food was located. *Right*: After 4 days of training, the sun-burst maze was substituted for the previous maze, and the previous route to the goal was blocked. Rats tended to choose the alleyway that most directly led to the goal, suggesting that they'd learned the direction in which the food was located, not just a series of stimulus–response associations.

two arms. Alternatively, the rat might learn that the food reward is in a certain place relative to the room. If it runs to that place, it will find the food reward. If the rat is always started from the same arm, these two possibilities cannot be distinguished: the rat may use a response strategy or a place strategy—both would be successful.

To distinguish between these, Tolman and his colleagues attempted to see which strategy was easier for the rats to learn. They trained one group of rats to make the same response (e.g. a left turn) when started from *two* different locations (start arm 1 and start arm 2). Thus, it was the rats' responses, not the food location, which were consistently reinforced. In the second group, running to the same place (e.g. food 1) resulted in reinforcement, regardless of the starting arm—and again, both start arm 1 and start arm 2 were used. In this group, the rats had to make a different response—a left or right turn depending on their starting location—to get to the food reward.

The results were dramatic: after 12 days of training, only three of the eight rats in the response group learned to make the correct responses consistently, whereas all eight rats in the place group learned to do so. Indeed, the rats

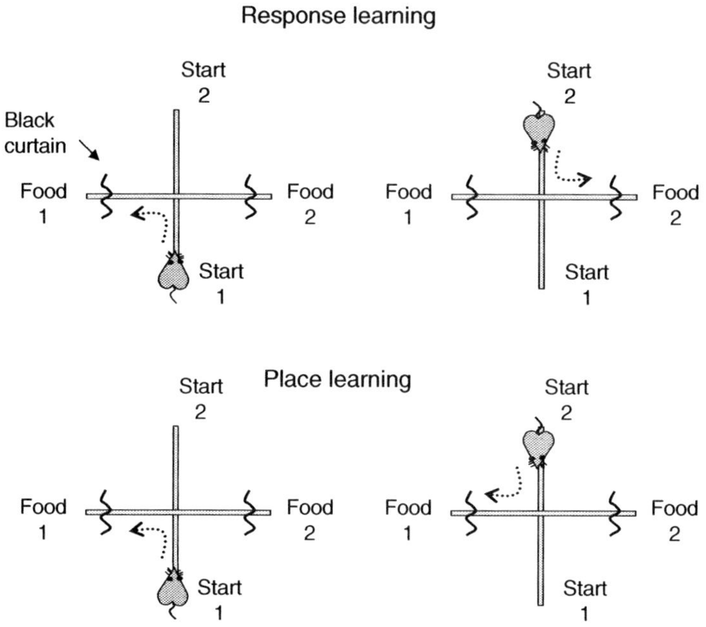

Fig. 2.8 Tolman and colleagues (1946b) trained two groups of rats to find food on a + maze. One group found food by making the same response, e.g. by turning left from different start positions (as shown in the upper two plots). The other group found food by going to the same maze location (lower two plots). All of the animals in this place group learned to find the food reliably, whereas only some of the animals in the response group did so. For Tolman and colleagues, this was evidence that place learning was easier than response learning.

learning to run to a single place required very few trials (range: 1–8) to do so consistently. Tolman *et al.* argued that, although the response strategy could be learned, it was much easier, and therefore perhaps more 'native', for the rats to learn to run to a place. Again, as in the sun-burst maze, this finding argues against a response-based account of maze learning, and suggests that the rats possess a more abstract representation of spatial location.

The logic of this experiment was not bullet-proof, however. Blodgett and McCutchan (1947) argued that in Tolman *et al.*'s place-learning rats, it was possible that the animals simply learned *two* responses. That is, when beginning at start arm 1, turn left, and when beginning at start arm 2, turn right. Blodgett and McCutchan showed that rats *could* learn to use a response strategy when the maze was placed in a dimly lit environment and moved on every trial. Moreover, this learning was comparable to that of rats trained in the same environment (a homogeneous dome-shaped room) without movement of the maze and with full illumination. The authors did however replicate the initial findings of Tolman *et al.* when they tested animals in an open laboratory room.

What can we take from these findings? The resolution of the place versus response debate is often placed with a review published by Restle in 1957. Essentially, Restle argued that rats on the T-maze are not inherently 'place' or 'response' learners. Rather, the extent to which they use one or the other strategy depends on the salience of stimuli outside the maze, frequently referred to as 'extra-maze' stimuli. When access to extra-maze visual stimuli is restricted by running the maze in a curtained enclosure, several studies show that a response strategy dominates. In contrast, when the maze is placed in an open room (where, presumably, the rats can see windows, doors, etc., from the goal arm), several studies find a place strategy dominance. Restle suggests that rats will use all available cues, but will ultimately ignore cues that are irrelevant to finding the goal.

The remaining Tolman studies deal with various implications of place learning. In 'Studies in spatial learning III', Ritchie (1947) used a T-shaped maze, and found that rats trained on two different paths to a single goal location learned the task somewhat faster than rats trained on two paths to goal locations in two different rooms (see Fig. 2.9). According to Ritchie, this

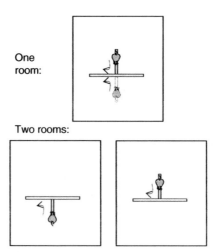

Fig. 2.9 Ritchie (1947) found that rats learned to go to a single location (upper plot) from two starting locations more rapidly than they learned to go to two locations (lower plots). On Ritchie's account, this provides evidence for place learning, as the number of responses is the same in both instances, but the number of locations differs.

provides support for place learning, as the required responses in both conditions were the same, and only the number of places to be learned differed. A complementary finding was observed in the ninth study in this series. Ritchie, Hay, and Hare (1951) trained rats on a *response* strategy on one maze with alternate start arms. They found that rats trained to always turn in one direction at the choice point of the T learned to do so more quickly if they were given training in two rooms, as opposed to having trials with alternating start positions on a single maze. Ritchie states that, when given training to two rooms, the rats learn to go to two places. However, it's possible that the one-room group learned more slowly than the two-room group because the rats in the one-room condition had to overcome a predisposition to go to the same place to find reward from alternate starting arms.

The fourth of the 'Studies' followed a prediction from the third: learning to go to a goal (one arm of a T-maze) from one start point will help learning to go to the same goal from a different start point (the same arm of the T, but with the start stem on the opposite side) (Tolman, Ritchie, and Kalish 1947a). The results here, however, were confounded by learning that a specific turn at the choice point would take the rat to the food. When this was removed by altering the training, rats trained to go to a specific goal location learned to go there more readily from a new start point than rats given comparable training in a different room. Thus, learning that a specific place has reward facilitates the learning of new routes to the same location. Again, the implication of this is that when running on a maze the rat develops expectations that a given location contains reward, and this expectation generalizes to new learning.

In the fifth study in spatial learning, Tolman, Ritchie, and Kalish (1947b) revisited the place versus response question for rats on a T-maze (as in Fig. 2.8, but using a T-shaped maze, instead of a + shaped maze). In this study, rats weren't permitted to correct an incorrect initial choice—that is, they weren't allowed to run down the opposite arm of the T after choosing the arm that wasn't reinforced. With this procedure, most rats trained on a response strategy eventually did learn the task (in contrast to the second study), although their learning wasn't nearly as rapid as that of rats trained to make a place response.

This study is also notable for a manipulation that is frequently used to pick apart the types of information used in solving spatial tasks. After training on either a response or place strategy, the rats were tested with the maze shifted by 90°. The logic of this is that, if rats have learned to turn in one direction at the choice point of the T, they should do so regardless of the position of the maze in the room. However, if rats have learned to go to a specific place relative to the room, movement of the maze with the room will cause problems.

What Tolman *et al.* found was that almost all of the response-trained rats make the correct response when the maze was rotated. However, they did hesitate considerably after making the turn, suggesting that they may have had an awareness of the changed location of the maze in the room. Six of the eight rats trained on a place strategy responded incorrectly (as defined by the maze arm's relation to light cue in the room) following rotation of the maze. Essentially, rats trained on a place strategy did not behave consistently following displacement of the maze, suggesting that they had indeed learned to run to a specific place when the maze was in its normal position. (I have found comparable results using a different variant of the T-maze task (Dudchenko 2001; see also Douglas 1966).)

In the sixth study of the series, Ritchie (1948) trained rats to find food at the end of one arm on a T-maze. His question was whether rats would tend to learn the place in which the food was located, or its direction in the room. To test this, after the rats had learned where the food was, the T-maze was replaced with a sun-burst maze that faced the opposite direction. The upper stem of the sun-burst maze—equivalent to the stem of the former T-maze—was blocked. However, the remaining maze arms were open. As the sun-burst maze was oriented in the opposite direction to the former T-maze, the rats had to make different responses on each maze to head in the same direction in the room. Ritchie found that rats tended to choose the maze arm that went in the direction (in the room) of the food, and not the arm that led to the former food location. Based on these results, Ritchie suggested that the rats have a disposition to seek food in a specific *direction* within the environment.

The seventh study (Tolman and Gleitman 1949) confirmed the earlier finding that, on a T-maze, rats learn to go to a place more readily than they learn to make a specific turn, and also showed that hungrier rats in both situations do better. Consistent with this conclusion, the authors found that rats who were deprived of sight after training on the T-maze were more impaired if they'd learned to go to a place, as opposed to having learned a response. This suggests that response learning isn't simply the learning of two different, visually identified places—one from each of the two different starting points—but truly is related to the physical turn made by the animal.

In the eighth study, Ritchie *et al.* (1950) argued that when a rat is trained on a T-maze, it first learns to go to a specific place, but later, if over-trained, it learns to make a specific response. This idea—that a shift in strategies occurs as a task becomes well learned—has been substantiated by subsequent neural systems experiments (see Chapter 7). (The ninth study in this series, as described earlier, was the complement of the third study.)

Cognitive maps in rats and men

Tolman summarized his arguments against the stimulus–response view of learning in a review entitled 'Cognitive maps in rats and men', in the July, 1948 issue of the journal *Psychological Review*. In this article, based on lectures given at Berkeley and Cleveland, Tolman described experiments whose findings suggested that rats learned more than a series of responses to the stimuli they encountered. Instead, rats actively explored their environments and formed mental 'field maps' of their environments. Such a view, as we will see in Chapter 6, received unexpected support from the discovery of neurons within the mammalian brain that encode specific locations.

Tolman's central question in this influential paper, like that of Watson earlier, was: how do rats solve mazes? Tolman writes that there are two camps on this issue. The first argues that maze learning is the product of a series of stimulus–response associations. In their view the rat's brain is like a telephone exchange, and a given stimulus is associated with a given 'outgoing' muscle response. For some in this camp, learning occurs because the stimuli associated with a correct response are more frequently paired than those associated with an incorrect response. Put another way, if the rat comes to a T-junction, and turning left will eventually take it to the end of the maze, whereas turning right will take it to a dead end, the rat may have more frequent pairing of the T-junction and the left response. Upon subsequent encounter of the T, the left response becomes more prevalent. There is a touch of circularity to this—why does the rat go left more often than right in the first place? But it is not central to Tolman's critique.

For others in the stimulus–response camp, learning is the strengthening of stimulus–response links that ultimately serve to reduce a drive. An example of this would be a hungry rat learning that a series of responses in a maze ultimately lead to a piece of food.

This account is most closely associated with Clark L. Hull, whose notable works include *Principles of Behavior* (1943), *Essentials of Behavior* (1951) and *A Behavioral System* (1952). For Hull, responses closer to a goal are learned more readily than those farther away. Thus, there is a *goal-gradient* in learning a maze, such that errors near the goal are eliminated first, and those earlier in the maze are eliminated later (Hull 1952). Maze learning reflects a series of stimulus–response links, and each response produces an internal reaction, which itself is associated with the next response in the sequence. With repeated experience, a habit is formed, such that a series of responses are triggered by an initial stimulus (Young 1950).

In *A Behavioral System*, Hull also writes of goal orientation, where organisms travelling towards a goal on a maze will tend to move in the direction of the goal, and tend not to head in the direction opposite of the goal, as in the experiment of Dashiell described earlier. Hull formulates these behavioural tendencies as theorems (112 and 113) within his theory of behaviour. As noted previously, the notion of a sense of goal orientation provides an intriguing link with a neurally based representation of direction.

Tolman does not accept these stimulus–response accounts of maze learning. He argues that when rats learn a maze, 'something like a field map gets established in the rat's brain' (p. 192). In support of this view, he describes results from five different types of experiments. In the first, 'latent-learning' studies, rats learned about the layout of the maze even if they weren't reinforced for doing so. For example, Blodgett (1929) compared rats that were reinforced for running a maze to those who weren't. The reinforced rats made fewer errors (dead end entries) across days, whereas the rats that weren't reinforced still made a high number of errors. However, if after a number of sessions the non-reinforced rats began to be reinforced, the number of errors they made dropped to the level of the group that had been reinforced from the start. Thus, the initially non-reinforced rats *had* learned something about the maze; they simply hadn't shown it.

The second and third types of experiments that Tolman marshals as challenges to the stimulus–response view of learning involve the rat's active sampling of its environment. In 'vicarious trial and error' (VTE) behaviour, the rat sways its head back and forth, hesitating before making a choice.[1] According to Tolman, this behaviour initially occurs more in simpler forms of a task, for example, telling the difference between a black card and a white card, as opposed to discriminating between a black and a medium grey card. VTE behaviour reflects the rat's learning of the discrimination rule. Subsequently, when the task has been learned, VTE behaviour occurs more for difficult discriminations, perhaps reflecting the additional stimulus sampling necessary for making a judgement. In 'searching for the stimulus' experiments, the rat actively attempts to identify the stimuli that predict, for example, the occurrence of a shock in a specific context.

The fourth set of experiments that argue against a stimulus–response account of learning are those in which rats appear to try out different 'hypotheses' to solve a maze. Here Tolman cites an experiment of Krechevsky (1932), where rats attempted a series of different strategies when faced with a series of

---

[1] Vicarious trial-and-error, and a more explicit contrast between Tolman's view of learning and that of Hull, is found Tolman's 1937 American Psychological Address 'The determiners of behavior at a choice point' (see Tolman 1938).

left–right decisions. Such a use of strategies suggests that rats don't passively associate a stimulus with a given response, but rather actively attempt to develop an overall solution to the problem.

Finally, Tolman describes the 'spatial orientation' experiments, such as the sun-burst maze, that were described earlier in this chapter. In learning a maze, and then being able to take a short cut to the goal location (as on the sun-burst maze), Tolman suggests that:

> As a result of their original training, the rat had, it would seem, acquired not merely a strip map to the effect that the original specifically trained-on path led to food but, rather, a wider comprehensive map to the effect that food was located in such and such a direction in the room. (p. 204)

We will return to this view later, but what does Tolman say about cognitive maps in humans? On this he is philosophical: the map in humans isn't just spatial, it instead is a means for a flexible and more tolerant way of thinking. 'Narrow strip maps' do not allow one to deal flexibly with one's surrounding and with others. Such maps may be the product of brain damage, inadequate cues within an environment, too much repetition of an initially learned path, and the presence of too much motivation or too much frustration. Broader, more rational maps allow one to see the bigger picture. They are the product of not allowing ourselves to become too emotional, hungry, or over-motivated. Tolman concludes:

> We must, in short, subject our children and ourselves (as the kindly experimenter would his rats) to the optimal conditions of moderate motivation and of an absence of unnecessary frustrations, whenever we put them and ourselves before that great God-given maze which is our human world. (p. 208)

Watson versus Tolman: who was right?

For Small, Watson, and Carr (and later Blodgett and McCutchan), rats solve mazes by making a response or a sequence of well-learned responses. This was based, in the early studies, on careful experimentation and the removal of different sensory abilities. For Tolman, a rat solving a maze experiences a series of sensory and motoric responses, but, in contrast to Hull's view, this doesn't just result in a stimulus–response habit. Rather, in running the maze, the rat develops an overall representation, which permits cognitive flexibility when faced with alternative configurations of the initial problem. For Restle, these views could be reconciled by suggesting that rats used whatever information is available within the environment.

However, Watson's observation that rats possessed a 'sense of orientation' when running the maze is quite similar to Tolman's notion that rats have a map that tells them that food is in a specific direction within the room.

Both imply that the rat has a representation of the maze relative to the extra-maze environment. Such a sense of place and direction maps well, as we shall see, with the subsequent discoveries of neurons in the brain that fire in specific places and neurons that fire when the animal faces specific directions.

Summary

An early question in the field of psychology was how, precisely, rats solve mazes. For the early behaviourists, frustrated with the wooliness of introspection, studying the behaviour of animals provided a concrete, tractable problem. The assumption of this work was that humans are not qualitatively different from other animals, and thus basic learning processes may be studied in the latter.

The results from early maze studies suggest that there are two strategies a rat, and likely most mammals, may apply to a spatial problem. One strategy is to develop a relatively automatic route-based approach, which is resistant to disruption following the removal of any one sensory cue or capacity (e.g. vision), and which depends on a response or series of responses that are well trained. A second strategy is to develop an overall knowledge of the layout of the environment—even extending to the environment beyond the maze. This map allows flexibility when aspects of the environment are altered. It is manifest in a predisposition to learn the location of a goal relative to the environment.

What, precisely, defines a 'place', and how spatial memory is assessed experimentally will be considered in the next chapter.

Chapter 3

Contemporary studies of spatial cognition

My laboratory is at the University of Edinburgh, and if you were to visit, I could show you a series of rooms that each contained a different type of apparatus for assessing, experimentally, learning, memory, and spatial cognition. In touring these rooms, you'd find students, postdoctoral researchers, and even, perhaps, a professor or two intently trying to answer specific questions on the nature of learning and memory, and its bases in the brain.

In this chapter I describe what you might find in these rooms: the contemporary tools used for answering experimental questions about spatial cognition in animals. This will, of necessity, be incomplete. As described in the previous chapter, maze use in psychology has a long history (Fig. 3.1), and an exhaustive review of all maze studies would require its own book (the interested reader should consult Munn 1950; Woodworth and Schlossberg 1954; Thinus-Blanc 1996). My aim in describing these tasks is to highlight what we know from experimental studies about the types of information used to find one's way.

The Olton radial arm maze

In 1976, David Olton and Robert Samuelson described a new method for assessing animal spatial memory in a paper entitled 'Remembrance of places past: spatial memory in rats'. The authors describe a radial-arm maze (RAM), which is a wheel-shaped apparatus with a central platform and eight, equally spaced radiating spokes (Fig. 3.2).

The basic procedure for running the radial arm maze is simple. A hungry rat is placed on the centre platform of the apparatus, and is allowed to enter different arms. At the end of each arm, a single piece of food is available. After some exposure to the maze, rats typically enter the arms, run to the ends, and gather each of the eight food rewards.

The remarkable aspect of the RAM is that rats, once they've retrieved the reward from a given maze arm, tend not to return to it. In fact, Olton and Samuelson found that if rats were permitted to make eight choices on the maze

Fig. 3.1 A photo of a rat at the end of a maze arm. As many 'rat-runners'—psychologists and behavioural neuroscientists who use rats to study learning and memory processes—would agree, rats aren't merely passive participants in an experiment. Rather, they appear to show curiosity and motivation in exploring their environment.

before being removed, they entered, on average, 7.6 different arms. The rats do this, the authors show, by remembering which spatial locations they've visited.

This conclusion was based on several clever control manipulations. First, sprinkling the apparatus with after shave (Old Spice or Mennen) did not disrupt the rats' accuracy at finding the arms with food, although it presumably covered up any odour cues from the food at the end of the maze arms, or olfactory trails left by the rats on visited arms. Additional controls were done by allowing the rat to enter a few maze arms (e.g. three), and then confining the rat to the centre platform while the maze arms were changed in some way. The rat was then released and allowed to make its remaining choices. If the visited and non-visited arms were interchanged while the rats were confined to the centre platform, the rats still chose the non-visited locations—indicating that they weren't avoiding visited arms based on their smell or any local cues. If, while the rat was confined to the centre platform, all of the arms were rotated about the central platform by 45° and the visited arms were re-baited, the rats still chose the arms in non-visited locations (relative to the room) when released. Thus, the rats appeared to remember which locations they visited and used this memory to choose arms which had yet to be visited.

For Olton and Samuelson, the rats' remarkable ability to remember which maze locations they've visited reflects an impressive memory for

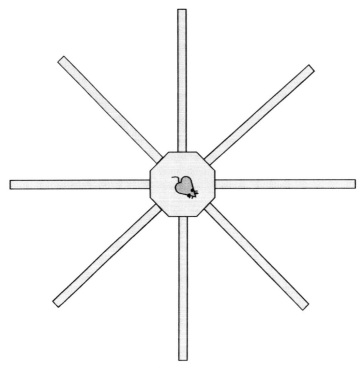

Fig. 3.2 A schematic of the Olton radial arm maze. In a typical experiment, a rat is placed in the centre of the maze, and its task is to find the food reward available at the end of each radiating arm. Rats show excellent working memory in this task, as they typically avoid re-entering arms that they've already visited on a given trial.

spatial locations. The rats' tendency to choose different arms was likely based on their tendency to alternate arm choices—referred to as spontaneous alternation (see later).

But what do the rats actually remember? An elegant study by Suzuki *et al.* (1980) examined this. The authors tested rats on a radial arm maze in an environment where they controlled the availability of landmarks. This was done by curtaining off the maze from the rest of the room with heavy black curtains, arranged in a circle. The ceiling was covered with a translucent board, and the environment was lit with a light in the centre of the ceiling. In the first experiment, the authors compared how well rats performed the RAM task when there were extra-maze cues (that is, cues not on the maze itself) in the environment, as opposed to when these weren't available. The cues were different stimuli (for example, Christmas lights, a fan, a toy bird) placed on the curtain walls or suspended from the ceiling beyond each maze arm (see Fig. 3.3). Rats tested with these stimuli made fewer errors—re-entries to already visited maze

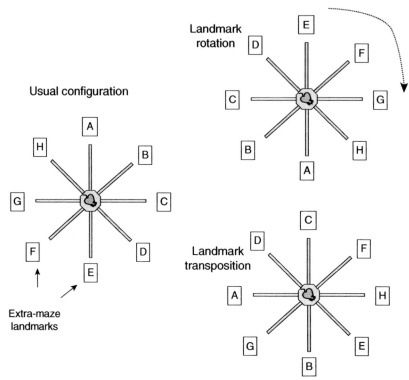

Fig. 3.3 An experiment by Suzuki *et al.* (1980) showed that rats use the spatial relationships between distal landmarks to remember which maze arms they've already visited and obtained food from. This was shown by shifting the landmarks by 180° after the rats had made their first three maze arm choices. The rats continued choosing arms based on the position of the extra-maze landmarks. In another manipulation in a different session, rats made three choices with the extra-maze landmarks in their usual configuration. The rats were then confined to the centre of the maze whereas the landmarks were interchanged with one another—disrupting the previous spatial relationships between different landmarks. When allowed to resume their search for food, rats appeared to make choices without reference to the previously selected arms or landmark positions. Thus, rats appeared to use the configuration of landmarks to guide their spatial memory.

arms—than those who were tested on the same maze without any extra-maze cues. However, even the no-cue animals learned the task; so extra-maze cues were not necessary for remembering which maze arms had been visited, though their presence was helpful.

Additional experiments showed that it was the spatial relationships between the cues, as opposed to the individual cues themselves, which the rats used to remember which maze arms they had visited. This was shown by allowing rats to visit three maze arms, and then confining them to the centre of the maze by closing the doors to the maze arms. While the rats were confined to the centre platform, the extra-maze cues were moved to the opposite side of the maze (that is, they were rotated by 180° around the maze) or transposed with one another. Shifting the cues preserved the spatial relationship between each cue, as cue A is still next to cue B, etc., although the whole array was in a different position relative to the maze. Transposition, in contrast, changed the spatial relationships between cues, as cues A and B, for example, were no longer next to one another.

Under normal conditions, after a rat had entered three maze arms and been confined to the centre platform, it would enter, on average, 4.5 of the 5 remaining unvisited arms in its next 5 choices. Thus, rats displayed excellent memory for the arms they had visited previously. When the extra-maze cues were rotated to the opposite side of the maze while the rat was confined to the maze centre, the rats still chose 4 correct (unvisited) arms in their next 5 choices, with the 'correct' maze arms being defined relative to the extra-maze cues. However, when the cues were transposed with one another, the rats made only 2.9 correct responses out of 5 choices, again defined relative to the extra-maze cues. Moreover, in a subsequent experiment, rats responded to the transposed cue array as if it was an entirely new trial. These results show that rats don't use individual cues to identify individual locations on the maze. Instead, they use the spatial relationships between landmarks (cues) to recognize locations. Thus, recognition of locations, in rodents at least, takes into account the entire visual scene surrounding the maze, as opposed to just individual elements of the scene (see also Zoladek and Roberts 1978).

As we'll see in Chapter 6, the radial arm maze task requires brain regions that play a crucial role in navigation. A full review of the history and many uses of the radial maze can be found in Foreman and Ermakova (1998).

An additional point to consider before we leave the radial arm maze is the capacity for spatial memory. As described earlier, rats are nearly perfect at remembering 8 maze arms. So is there a limit to how many places they can remember? Other versions of the radial maze answer this question. On a 12-arm radial maze, rats make approximately 11 correct choices; on a 17-arm maze they average ≥ 14 correct choices; and on a 24-arm maze rats make ≥ 20 correct choices (Buresova and Bures 1982; 17-arm maze from Olton *et al.* 1977). In the Buresova and Bures's estimate, the spatial working memory capacity is 40 to 50 items.

But there is also evidence that the capacity for spatial memory is nearly limitless. Clark's Nutcrackers, a North American bird that caches pine seeds in the fall to see it through the winter, can relocate 2,000 to 3,000+ cache locations, and appears to do so by remembering these locations relative to large landmarks nearby (Vander Wall 1982; Kamil and Jones 1997). In humans, the capacity for visual memory in humans is impressive: people can remember at least 10,000 different pictures after a single exposure (Standing 1973). So, it is possible that the capacity to recognize previously visited locations is unlimited. This may imply that a lack of spatial orientation isn't the product of a limit on how many locations we can recognize, but rather to other factors—inattention, loss of visibility, or a lack of distinctive visual landmarks.

Alternation on the T-maze

We've encountered the T-maze in the previous chapter with the work on place versus response learning. In those experiments, rats were typically trained with food in the same location, one arm of the T, and the question was how the rats learned to go to the food.

Another common version of the T-maze is the alternation task. In this task, the rat first runs up the stem of the maze and enters one arm of the T. The experimenter then picks up the rat and places it back at the beginning of the stem, and the rat may be kept there for a specified delay. It is then allowed to run up the stem again and enter either arm of the T. Usually, the rat will choose the arm opposite to the one chosen in its first run. In its simplest version, reinforcement is not present at the end of the T arms—rats, and many other species, will *spontaneously alternate* arm choices on adjacent runs. The motivation for spontaneous alternation may lie in the animals' predisposition to encounter new stimuli, or to forage in different locations for food (for review see Dember and Fowler 1958; Richman *et al.* 1986). Rats appear to alternate locations or directions, as they'll alternate at an 86% rate on a T-shaped maze, but will only do so at a close-to-chance rate of 55% on a maze where the two choice arms at the top of the stem are parallel to one another (Douglas *et al.* 1972).

To select the alternate arm of the T on consecutive runs, the rat must remember which arm it has already entered. How does it do this? A series of experiments by Douglas (1966) examined this question. To control for odour cues, Douglas gave rats a first run on one T-maze, and then took them to a second room for a second run on a second T-maze. Thus, the rats couldn't choose alternate arms of the T based on any odour cue left on their first run, as the second run was on a different maze.

What Douglas found was that rats tended to choose alternate arms of a T, even when the consecutive runs were given on separate mazes. However, this only occurred when the mazes were oriented in the same direction in both rooms. When the mazes were perpendicular to one another, the incidence of alternation fell to a chance level. From this he concluded that rats alternate directions (e.g. west, east), and not responses (left and right turns at the choice point of the T). As in the Tolman experiments described in the previous chapter, this finding suggests that animals have a predisposition to use the overall orientation of an environment to identify locations.

A popular variant of the spontaneous alternation task is a 'forced-sample' version (see Fig. 3.4). Here, one arm of the T is blocked when the rat makes its first run, and thus the experimenter specifies which arm of the T the rat 'samples'. The rat is then returned to the start arm, and, after a delay, allowed a second run with both arms of the T open. The rat is only rewarded for selecting the arm opposite to the one entered on the first run.

T-maze alternation has been used in many studies examining the role of different brain areas, neurotransmitter systems, and drugs on memory. In the context of this chapter, however, I will describe an experiment that I conducted looking at what rats remembered in a forced-sample alternation task (Dudchenko 2001).

The starting point of this experiment was the observation that removal of a specific brain region, the hippocampus, abolishes the rat's ability to perform this memory task. Importantly, memory for other types of information is still present (Dudchenko et al. 2000), so there is something specific about the memory demands of the alternation task that makes it particularly sensitive to damage to this brain region.

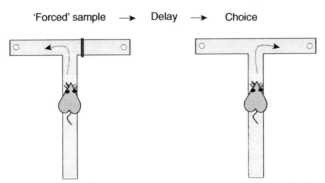

Fig. 3.4 In the working memory version of the T-maze alternation task, the rat, on its first run, is only permitted to enter one arm of the T. It is then removed from the end of the arm by the experimenter and placed at the bottom stem of the T for a short period of time. The rat then makes a second run up the maze, and on this run both arms of the T are accessible. Reward, however, is only available on the arm opposite to the one the rat entered on its first run. Thus, the rat has to remember which arm it entered on its first run, and use that memory to select the alternate arm on its second run.

My approach was similar to the Douglas (1966) and Suzuki *et al.* (1980) experiments described earlier. What I found was that rats could alternate on a T-maze even when no extra landmarks were present in the testing environment. Rats tested with landmarks, however, used them. So, a variety of cues could be used to remember which arm was visited. In a subsequent study, Dr. Larissa Zinyuk and I found evidence that in the absence of extra-maze landmarks, the rats derive their orientation from the position of the maze itself (Dudchenko and Zinyuk 2005).

The use of direction information, as well as a predisposition not to return to a previously visited place, has been shown in a thorough study by Futter and Aggleton (2006). They observed that it was difficult to get rats to use an egocentric (response) strategy in an alternation task. This is consistent with the assumptions underlying the RAM and with the evidence for a bias towards place learning described in the previous chapter.

Richard Morris's water maze

A particularly influential tool for assessing memory and spatial cognition is the Morris water maze (see Fig. 3.5).The maze comprises a large, circular pool of water, with a small, submerged platform often located at a fixed position

Fig. 3.5 A photo of a Morris water maze. Note the presence of distinctive extra-maze landmarks within the testing room. Rats presumably rely on an association between the landmarks and the position of the submerged platform to guide their navigation towards the platform when placed in the water.

within the pool. The water of the pool is made opaque, and the submerged platform rests just below the surface, and so is not visible to the rat. Rats placed in the water attempt to 'escape', and will climb on to the platform readily if they encounter it.

The first paper describing this maze, 'Spatial localization does not require the presence of local cues' (Morris 1981) repays reading. In the first experiment, Morris compared groups of rats trained with a submerged platform or a visible platform within the maze. On different trials, one group was trained to find the submerged platform in a constant location—referred to as the place group. A different group encountered the same platform in different places on every trial. A third group sought the visible platform in a constant place, and a fourth group was trained with the visible platform in different positions on every trial. The results showed that rats learned to swim rapidly and directly to the submerged platform when it was in a constant location. Likewise, the rats trained with the visible platform swam directly towards it. Rats trained with a random positioning of the submerged platform, not surprisingly, took the longest to find the platform.

Two probe sessions provided support for the view that rats learn the spatial location of the submerged platform. In the first probe, the platform was removed for all groups, and the paths of the rats were recorded as they swam around for 60 seconds looking for it. Rats in the place group spent a disproportionate amount of time swimming in the portion of the pool that had previously contained the submerged platform. Interestingly, rats trained with a stable visible platform position also showed a tendency to spend more time in the previously correct region of the pool, suggesting that they too had learned something about the platform's location, even though this wasn't necessary to solve the task. The remaining groups, trained with variable platform positions, searched throughout the pool for the platform when it was removed. In a second probe session, the platform was moved to a new location. Rats previously trained to find the submerged platform in one location continued to look in that place for the platform, and thus took longer to discover the platform's new position. This again suggests that the place-trained group had learned where the platform was.

The second experiment in this paper addresses the place-versus-response controversy that we considered in the previous chapter. Specifically, do rats learn a response (e.g. when put in the maze, always swim left), or do they learn a place? Is performance in the Morris water maze based on stimulus–response learning, or a flexible cognitive map? To test this, Morris trained rats to find the submerged platform in a constant location, with the rats starting each trial from the same point at the periphery of the maze. In a test session, one group of rats was started from new locations along the maze periphery. These rats swam as readily to the hidden platform as they had when released from the old start location, suggesting that they could take a novel route to the hidden platform. Another group was started from novel positions, but also had the platform move on each trial so that it was in a constant position relative to the start point. These rats were terrible, and tended to search for the submerged platform in its previously trained location. These findings suggest that place learning, and not response learning, underlies localization of the hidden platform.

We can ask the same question of the Morris water maze that we have of the previous tasks: what do rats learn? A handful of studies have examined this issue. In a methodological paper, Morris (1984) found that drawing a black curtain entirely around the water maze reduced performance to a chance level. When the curtain was pulled some of the way around the maze—obscuring the view of distal landmarks in ¼ of the maze near the training quadrant— performance was slightly diminished. These observations suggest that visual landmarks in the training room beyond the maze allow the rat to identify the platform's location within the pool.

Fenton et al. (1994) tested rats in a cue-controlled version of the maze. The rats were trained in darkness with four illuminated, shaped landmarks. Rats readily learned the maze with either two or four landmarks, and rats trained with four landmarks still did well if two landmarks were removed. Rats were impaired in the two-landmark situation if the two familiar landmarks were exchanged for two new landmarks. Fenton et al. also found that new land- marks weren't learned as well if other landmarks were already present. This finding is consistent with the phenomenon of *blocking*, where a previous asso- ciation between stimuli lessens the tendency to learn new associations (Kamin 1968). Overall, the Fenton et al. study shows that rats use specific extra-maze visual landmarks to find the hidden platform.

A similar study by Prados and Trobalon (1998) found that rats could learn where the hidden platform was located when two or four extra-maze cues were visible within a curtained enclosure surrounding the maze. If only one cue was available, however, rats didn't show a preference for the region of the pool where the platform was typically located. The authors found that after learning the platform with four extra-maze cues, the rats could still find the platform when any two cues were removed. That is, no specific cue or cue combination guided behaviour—and thus the rats must have learned the platform location relative to all four cues. This, indirectly, supports the idea that the configura- tion of extra-maze cues, and not individual cues themselves, guide navigation on the maze.

Chamizo *et al.* (2006) trained rats with two different landmarks suspended from the ceiling at the periphery of the maze. The landmarks were within a circular curtain that surrounded the maze, and one landmark was always present within the environment, whereas the second was one of two alternative landmarks, each in a different position. When the consistently present landmark was close to the platform, rats relied on it, and not the remaining landmarks, to find the platform. If the consistently present landmark was far from the platform, rats still used it, but could also use the alternative landmarks when they were presented together. Thus, a landmark near the hidden platform can *overshadow* learning of other landmarks.[1]

What hasn't been explicitly shown—as in the Suzuki *et al.* studies in the radial arm maze—is that disrupting the spatial relationships between landmarks disrupts performance. The Fenton *et al.* study shows that the rats use landmarks, but in their study it was still possible that rats simply swam towards or away from a single landmark. The studies by Prados and Trobalon and Chamizo *et al.* show that the rats follow rotation of the landmarks, although in this instance the landmarks and the platform were rotated on every trial, so they were thoroughly dissociated from any other potential room cues. Indeed, Mackintosh (2002) notes that this strategy is necessary to keep the rats from using uncontrolled cues, or 'perhaps even some compass sense' (p. 168), to find the platform.

Three studies have manipulated the extra-maze landmarks in the water maze environment. In the first, Eichenbaum *et al.* (1990) trained rats with or without a specific brain lesion to find a submerged platform from a fixed starting location. The maze was in an open room, but there were two salient visual landmarks in the line of sight of the rats as they swam to the platform. Eichenbaum *et al.* rotated these specific landmarks by 180°, and also started

---

[1] The reader may ask, and I did when writing this, what the difference is between overshadowing and blocking. Luckily, my neighbour in the department, Dr David Lieberman, is an expert on learning and learning theory, and so I asked him. In blocking, a prior association weakens the formation of a new association. This is in accordance with the Rescorla–Wagner theory of associative learning, which holds that the associative strength available to link two stimuli is finite. Thus, stimuli compete for associative strength. If one stimulus has already formed a strong association with another—say the ringing of a bell with the presentation of food to a hungry dog—adding another stimulus, like a short whistle, it will yield little learning. Overshadowing is based on the same assumption, but in this instance both stimuli (i.e., the bell and the whistle) are presented at the same time, but one is much more salient than the other. So, if the bell is really loud, the dog may form a stronger association between it and the food, than the whistle and the food. In the Chamizo *et al.* experiment, a landmark close to the platform tended to be better learned than landmarks that were present at the same time, but were farther away.

the rats from a point 180° from their usual starting position. Normal rats continued to swim directly to the platform (whose position had not been changed), and this suggests that other landmarks in the room guided behaviour. Conversely, the rats with a specific brain lesion tended to swim in the location dictated by the rotated landmarks—suggesting that they did pay attention to these landmarks. From this study, then, it's not entirely clear which cues intact animals use to find the submerged platform.

In a second study, Maurer and Derivaz (2000) positioned three thin grey cylinders near one another at the side of a water maze with transparent walls. Great care was taken to ensure that these were the only landmarks available in the testing room. Rats were trained to find a hidden platform within this water maze, and its position was kept constant across training days. Probe trials showed that when the cylinders were shifted to a position 180° away from their initial position on the periphery of the maze, the rats shifted the location where they searched for the platform by 180°. When the array of cylinders was 'pivoted' away from the water maze (keeping the array together, but moving two of the cylinders away from the maze walls), the rats also shifted where they searched for the hidden platform. However, this shift appeared to be based on both the position of the displaced array of cylinders and the distance to the maze walls. The results from manipulations of the cylinder size and spacing were less clear-cut, but appeared to show that rats were sensitive to these factors as well. Overall, these findings suggest that extra-maze landmarks guide the direction in the pool where the rat searches for the platform.

In a third study, Young et al. (2006) looked at the cues used to solve the water maze, but their findings suggest the use of subtle intra-maze cues, as opposed to presumably salient extra-maze landmarks. In this study rats were trained to find a hidden platform in a maze curtained off from the remainder of the room, with four extra-maze cues (different dark shapes on a white background) positioned in different locations within the curtained enclosure. Once the rats had learned the platform location in this environment, removal of the four landmarks did not disrupt behaviour—in this case, measured solely by the time taken to find the platform. Rotation of the pool itself, in the absence of the landmarks, did increase the time it took for the rats to find the platform, still in its original location. It's not clear whether the authors also rotated the visual landmarks in this study—they mention rotation of the curtains—but even if so, this did not increase the latency to find the platform. So, in this study, there was little evidence to show that the extra-maze visual landmarks used were necessary to locate the submerged platform. Rather, it seems like some intra-maze landmark may have been used.

Overall, it is not entirely clear how extra-maze information guides behaviour on the water maze. That the information from outside the pool is used is clear from the majority of studies I've described, the Young *et al.* (2006) study being the exception. The best evidence that the spatial array of landmarks is used was found by Maurer and Derivaz (2000), but their data also suggest that rats learn the distance of the hidden platform to the maze walls. There are a few additional studies worth noting in this regard, each with rather different testing conditions.

In the first of these, Moghaddam and Bures (1996) found that rats can learn to solve the maze in complete darkness if they are trained to swim from a fixed start location to a fixed platform location. This learning is much slower than that of animals trained on the same task in the light. Although the authors suggest that learning the maze in the dark is egocentric, they also found that when the start location and platform location were shifted by 90°, some animals returned to the previously correct platform location. This suggests some use of allocentric cues to find the platform, even in the dark.

In a second study, Hamilton *et al.* (2004) carefully examined the behaviour of rats as they swam to a visible platform—that is, a platform that stuck out from the water. Using the distinctions of O'Keefe and Nadel (1978; see Chapter 6), rats could find the platform by identifying its location in the environment, or they could simply use the platform as a beacon and swim towards it. What Hamilton *et al.* found was that rats appeared first to use an allocentric strategy to orient to the direction of the platform when placed in the pool. There was then a slight dip in their speed—referred to as a shift point—when the rats looked around. Once they saw the platform, they swam directly towards it. Thus, the rats appeared to use both a spatial- and a beacon-approach strategy, even when the platform was always visible. A similar strategy of orientation based on extra-maze cues followed by a beacon-led approach was observed in the normal rats tested by Clark *et al.* (2007).

Finally, McGregor *et al.* (2004a) found that rats learn to locate a hidden platform using both intramaze landmarks (a black and white sphere and a grey pipe in the maze) and extra-maze landmarks. This again suggests that rats will learn about distal extra-maze cues, even in the presence of obvious intra-maze landmarks.

Landmark use in an open field

A simple way of examining spatial learning and memory is to look at the behaviour of experimental animals, usually rodents, as they search for a hidden reward or explore objects in a large, open arena. Such an arena usually has walls, and may contain landmarks. Typically, when introduced to a large environment for the first time, rats will explore its perimeter. This 'wall hugging' is referred to as *thigmotaxis*. As the rat becomes more familiar with the enclosure, it tends to explore the centre of the enclosure. If the rat is familiar with the arena and a new landmark—for example, an object of some type—is introduced, the rat will typically move towards the object and 'explore' it. With extended exposure, the rat habituates to the object and spends less time exploring it.

This spontaneous exploration of objects can be used to assess memory (Berlyne 1950; Ennaceur and Delacour 1988). If multiple objects are present in the arena and the animal has explored these, spatial memory can be tested by moving one of the objects relative to the others, or by interchanging the positions of a subset of the objects (Poucet *et al.* 1986; Thinus-Blanc *et al.* 1987; Dix and Aggleton 1999). Re-exploration of the displaced object indicates that the animal has noticed that the object has changed position, and therefore must remember the object's original position.

What about the use of objects as spatial landmarks? Using a 3.5-metre diameter circular arena, Tom Collett and his colleagues (Collet *et al.* 1986) examined how Mongolian gerbils used landmarks to find a hidden location which contained sunflower seeds. In a previous study, Cartright and Collett (1983) had shown that bees recognize a location by matching their current view to that observed previously at the same location. With gerbils, the question was in part whether mammals did the same thing. What the authors observed was that the gerbils readily found hidden seeds that were repeatedly placed in a specific direction and distance from a white cylindrical landmark (Fig. 3.6). Because the gerbils searched in one location, and not in a circle the correct distance from the landmark, they knew not just how far away the seeds were from the landmark, but also in which direction the seeds were placed. The animals did this by establishing their directional orientation from the start box used to release the animal into the enclosure. If two different landmarks were placed at a fixed distance from one another, with the seeds a certain distance away, the gerbils learned about the location of the hidden food with respect to each landmark. Thus, if the space between the landmarks was subsequently increased, the gerbils searched in two locations—each the correct distance from one of the landmarks.

If three landmarks were available and arranged in a triangle, the gerbils could use a subset of the landmarks to find a fixed, hidden reward location. They could also use the array itself as a directional cue if their start box was placed in different locations on different trials (and was thus an unreliable source of initial orientation). Interestingly, the gerbils appeared to 'know'

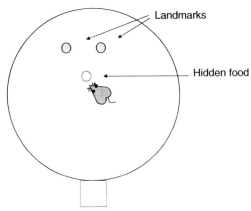

Fig. 3.6 Schematic of the testing environment used by Collet *et al.* (1986) to assess how landmarks are used to identify the location of hidden sunflower seeds. The searching pattern of gerbils on this task suggests that they learn the distance and direction of the hidden seeds from each landmark.

where they were going to go before they arrived, as they would go to the correct location—the location of the hidden seeds—even if the lights were turned off on their way there.

For Collett *et al.* these experiments suggest that gerbils learn a reward-location vector (direction and distance) relative to a landmark. The gerbils must also recognize where they are relative to the landmark when they begin a trial from the start box. Thus, to find the hidden reward location from the start box, the gerbils take into account their current location relative to the land-mark (the 'seen' vector), and the reward's location relative to the landmark (the 'stored', or learned vector). This use of stored vectors to identify locations is an alternative to an overall map-like representation of the environment. However, as the authors suggest, these alternatives are difficult to separate in an animal that has learned the distance and direction of a reward location rela-tive to all of the landmarks in the environment. A counter example, perhaps, is the finding that dogs can take a direct shortcut between two rewarded loca-tions that they've only experienced separately (Chapuis and Varlet 1987). Such flexibility is consistent with the use of a cognitive map of the entire environ-ment, but is slightly more difficult to explain with respect to learned vectors, as the vector between reward sites has not been previously experienced.

Another important study tested whether learning of a spatial landmark in an open environment could be blocked by previous learning of a different land-mark. Biegler and Morris (1999) found that rats could learn to find a hidden reward site based on its location relative to distinctive landmark, or to be precise, an array consisting of a distinctive landmark and two identical, ambiguous landmarks. When an additional distinctive landmark was added to the arena, the rats readily explored it. However, when the rats were subsequently tested with just the added landmark, they could not find the hidden reward site. Thus, the rats had failed to learn where the reward site was in relation to the added landmark. Control rats, trained in the presence of both distinctive landmarks from the start, could use either. This demonstration of blocking suggests that spatial learning obeys the rules of associative learning, and contrasts with the view that new information is readily incorporated into a cognitive map of the environment (O'Keefe and Nadel 1978; see later).

The Barnes maze

Carol Barnes developed a maze that takes advantage of the rats' natural preference for dark, enclosed locations and their dislike for open, brightly lit situations. The maze is made up of a circular table with 18 holes on its periphery (Fig. 3.7). Beneath one of the holes is a dark tunnel that the rat can enter. The location of the 'correct' hole—the hole that leads to the tunnel—can

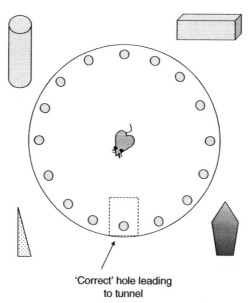

'Correct' hole leading
to tunnel

Fig. 3.7 Schematic of the Barnes maze. Rodents prefer dark, enclosed environments, and, when placed at the centre of an open table top, will search for the hole on the periphery that will take them to a darkened tunnel. Only one hole leads to the tunnel, however, and the animals identify its location based on its spatial relationship to extra-maze landmarks.

be identified by its spatial relationship with extra-maze landmarks in the environment (Barnes *et al.* 1980; Harrison *et al.* 2006). The rat begins each trial by being placed in a small cylinder in the centre of the table. The cylinder is raised, and the rat is then free to go where it wishes. Again, rats prefer the darkened tunnel to the open table top, and, with training, will head relatively directly to the hole that leads to the tunnel.

Using this maze, Barnes showed that old rats were not as accurate as young rats in finding the correct hole. Young rats would make an average of just over three errors (looks at the incorrect holes) before finding the correct hole, whereas old rats made an average of over five errors per trial (Barnes 1979; Barnes *et al.* 1980).

The Barnes maze also works well with mice, and a study by Bach *et al.* (1999) found that old mice, like old rats, aren't as good as younger animals at finding the correct hole based on extra-maze landmarks. However, if a cue was placed right behind the correct hole, both old and young mice were equally able to run directly to it. Thus, older mice were impaired on a spatial version of the task, but not on a beacon version. This impairment correlated with a decrease in longer-term changes in the strength of the connections between neurons.[2]

Homing by path integration

The tasks that I've described thus far capitalize on adaptive aspects of the rats' behaviour. The RAM and T-maze task likely work well because the rat has a propensity to forage in different locations for food. It may be adaptive for the rat to remember the locations where food sources have been exhausted, and to conserve energy by not revisiting them. For the Morris water maze, the

---

[2] Such changes are thought to be the basis for learning and memory. A review of this work, for which spatial learning has been an invaluable tool with experimental animals, is a book in itself (see Squire and Kandel's *Memory: From Mind to Molecules*, or Kandel's *In Search of Memory*). The starting point, briefly, is 'Hebb's Rule', a formulation by the Canadian physiological psychologist Donald Hebb in his 1948 book entitled *The Organisation of Behavior*. The rule is that, if one neuron repeatedly takes part in the firing of a second neuron, some growth process takes place whereby the connection (the synapse) between these is strengthened. A subsequent discovery by Bliss and Lomo (for review see Bliss, Collingridge, and Morris in *The Hippocampus Book*) has shown that in one brain region (the hippocampus), a long-lasting strengthening of the synaptic connection between neurons occurs with repeated stimulation. The strengthening is termed long-term potentiation (LTP). LTP has two phases: a shorter phase, which depends on a biochemical cascade within the neuron, and a late phase, which depends on the production of proteins. Mice that are genetically engineered to have impaired late LTP in the hippocampus are significantly impaired in learning the spatial location of a submerged platform in a Morris water maze (Abel *et al.* 1997).

adaptive response is perhaps more immediate: if the rat doesn't escape from the water, it will drown. For the Barnes maze, the motivation is the rats' preference for dark, enclosed environments as opposed to brightly lit, exposed situations.

A further type of spatial task capitalizes on the rodents' propensity for returning to a 'home' site. In a typical homing task, the rat leaves its nest and forages for food on a large platform or in a large arena. Once it encounters a piece of food that is too large to consume immediately, the rat will take the food back to its nest by a direct route (Fig. 3.8). As rats are able to return to their nest directly from any point along their foraging route, they must keep track of where they are relative to the home site. From an adaptive standpoint, the ability to make a beeline to the nest may be useful when the rat encounters a predator or wishes not to share any large food discoveries.

From a way-finding perspective, homing is of interest because it speaks to how well orientation can be maintained in the absence of landmarks. This maintenance of orientation by the (putative) integration of distance and

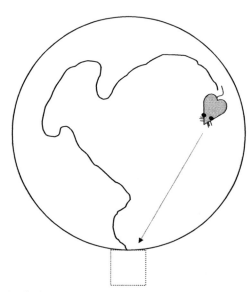

Fig. 3.8 Schematic of a homing task. In such a task, the rat leaves a 'home' at the periphery of the circular platform and searches for a food morsel on the platform. Upon encountering the morsel, the rat will typically head directly back to its home with the morsel. The ability to make a direct return to the home after a meandering path on the platform suggests that the rat continuously updates its direction and distance relative to the home.

direction travelled is referred to as *path integration*.[3] It is thought to be an internal process, although external information may be used in a non-landmark-based way. Path integration (PI) is hypothesized to rely on an ongoing integration of self-motion information provided by vestibular cues, motor efference copy (copies of the brain motor signals that command movement), and an integration of optic flow—that is, a sense of movement as objects pass across the retina.

One of the original demonstrations of path integration is reported in two papers by Mittelstaedt and Mittelstaedt (1980; 1982). The authors tested the ability of female gerbils (desert mice) to retrieve their sucklings and return to a nest on the periphery of a circular arena. The authors found that after the gerbil searched the platform and found the suckling, it returned directly to the nest. As the sucklings were found in different locations on different excursions, the gerbils' ability to return directly to the nest suggests that they knew where they were, relative to the nest, at all times. The gerbils did this in complete darkness, and persisted in their search for the nest if the nest was moved during the gerbil's outbound journey. The strongest evidence that this task was performed by PI comes from manipulations of the gerbil before it commenced its homebound journey. If the cup on which the suckling was found was placed in the centre of the arena, and was rotated slowly while the mother was in the cup fetching the suckling, the gerbil returned to an incorrect location that corresponded to the amount of rotation. Specifically, if the gerbil was slowly rotated by 37°, it searched for its nest site in a location about 37° off the true location. This 'fooling' of the gerbil suggests that knowledge of the direction or location of the nest was internal, and not specified by any extra-maze cues. Faster rotations of the gerbils didn't fool the animals, presumably because such rotations were detected by the animals' vestibular system and corrected for. Essentially, with faster rotations, the gerbils 'knew' that they'd been rotated and adjusted their homing trips accordingly.

....

[3] Path integration is also occasionally referred to as *inertial navigation*. That is, it's a form of navigation that depends on changes in the inertia of the organism, and, presumably, some form of time estimation. Sensitivity to inertial changes immediately suggests the involvement of the vestibular system, and there is evidence that this system is indeed critical for the maintenance of orientation (Matthews *et al.* 1989; Whishaw *et al.* 2001). A related term is *dead reckoning*, which refers to a calculation of one's current location based on the knowledge of the distance, speed, and direction one has travelled from a start point or previously known location. Dead reckoning is different from path integration in that the latter in an ongoing process—an organism is continually integrating its travelled path relative to its start point—whereas a reckoning of a position is a periodic calculation based on time, speed, and direction (Cornell and Heth 2004). Finally, *idiothetic* navigation refers to maintenance of orientation based on the knowledge of one's own movements.

A series of experiments from the laboratory of Ariane Etienne have systematically explored homing ability with golden hamsters. In the initial demonstration of homing, Etienne (1980) showed that hamsters would go from a nest site to a location with food, fill their cheek pouches, and then return directly to their nests. In this way, they'd hoard food.

In a paper published in 1986, Etienne and colleagues provided some of the strongest evidence for path integration in animals. They tested individual hamsters in a large circular arena that was equipped with 12 equally spaced doors on its periphery. Behind one of the doors was the hamster's nest, and the remainder of the doors were closed. Individual hamsters actually lived in these nests during the period of testing. The floor of the arena was covered with sawdust, and during test sessions this was raked about so potential olfactory cues associated with a specific location would be disrupted. In addition, the hamsters were tested under infrared light, and 'pink' noise generators masked any uncontrolled sounds.

Etienne *et al.* observed that hamsters made a direct return to the nest site even if they were taken from the nest to the centre of the arena in a box. Thus, the hamsters didn't actually have to walk to the centre of the arena to be able to return home accurately, although on trials in which they were permitted to do so their accuracy was considerably better. In a first experiment, the authors carried individual hamsters to the centre of the arena in a box, and, while doing so, rotated the arena and the attached nest site by a fixed amount (90°, 135°, or 180°). Thus, any local cues in the arena or nest were rotated relative to the hamster's possible expectation. What Etienne *et al.* observed was that 7 of the 14 hamsters returned to the former direction of the nest. The remaining hamsters homed to the correct side of the arena, but their responses were not statistically significant.

In a second experiment in this impressive study, the authors showed that hamsters transferred to a second arena before making their homebound journey tended to head in the correct direction—that is, the direction that would have taken them to the nest site if they'd remained in the original arena. A third experiment ruled out the possibility of magnetic cues as a source of orientation. In a final experiment the arena and nest box were rotated by 90° or 180° before the hamster left the nest. Under these circumstances, the hamsters returned directly to the nest after visiting the centre of the arena, and not to the former nest location. This suggests that the animals maintained their orientation from the nest, and not from any cues in the testing room. Together, these results suggest that the hamsters were able to keep track of the location or direction of their departure point—the nest box—without using external cues like vision or smell. This ability to home in the absence of external information suggests that the hamsters were path integrating.

In a 1988 work, Etienne *et al.* found evidence that supports the predictions that follow from a path-integration explanation of homing. First, if PI reflects the integration of self-movement information, it should be prone to accumulating error. That is, unless the rodent is perfectly able to keep track of its movements, some slippage in its knowledge of orientation is likely to occur the more it moves. So, homing after a long and convoluted excursion should be less accurate than homing after a very short excursion.

The authors tested this by leading (or passively transporting) the hamsters from their nests on the periphery of a circular arena to the centre of the arena, in infrared light. At the centre of the arena, the hamsters were led on a series of either three, five, or eight full turns before being allowed to fill their cheek pouches with food and to return to their nests. Hamsters reliably found their nests after three rotations in the centre of the arena, but were less accurate after five rotations, and even worse after eight rotations. In addition, the errors in their return direction were in the same direction as the turns, suggesting that the animals didn't fully compensate for the rotations when more than three were done. In a separate manipulation, the authors also showed that changing the point at which the PI process starts yielded a corresponding change in the hamster's homing direction.

As in their 1986 study, Etienne and colleagues observed that if the hamsters were transferred to a second, adjacent arena immediately before their return journey, they would head in the same direction as in the first arena. Thus, the hamsters did not appear to compensate for the passive movement associated with the transfer from one arena to the other (in which case they'd head for absolute location of the 1st nest site), but did compensate for changes in their angular heading. This maintenance of angular or directional orientation across adjacent arenas is consistent with the maintenance of direction across adjacent T-mazes, as described in the previous section (see also Dudchenko and Davidson 2002). Together, these findings suggest that rodents may be able to maintain a sense of direction across environments.

Another study from the Etienne laboratory (Etienne *et al.* 1998b) examined the ability of gerbils to use path integration to go to a reward site from a nest site. In the task, gerbils were led by an experimenter (holding a bait) from a nest site at the periphery of a circular arena to a different point along the periphery of this arena. From there, the gerbils' task was to head to the interior of the arena, where four identical cylinders, equidistant to one another and about halfway from the periphery to the arena centre, were found. One of these cylinders consistently contained food, the others did not.

Etienne *et al.* found that gerbils reliably selected the correct cylinder after being led to different points along the arena periphery. They chose the correct cylinder even if it was unbaited, suggesting that the smell of food wasn't necessary to find it. They were also able to find the correct cylinder in the dark. If the nest was moved to a different location prior to the outbound journey, the gerbils searched for the goal cylinder based on the location of the nest, not on room or uncontrolled arena cues. The authors suggest that gerbils, in their initial experience of going from the nest to the cylinder, learned a nest-to-goal vector. When the animals were subsequently led to different positions along the arena periphery, they combined their knowledge of their position relative to the nest (their current-position vector, assumed to be based on path integration), with the learned nest-to-goal vector, and then proceeded to the goal cylinder by subtracting one vector from another.

These results are clear, although one concern is that for three of the six peripheral test locations, the nearest cylinder was the correct one. Secondly, from some of the other peripheral locations, the gerbils seemed to pass close to or directly underneath another cylinder. Though they didn't sample these cylinders by climbing in them, it seems possible that the gerbils could have detected their lack of a food scent.

Some of the clearest evidence for path integration is found in the experiments of Ian Whishaw and colleagues at the University of Lethbridge. Although I'll consider the neuroscience aspects of this work in Chapter 6, their data from control rats provide evidence for the use of path integration in rats. Whishaw and colleagues trained and tested rats on a circular table top with escape holes on the periphery, as in the Barnes maze (for review see Whishaw *et al.* 2001). In the task, rats emerged from their 'home' hole, foraged on the open table until they encountered a food reward and then returned directly to the correct (home) hole. If the rats were trained with a constant 'home' location in a room with extra-maze cues, they used these cues to identify the correct hole (Maaswinkel and Whishaw 1999). However, rats were equally capable of doing the task in complete darkness (under infrared light), and their home journeys continued to be direct. Moreover, if the rats were started from a new hole in the darkness, they tended to return to this hole after they'd found the food, and not the previously trained hole. This suggests that the rats were able to maintain their orientation relative to the start hole in darkness, indicative of path integration. In another version of the task, rats started from a dark box that was placed on the periphery of a large (155 centimetre diameter) table. The rats left the box, foraged on the table until they encountered a food reward, and then made a direct return to the box to consume the food. Again, they did so readily in the dark, and even returned to the box's location if the box was removed right after the rat began its outbound journey.

Intriguing evidence for path integration is found in a study by Wallace and Whishaw (2003). These authors looked at how rats explored a circular table after leaving a small box located at the periphery of the table. Rats were tested both in the light and in darkness (under infrared light), and normal animals usually made circuitous exploratory trips from the 'home' box. At some point in a given trip the rat would decide to go back home, and would do so with a direct home-bound run. Not only were these runs directed towards the home box, even in darkness, but the peak speed of the rat's running occurred at the mid-point of the home-bound journey—regardless of how far the rat was away from the home box. Thus, in darkness, the rats appeared to 'know' how far away they were from the home box, and would speed up and slow down appropriately. As we'll see later, this capacity depends critically on a specific brain region.

The use of path integration has also been assumed in an experiment by Shettleworth and Sutton (2005). The authors tested homing in a 16-sided arena with 16 doors on the periphery. One door led to the animal's 'home' box, and the remaining doors could not be opened. The rat's task was to leave the home box, find food within the arena, and then return to the home box. The floor of the arena was covered with bedding, and the rats were disoriented before starting the task by being rotated eight times in a minute on a turntable. The arena was curtained off from the remainder of the room.

In a first experiment, rats trained on the task with or without a beacon (a black panel surrounding the correct door) homed accurately. In a second experiment, one group of rats was trained with the beacon at the home door, whereas a second had the beacon placed at a different door, relative to the home door, each day. Again, both groups homed accurately, and both continued to do so even when the beacon was removed. In a third experiment, the authors show that initial exposure to the environment without the beacon did not block subsequent use of the beacon when it is later placed at the home door.

The authors' interpretation of these findings is that, in the absence of a beacon, or in the presence of an unreliable beacon, rats found the home door by dead reckoning. The fact that rats trained with a reliable beacon could still find the home door when it was removed suggests that the beacon did not overshadow the animals' dead reckoning. Finally, the lack of blocking suggests that dead reckoning does not compete with beacon use in homing behaviour.

These conclusions may be correct. However, the authors assume that if the rats aren't using the beacon, then they must be using dead reckoning. They argue against the use of any (presumably) subtle extra-maze cues based on prior demonstrations of path integration in other labs. A more explicit way of demonstrating the use, or lack of use, of path integration is to manipulate the animal at the point at which it begins its homing journey. It is to these studies that we turn next.

Manipulating path integration

If animals find their way back to a nest site by using an internal sense of their direction (and possible distance) relative to the nest, it should be possible to fool the animals in the following way: at the point at which the animal gathers food at a food source, but just before it begins its home-bound journey, it could be rotated very slowly. If just the animal is rotated independently from the arena (by rotating the platform upon which the food source is located), and if the homing is via internal path integration, the animal should home in the wrong direction (Fig. 3.9) The magnitude of its error should correspond to the amount that the animal has been rotated.

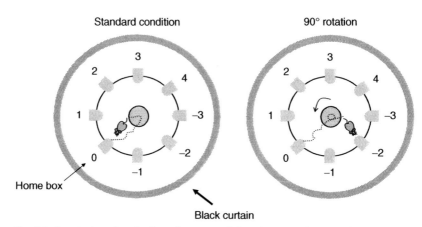

Fig. 3.9 A technique for 'fooling' the sense of direction. *Standard condition*: Rats are trained to retrieve a food morsel from the centre of a circular platform and return with it to their home box (box 0). The remaining home boxes, numbered relative to their distance from box 0, are closed. The platform is surrounded by a black curtain to prevent access to any extra-maze landmarks. *90° rotation*: once an individual rat returns to box 0 readily under the standard condition, it is given probe tests to attempt to fool its sense of direction. In these tests, when the animal is at the centre of the platform gathering its food morsel, a tube rises from the platform floor to confine it to the centre temporarily. Then, the centre floor is rotated slowly by 90°. If the rat uses internal information to guide its navigation to the home box from the centre of the platform, and if it can't detect the slow movement of the floor, the rat should be fooled by this rotation, and, once the confining tube is lowered, should head to a home box 90° away from the actual home box.

As described earlier, this is what the initial Mittelstaedt and Mittelstaedt experiments found. Rotating the gerbils by 37° caused a corresponding shift in the direction of their homing. In hamsters, Séguinot *et al.* (1993) also rotated the animals slowly (one rotation per minute) prior to a homing journey. This produced a misorientation of the homing journey, although the authors did not relate the amount of rotation to the amount of error. A lack of orientation towards the nest site in the dark was also produced if hamsters were rotated 10 times quickly (0.8 rotations per second) before they started their homebound journey (Griffin and Etienne 1998). Presumably, the hamsters weren't able to compensate for such a rotation. However, if the same rotation was followed by the lights being turned on for 10 seconds, the hamsters were able to reorient to the nest site. Thus, a brief exposure to the visual landmarks in the environment allows a presumably misoriented animal to reorient (see also Etienne *et al.* 2000).

As manipulation of the animal, and presumably its internal sense of the direction, has the potential to provide strong evidence for the use of path integration, I sought to establish it in the rat. In two experiments, Ms Catriona Bruce and I (Dudchenko and Bruce 2005) trained rats to run from a home box on the edge of a circular platform to its centre, where the animal found a large piece of food. The home box was one of eight identical sites, the remainder of which couldn't be entered because their entranceways were blocked with clear Plexiglas.

Rats reliably returned to their specific home site, even if they were kept in the centre of the circular platform for a short period of time. Thus, the rats could remember the direction or location of their home sites reliably. To show that the animals were using path integration, we rotated the rats slowly by 90° while they were in the centre of the platform gathering their food. The centre of the circular platform moved independently, so the home site and the remainder of the maze did not change positions. However, to control for any olfactory cues associated with the home site or the circular platform surface, we moved the home box to a different position while the rat was being slowly rotated. We also wiped the platform surface with a detergent-soaked cloth. The rats were then permitted to return to their home site, and the sites chosen are shown in Fig. 3.10. As is evident from Fig. 3.10a, despite having been slowly rotated, the rats returned to their original home site. In another manipulation (Fig. 3.10b), we rotated the rats in one direction while they gathered their food from the centre of the platform, and the platform itself in the opposite direction. Here again, the rats were not fooled, and returned reliably to their original home site.

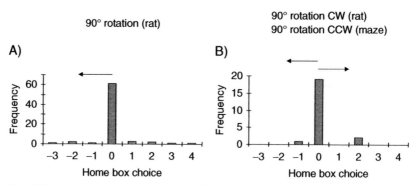

Fig. 3.10 Even under the controlled conditions shown in the previous figure, fooling the rats' sense of direction is difficult. In one set of experiments, Catriona Bruce and I (Dudchenko and Bruce 2005) failed to fool the rats when we rotated them by 90° slowly (*left plot*). Under these conditions, the rats did not use uncontrolled cues on the platform surface, because if we rotated the platform itself (while the rat was slowly rotated in the opposite direction), the same result was obtained (*right plot*).

In our hands, rats were not misoriented by slow rotations. In a subsequent experiment (van der Meer *et al.* 2007), evidence that the rats' sense of direction could be fooled was observed in a subset of animals that were disoriented before each training session. Together, these findings suggest that PI may be used in homing in some circumstances, but in others, rats can, presumably, use quite subtle extra-maze cues to home. This variability in homing behaviour, or perhaps the motivation to home, may be genuine: in studies with hamsters (Séguinot *et al.* 1993; Griffin and Etienne 1998) 60% or more of the animals either failed to return directly to the nest site or to hoard food reliably.

Geometry and spatial learning

In the final portion of this chapter, I turn to research on the use of the shape (geometry) of the environment as a way of recognizing locations. The essential phenomenon is that a variety of animals (including people, as we'll see in Chapter 5) can find a goal location by using the shape of the environment to distinguish places within it. A strong version of this idea is that the shape of the environment is used even when other information, for example, an obvious landmark, is present. Based on the evidence for this, researchers have suggested that a 'geometric module' for spatial processing occurs in the brain (Cheng and Newcombe 2005). If such a feature does exist, it may allow us to remain oriented in enclosed environments without many features, although it may also lead us to discount reliable landmarks in favour of the overall shape of the enclosure.

Evidence for the use of environmental shape to identify locations was initially presented by Ken Cheng (1986). He trained and tested rats in a rectangular enclosure with small panels in each corner of different texture, colour, and smell. A food bowl was buried in one corner of the enclosure under the bedding that covered the floor, and the hungry rats' task was to find it. Control trials showed that the rats could not find the food based on its smell. In one version of the task, rats were first exposed to food in a given location and then tested for their ability to return to that location on a subsequent trial. In another version, the food was in a fixed location across trials, so the rat just had to learn where the food bowl was hidden. In both versions of the task, rats readily learned to find the food, but made interesting errors. If, for example, food was found in one specific corner of the enclosure, rats would tend to look for the food either in this corner *or* the corner diagonally opposite it. That is, when making mistakes, rats often chose the corner that would be correct if the rat was facing the opposite direction (the rotationally equivalent corner; see Fig. 3.11). This finding suggests that the rats did not just rely on the distinctive panels in the corners of the enclosure as landmarks or beacons, but also used the shape of the environment to find the food location. Thus, if the rats have

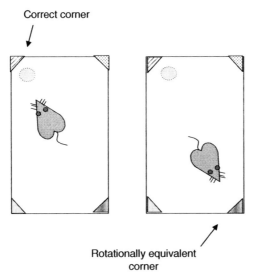

Fig. 3.11 In a rectangular environment, Cheng (1986) and others have shown that rats trained to find food in one corner of apparatus will search both the trained corner and the rotationally opposite corner. Thus, rats appear to use the shape of the environment, and not the distinctive features of individual corners, to guide their spatial behaviour.

the capacity to distinguish their left from their right, the shape of the environment alone is sufficient to narrow down the possible locations of reward to the correct corner and its rotational equivalent. Wall *et al.* (2004) confirmed this using a rectangular environment without landmarks in rats, and Gouteux *et al.* (2001a) did so in disoriented rhesus monkeys.

What's surprising about Cheng's finding is that the rats didn't just use the distinctive corner panels in the enclosure to find the hidden food. The rats appeared to use these features to an extent to distinguish the correct corner from its rotational equivalent, as they tended to choose the correct corner on the majority of trials. However, when they made mistakes, they tended to choose the rotationally equivalent corner. Further, if the panels were shifted one corner over, the rats were much less accurate, and tended to make errors by selecting the previously correct corner. Thus, the corner panels were used by the rats in this task, but not exclusively, and the rats' errors suggested that they also paid attention to the shape of the enclosure.

Similar results were observed by Margules and Gallistel (1988). Using a nearly identical task and environment to Cheng, they found that rats could distinguish the 'correct' corner of the rectangle (the corner containing the hidden food) from the remaining three corners if they had access to cues outside the enclosure. For the authors, this confirmed the rats' tendency to use, preferentially, distal cues or landmarks for orientation. However, when access to these cues was prohibited, the majority of rats chose the correct and rotationally correct corners equally. Thus, even in the presence of distinctive corner panels, the rats used the shape of the environment to determine their orientation.

Another example of the use of shape, as opposed to distinctive landmarks, is found in a study by Benhamou and Poucet (1998). They placed three distinctive cones in a triangular arrangement in a Morris water maze. A first experiment demonstrated that the rats could distinguish the cones from one another. In a second experiment, rats were trained to find the hidden platform located between two of the three cones. However, when the cones were arranged as an equilateral triangle, the rats showed no preference for the correct platform location: they spent as much time there as they did in each of the geometrically equivalent incorrect locations. This suggests that the rats weren't paying attention to the distinguishing features of the landmarks, but were rather using the overall 'shape' of the cue configuration. If the cones were arranged as an isosceles triangle (i.e., one 'side' of the triangle is longer than the other two), rats searched for the platform in the correct location. Again, this suggests that the rats used the overall shape produced by the arrangement of the three cues.

Muddying these waters somewhat are findings that if one wall of a rectangular environment is a different colour from the other (and thus serves as a distinguishing landmark), the geometry of the environment may not serve as a prominent cue for orientation. For example, Golob and Taube (2002) found that disoriented rats could learn the location of a submerged platform in a rectangular water maze where one of the short walls was of a different color. Under these circumstances, disorientated rats used a landmark to reorient. A caveat to this, however, was the finding that when the same rectangular environment was used as a 'dry' maze and the rats' task was to remember which corner contained a reward, the rats did not distinguish between corners very well. Thus, in a different task in the same environment, a landmark was not used for reorientation. These, and earlier findings (Martin *et al.* 1997; Dudchenko *et al.* 1997b; Gibson *et al.* 2001), suggest that the use of a landmark for reorientation depends on the nature of the task. If the task is appetitive—the rat is seeking a reward—then disoriented animals may reorient based on the shape of the environment. If the task is aversive—the rat is trying to avoid something it doesn't like—then reorientation can occur based on a landmark.

The use of a landmark for reorientation has been tested in human adults (Hermer and Spelke 1994) and rhesus monkeys (Gouteux *et al.* 2001a). In monkeys, a methodical series of experiments showed that monkeys use large landmarks—like a coloured wall or a larger corner panel—to reorient in a rectangular environment. If these landmarks are small, however, monkeys rely on the shape of the environment for orientation.

Can shape be ignored?

The results of Cheng, and Margules and Gallistel (and additional findings in human children that I'll present in Chapter 5) suggest that the shape of the environment is sometimes used for orientation even in the presence of other reliable cues. This is counter-intuitive, and may suggest that the mammalian brain can't help but pay attention to the shape of the environment when attempting to orient. It also runs contrary to what would be expected from an associative learning account: if stimuli compete for associative strength, the stimulus that best predicts the occurrence of another is the one that should garner the most attention. For spatial learning, if a landmark is in a fixed location relative to a hidden platform, the rats should use it, and not the shape of the environment, if the shape permits more than one solution (e.g. as in a rectangular environment). An alternative account is that of O'Keefe and Nadel (1978). Their idea, described in more detail in Chapter 6, is that spatial learning differs from strict associative learning in that new information, detected by

exploration, is readily added to a cognitive map, even if the existing information in the 'map' is sufficient to identify the location of a goal.

A number of experiments have examined these alternatives. Pearce *et al.*
(2001) trained rats to find a hidden platform in a triangular water maze. For
some rats, a black rod with a white disc was attached to the platform and served
as a 'beacon' to tell the rats where the platform was located. For others, no
beacon was available. What Pearce *et al.* found was that rats trained with a
beacon still looked for the hidden platform in the correct location even when
the beacon had been removed. Thus, these rats had apparently learned where
the platform was relative to the shape of the environment, even though they
could have relied just on the beacon. Beacon learning failed to completely
overshadow shape learning. A similar result was observed by Hayward *et al.*
(2003): rats trained to find a hidden platform in a rectangular environment
with a landmark (a 12 centimetre sphere near the hidden platform) still showed
that they had learned about the geometry of the environment when tested in
the landmark's absence. The authors also showed that rats learned about the
shape of the enclosure even when extra-maze cues outside the enclosure were
visible during training. Finally, Wall *et al.* (2004) showed that a landmark
established clear stimulus control over rats' spatial behaviour in a rectangular
environment. However, in a blocking paradigm (training with the same landmark across two environments so that the landmark, and not the shape of the
environment, was the best predictor of reward location) rats nonetheless
learned to find the reward based on the environment's shape. Together, these
findings are consistent with the idea that some attention is paid to the shape of
the enclosure regardless of what other information is available. In this way,
learning about the shape of the environment may reflect the cognitive map
learning proposed by O'Keefe and Nadel.

A related set of experiments by Pearce *et al.* (2006) (see also Graham *et al.*
2006) looked at shape learning in the presence of distinctly coloured walls. The
take-home message from these experiments was that learning about shape was
not independent of learning of a non-geometric cue. The authors found that
coloured walls helped shape learning in kite-shaped pool—where, potentially,
the shape may not have been a particularly distinctive cue. However, in a
rectangular pool, having two adjacent black and two adjacent white walls
prevented learning about the shape of the environment. That is, the distinctive
combination of coloured walls (e.g. a corner where two black walls met) was
learned on the basis of the colour of the walls, with no attention to the shape of
the environment. Even in a more ambiguous situation where the long walls of
the rectangle were black and the short walls white, the colour of the walls over-
shadowed learning of the environment's shape. In addition, prior training in a

square environment with two adjacent black and two adjacent white walls blocked shape learning for animals subsequently trained with the same combination of coloured walls in a rectangle.

But do rats, in using the shape of the environment, use the entire shape to orient, or just some aspect, like a distinctive corner? Pearce *et al.* (2004) sought to distinguish between these two possibilities, which they termed the *global solution* and the *individual corner solution*. They found that learning in a rectangular water maze transferred to a kite-shaped environment that possessed a similar local feature (a corner that looks the same in both environments). Thus, rats appear to use an individual corner solution to find the hidden platform. This conclusion, and similar results in chicks by Tommasi and Polli (2004), resulted in an interesting and well-reasoned debate. Cheng and Gallistel (2005) argued that, although it was true that the animals in these two experiments did not use the overall shape of the environment when generalizing between two contexts, there were alternative global solutions that could be invoked. One possibility was that the animals used the principal or long axis to identify the correct location across different environments. The principal axis is, essentially, a line that one could draw through the centroid of the figure that would divide it into two equal halves. In the Pearce *et al.* experiment, use of the principal axis would direct the rat to the common corner in both the rectangle and the kite mazes. Cheng and Gallistel suggest that this is a more parsimonious account of the data.

McGregor *et al.* (2006) responded to Cheng and Gallistel's challenge by conducting a simple, yet elegant, experiment. Rats were trained to find a hidden platform at a corner at the base of a simple house-shaped (pentagonal) maze. Following this, they were tested in a rectangular-shaped maze. In the rectangle, one group of rats was trained with the hidden platform in the two corners that were identical to a corner found in the house-shaped maze. In the second group, the rats were trained in the rectangle to find the hidden platform in the corners that were not common to the house-shaped maze, but agreed with the principal axis of both environments. The authors found that rats trained to find the platform in the identical corners significantly outperformed the rats trained to find the platform in the corners defined by the principal axis. This suggests that the rats used some local feature of the corner, common to both environments, and not the principal axis, to learn the hidden platform's location.

To summarize, rats and a number of other animals are able to use the shape of the environment to identify spatial locations. In some instances, the use of shape overshadows the use of other non-geometric landmarks, particularly if these landmarks are small. In other situations, clear evidence for the use of landmarks, and for competition between landmarks and geometry, has been demonstrated. These results suggest that, although environment shape may be a salient orientation cue in some situations, an obligatory and impenetrable 'geometric module' may not exist.

Maze tasks and real world spatial orientation

In this chapter I've described a number of experimental approaches for assessing spatial cognition in experimental animals. Given the rodents' propensity for solving spatial tasks, it is of course possible that our tools have been shaped to play to their strengths. Nonetheless, these tasks indicate that three types of information can be used to identify a location: beacon landmarks, spatial landmarks (including the shape of an environment), and path integration.

Beacon use is perhaps the simplest way to identify a location. For rats, an example of a beacon task is the visible platform condition in the Morris water maze. If the platform is visible, the rat simply has to swim towards it. More generally, if a destination is visible and recognized, it's relatively difficult to envision how one might lose their way. Once I leave the lab and see Edinburgh castle, I'd have little difficulty in finding my way there—I just have to keep it in view.

The second way in which rats identify a spatial location is by the use of spatial relationships between landmarks. On the radial arm maze, rats identify specific maze arms by their spatial relationship to extra-maze landmarks. On the hidden platform version of the Morris water maze, rats learn where the platform is hidden by its relationship with the constellation of landmarks outside the pool. In contrast to beacons, spatial landmarks themselves are not the destination, but specify a location by their constant direction and distance from the destination. Navigation based on spatial landmark use requires recognition of the landmarks and knowledge of the spatial relationships between the landmarks and the intended destination. In some situations, an added landmark isn't used if the animal has previously learned to identify a location based on an existing landmark.

A variant on the use of spatial relationships between landmarks is the use of the shape, or geometry, of the environment as an orientation cue. Lacking other cues, or even in the presence of some non-geometric landmarks, animals can reorient based on the shape of the enclosure in which they find themselves.

The third means of identifying a location, again based on studies in animals, is by maintaining orientation with respect to the to-be-remembered location at all times. For rodents, this likely underlies some forms of homing when landmarks are unavailable. The benefit of this system lies precisely in the circumstances in which it is observed: it permits the maintenance of orientation in 'cueless' environments or the dark (and, as we'll see in Chapter 8, in exploring new environments). The downside of PI is that it may be prone to accumulating error. In humans, if analogous processes occur, they may give rise to a mistaken sense of orientation in the absence of familiar or distinguishable landmarks.

Chapter 4

Human navigation

I also recall a story about a Northern Saskatchewan
trapper who was familiar with his walking pattern–
he knew that he veered left when trying to walk in a
straight line. One day he was caught in a white-out
on a lake. By walking ten steps straight ahead then
taking one to the right he was able to make the shore
and take cover among the trees and avoid making the
dreaded circle so many people do when trying to go
in one direction.
Usne J. Butt (2002)

I've only been lost once as an adult. I was hiking with my wife in the hills
in Scotland, and, as William Naismith experienced (Chapter 1), a thick mist
descended. We were high on the hill, a bit tired, and could only see a little
of the trail in front of and behind us. As any walker of the Scottish hills will
confirm, there are often multiple paths on the hills created by the sheep that
freely roam there. The trail that we were attempting seemed wrong. It was
much longer than anticipated, and didn't seem to be taking us down off the
hill. We had a map and compass, and so could establish our orientation, but
not where we were. Eventually, we encountered other hikers, and learned our
precise whereabouts. We descended in the correct direction, and once below
the mist, were able to see where we were and the way back to the car.

How did we come to feel lost? We were on a route that we'd not travelled
before, and the visibility was limited. So, distant landmarks couldn't be used.
However, had we possessed a strong magnetic sense of direction, or the capacity to path integrate over long distances, we may have retained our sense of
orientation. Setting aside personal deficiencies in cognitive ability (although
these are undoubtedly significant), how well are humans able to stay oriented
when a destination can't be seen? The studies I'll review in this chapter suggest
that humans are quite limited in their way-finding abilities when landmarks
are unavailable (Fig. 4.1).

Fig. 4.1 In New York City, authorities have experimented with placing decals showing directions on the sidewalks (pavements) outside subway stations. These are to help people emerging from the subway to 'get their bearings'.

Reproduced with permission from the *New York Times*, 17 October 2007 (Surface help for subway riders). The photo is by Ruby Washington.

Taxonomies of wayfinding

An assumption that I make throughout this book is that people typically don't get lost when in the presence of familiar landmarks. Basically, if we recognize our surroundings, we know where we are. Thus the main subject matter of this chapter is how we find our way in the absence of landmarks. However, before considering this subject, it is worth mentioning the ways in which we likely find our way under normal circumstances.

On the account of Gary Allen (1999), there are three types of wayfinding. The first is an 'oriented search' strategy, whereby we start from a known orientation, say our hotel in an unfamiliar city, and search for a destination or explore a location relative to this. This may resemble a homing strategy, where exploratory trips from a known, and presumably visible, base are followed by a return to the base. A second means of wayfinding is route following. Here Allen gives the example of painted lines on a hospital floor that guide the visitor to specific destinations (e.g. the maternity unit). Obviously, following a route isn't terribly taxing, and, of course, this is precisely the point. A third category of wayfinding is piloting from landmark to landmark. This, essentially, is the list of directions someone might give us to get to a destination: turn left at the first light, turn right at the tall building, go straight towards the harbour, etc. One landmark leads to the next, until the destination is reached. An unusual variant of this, cited by Loomis *et al.* (1999), is the use of an imagined reference island—an etak—as a landmark by Micronesian boaters travelling from island to island in the Pacific Ocean. In their conception, the boat is visualized as being motionless, and the etak changes location as the voyage progresses (see Lewis 1994).

An extension of Allen's three types of wayfinding has been proposed by Wiener *et al.* (2009). They describe different types of wayfinding based on the information available to the navigator, and the purpose of the journey. Their first distinction is between *aided* and *unaided* wayfinding. In aided wayfinding, the navigator follows signs, a map, or a GPS to get to a specific location. For example, a backpacker attempting to walk the Appalachian Trail (a 2,175-mile footpath in the eastern United States) simply needs to follow the white 'blazes'—square white marks on trees or rocks along the trail—that mark the entire route.

In unaided travel, Wiener *et al.* make a distinction between *undirected* and *directed* wayfinding. Undirected wayfinding includes exploration of new environments and also trips within familiar locations without a particular destination in mind. Directed wayfinding, in contrast, occurs when one has a specific destination in mind. If one doesn't know the precise location of the destination, the individual may perform a *search*, which is *informed* if there is some rough knowledge of the environment, or *uniformed* if the environment is unfamiliar. If the location of the destination is known, then the task becomes one trying to get there, or *target approximation*. If the route to the destination is known, then the task is simply that of *path following*. If the route isn't known, then one engages in *path finding*, either by searching for a path that will take one to their destination, or by planning a path to the destination through the intermediate unknown territory.

Walking in circles and veering

Although our wayfinding usually relies on landmarks or aids, what happens when landmarks aren't available, or our surroundings are unfamiliar? Anecdotal accounts, like that of the Canadian trapper that heads this chapter, suggest that disoriented people wander in circles. An early and curious explanation for this was that all organisms—from amoebas to humans—have an innate spiralling tendency (Schaeffer 1928). Schaeffer's results suggested that if blindfolded, humans will travel in repeated circles, and they will do so when walking, swimming, or even driving a car. He first observed this when attempting, together with students, to walk in a straight line with blindfolds on after a light snowfall. The tracks they left in the snow showed that they'd walked in regular spirals. In one example (Figure 4.2a), a university instructor veered to the left or right (usually until reaching a fence) when attempting to walk in a straight line on a race track. Others showed spiral paths, and Schaeffer argued

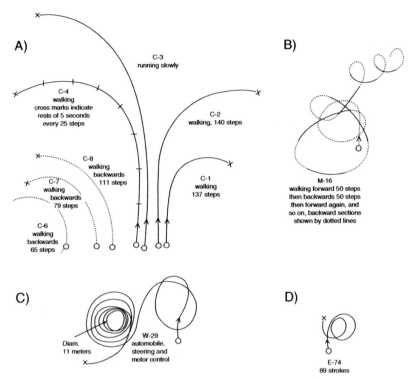

Fig. 4.2 Examples of circling behaviour described by Shaeffer (1928). *A)* Veering while attempting to walk, with a blindfold, in a straight line on a race track. *B)* Circling is still observed when a person alternates between walking forwards and backwards, suggesting that it isn't due to differences in leg length. *C)* Example of circling when driving while blindfolded *D)* Example of circling while swimming.

Reproduced from Schaeffer (1928) Spatial movement in man. *Journal of Morphology*, **45**: 293–298.

that these weren't due to physical asymmetries in the legs as some people still 'spiral' when alternately walking forward and backward (Fig 4.2b). In addition, people also showed spiralling when driving blindfolded (in a Ford coupe at 13 kilometers per hour, Figure 4.2c) or giving instructions to a driver while sitting in the passenger seat, blindfolded. Thus, for Schaeffer, the mechanism underlying spiralling was above the level of the spinal cord, and underlies our behaviour when lost:

> Persons who lose their way in forests, snow-storms, fogs, etc., go 'round in circles', because in these persons the orienting senses are not functioning, and then the spiralling mechanism guides the path. (p. 394)

In a footnote, Schaeffer suggested that:

> The circles made by persons losing their way are of course much larger than these experimental circles with the eyes blindfolded; for with the eyes open it is possible to walk straight stretches as far as one can see clearly, which may be 10 or 20 meters in a snowstorm or fog, to several hundred meters in a forest. The circles in the latter cases are really irregular polygons and may have circumferences of 10 or even 30 kilometers, according to some accounts. (p. 310)

For Shaeffer, we get lost because we are unable to orient using our senses—such as vision—and an innate mechanism for spiralling then is revealed.

Lund (1930), however, argued that the notion of a spiralling mechanism was unnecessarily mysterious. As Schaeffer did not record physical asymmetries, his study failed to rule out the simpler interpretation that walking in circles is due to differences, for example, in leg length. Lund tested this alternative explanation by having 125 blindfolded undergraduate students walk in a straight line on a flat playing field. He found that the students began to veer from a straight line before they'd walked 100 feet, and they continued to do so up to the farthest point measured (300 ft.; see Fig. 4.3). About 55% of the

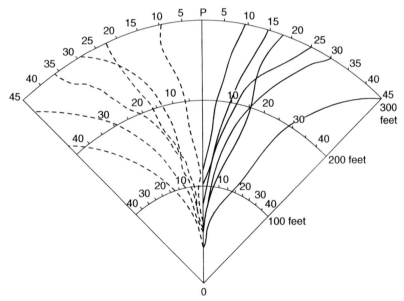

Fig. 4.3 Examples of veering while walking blindfolded on a flat playing field. Lund (1930) found that the students tended to veer after about 100 feet.

Reproduced from Lund (1930) Physical asymmetries and disorientation. *American Journal of Psychology*, **42**: 51–62.

students veered to the right, and 45% of the students veered to the left. Lund measured the length of the students' legs and found that one leg was often slightly longer than the other. If the student's left leg was longer than their right, they tended to veer to the right. If the right leg was longer, they veered to the left. If the blindfolded students walked backwards while trying to maintain a straight line, they veered in the opposite direction. Larger differences in leg size led to greater deviations from the straight line. Thus, in contrast to Schaeffer, these results suggest that because our legs aren't perfectly equal lengths, we tend to veer in the direction of the shorter leg—presumably because we cover slightly less ground with the shorter leg stride.

Results from an experiment by Klatzky et al. (1990) showed that we veer less the faster we walk. Blindfolded participants who walked slowly veered by an average of 12.7° over a 14 metre walk, whereas those who walked at a normal rate veered by 10.1°, and those who walked fast veered by 8.9°. Over 100 feet, the authors calculated, walking at a normal speed would produce a veer of 22°. Using a relatively strict criterion (veering in the same direction on at least 12 of 15 trials), 59% of the participants veered consistently.

Veering has been observed in other situations. Boyadjian et al. (1999) had people try to keep a straight line for 15 metres, while blindfolded, by walking, pushing themselves in a wheelchair, or directing someone else who pushed their wheelchair. In all three conditions, people veered. When walking, they veered by 2.5 metres on average, and when pushing themselves in a wheelchair they veered by 3.2 metres. In both of these conditions, individuals tended to veer in a consistent direction across trials, although different individuals veered in different directions. People veered in the same direction when walking and travelling in a wheelchair about half the time. When guiding someone else who pushed them in a wheelchair, people were 4 metres off, but veered inconsistently across trials. These results are consistent with the Lund findings, and suggest that physical differences between limbs may also account for veering when using one's arms. Veering that occurs without the use of limbs (when directing someone who is pushing you) isn't based on fixed differences between appendages, and thus is not consistent across trials.

However, some have argued that veering isn't simply due to physical asymmetries. In a review of veering studies, Guth and LaDuke (1994) cite data from a monograph by Cratty (1965) indicating that veering may not be due to simple differences in leg or stride length. In one experiment, blind people attempted to walk in a straight line across an athletic field. Of the participants, 65% veered, but the veers were unrelated to difference in leg length or stride. In a 1966 study, Cratty and Williams asked 43 blind participants to walk a straight line, and 91% of these veered consistently (that is, in the same direction) across trials. Consistent veering was also observed in two of the four blind participants that Guth and LaDuke (1995) tested, but in this study, no attempt was made to relate veering to physical asymmetry. Similarly, consistent veering was observed by Day and Goins (1997), but they did not find a consistent reversal of veering direction when the participants (13 blindfolded women) walked backwards.

Veering can also be influenced by changes in posture or the presence of distracting stimuli. A study by Millar (1999) found that blind children veered towards a sound of a brief handbell ring when attempting to walk straight across a room. Blind children also veered from a straight line if they carried a 2-pound bag in one hand. In this instance, children veered in the direction opposite to the load bearing arm, presumably because they leaned slightly away from the load as they carried it. In a control condition, blind children were able to walk directly across a 2 metre room to an experimenter if they heard her voice prior to the start of the walk. Thus, blind children can walk in a straight line across 2 metres, but veer away from this if an irrelevant sound is presented to one side, or veer if their posture is altered by carrying a load in one hand. Surprisingly, it has also been shown that concentrating on one's gait while walking leads to an increase in veering, while engaging in a distraction task (reciting male, female, or animal names to oneself) leads to a decrease in veering (Vuillerme *et al.* 2002).

One account of veering suggests that it is due to small errors in the angle of our steps. Kallie *et al.* (2007) tested the ability of blind and blindfolded participants to walk in a straight line over 9.14 metres. Both groups veered from a straight line, on average by about 0.82 metres, and there was no difference between blindfolded and blind participants. Kallie *et al.* showed that this veering wasn't due to an inability to detect a curved path, as the participants' threshold for detecting curvature in paths did not correlate with their veering. Based on a model, the authors conclude that direction of an individual step varies by about 1°. As this error accumulates with each step, veering will occur as a person walks further.

Significant variability in step direction, and consequent veering, is observed in individuals with damage in their vestibular system when they try to walk in a straight line to a previously seen target while blindfolded (Glasauer *et al.* 1994). The authors suggest that this is likely due to a loss of balance while walking. However, this veering may also be due to an inability to maintain locomotion in a specific direction. This is an intriguing alternative because, as we'll see in a subsequent chapter, disruption of the vestibular system severely disrupts the brain's representation of direction.[1] Although individuals with vestibular system damage veered, they were as accurate as control subjects in estimating the distance to the previously seen target. This suggests that the vestibular system may not be necessary to keep track of the distance one travels in the absence of vision.

In another study, little evidence for veering was found when participants wearing opaque glasses attempted to walk in a straight line over 8 metres (Paquet et al. 2007). Little average directional error was also observed when participants walked backwards over the same distance, although greater error was observed when they walked sideways. When re-tested on the same task a week later, the participants' errors weren't strongly correlated with their performance on the initial test. It's not clear why veering wasn't observed in this study, although the distance walked was somewhat less than that used in other studies with adults.

Finally, an intriguing recent study has confirmed Schaeffer's earlier observations that people tend to walk in circles when lacking orientation cues. Souman et al. (2009) had six university students attempt to keep a straight course over several hours in an unfamiliar German forest. Four of the students walked in cloudy conditions, and all four walked in circles. The two remaining students walked when the sun was out, and their paths were relatively straight. The authors tested three participants in the Saharan desert, and found that two of the subjects, tested during the day, veered from a straight line but didn't walk in circles. The remaining subject, tested at night, ended up heading in the opposite direction when the moon was obscured by the clouds. Additional tests examined the ability of blindfolded participants to walk in a straight line for 5- or 10-minute trials on an airstrip. On average, after a few minutes of walking, participants had veered by approximately 100 metres. Some participants did walk in circles, but the direction of veering was not consistent across trials for the same subject.

In contrast to the results of Lund described earlier, Souman et al. found that physical asymmetries could not account for the direction of veering. Differences in the strength of each leg did not correlate with veering, and even manipulating the relative lengths of individual legs (by varying sole size) did not produce systematic changes in veering. On their account, veering and walking in circles is caused by a cumulative error in the subjective sense of direction.

---

[1] Berthöz et al. (1999) attribute this difficulty to a lack of input from the head direction cell system (see Chapter 8). The results from Glasauer et al., I suggest, may imply that linear path integration (estimating how far one has moved), and angular path integration (estimating how one's change in direction) rely on separable parts of the nervous system.

It's clear from this brief review that veering is frequently observed when people try to walk in a straight line without vision (the exception being the Paquet *et al.* study). There is less of a consensus about how this occurs. An unusual, early explanation was that an innate spiralling mechanism is responsible for walking in circles, although subsequent studies suggested that differences in leg length produce veering when walking, and differences in the arms presumably underlie the veering that occurs when self-propelling a wheelchair. Others have suggested that error in the direction of individual steps is to blame. If physical differences cause veering, then a consistent drift in the same direction would be expected when walking without vision. However, in some situation consistent veering is not observed. Veering can be influenced by postural shifts and by the presence of incidental stimuli during the walking attempt, so it's likely that in real world situations, veering may be influenced by a person's physique, aspects of the external environment, and perhaps most intriguingly, drift in one's subjective sense of direction.

Walking towards a target you can no longer see

Imagine that you're in a snowstorm, looking for your tent, and the snow pauses for a few seconds allowing a brief view of the tent in the distance. The snow then resumes with its full fury, and you can't see a thing. How long would the memory of this view be sufficient to guide your subsequent search in the snow?

The answer, according to an elegant study by Thomson (1983), is 8 seconds. If you haven't found your tent in 8 seconds, there's a good chance you are going to miss it, unless you happen to be within 5 metres of it. Thomson showed this limit in human wayfinding by having undergraduate students view a wooden marker that was placed at distances ranging from 3 to 21 metres away. They then closed their eyes, and walked to the marker. The students were accurate in walking to the marker with eyes closed when it was up to 9 metres away, but beyond this their performance was significantly more variable (see Fig. 4.4). Thus, if walking 12 metres, on one trial they might walk beyond the marker, and on another they might stop well before the marker.

It turns out, however, that it wasn't the distance to the marker that was critical, but rather the time taken to get there. The students could get to a marker 9 metres away in about 6.6 seconds, but going to a marker 12 metres away took about 9 seconds. If the students were allowed to run, they could accurately get to a marker 21 metres away. Conversely, if the students had to close their eyes and wait for a few seconds before starting out, they could only reach a target 3 or 6 metres away, depending on how long they had

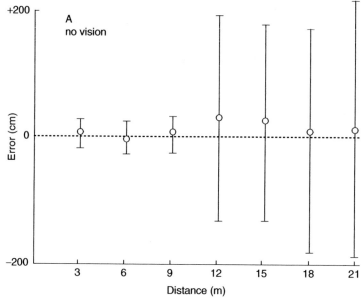

Fig. 4.4 Thomson (1983) found an increase in the variability of distance estimations when walking without vision to a previously viewed target more than 9 metres away. This increase, on Thomson's evidence, was due to the amount of time it took to walk 9 metres or more.

Reproduced from Thompson (1983) Is continuous visual monitoring necessary in visually guided locomotion? *Journal of Experimental Psychology: Human Perception and Performance* **9**(3): 427–443. Published by the American Psychological Association, and reprinted with permission.

to wait. The critical cut-off time was 8 seconds. Students were accurate at getting to the target if it took 8 seconds or less, and inaccurate if it took more than 8 seconds.

There was one caveat to these findings. If the distance to the target was 5 metres or less, the students were accurate, regardless of the 8-second cut-off. Thomson suggests that for this 'near space', people execute a motor programme—a set of 'motor instructions'—that isn't as sensitive to decay as the memory for targets farther away. For targets beyond 5 metres, however, a simple motor programme isn't sufficient. Here, the person must remember where the target is, and that memory starts to become inaccurate after 8 seconds.

A subsequent study by Elliot (1986) claimed to be unable to replicate Thomson's findings. However, as pointed out in a reply by Thomson (Thomson 1986), Elliot's study did not directly speak to the previous findings because participants took longer than 8 seconds to reach targets beyond 'near space'.

As argued by Thomson, introducing a short delay before going to the target should not impair performance in near space, and thus no delay effects were seen in Elliot's study when participants attempt to reach targets 3 or 6 metres away. For distances beyond this near space, introducing a delay should result in reduced accuracy, but only if the distance could be covered in less than 8 seconds. In Elliot's study, this wasn't the case. Thomson suggests that this may be related to a lack of feedback provided to participants in practice sessions—walking with one's eyes closed is unnatural, and providing feedback in practice sessions may instil confidence in the participant, and may allow them to 'calibrate their system' to their gait.

A study by Riesser et al. (1990), however, also attempted to replicate Thomson's 8 second limit finding, this time with participants who were given practice sessions with feedback. Participants were asked to walk to targets 2–22 metres away with their eyes closed. Riesser et al. found that the amount of variable error (the absolute distance from the target) increased proportionally with increasing target distances, but there wasn't a jump in error after 9 metres. Instead, error was about 8% of the target distance for most distances. Interestingly, the authors also measured the participants' veer while walking with closed eyes, and found that: (1) veer wasn't consistent across trials—both left and right veers were observed in the same subjects; and (2) the amount of veer was about 4% of the distance to the target, and increased linearly with the target distance. A further finding was that, when participants were asked to walk quickly, they tended to overshoot the target location.

It's not clear how the Thomson and Riesser et al. findings can be reconciled. From a psychological perspective, they point to different mechanisms for finding one's way in the absence of vision. For Thomson, we have an 8-second window for accurately remembering a target's location, and beyond this a sharp increase in variability is observed. For Riesser et al., variable error in finding a target without vision depends simply on how far away the target is—the farther away, the more error. From a wayfinding standpoint, however, both studies suggest that error in walking to a target without vision increases when one walks more than 10 metres or so. The Riesser et al. findings further suggest that veer creeps in with longer distances. Given these limits, it's easy to see how quickly we might have problems getting to a previously seen target in fog, darkness, or snow, or when we are in an environment lacking distinguishing features.

Estimating target location

Another approach to the study of orientation in the absence of vision is to ask people to point to a previously seen target. Böök and Gärling (1981) found that people exhibited a fair bit of error in their ability to remember the direction and distance of a target light in a dark room. In their study, in one condition, a small red light was illuminated for 5 seconds, and after it was turned off, the participants were guided to a stopping point between 1.4 and 11 metres away. They were then to estimate the distance and direction to the previously seen red light. Error in these estimates increased with increasing distances, and the authors concluded that the participants' 'maintenance of orientation is far from accurate' (p. 1004). They suggest that forgetting, and the recurrent processing of target's location and the distance walked, contribute to this inaccuracy.

More accurate estimates of the distance to a previously seen target were seen using a 'triangulation' approach. Fukusima *et al.* (1997) had participants look at a target—a white ball on top of a tripod—in an open, grassy field on the University of California Santa Barbara campus. In one condition, participants pointed to the target, and then closed their eyes and walked 5 or 10 metres parallel to the target, while still pointing at it. By using the beginning pointing direction and the end pointing direction, the authors were able to triangulate the participants' perceived target location. Participants were quite accurate at pointing to targets up to 15 metres away, with mean errors of usually less than 1 metre. This occurred both when the participants pointed to the target, and in a different experiment when they faced the target after moving to its left and right. In a final experiment, Fukusima *et al.* found that subjects were also accurate in walking directly towards the target with their eyes closed, as in the experiment of Thompson described earlier. Although the results were consistent with those of Thompson in that participants, on average, walked about the correct distance, they differed from his results in that a sharp increase in variance was not observed after 10 metres.

Going back to the start: triangle completion tasks

Another way of testing how well people find their way in the absence of vision is to blindfold them, lead them in one direction, and then in a second, and then ask them to return directly to their starting location (see Fig. 4.5). Essentially, the participant is led over two sides of a triangular route, and then completes the triangle by returning to the start. The studies that I'll summarize below indicate that humans show a fair amount of error in this task, even over short distances.

A 1951 study by Worchel used this technique with blind children and sighted children wearing blindfolds. In one task, the children were led by the experimenter over two legs of a right isosceles triangle, and were then asked to return to the start point. Several different sized triangles were tested, and the route back to the start, the hypotenuse of the triangle, varied between 8 and 22 feet.

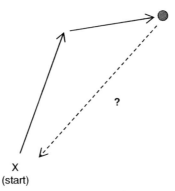

Fig. 4.5 The triangle-completion task is one way of testing the ability to keep track of changes in distance and direction. In the task, the participant, often blindfolded, begins at a start point ('X'), and is led by the experimenter in one direction, and then another. The participant's task is to return in a direct line to the start point.

For both blind and blindfolded children, the average error—the distance between the actual start-point and where the children thought it was—increased with the size of the triangle (Fig. 4.6). Blind children were somewhat worse than sighted children with blindfolds, and this was attributed to the blind children's tendency to head in the incorrect direction. Worchel suggests that the differences between the blind and the sighted children in this task may relate to the latter group's ability to visualize the overall shape of the route.

A subsequent study suggested that accurate completion of the triangle task without vision does not depend on the vestibular system. Worchel (1952) compared deaf children with or without impaired vestibular function on the

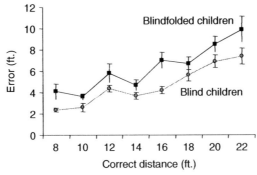

Fig. 4.6 Worchel (1951) found that both blind and blindfolded children showed an increase in error on the triangle-completion task with increasing triangle size. Blind children were slightly worse at the task than blindfolded children, and Worchel ascribes this to the ability of sighted children to visualize the route.

triangle task as described earlier. Surprisingly, the children with impaired vestibular function were better than those with intact vestibular function. A similar lack of impairment on this task has been seen in adults with unilateral vestibular loss (Péruch *et al.* 2005). In both studies, the intact performance by those with vestibular loss was attributed to a compensatory use of kinaesthetic/proprioceptive cues.

In an important study, Loomis *et al.* (1993) tested blind and blindfolded sighted participants on smaller-scale triangle completions. They were first led in one direction for 2, 4, or 6 metres, and then in a second direction for 2, 4, or 6 metres. The participants' task was to then return to the start position, marked as an 'X' in Fig. 4.7. As is apparent in this figure, although the participants headed in the right general direction, they often missed the starting point, even over these short distances. Loomis *et al.* present the data from every participant, and the figures show that participants frequently missed the starting point. They state that 'no single subject came close to exhibiting negligible

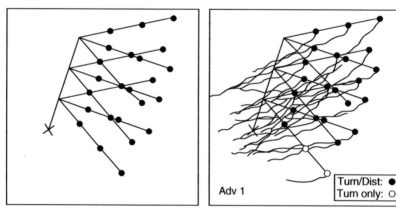

Fig. 4.7 In a study by Loomis *et al.* (1993), blind and blindfolded individuals were tested on a triangle-completion task. *Right figure:* Participants began at the 'X' and were led along one direction for 2, 4, or 6 metres, and then another until they reached a stopping point—shown as a dot. The lengths of the two legs of this outbound journey were varied, and thus a number of different routes are shown. *Left figure:* When attempting to return to their starting point (curvy lines), participants tended to head in the correct direction, but, even over these short distances, usually missed the target.

Reproduced from Loomis *et al.* (1993) Non-visual navigation by blind and sighted: assessment of path integration ability. *Journal of Experimental Psychology: General* **122**: 73–91. Published by the American Psychological Association, and reprinted with permission.

errors over the 27 triangles' (p. 83), and that even given the short distances of the triangles, participants couldn't use path integration accurately. On this task there was no difference between blind participants and sighted participants who were blindfolded. The average absolute error in direction was 22° and 24° for the two groups of blind subjects (one group was congenitally blind; the other became blind at a later point in life). The error for the sighted participants with blindfolds was also 24°. The absolute distance error (that is, how far from the start point they finished when trying to complete the triangle) was on average 1.37 metres for the congenitally blind participants, 1.07 metres for the adventitiously blind participants, and 1.68 metres for the sighted/blindfolded participants.

A comparison of different species on the triangle completion task, including spiders, bees, ants, hamsters, dogs, and humans, reveals a common type of error. Etienne *et al.* (1998a) showed that all six species tended to undershoot the start location when attempting to return to it. As pointed out by Cornell and Heth (2004), this type of error—walking a smaller triangle than the actual route—has the advantage of re-crossing the initial outbound leg of path, which may permit the encounter of previously seen cues.

A variant on the triangle completion task was used by Sholl (1989) with blindfolded undergraduates. The starting point of her experiment was the surprising observation that some female participants make errors when asked to estimate the orientation of a water surface in a tilted container. This is Piaget's 'water-level' task. Sholl's hypothesis was that error on this task—indicating that the water tilts with the container—may arise from difficulties using information from the otolith organs. These are the part of the vestibular system that detects the orientation of the head relative to gravity. To test this, Sholl first identified participants who either did or did not make a number of errors on the 'water-tilt' test. She then tested their ability to maintain their directional orientation after being pushed in a wheelchair, while blindfolded and wearing headphones, over a path with two, three, or four segments (each of which was 2.4 or 4.9 metres long). The participants' task was to point to the start of the route after travelling the various segments. Under these conditions, putatively, the only information available for orientation was that coming from the vestibular system. Participants who were poor at the water-tilt test were particularly poor at keeping track of their orientation in this task—even over just two segments. However, if blindfolded participants walked the segments, they were much more accurate in pointing to their start point. Thus, information from self-movement substantially improved the participants' ability to maintain their orientation.

A task similar to Sholl's was used by Klatzky *et al.* (1990) with blindfolded participants. Participants were led over routes that had one, two, or three segments, and then asked to return to their starting point. Of course, for the one segment route, the participant simply had to turn 180° around and retrace the line that they'd just walked. The two segment paths were triangle completions, and the three segment routes were more complicated 'shapes' including one route that crossed over itself. Identical routes were constructed of a short length (< 3-metre segments) and a longer length (< 10-metre segments). Participants showed nearly a 20° absolute error when simply turning around and heading back over a one-segment route. Over two segments, they had a 22° error, and they showed a 35° error over routes with three segments. There was no difference between the short and longer length routes, but some routes were more difficult than others, even with the same number of segments.

Another variant of triangle task was used by Professor Alain Berthöz and his colleagues. In a review of these experiments, Berthöz *et al.* (1999) describe a task (Glasauer *et al.* 1995) in which participants viewed a short triangular route and then attempted to reproduce it while blindfolded. The nature of this task was different from that of Loomis *et al.* in that it measures the accuracy of reproducing a previously viewed triangle, as opposed to the 'online' processing of one's location relative to a start point. However, the task used by Berthöz and colleagues also allowed measurement of error in the distance walked for each leg of the triangle, and the direction of each leg of the triangle. Distance errors increased over the three sides of the triangle, and participants made an angular error of –7° on the second and third legs of the triangles. Thus, participants tended to underestimate how much they needed to turn in order to reproduce the previously seen triangle.

Triangle completion in virtual space

A different way of testing how well people can maintain their orientation is to test them in virtual environments. In these studies, participants view their virtual environment on a large screen, or on a head-mounted display. An advantage of this technique is that it allows the experimenter to reduce an environment to its elements, and then manipulate these. In an elegant study using this technique, Kearns *et al.* (2002) tested how well people were able to complete a triangle when the only information available was from optic flow. This was done by presenting a virtual environment where the floor, the walls, or both had a visual 'texture'. Participants moved through the virtual environment, via a joystick, to temporary posts which marked the end of each of the first two legs of a triangular route. Once the post disappeared, the participants' task was to return to the beginning of the triangle. The triangles were similar in size to those used in the Loomis *et al.* study (4.25 metre for one leg and 2.25 or 4.25 metres for the second leg). Across the different virtual environments, participants tended to head in roughly the correct direction, but as in the Loomis *et al.* study, with substantial error. They typically under-turned and headed in directions that were off by between 10° and 43°, and ended up more than 3 metres or more away from the start point, on average. Thus, the perception of movement provided by optic flow allowed only a coarse estimate of orientation. In a subsequent experiment, subjects walked the triangles while viewing the virtual environment with a head-mounted device. (Interestingly, no subject reported 'simulator sickness' in this condition, whereas several subjects dropped out of the experiment when watching the virtual environment without self-movement. This suggests that the optic-flow induced perception of movement, without the matching physical sensation of movement, can be disagreeable.) When completing virtually viewed triangles by walking, subjects typically overturned, but they missed the starting point of the triangle by less (2 metres or more on average) than when performing the same task without walking. Under these circumstances, the presence or absence of visual texture in the virtual environment didn't have a strong effect on performance, and the authors conclude that when self-motion information is available, it is used in preference to optic flow information.

How the path integration process takes place during these tasks isn't entirely clear. One possibility is that people continuously update their orientation relative to the start point as they move away from it. Alternatively, orientation relative to home may be based on memories for the segments of the route. Wiener and Mallot (2006) attempted to distinguish between these possibilities by testing people on virtual path completion tasks over a single distance (18 metre) with two, three, four, or five segments. They reasoned that if the orientation to the start point was based on memory for its segments, then orientation following travel over more segments should be slower and less accurate. However, Wiener and Mallot found that pointing error was similar regardless of the number of segments in a route, and response time was faster with more segments. Thus, in this study, the complexity of the route didn't influence path integration. The difference between these findings and those of Klatzky *et al.* (1990) described earlier is that in the Klatzky *et al.* study routes with more segments were also longer.

Virtual space with landmarks

Perhaps not surprisingly, the most accurate demonstrations of orientation appear to occur when landmarks are available. For example, Riecke *et al.* (2002) found that in a virtual small town, complete with streets, trees, and houses, participants were quite accurate at returning to a start position, with an average absolute error of 4°. In contrast, when the virtual environment only contained 3D blobs (to allow the perception of optic flow), participants had an absolute error of 18.6°.

A second demonstration of the superiority of landmarks for orientation is found in a study by Foo *et al.* (2005). This wasn't a triangle-completion study, but rather an experiment on the ability to take a shortcut between two virtual locations that had been experienced independently. Foo *et al.* found that participants were off by about 30° when attempting to take a shortcut of just 9.5 metres between two locations in a virtual desert. When the virtual environment contained stable landmarks, participants were much more accurate— particularly if the landmarks were near the goal location. Such was the reliance on landmarks that if they were surreptitiously moved after the participants' initial exposure to the environment, the participants still used them and deviated in their shortcut route. From these results, Foo *et al.* conclude that people aren't very accurate at calculating the distances and directions between locations that they have experienced separately. However, people readily use visual landmarks to make shortcuts when these are available, even early in learning (Foo *et al.* 2007). Together, the results from Foo and colleagues and those from Riecke *et al.* show that people use visual landmarks instead of other sources of information to find their way when landmarks are present.

Interim summary

The results from triangle completion tasks suggest that humans aren't terribly accurate in returning to a start point in the absence of visual landmarks. They exhibit errors 20–30° after travelling relatively short distances, and even show a 20° error when turning around after walking in one direction. A hierarchy of information for orientation is suggested by several findings. If one attempts to keep track of their orientation based solely on optic flow or vestibular information, only a rough maintenance of orientation is possible. However, if one walks two sides of a triangle in a triangle completion task, their ability to keep track of their orientation is somewhat better. The most accurate means of determining one's orientation is by the use of stable landmarks.

The significant error shown by humans when attempting to maintain orientation in the absence of vision contrasts with the impressive path integration capacity of rodents described in the previous chapter. One possibility is that rodents, as nocturnal foragers, have developed a better sense of self-motion tracking and homing than humans. Whereas visual perception of landmarks is central for humans and other primates in perceiving and orienting to their surroundings, it may be less so in animals, such as rodents, that have a more limited visual acuity. In the next section, however, I review the evidence for an alternative means of orientation.

Orientation over long distances: do humans have a magnetic sense?

The earth, in essence, is a giant magnet. If you pick up a compass and place it on your desk, you can detect this by watching the red tip of the needle swing towards the magnetic north pole. The magnetized metallic needle of the compass is suspended in a fluid (to remove jitter), and the needle detects the magnetic polarization of the earth.

As humans have evolved in the presence of this magnetic field, it's reasonable to wonder whether we have some sense of magnetic fields. Such a 'sixth sense' would be useful in finding one's way around, particularly in environments with few distinctive landmarks. Additionally, there is considerable experimental interest in whether other animals, particularly birds, can make some use of the earth's magnetic fields to navigate (Wiltschko and Wiltschko 2005; Mora *et al.* 2004). As I'll review next, the evidence for such a sense in humans has not been supported.

In 1980, Dr Robin Baker published a description of an intriguing experiment on the ability of humans to maintain a sense of direction. He conducted the experiment in Manchester, England and used university students as subjects. Baker blindfolded the students, placed them on a bus, and had them driven by an indirect route to locations 6 to 52 kilometres from Manchester University. The students were then taken off the bus one by one and, with blindfolds still on, asked to indicate which direction they thought they had been taken relative to the University.

The results were surprising in light of the data I've reviewed on the maintenance of orientation over short distances without vision. Even though the students had been blindfolded and asked not to talk with one another during the journey, they were fairly accurate at estimating the direction in which they'd been taken, and thus their homeward orientation. Baker's results suggest that people are able to maintain a sense of direction over not just metres, but also kilometres.

Another experiment in this study produced an even more controversial result. Students aged 16 and 17 years were taken from their schools on a bus to sites 5 kilometres (~3 miles) away. The route they took was indirect (16 kilometres in length) and involved many 'twists and turns' through a town. The students were all blindfolded, and half wore magnets in the elastic of their blindfolds. The other half of the students wore a brass bar of the same size.

The students wearing the magnets were unable to estimate the correct direction of the school from the drop-off point, whereas the students wearing the non-magnetic brass bar were able to do so. The implication of these results was that students estimated their direction after the bus journey by using a magnetic sense. Equipping the students with a magnet interfered with this sense.

Gould and Able (1981), however, were unable to replicate these results with university students from Princeton and from the State University of New York at Albany. They first took 40 Princeton undergraduates on an indirect drive in a school bus or in a van. The windows in the bus and van were covered, and the students were blindfolded and wore black felt hoods. Half of the students had magnets attached to the front of their blindfolds, whereas the other students had non-magnetic weights. They were driven to a site 20 kilometres from Princeton, and asked to write down the direction in which they thought Princeton could be found. Neither of the groups reliably pointed in the correct direction.

A single failure to replicate a finding can happen for many reasons. But Gould and Able also failed when they tried again. In a second experiment, with 15 blindfolded students and staff, they stopped at six locations along a route and asked the study participants to estimate the homeward direction. Of the six estimates, five were random (that is, as a group, the estimates were not centred on any specific direction), and the remaining, non-random estimate was 175° away from the correct direction. In three additional attempts with slight variations in the procedure, estimates from almost every site were random, and the few non-random estimates were well off the correct direction.

The authors next invited Dr Baker to join their efforts. They made three more attempts to observe the ability of people to correctly indicate the direction from which they had come after being blindfolded and transported to a different location. Dr Baker ran two of the three attempts. None of the attempts provided evidence for correct orientation towards the start location. Gould and Able concluded that:

> ... the students in Baker's studies either had cues available to them which were absent in the Princeton and Albany experiments, or are dramatically better than Americans in using whatever cues may be involved in judging displacement. (p. 1062)

Efforts by other authors also failed to show the humans possess a magnetic sense. In a study using 103 Australian university students, Fildes *et al.* (1984) went to extraordinary lengths to eliminate any possibility of detecting direction-based sight, sound, or sensation on the skin. They had the students wear surgical overalls, boots and aprons, and then black velour mittens and face masks. Noise protectors were placed over the students' ears, perfume was dabbed below their noses, and a wicker basket with a black cover was placed over their heads. The students were walked via a complex route to a platform on one of the university's playing fields. They were asked to point to the north, to their homes, and to Melbourne (~20 kilometres away). Under these conditions, not surprisingly, the directions in which the students pointed were random. When the students were allowed to repeat the tests after taking off all their insulation from the world, they were able to indicate which direction was north. Thus, this study provided no evidence for a magnetic sense of direction, although students were oriented when they had access to normal sensory information.

A subsequent study by Westby and Partridge (1986) found a consistent result. In three experiments, they tested the ability of Sheffield University undergraduates to estimate absolute direction and homeward direction following transport in a blacked-out mini-bus or Land Rover to a site 4 to 14 kilometres from the University. At almost all of the 'release' sites (places where students were asked to estimate the homeward direction), the students' estimates were random. Westby and Partridge concluded that there was no evidence for 'blind homeward orientation' (p. 330). They too add a tongue-in-cheek explanation for their results:

> There is no support either for Gould and Able's alternative explanation that British students are better than Americans at this task. Perhaps it depends on which side of the Pennine Hills the experiments are conducted?[2] (p. 331).

Taken together, these findings provide little support for the view that humans are able to keep track of their directional orientation following larger-scale passive movement in the absence of visual information.[3] A similar conclusion was made by Harold Gatty in his instructive book on navigation entitled *Nature is Your Guide* (1958):

> Some people . . . will even go farther, and imply that the sense of direction is a sixth sense, a quite special sense to be added to the five senses with which the ordinary man or woman (and many another animal) is born.

---

[2] The Pennine Hills are a north to south mountain range in northern England. Manchester University, where Robin Baker conducted his experiments showing support for a human magnetic sense, is on the west side of the Pennines. Sheffield University is on the east side.

[3] In a subsequent paper, Baker argued that if you consider several sources of data together using a specific statistical technique, his claim that people are able to maintain their sense of direction in the absence of visual information is supported (Baker 1987). He argued that, even if results from individual experiments are not always significant, the observation of several nearly significant findings is itself unlikely to occur by chance. Baker is correct on this last point; but the inability to directly confirm the initial finding he makes is, in my opinion, more persuasive.

I do not believe that there is any such sixth sense. A man with a good sense of direction is, to me, quite simply an able pathfinder—a natural navigator—somebody who can find his way by the use of the five senses (sight, hearing, taste, smell and touch—the senses he was born with) developed by the blessing of experience and the use of intelligence. (p. 17)

A good sense of direction?

Although there is no strong evidence for a magnetic sense in humans, there is evidence that we can keep track of our orientation when we can see our surroundings. Bovet (1994) drove 97 undergraduate students from Laval University in Quebec to a specified destination by a relatively direct route. The students were told before they left where they would be going (although on average only 15% of the students had experienced the release location before), and told that they'd be asked to estimate north and the direction of the campus once they'd arrived. At seven of the ten sites where the students were questioned, their estimates of the direction of the campus were reasonably accurate (within 23° of the actual direction). Bovet suggests that the students may have oriented in part by using the orientation of the major roads in the area (running north–south or east–west) and by using landmarks during the outward journey to detect the direction in which they were travelling.

An interesting study by Kozlowski and Bryant (1977) showed that people who report having a good sense of direction are better at estimating the direction of familiar landmarks, and faster at learning the layout of a new environment. The authors asked undergraduates at Wesleyan University to rate how good their sense of direction was on a scale of 1 (poor) to 7 (good). They found that students who had a better sense of direction were more accurate at representing the direction of familiar buildings on campus. In another experiment, the authors led students on a route through relatively unfamiliar tunnels underneath a university dormitory. After being led to the end of the tunnel and back, the students were asked to indicate the direction of the tunnel end. Interestingly, students with a good sense of direction were no better than those with a poor sense of direction on their first time through the tunnel—both groups were at least 40° off. However, with repeated trials, the students with a good sense of direction showed a sharp drop in their error, whereas those with a poor sense of direction showed no change. There are many possible explanations for these findings, but they do suggest that the common usage of a 'sense of direction' relates to actual orientation abilities.

A related study was conducted by Sholl (1988; study 2). She asked students at Boston College to rate their sense of direction on a 9-point scale, which ranged from 'easily lost' to 'easily find my way'. On this basis, students were classified as having either a good sense of direction or a poor sense of direction. On paper and pencil tests (also called psychometric tests) of spatial abilities, there was no difference between these two classifications of students. However, when asked to point to out-of-view landmarks from different imagined perspectives, students with a poor sense of direction took longer and were less accurate than those with a good sense of direction. For Sholl, this supports a distinction between a primary frame of reference—one's immediate surroundings—and a secondary frame or reference—where one must imagine oneself in a different location.

A similar approach was taken by Cornell *et al.* (2003) in their assessment of self-reported sense of direction and wayfinding and landmark representation abilities. University of Alberta undergraduates were asked to rate how good their sense of direction was on a 9-point scale, and, as in the Kozlowski and Bryant study described earlier, students with a better sense of direction were more accurate in pointing to landmarks that they couldn't see. Similarly, student and non-student participants with a better sense of direction were more accurate in identifying a location within an unfamiliar building that had only been pointed out to them from outside the building. Those with a good sense of direction tended to use external landmarks—the sun, or a prominent building on campus—to orient themselves. However, students with a good sense of direction were no better than those with a poor sense of direction in taking a direct shortcut after being led on a route through an unfamiliar neighbourhood. Having a good sense of direction did reduce the error in pointing to out-of-sight locations in adults led through the campus for the first time.

Together these findings indicate that we are able to keep track of our direction, and this is likely done by orienting to salient landmarks—familiar roads or distinctive buildings. Our self-ratings of our sense of direction are reliable and predict how well we are able to recall the spatial layout of familiar environments, particularly if we have to imagine these from different perspectives. Having a good sense of direction is also beneficial in learning the correct layout of a new environment, and in following directions (Hund and Nazarczuk 2009). However, it may not help with the ability to take a shortcut in an unfamiliar setting.

An intriguing alternative: egocentric representation of space

When we consider how we represent locations beyond our immediate perception, we usually think in terms of a cognitive map—a stable, Euclidean representation of the distances and directions between landmarks and locations. An alternative view, however, is that humans don't have an overall cognitive map of their environment. Instead, we may represent our location by updating our position, in an ongoing way, relative to individual landmarks.

Wang and Spelke (2000) hypothesized that humans maintain orientation by keeping track of how far they have moved relative to individual landmarks in the environment, or, equivalently, how far the landmarks are displaced relative to the person once he or she has moved (Fig. 4.8). In vector terms, one's movement can described as a vector of a certain distance and direction. The initial position of a given landmark, for example landmark 'C' in Fig. 4.8, can also be specified as a vector (that is, the landmark is a certain distance and direction

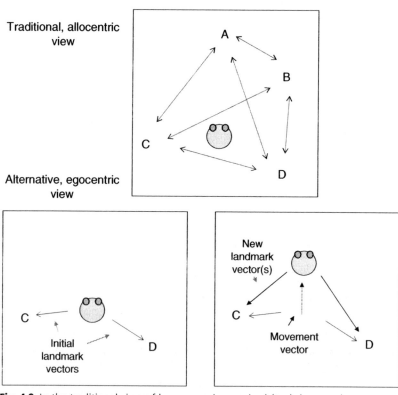

Fig. 4.8 In the traditional view of how space is perceived (*top*), humans have a representation of the spatial relationships between landmarks, and this is independent of position. In the view of Wang and Spelke (2000; *bottom*), humans encode the spatial relationship between themselves and individual landmarks, and then calculate changes in these relationships by keeping track of the distance and direction they've moved.

away from the person's initial position). If the initial landmark vector is subtracted from the vector specifying one's movement, the resulting new vector would specify the current position of the individual relative to the landmark.

The crucial distinction between the traditional view of a fixed, Euclidean map and an egocentric updating system is in the relationship of the navigator and the landmarks. In the traditional view, we remember the spatial relationships between landmarks, and we also keep track of the distance and direction that we've travelled. We then calculate where we are relative to the unchanged spatial array of landmarks. If we become disoriented, we might not know how *we* are oriented relative to the landmarks, but we should still be able to recall how the landmarks are related to one another. In the egocentric view, we update our position relative to landmarks on an individual basis, and we don't possess an overall cognitive map of the environment. Under this view, if our updating system were disoriented, our ability to specify the relationships between landmarks would likewise be disrupted.

To test this, Wang and Spelke (2000) conducted a series of experiments where participants pointed to landmarks outside a curtained enclosure. The participants were familiarized with the landmarks before entering the enclosure, and could point in their direction from within the enclosure, even though they were no longer visible. Participants also closed their eyes and were disoriented (by turning themselves around for 1 minute while standing or while sitting in a swivel chair). Following this, the participants were no longer oriented relative to the landmarks, as one would expect. Remarkably, participants also showed significantly more error in specifying the relationship of the landmarks to one another. Additional experiments showed that this 'configural' error was not due to any after-effects of the disorientation procedure, and was not due to an inability to reliably point in the same direction. It seemed to depend on the disruption of the ongoing updating of the individual's location relative to each landmark. In addition, disoriented subjects were still able to correctly specify the relationship of the corners of the environment relative to one another, suggesting that knowledge of the shape of the enclosure was not disrupted.

These results, together with additional findings, led Wang and Spelke (2002) to suggest that humans don't use cognitive maps to find their way. Instead, they use an ongoing egocentric updating of themselves relative to locations or landmarks in the environment. Locations are recognized by their local view— that is, the view previously experienced by the individual—similar to the way in which bees and ants find locations. Allocentric information, in the form of the fixed spatial relationships between landmarks, is not represented, although the fixed relationships comprising the shape of the environment (its geometry) are used to reorient after disorientation.

An attempt to reconcile the egocentric and allocentric views of orientation is provided by Burgess (2006). He reviews some of the evidence supporting the egocentric view of orientation, but also points out some of its difficulties. For example, egocentric orientation gets complicated when distances or the number of locations to remember increase, as the individual presumably has to update their orientation relative to each location. Secondly, one can recall the spatial relationships in one's neighbourhood even while travelling to another destination, and thus egocentric views and current self-motion information aren't strictly necessary for spatial memory. Finally, in the brain there are spatially tuned neurons that appear to encode allocentric features of the environment (see Chapters 6 and 8), and these appear to guide spatial behaviour.

Burgess also describes evidence that landmarks and external cues aid orientation and spatial memory. A particularly important finding is that of Waller and Hodgson (2006) who replicated the findings of Wang and Spelke, and also showed that disorientation failed to increase pointing errors in a very familiar environment. Thus, people possess a stable representation of the spatial relationships of familiar landmarks. For Waller and Hodgson, disorientation caused a shift from the use of a temporary, egocentric representation of space, to a more permanent, less precise memory for the layout of a given space. They termed this the *disorientation effect*.

To account for these findings, Burgess proposes a two-system model where egocentric and allocentric information are processed at the same time. Functionally, egocentric orientation may work for current orientation, and stored allocentric representations guide navigation over large-scale, familiar environments.

Psychometric tests versus real world spatial orientation

For the purposes of this book, I have equated spatial abilities with wayfinding and navigation. However, assessment of spatial abilities is also common with a number of 'table-top' tasks. For example, in the Weschler Adult Intelligence Test (one type of IQ test), test-takers attempt to reproduce visual patterns with 3D coloured blocks, and to assemble jigsaw puzzle figures. Other tests examine the ability to mentally rotate 2 or 3D objects, and there is a large literature on sex differences in this capacity (for review see Voyer et al. 1995).[4] The capacities

---

[4] In their meta-analysis of 286 studies with tests of mental rotation, spatial perception, or spatial visualization, Voyer et al. (1995) found that the greatest difference between

measured by these types of spatial tests are undoubtedly complex, and they may or may not apply directly to wayfinding abilities or a sense of direction (e.g. Sholl 1988; Riecke *et al.* 2002).

An attempt to bridge the gap between paper and pencil tests of spatial ability and wayfinding is found in a study by Allen *et al.* (1996). The context of this work was an earlier demonstration that the factors that predicted performance on tests of wayfinding and orientation were independent of the 'spatial ability' factor identified in tests of spatial relations and visualization (Lorenz and Neisser 1986, cited in Allen *et al.*). To address this, Allen *et al.* tested spatial abilities with psychometric tests, 2D maze learning, perspective matching, and route learning through a small town. Overall, their results suggest that the relationship between visual–spatial abilities assessed in some paper and pencil tasks don't apply directly to real world knowledge of distance, direction, and location recognition. However, they can be related via a relationship of both types of tasks to performance on 2D maze learning and reversal, and to the speed for matching visual perspectives.

Summary

The findings reviewed in this chapter show that humans are not terribly good at maintaining their orientation when they can't see where they are going. In the absence of vision, we tend to veer when trying to walk in a straight direction. Although it's not entirely clear why this is so, it doubtless contributes to a disparity between where we think we are, and where we actually are. Further, at least some evidence suggests that the fidelity of our memory for a previously seen target destination rapidly decays. One can easily envision how this may play out in a situation where previously visible landmarks are obscured by darkness, fog, or snow. We may think we remember where our target is, but our memory is likely to be inaccurate after a short period of time or after travelling a short distance.

An alternative perspective on spatial orientation maintains that there are two ways in which we know where we are. One, as I've considered in previous chapters, is a cognitive map—an allocentric memory for the spatial layout of a given environment. The second is an egocentric updating of one's current position relative to individual landmarks in the current environment. This process is sensitive to disorientation. One view is that, following such

men and women was in mental rotation. This difference was 0.6 standard deviation units in favour of men. Spatial perception tests also showed significant sex differences (0.4 standard deviation units). There wasn't a significant difference between men and women, overall, in tests of spatial visualization.

disorientation, people can reorient based on the shape of the environment. Another view is that people switch between an egocentric updating strategy and the use of an allocentric memory for the environment when disoriented. A third view is that egocentric updating is used for orientation in one's current environment, but an allocentric representation is used for navigation over larger distances. Essentially, these two mechanisms or spatial orientation may give rise to two different forms of being lost: *misorientation* and *disorientation*. In misorientation, one may retain knowledge of the spatial relations between landmarks that are out of view, but one's heading relative to this representation is misaligned. An example of this is Naismith's experience of getting turned around on the mountain top. He presumably retained a representation of the layout of the village to which he was heading from the top of the mountain, even though his heading sense of direction was turned around. Disorientation, in contrast, would refer to a breakdown in the map itself. The knowledge of the spatial relationships themselves becomes unstable.

In the absence of visual landmarks, we are able to maintain only a coarse orientation over short distances. Optic flow and vestibular information may provide some limited orientation information, although self-movement information appears to be more important. Over longer distances, there isn't consistent evidence for a magnetic sense. So, one of the reasons we get lost is because, in the absence of vision, our capacity for keeping track of our own orientation or that of a target location is limited.

Chapter 5

Spatial cognition in children

On October 14, 2000, Cameron Munro, a 3-year-old boy, wandered away from his parents into the woods in a remote part of the Scottish Highlands. He had been in a play area adjoining the woods, and entered the woods when briefly out of his mother's view. His parents could not locate him, and at 4.30 p.m. he was reported missing. A large-scale search operation involving volunteers, mountain rescue teams, and British Royal Air Force helicopters began. The search continued through the night, and at 8.30 the next morning Cameron was found by a searcher with a dog, having curled up and slept in an upturned tree. The boy had apparently slept through the night, and told rescuers that he'd wandered into the woods to look for dinosaurs.

Such occurrences are not uncommon, and search and rescue teams use the typical behaviour of lost children (and adults) to know where to concentrate their searches (Hill 1998; Syrotuck 2000). Data gathered by Ken Hill from search and rescue call-outs in Nova Scotia indicate that the median distance covered by lost children aged 1 to 6 is ½ mile. This median fits well with Cameron Munro's misadventure, as he was found approximately ½ mile from where he'd wandered off.

Why do children get lost easily? Do they perceive space in a different way? How does spatial intelligence develop? In this chapter I review what is known about how children perceive locations and spatial relations.

Piaget and early studies on spatial cognition in children

Jean Piaget was a Swiss psycholoigst who achieved renown for his ideas on the development of cognition in children. Piaget himself was a precocious child, and published his first scientific paper at the age of 10 (Thorne and Henly 2005). Piaget's early research interest was in molluscs, and he received his Ph.D. in biology based on mollusc work. He then turned to the study of children, and his work led to the idea that, as children develop, their thinking changes qualitatively. This was formalized in his notion that children go through four stages of cognitive development. These range from the senso-rimotor stage, where infants learn about the relation between their senses and

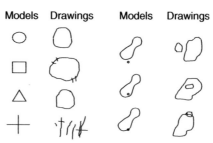

Fig. 5.1 Piaget and Inhelder (1948) tested the ability of children to reproduce models of geometric figures. Three- and four-year-olds were able to reproduce topological relationships (right drawings), but were unable to accurately represent distances and directions (left drawings).

Adapted from *The Child's Conception of Space* with permission from the Jean Piaget estate.

their motor actions, to the formal operational stage, where teenagers and adults are capable of abstract thinking.

Piaget was a prolific writer and experimenter, and in 1948, together with Barbel Inhelder, published a book entitled *La Representation de l'Espace chez l'Enfant* (*The Child's Conception of Space*). In Part 1 of this work, Piaget and Inhelder describe how children show an understanding of *topological space*. This type of knowledge refers to the relative relation between aspects of a figure independent of their precise shape. For example, Piaget and Inhelder asked children to copy a figure that resembled a blob with a small circle either near the blob, wholly within the blob, or on the blob's surface. Three- or four-year-old children could do this, even though they were unable to copy squares or triangles—drawing circles for these instead (see Fig. 5.1). Thus, children were able to represent the relative relationship between parts of a figure—the circle and blob—before being able to represent the distances and angles that define specific shapes.

In the second section of the book, Piaget and Inhelder turn to *projective space*—the location of objects relative to one another based on their distances and directions. This can take the form of an awareness of where objects are located relative to one another from different points of view.[1]

To look at this, Piaget and Inhelder showed children of different ages a pasteboard model of three mountains of different sizes (see Fig. 5.2). The child's task was to imagine what these mountains look like from different perspectives.

---

[1] This is a big step, psychologically. It resonates with the ability of the child to recognize that others have different mental states or perspectives. This ability is similar to a 'Theory of Mind'.

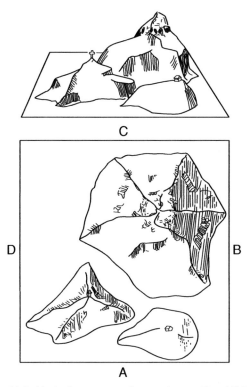

Fig. 5.2 Piaget and Inhelder's three-mountain experiment. The child's task was to identify the view of the mountains that a doll would have when it was placed on different sides of the model. Children under the age of 8 years would frequently identify their own view as that of the doll, even when the doll and the child faced different views.

Reproduced from *The Child's Conception of Space*, with permission from the Jean Piaget estate.

To facilitate this, a small doll was placed at different vantage points relative to the mountains—either in front (where the child was), behind, to the left or right—and the child was asked to select a picture, from a set of 10 taken from different vantage points, that matched the view as seen by the doll.

What Piaget and Inhelder found was that children between 6 and 8 years of age would frequently say that the doll's view was the same as their own. For example, when Gil (a 7-year, 4-month-old boy) was asked to choose a picture that matched that of the doll seated to his right, he chose a picture that represented his own view. Zan, a 6-year, 6-month-old boy, chose a picture with his own view and a very similar view when asked to match the doll's view from the left of the model. When the doll was moved to the right of the model,

Zan again picked the picture matching his own view. However, by ages 8 to 9, Piaget and Inhelder found that children develop the ability to coordinate different viewpoints. For example, when Dar, a 9½-year-old, was asked to place the doll in a position that matched the view shown in a specific picture, he was able to do so immediately and correctly. When asked whether there wasn't some other place the doll might have the same view he answered (correctly) 'No, there isn't any other' (p. 240).

This work suggests that younger children have difficulties imagining the perspectives of others. One may speculate that, in terms of navigation, this inability may make it more difficult to envision locations based on different views of the same landmarks. For example, if a child lived in a location where mountains were visible in the distance, the child might have difficulty inferring the location of his home if he found himself on the other side of these mountains (Fig. 5.3).

In another work, *The Child's Conception of Geometry* (English translation, 1960), Piaget, Inhelder, and Szeminska describe an experiment in which the child's knowledge of a familiar, large-scale space was tested using a model town. Children were first asked to look out of a window at their school and point to well-known locations. Having confirmed each child's familiarity with the neighbourhood, the experimenter then had the children turn away from the window and recreate the neighbourhood on a sand tray. The experimenter placed a model building representing the school in the centre of the sand tray, and asked the child to complete the school neighbourhood with model objects representing other buildings and physical features of the town, for example, the river.

Children under the age of 7 arranged the model objects incorrectly. One 4-year-old placed the kindergarten building, where he was attending school,

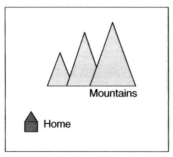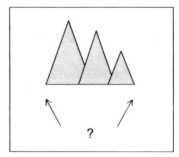

Fig. 5.3 Difficulty imagining the view from other perspectives may make it more difficult to infer the location of a goal, such as a child's home (*left plot*), when approached from a different perspective (*right plot*).

quite close to his home, and the main school building much farther away, even though the two buildings were next to one another. He also placed two bridges over the local river right next to one another, presumably because they were 'conceptually similar'. A 5-year, 11-month old child grouped locations that he liked—the football ground and the general store that sold toys—quite close to his school, even though this was incorrect. In these and other examples, Piaget and colleagues found that children grouped locations based on their similarity, the child's personal interests, or because they had repeatedly travelled from one to the other. Occasionally objects were correctly placed relative to one another, but these local placements were incorrect relative to the other landmarks. If asked to describe routes between locations in the neighbour-hood, the children often referred to their own motor responses (*I go straight along, I turn there, I go straight along again . . .* (p. 11)), and these weren't necessarily anchored to landmarks encountered on a given route.

Children in the next stage of development (beyond 7 years of age in the examples Piaget describes) began to arrange sub-groups of landmarks correctly in their models. However, the positions of the sub-groups relative to one another and to the overall space were incorrect. The sub-groups appeared to be based on views or routes that were familiar to the children, although they were unable to link these independent views. At this stage the children made reference to landmarks when describing routes.

Finally, at around the ages of 8 or 9, children showed the correct coordination of the entire neighbourhood. They were able to describe routes correctly when imagined in one direction or its reverse.

For Piaget and his colleagues, the development of large-scale spatial knowledge isn't simply the accumulation of additional information about an environment. Rather, it reflects a qualitative change in the way the child thinks about his or her environment. Initially, the child's representation is egocentric, and based on his or her own movements. Gradually, their representations become less self-centred, and come to reflect the relations between landmarks themselves. Ultimately, the child views him- or herself as a moving object within a fixed spatial framework.

This view of spatial development largely agrees with that offered in a comprehensive review by Siegel and White (1975). For them, the first step in the development of the child's spatial knowledge is the detection and recognition of landmarks. This is a slight departure from Piaget's views, as he held that self-centred routes comprised the child's early representation of space, with landmarks added to these descriptions as an afterthought. Next, in Siegel and White's account, children begin to use landmarks as the anchor points for their routes. Following this, children form 'mini-maps', clusters of landmarks that are locally consistent, but which are not consistent between clusters. These mini-maps are akin to the sub-groups of landmarks described by Piaget and colleagues. In the next stages of development, children develop a frame of reference that is anchored to the outside world, as opposed to themselves. Ultimately, different routes that children are familiar with are coordinated in an objective frame of reference to create a survey map.

Children's knowledge of distance and direction

Piaget and Inhelder's observations that young children are unable to copy shapes such as squares and rectangles suggests that children do not have a sense of the angles or distances between lines.[2] Such information is sometimes referred to as *metric* knowledge, and is in part the subject matter of Euclidean geometry. However, Piaget and Inhelder's results imply that young children can use topological information—that is, they can tell whether one figure is within another, or whether figures are close together or far apart. This notion has presented a challenge to subsequent researchers: are young children able to use distance and direction information to find their way about environments? An interesting series of experiments in blind and blindfolded children has provided evidence that children can learn about the distances and directions between objects within an environment.

In 1981, Landau, Gleitman, and Spelke tested the spatial abilities of a 2 ½-year-old girl by the name of Kelli, who had been blind since shortly after birth. The task for Kelli and five blindfolded children, tested individually, was to find their way between four different objects in a laboratory playroom. These included the child's mother (sitting in a chair), a stack of pillows, a basket of toys, and a table (see Fig. 5.4).

Kelli was first walked by the experimenter from her mother to the pillows and back. Next she was walked from her mother to the table and back, and then from her mother to the toys and back. She was then asked to go from one landmark to a second, for example from the toys to the pillows. As Kelli had only experienced each of these landmarks in relation to her mother, the ability to take a novel route between them would show that she was able to represent the directions between each of the independently experienced landmarks.

Kelli was given 12 tests (e.g. go from the table to the toys), and on 8 of these 12 she walked to the correct location. On two of her four errors, she was only off by a small amount (15°). When the five children who were sighted

---

[2] For a more extensive review of Piaget's thinking, see Hart and Moore (1973).

Training

Test

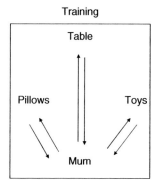
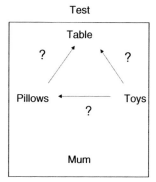

Fig. 5.4 Landau *et al.* (1981) tested the ability of a 2½-year-old blind girl, Kelli, to infer the spatial relationships between landmarks in a testing environment (*right plot*) following exposure to each landmark separately (*left plot*). Kelli was able to navigate between the landmarks successfully, suggesting that she had the ability to represent distance and direction information.

but wore blindfolding goggles performed this task, they also were correct on 8 of 12 trials.

These results suggest that, in the absence of visual information, young children *are* able to use the relative direction of landmarks to get from one location to another. A convincing demonstration of this is a manipulation in which Kelli was first exposed to the landmarks and tested in a way similar to that described earlier, and then taken out of the room to get a drink of water (Landau *et al.* 1984). While Kelli was out of the room, the experimenters shifted the location of each of the objects within the room by 90°. Thus, if the table previously had been in the north of the room, it was moved to the west, and the same for the remaining landmarks. When she returned to the room, the experimenter placed her at one of the landmarks, and Kelli was asked to go to the other landmarks.

This is an important control condition for the following reason. Kelli might have been able to find her way between landmarks not on the basis of where the landmarks were relative to one another, but on the basis of some other uncontrolled cue in the room. For example, if background noise from outside the room was slightly louder on one side of the room relative to the other, she might associate the 'louder' side of the room with a specific landmark (e.g. the table). By moving all the landmarks to different positions within the room, while maintaining their spatial relationship to one another, it was unlikely that any unintentional room cues could help with performance. If Kelli was able to navigate to specific landmarks even after they've been displaced in the room, she was likely using the spatial relations between the landmarks, and not any other cue, to solve the task. Indeed, Kelli was able to turn towards the correct direction and end up in the correct position on the majority of trials.[3]

Some criticisms and replication attempts

The strongest interpretation of Kelli's ability to find her way between landmarks in the testing room is that she, like children beyond the age of 2 years, can create an internal representation of a room that includes the distances and directions between landmarks. However, Liben (1988) argued that this conclusion might be premature. First, it was possible that Kelli was able to find the landmarks by some form of trial-and-error learning with perceptual feedback. Second, if it was true that Kelli has an internal cognitive map of the room and its landmarks, she should have taken a direct path when going from one landmark to another. Finally, as the testing took place in a room, it's unclear whether Kelli necessarily needed to know the distances between the objects: she could have simply set off in the correct direction and eventually reached the object or the wall.

These points were addressed in subsequent experiments by Landau *et al.* (1984). When tested in a similar task in the absence of a subset of the landmarks, Kelli was still able to find her way to the correct locations on the majority of trials. When tested in the absence of any sound cues or feedback from the experimenter (a different experimenter was used during the training and testing phases), Kelli was still accurate. Thus, she was able to go to the location where the object should be, even when it wasn't present. This suggests that Kelli didn't solve the task by some sort of perceptual feedback.

If Kelli knew the spatial relationships between the landmarks, why didn't she move directly between them? Landau and colleagues argue that she might have been distractible, or that it might have been more difficult to maintain a straight line because she was blind. Evidence in support of this comes from trials in which the authors played 'hide-and-seek' with Kelli in the testing room. The experimenter called out to Kelli ('come find me') once from a location within the testing room, and Kelli's task was to go to where she thought she'd heard the experimenter. On 8 of 12 trials, Kelli was able to do so, but on some of these successful trials she took a rather indirect route. Even though she

---

[3] Kelli was slightly worse at ending up in the correct location after displacement of the landmarks relative to her performance before the landmarks had been moved. However, the authors observed that she turned towards the goal location on every trial after the landmarks had been moved, and that her slightly poorer performance may in part be due to forgetting or distraction when she was out of the room.

was simply going to a location where she heard a voice, she still occasionally took indirect routes.

An attempt to replicate the findings with Kelli in a larger number of subjects was done by Barbara Morrongiello and colleagues (1995). They tested 36 sighted children and 12 congenitally blind children on a task similar to the one used with Kelli. In a rectangular test room, a table with a distinctive toy was placed against the centre of each wall. The sighted children were given swimming goggles that had been made opaque, so they were unable to see. All children were given two to three trials in which they were walked by the experimenter from the first table (table A) to the remaining tables (B, C, and D) individually. The children were trained until they could point in the direction of the tables when situated at the 'home' table A. The children were then tested for their ability to take a novel route, for example, going from table B to table D.

The results do not wholly contradict the findings with Kelli, but provide less support for the idea that small children can navigate accurately between landmarks. Some children of all age groups (4 to 9 years of age) made relatively direct novel trips between specific tables. However, children of all age groups also exhibited indirect routes. There was no difference in the efficiency (directness) of the routes between the blind and sighted (but blindfolded) children, and, surprisingly, there was no difference in directness across age groups. However, older children displayed significantly more accuracy in terms of their initial turn towards the goal table, their closest position to the table during the route, and their proximity to the table at the end of the route. Blind children were as accurate as sighted children in their initial turn towards the goal table, but were worse when it came to the accuracy of where they ended up at the end of the route. In support of the idea that knowledge of the spatial layout of the environment should be reflected in an initial orientation towards the correct goal, Morrongiello *et al.* found a strong correlation between the accuracy in the initial turn towards the goal and the accuracy of the final position in the route. The authors suggest that 'only a minority' of children accurately display distance and direction information, and thus their results do not support the findings of Landau *et al.* (1984).

A different approach to the question of whether children can use distance information was taken by Huttenlocher *et al.* (1994). They found that children of at least 16 months of age were fairly accurate at specifying the location of a hidden toy in a 5-foot-long sand trough. Young children showed a slight tendency to estimate the location of the toy towards the middle of the trough, whereas the bias of older children suggested that they sub-divided the trough into left and right portions. The accuracy of the children in remembering the hidden toy's location suggests that they were able to perceive and remember distances in near-space (within a few feet of the observer). A subsequent study with this task showed that young children could compensate for their movement to the opposite side of the sandbox before searching for the hidden toy, and only benefited from the presence of extramaze landmarks after the age of 22 months (Newcombe *et al.* 1998).

So what can we take from these findings? The results with Kelli may not be representative of 2-year-olds in general. However, together with the results of Morrongiello *et al.* they suggest that least some children are able to take direct, novel paths between locations that they have experienced independently. In general, the older the child is, the better they are at doing this, and this is perhaps consistent with the development of spatial perspective found in the Piaget and Inhelder studies. However, the experiments with the hidden toys in the sandbox show that children are able to represent nearby distances. Young children are also able to track their self-motion, but don't rely on landmarks until they are nearly 2 years of age.

Do disoriented children only pay attention to the shape of the environment?

If you were to place a child in a rectangular shaped room and, in front of the child, place an object in a container in one of the room's corners (all of which had a container)—would the child, after being turned around a few times, be able to find the object? The remarkable answer, from a 1994 study by Linda Hermer and Elizabeth Spelke, is 'no'. They found that children who were placed in the room, disoriented slightly by being turned around a few times with their eyes closed, would search for the hidden object in either the correct corner of the room, or the corner 180° opposite, equally (see Fig. 5.5). This occurred even when one of the walls of the room was a different colour than the others, when landmarks (a toy truck and a teddy bear) were added to the room, or when visually distinct containers were used. In contrast, adults tested in the same task used the coloured wall to orient correctly. The children, in all instances, appeared to ignore the landmarks or the different coloured wall and to use the *shape* of the room to guide their search for the hidden object. As the reader will recall from Chapter 3, this same effect has been shown in rodents. Hermer and Spelke's interpretation of their findings is that children's reorientation is based on the geometry of their environment, and is insensitive to landmarks. Essentially, children rely on a 'geometric module' in their brain that establishes orientation based on the shape of the environment.

A confirmation of this finding was obtained by Linda Hermer in 1997. She tested children between the ages of 3½ and 4 years in a rectangular room

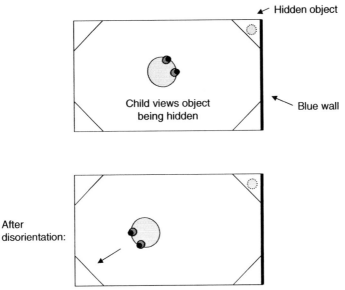

Fig. 5.5 Hermer and Spelke (1994) found that disoriented children searched for a toy that they had seen hidden in a corner of a rectangular environment (prior to disorientation) in both the correct corner, and the rotationally equivalent corner. Thus, the children appeared to use the shape of the environment to reorient, despite the presence of a polarizing cue, a blue wall.

in which one of the short walls was covered with a blue fabric. As in the previously described experiment, each corner of the room was equipped with a container in which objects could be placed. Children entered the room via a door that, when closed, could not be distinguished from the wall. Once inside the room, the children were shown two different objects, and these were hidden in separate containers in different corners of the room. The children were asked whether they knew where the objects had been hidden to ensure that they had seen them being hidden. They were next disoriented, presumably by being turned around a few times with their eyes closed (the exact process isn't described), and then asked to identify where the two objects and the door to the room were.

The results were the same as in the initial Hermer and Spelke study: when asked to find the first hidden object, disoriented children used the shape of the room to reorient, and thus chose either the correct corner or the geometrically equivalent corner 180° opposite. Thus, despite the presence of an obvious landmark—a blue wall—the children used the shape of the room to reorient.

The significant new finding in this study concerned the children's subsequent decisions. After deciding where the first object was hidden (and they weren't told whether this choice was correct or not), the children indicated where they thought the second object and the door to the enclosure were. These agreed with the location chosen for the first hidden object. That is, even though the children chose the 180° corner as often as the correct corner on their first choice, their subsequent choices were all correct relative to this initial choice. Thus, if the children had a representation of the spatial relationship between the locations where the two objects were hidden and the door, the entire representation was reoriented based on the shape of the room. The children's 'memory for the layout of the environment was internally coherent', although it did not necessarily correspond to the true locations of the objects and the door.

Evidence for the use of room geometry for reorientation has also been seen in other environments. Wang et al. (1999) tested disoriented children in a square room with a single red wall. The children had extensive exposure to this environment, yet still used the shape of the environment, as opposed to a landmark, to reorient. However, if the authors changed the shape of the room by causing one of the walls to stick out slightly into the room, the disoriented children reliably chose the correct corner of the room significantly more often than any other corner. In an isosceles triangular environment without landmarks, Huttenlocher and Vasilyeva (2003) found that toddlers used the shape of the environment to find a hidden toy following disorientation. They further showed that this reorientation wasn't achieved by simply matching the view of the correct corner, but rather appeared to be due to the toddler's representation of the entire space.

One remarkable aspect of this phenomenon is that it appears to depend on language use. Hermer-Vazquez et al. (1999) tested this by looking at the reorientation of adults in a rectangular room with a single blue wall. Recall from the initial Hermer and Spelke work that adults, in contrast to children, successfully used the blue wall to identify the corner in which the object had been hidden. In this study, as previously, Hermer-Vazquez et al. had adults watch as a set of keys was hidden in one corner of the room. They then closed their eyes and were disoriented by making at least ten full turns. Upon opening their eyes, their task was to find the corner in which they'd seen the keys being hidden. As before, adults used the blue wall as a landmark, and successfully searched for the keys in the correct corner. However, if they engaged in verbal shadowing during the trial—repeating a taped passage that was played through overhead speakers—the adults failed to use the blue wall to reorient. Instead, they searched in the correct and the rotationally equivalent corners equally. Thus, when engaged in a verbal distraction task, adults fell back on the use of the room's shape to reorient, as opposed to the blue wall. This, the authors argue, suggests that the geometric module assumed to be present in children is also present in adults, but in adults other abilities are layered over it. Additional support for the view that the use of language mediates the use of landmarks for reorientation is found in a subsequent study with children of approximately 6 years of age. Hermer-Vazquez *et al.* (2001) found that the ability of these children to use a salient landmark for reorientation, as opposed to just the room geometry, was predicted by their ability to verbally produce (and presumably comprehend), the words 'left' and 'right'.

Subsequent experiments have shown that whether children use the shape of the environment to reorient depends on the size of the environment and the children's age. In one set of studies, Learmonth *et al.* (2001) tested children just under the age of 2 in an 8×12-foot, rectangular environment. This was larger that the 4×6.25-foot environment used in the Hermer and Spelke experiments. The children watched as the experimenter hid a toy in one of the four corner boxes in the environment. They were next disoriented by their parents, and then released to seek the hidden toy. Learmonth *et al.* found that if the room contained no polarizing landmarks, the disoriented children searched for the hidden toy in the correct and rotationally equivalent corners equally. Thus, the children used the geometry of the environment to reorient when alternative spatial cues weren't available. However, when landmarks (e.g. a bookshelf, a door) were added to the environment, the children chose the correct corner more frequently than any other corner. In a direct attempt to replicated Hermer and Spelke's findings, Learmonth *et al.* tested children on the task when the environment was equipped with a blue wall. Here again, disoriented children chose the correct corner significantly more often than the rotationally equivalent corner. Thus, in the larger environment used in this experiment, disoriented children did not reorient based on the shape of the environment, but instead used landmarks contained therein. In a subsequent experiment, Learmonth *et al.* (2002) tested children in both a 4×6-foot environment, and an 8×12-foot environment. Following disorientation, children under the age of 3 used the shape of the environment to reorient in the small room, but not in the larger room. Further, disoriented 6-year-olds used a landmark within the environment—a blue wall—to reorient, regardless of the size of the environment. Five-year-olds used the shape of the room if it was small and the blue wall if the room was larger.[4]

---

[4] On a table top, 'model' rectangle, a different pattern of findings was observed. Gouteux *et al.* (2001) showed that three-year-olds were unable to use either the shape of the environment or a landmark (a yellow wall) to distinguish corners of this environment. In contrast, 4-year-olds, 5-year-olds, and adults, were able to use the shape of the

The size of the environment and the age of the child also appeared to be factors in the use of environment geometry for orientation in a rhombic- (leaning rectangle) shaped environment. Hupbach and Nadel (2005) tested the reorientation ability of disoriented children of different ages in a 7×7-foot rhombus. They found that 2- and 3-year-olds could not use the shape of this environment to reorient, and searched for a hidden target in all four corners of the environment relatively equally. Four-, five-, and six-year-olds, in contrast, did use the shape of the environment to reorient, and searched for the hidden target in both the correct and rotationally equivalent corners of the environment. When a salient landmark—a yellow curtain—was added to one wall of this environment, 4-, 5-, and 6-year-olds used it to successfully select the correct corner. Two- and three-year-olds continued to perform at a chance level. The results from the older children in this study are consistent with those achieved by Learmonth and colleagues, and show that in a larger environment, a salient landmark is used for reorientation.

A further point that isn't clear about the geometric module view is whether it applies when objects, as opposed to walls, define a space. Gouteux and Spelke (2001) found evidence that objects were insufficient to define an overall shape. They tested the ability of disoriented 3- to 4-year-old children to find a target object within a spatially arranged array of three or four identical containers. The testing environment was a circular enclosure, and the containers were spaced relative to one another to form either a large triangle or a large rectan- gle. After hiding the target in one of the containers, the children disoriented themselves by closing their eyes and turning around four times. They then sought the target. Although the location of the target could be deduced from the shape of the array when it was triangular (or the correct and 180° con- tainer when it was rectangular), the children chose randomly. Only when partial walls were added to the array did children use the geometric layout of the situation to guide their choices. These findings suggest that objects are insufficient to define a geometry that can be used to provide reorientation in children. Rather, some aspects of an *enclosed* space appear necessary for the use of shape as a reorientation cue. An intriguing speculation is that enclosures function as boundaries and, as will be described in Chapter 7, these are encoded by specific neurons in the brain.

In contrast to these results, however, Garrad-Cole *et al.* (2001) found that children could use the arrangement of objects to define a geometric space.

environment to find a previously viewed reward when it was the only cue available. When a landmark was available, it was used by each of these three age groups. Comparable results were found by Hupbach and Nadel (2005).

They tested whether disoriented children could use four hiding boxes, arranged as a rectangular array, to reorient. When the boxes were arranged to form the corners of a rectangle, disoriented children (just under 2 years of age) searched for a previously hidden toy in either the correct 'corner' or the corner that was rotationally equivalent to this to a greater extent than the remaining two corners. Thus, in contrast to the results of Gouteux and Spelke, the children in this study used the implied geometry created by four objects.[5] When tested with distinctive boxes, as shown by Gouteux and Spelke, disoriented children chose the correct corner over all other corners. For Garrard-Cole *et al.* this result suggests that geometry does not overshadow non-geometric information.

Together, these findings suggest that children may reorient in a way that is qualitatively different from that of adults. Children may rely on geometric information in some instances, whereas adults may preferentially use landmarks. On one account, the shift from the use of geometry for reorientation to the use of landmarks depends on the development of spatial language. Moving from these experimental observations to an account of why children get lost is, admittedly, a speculative exercise. However, it is possible that disoriented children may erroneously orient to the boundary features of an environment, and overlook potentially informative landmarks.

Children's wayfinding

What strategies do children use in wayfinding? One way of answering this question is to test spatial abilities in larger laboratory or real world environments. This approach may speak more directly to the question of how children find their way as testing with smaller-scale maps or models requires not just spatial knowledge, but also the ability to translate that knowledge into a different scale representation (Acredolo *et al.* 1975; Herman and Siegel 1978). However, it is worth noting the direction of influence can be reversed: exposure to maps may itself influence the development of spatial representations (for review see Uttal 2000).

An elegant set of experiments by Acredolo, Pick, and Olson (1975) showed that children were better able to remember locations if they were told that they should try to remember them and if the locations were within a familiar spatial context. Children between the ages of 4 ½ years and 5 years, 7 months were taken for walk in two environments: a familiar outdoor playground at the children's nursery, and an unfamiliar hallway in a building next to the

---

[5] There is also evidence that non-disoriented infants as young as 8 ½ months notice changes in the geometric arrangement of objects (Lew *et al.* 2005).

children's nursery. During the walk, at a predetermined spot, the experimenter dropped a card that she was holding. In one condition, the children were told to remember the location where this occurred, so that they could later return to it. In the other condition, the children weren't told anything. At the end of the walk, children in both conditions were asked to return to the location where the card was dropped.

Children who were told they should remember where the experimenter dropped the card were much more accurate at returning to this location. Moreover, they were better at doing this in the playground than in the unfamiliar hallway. In a second experiment, a different group of children (4 to 5 years of age) were tested in the same task, but in familiar or unfamiliar hallways that either contained distinct landmarks (distinctive chairs in the unfamiliar hallway; play equipment in the familiar hallway) or did not. If the presence of landmarks helps to make the environment more differentiated, one would predict that children would be more accurate at remembering the location where the experimenter dropped the object (in this case a key ring). The results again show that children were more accurate at remembering a spatial location when told they needed to remember it, although the evidence for a difference between familiar and unfamiliar contexts was less pronounced. Children were more accurate when distinct landmarks were present in both environments. These results suggest that children are better able to remember locations if:

(1) they intend to remember them;

(2) there are distinctive landmarks nearby; and

(3) the general spatial context is familiar (at least in some cases).

In support of this first point, a subsequent experiment revealed that 8-year-olds were much more accurate than 3 ½year-olds or 4-year-olds at remembering specific locations, and they too benefited from being told to remember a location. In support of the third point, Cousins *et al.* (1983) found that in a familiar environment, the children's school campus, wayfinding was error free (see also Lehnung *et al.* 2003).

Similarly, there is evidence that the more experience a child has with their environment, the better their memory for its layout. Herman and Siegel (1978) tested children in a model town that they could walk through. The town contained 19 different miniature buildings about 6.4 centimeters high. Children who had walked through the town three times were better at remembering the location of buildings than those who had only walked through once, and older children (mean age: 10 years, 7 months) were better than two groups of younger children (mean ages: 5 years, 7 months and 7 years, 7 months). Findings consistent with this have also been observed by Presson (1987).

For Herman and Siegel, the children's ability to remember the locations of buildings within the model town indicates that they were able to recognize distances and directions. In a subsequent experiment, it was shown that the children benefited from repeatedly viewing the experimenter walking through the environment—they didn't need to walk through themselves. Also, if the model town was in a classroom as opposed to a gymnasium, the children performed more accurately—presumably because additional local cues along the classroom walls aided the memory for where the model buildings were located. Newcombe (1988) suggests that the Gestalt principle of proximity—the perceptual grouping of items that appear to be close to one another—may in part account for the better performance of children in the classroom versus the gymnasium.

Repeated experience of being driven through an unfamiliar neighbourhood also improves the learning of landmarks therein. Herman et al. (1987) found that both children and young adults were more accurate at specifying the direction of out-of-view landmarks when they had been driven through the neighbourhood three times compared to when they'd been driven through it once. In this study, 8-year-olds exhibited considerable error ($>60°$) in pointing to three of four landmark locations, despite having these pointed out to them on the drive. Eleven-year-olds and nineteen-year-olds were significantly better than this. According to the authors, this result suggests that 8-year-olds have difficulty in integrating spatial information in large-scale space.

Knowledge of out-of-view items was also assessed in an interesting experiment by Hazen et al. (1978). They argued that young children's representation of large-scale spaces is route-like and not well integrated compared to that of older children. They tested 3-, 4-, and 5-year olds in a four-room environment, arranged as a square (see Fig. 5.6). Five- and six-year olds were also tested in a six-room environment. Each room had a door centred in each wall, and was equipped with a different toy animal in the centre of the room. The children were led through the rooms in a specified sequence repeatedly until they learned the sequence of rooms. They were then asked to reverse this route, and to tell the experimenter which toy animals were to be expected in each upcoming room on the reverse route. Some rooms were adjacent to one another, but not explored in sequence (e.g. rooms A and D in Fig. 5.6). Here, the children were asked if they could infer what toy was located in the adjacent room. This, essentially, is the equivalent of being able to take a shortcut between independently experienced locations. What Hazen et al. found was that the older the child was, the more readily they learned the sequence of rooms. However, once they'd learned the sequence, all children readily reversed these routes. When probed for their ability to anticipate the toy in the next room in

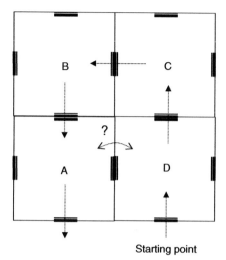

Fig. 5.6 Hazen *et al.* (1978) led children from a starting point through a fixed series of rooms (D–C–B–A). Children under the age of 5 years had difficulty inferring the location of toys encountered in adjacent rooms (A–D) that they'd only experienced separately. Six-year-olds, however, were much better at this.

the reversed route, 3-year-olds were worse than 4- and 5-year olds. When tested for their ability to make a spatial inference, children under the age of 5 did poorly, whereas 6-year-olds did significantly better. These results suggest that as children develop, they are better able to learn a route through an environment, and to anticipate upcoming landmarks when the route is reversed. However, children under the age of 6 don't readily form a representation of the overall layout of a repeatedly experienced environment.

Route learning was also assessed by Cornell, Heth, and Broda (1989). They tested the ability of children to learn a route through an unfamiliar, real world environment. The authors led 6- and 12-year-old children from the edge of the University of Alberta campus to a point approximately 1 kilometre inside the campus. They then asked the children to lead the experimenter back to the starting point. Some children were informed that they would have to lead the experimenter back before the experiment started, and others were not. In addition, for some children, salient local landmarks (a telephone booth; a mailbox) were pointed out to the children and they were told that these would be useful things to remember for their return journeys. For others, distal landmarks including a large building and a smokestack were pointed out.

Some of the results in this study were surprising: children who were told that they'd have to remember the route they travelled were no more accurate at finding their way back to the starting point than those who hadn't. On the face of it, this might appear to be at odds with the results of Acredolo *et al.* (1975), where children who were told to remember where an object was dropped were better at doing so than children who weren't explicitly told to attend to this event. However, Cornell *et al.* also noted that the children were instructed to pay attention to specific local landmarks on the outbound journey and this helped them in choosing the correct route on their return journey. As in previous studies, older children outperformed younger children, and an additional finding was that, when the children were off-route on their return journeys, they still tended to head in the correct direction (that is, the direction of the start point).

In agreement with these findings, Golledge *et al.* (1992) observed that children between the ages of 9 and 12 rapidly learned a route through an unfamiliar neighbourhood. Each child was first led through the route and back by the experimenter, and then the child's task was to lead the experimenter through the route. The experimenter corrected the child if they made an error. After three out-and-back traversals of the route, the children were nearly error-free. Their memory for views along the route improved over trials, with the best recognition occurring at intersections. Interestingly, sketch maps of the routes drawn by the children generally did not include many landmark features, although the number included did increase with more route experience. These results may be consistent with Piagetian view of spatial knowledge development. Children at the age of 9 or so were able to accurately integrate routes into allocentric representation, and this began with knowledge of routes, to which landmark representations were subsequently added.

Children may also be worse than adults at keeping track of a previously seen target location after moving with their eyes closed. In a study by Riesser and Rider (1991), 4-year-olds and adults first viewed a target object in an experimental room. Both groups accurately pointed to the object when asked to do so with their eyes closed. However, children showed significantly more error than adults when pointing to the target object after being led to a new position within the room with their eyes closed. The precise nature of this less accurate performance is unclear, although Riesser and Rider show that it was unlikely to be due to differences in the ability to remember the target. As performance decreased when the complexity of the route increased—again with the participants' eyes closed—it was possible that the children were less able to track their movement.

Children's spatial working memory

Evidence also suggests that the ability to use landmarks to identify locations develops after 2 years of age. DeLoache and Brown (1983) found that children with an average age of 21 months (range: 18–22 months) and children with an average age of 26 months (range: 24–29 months) both remembered the location of a hidden stuffed animal within their homes when the toy was closely associated with a specific cue (for example, directly underneath a sofa cushion). Only the older children, however, were able to find the hidden toy when it was placed in one of four identical containers near different landmarks (e.g. a chair) within the home. Thus, children under the age of 2 could use a cue that was part of the hiding location, but could not associate a landmark and nearby hiding location.

Cornell and Heth (1983) found that 3- and 5-year olds readily remembered the location of hidden puzzle pieces in the reception area of a laboratory. Their task resembled the radial arm maze task used in rodents (see Chapter 3), in that the child sat in a chair in the middle of the room, and the experimenter hid the puzzle pieces in 12 different containers equidistant from the chair. A further 12 hiding locations were also available, and these consisted of identical envelopes at a fixed distance to each container. Three-year-olds searched in an average of 16.3 locations to find the puzzle pieces; five-year-olds found all of the pieces within 14.6 searches. Younger children made slightly more working memory errors—repeated visits to previously searched locations—than older children. The authors' analysis of the response patterns showed that whereas all children relied on memory for visited locations when searching for the puzzle pieces, the older children also tended to discriminate between the class of hiding location (envelope versus hidden container) and to use a strategy of visiting adjacent locations, particularly for the identical envelopes.

Evidence for the use of a search strategy was also observed in a study by Aadland et al. (1985). Using an actual radial arm maze, they found that children under 30 months of age performed at a near-chance level when remembering which arms they'd visited and which they had not. Performance improved for children up to 60 months of age. However, this increase in accuracy was accompanied by a corresponding increase in choices of adjacent arms. Thus, the developmental change revealed in this study, as in the Cornell and Heth work, was a move towards strategy use.

Studies that have attempted to block the use of a response strategy, however, also show that older children appear to have better spatial working memory than younger children. For example, Foreman et al. (1984) tested the spatial working memory of 2- and 4-year-olds in a task where they had to retrieve chocolate sweets from eight radially arranged locations within a testing room with landmarks. Measures were taken to prevent the children from using a response strategy when it became evident on the first day of testing that the

4-year-olds tended to do so. Across the subsequent testing days, 4-year-olds made significantly more correct responses (visits to previously unvisited reward locations) than 2-year-olds. This younger group performed at a near-chance level throughout testing. When the reward locations were shifted relative to the room landmarks, 4-year-olds showed a sharp drop in the number of correct responses they made, and performed at the same level as 2-year-olds. Thus, 4-year-olds appeared to remember which locations they had visited based on the spatial relationships between these reward locations and the landmarks in the room. Two-year-olds, in contrast, did not use these landmarks. In a subsequent study (Foreman *et al.* 1990), 18- to 24-month-old children were found to perform worse than older children (33 to 42 months of age and 47 to 58 months of age) on a task where only a subset of identical locations were regularly baited. The younger children made more errors both in visiting locations that had never been baited (reference memory errors), and in re-visiting previously sampled locations (working memory errors).

Using a procedure that was designed to resemble another rodent task, the Morris water maze, Lehnung *et al.* (1998) tested the spatial memory abilities of 5-, 7-, and 10-year-olds. The maze was a circular curtained arena that was 3.6 metres in diameter. Four different 'distal' cues (e.g. a sun, a shooting star) were attached to the curtains, and spaced at 90° intervals. In addition, a toy rabbit and mouse served as two intra-maze landmarks. The arena had a double floor, and was equipped with 20 magnetic sensors in different locations, each of which was detectable by a thin light point in the carpet. The task was presented in the form of a 'squirrel game', where children had to detect which locations contained nuts. When the child visited a location with an imaginary nut, a tone was sounded. The task contingencies were based on a working-reference memory radial arm maze task, where only a subset of the locations was 'baited', and where repeated visits did not produce re-inforcement. Across trials, the same locations were baited, and the remaining locations were never baited.

All three groups of children learned the task over 10 trials. However, the cues used by the different age groups differed. Probe trials revealed that 5-year-olds solved the task by relying on the intra-maze landmarks. Some 7-year-olds also used these, whereas the 10-year-olds relied on the distal landmarks. The authors describe some of the 5-year-olds as being 'lost' within the arena when the intra-maze landmarks were removed—even though the distal landmarks were still present. These results suggest that young children focus on intra-maze landmarks within this type of situation, whereas older children focus on landmarks at the environment's periphery.

Summary

Children may get lost because their representation of the outside world differs from that of adults. For Piaget, the child's knowledge of large-scale environments begins with a knowledge of familiar routes, and the addition of landmarks to these representations is only incidental. Children then develop accurate representation of localities, likely based on familiar views. In their final phase of development, children are able to integrate representations of sub-groups of landmarks together to form coherent overall representation. Thus, children move from a self-centred perspective of the world to a more universal view. This development may underlie the repeated finding that older children are better than younger children on many spatial tasks.

Piaget and Inhelder also argued that young children possessed only a topological representation of spatial relationships. However, work with a blind child by the name of Kelli, as well as with blindfolded children, provides evidence that the children are able to infer the distance between landmarks and their relative directions. From both perspectives, however, there is support for the view that as children develop, their spatial abilities increase.

In smaller enclosed spaces, children appear to pay attention to the shape of the environment when reorienting. In some instances, they do this even in the presence of a salient, non-spatial landmark. Though this may not apply to getting lost in larger-scale, unenclosed spaces, it may contribute to children's disorientation within man-made enclosures.

There is also evidence that younger children do not use landmarks to the same extent as older children and adults. This evidence is based on spatial memory tasks within a home or laboratory. However, it is easy to imagine that inattention to distal landmarks might make it more difficult to reorient when in a larger-scale space.

Related to this, Cornell et al. (1989) offer some advice for helping children to stay oriented based on their findings. They suggest that the 'use of near landmarks for wayfinding is probably fundamental for younger children' (p. 762), and thus adults shouldn't just tell children to pay attention in general, but rather they should 'consider the route, select distinctive and reliable cues near intersections, and remind the child of the actions to be taken at those intersections' (p. 763). This process, it may be presumed, would increase the child's awareness of specific landmarks, and would make explicit the association between a specific landmark and the appropriate response. For adults, it is possible that incidental attention to landmarks is sufficient to guide subsequent recall of a route.

Chapter 6

The hippocampus as a cognitive map

[H.M.] still exhibits a profound anterograde amnesia, and does not know where he lives, who cares for him, or what he ate at his last meal. His guesses as to the current year may be off by as much as 43 years. . . In 1982, he did not recognize a picture of himself that had been taken on his 40th birthday in 1966. *Corkin (1984)*

The quote above describes the severe memory impairment of patient H.M., an individual who, as a young man, underwent an experimental brain surgery to relieve his severe epilepsy. H.M.'s relevance for studies of spatial cognition lies in the focus his case brought to understanding one of the key brain structures removed in his surgery, the hippocampus. This structure is central to the most influential theory regarding the neural bases of spatial cognition. This theory, as presented in O'Keefe and Nadel's 1978 book *The Hippocampus As a Cognitive Map*, holds that in the mammalian brain, in the hippocampus, a neural representation of the world exists.

In this chapter I will begin our consideration of the neuroscience of spatial cognition. Before doing so, I will consider the story of H.M., the motivation for much subsequent basic research on the brain bases of memory, and also provide an overview of the brain's anatomy. From there I will consider the cognitive map hypothesis, as described by O'Keefe and Nadel, and subsequent work on the role of the hippocampus in animal and human spatial memory.

The story of H.M.

H.M. was born in Connecticut in 1926, and suffered his first minor seizure at 10 years of age, and his first major seizure at 16. When he was 27, his family contacted Dr William Beecher Scoville about an experimental surgery that might relieve his epilepsy. At the time, the medications H.M. took were not particularly effective (Corkin *et al.* 1997).

H.M. underwent the removal of a portion of his temporal lobe in both hemispheres of the brain (see box for anatomy primer). From the standpoint of his epilepsy, the surgery was a success: the frequency and severity of his seizures decreased. But the surgery had an unintended side-effect: afterwards, H.M. was unable to form new, everyday-type memories. This deficit, termed *anterograde amnesia*, lasted H.M.'s entire life. Apparently, H.M. wasn't even able to recognize a researcher who had tested him repeatedly over several years. H.M. also had a small period of *retrograde amnesia*—impaired memory for events that happened prior to his surgery. Evidence suggests that damage restricted to the hippocampus and the adjacent subiculum may be associated with temporally graded retrograde amnesia—an impairment that is worse for memories closer to the time of the brain damage as opposed to older memories (Squire and Bayley 2007). There are, however, situations in which this is not seen (e.g. Martin *et al.* 2005; Clark *et al.* 2005a, b).

The case of H.M. has highlighted important distinctions with respect to the brain bases of memory. Firstly, the finding that selective damage to a small part of the brain produces a memory impairment indicates that portions of the brain are likely to be specialized for forming new memories, and these regions lie within the temporal lobe. Subsequent work has suggested that it is not just the hippocampus that is critical for memory formation, but also the adjacent cortical brain regions that provide input to the hippocampus (Squire 1992; Zola-Morgan *et al.* 1993, Murray 1996).

A second lesson from H.M. is that there are different types of memory. H.M. is severely impaired at making new *declarative memories*—memories for everyday facts and events. However, he is able to learn new skills, such as tracing an

A neuroanatomy primer

The brain is one of the major components of the nervous system. The nervous system is divided into the *central nervous system*, which refers to the brain and spinal cord, and the *peripheral nervous system*, which refers to the neuronal innervation of the body (for example, one's skeletal muscles) and organs outside the brain and spinal cord. The peripheral nervous system comprises the *somatic nervous system*—the nerves that innervate the muscles we use to move—and the *autonomic nervous system*. Neural control over much of our body occurs without conscious awareness, and the autonomic system is divided into the *sympathetic* and *parasympathetic* divisions. The sympathetic nervous system, to a first

A neuroanatomy primer

approximation, prepares the body for 'fight or flight' via increases in heart rate and palm sweating, and other body responses. The parasympathetic nervous system has something of the opposite effect: for example, it decreases heart rate. These distinctions are only approximate, however, as the sympathetic and para-sympathetic systems interact in a more complex way (Berntson *et al.* 1991; 1994). Finally the *enteric nervous system* is the component of the autonomic nervous system controlling smooth muscles, for example, the muscles surrounding one's intestines.

The central nervous system, the brain and spinal cord, are encased in bone (the skull and the vertebrae), and are somewhat isolated from the rest of the body by the *blood–brain barrier*. This functional barrier surrounds the blood vessels and only allows certain essential molecules—oxygen and glucose, for example—to get into the nervous tissue, while shielding the brain and spinal cord from potentially damaging molecules that might circulate in the blood. The existence of this barrier is something of a mixed blessing, for though it protects the brain and spinal cord, it also means that some potentially beneficial drugs or treatments can't get to the brain.

The outer surface of the brain is the cortex, and the bumps of the convolutions are called *gyri*, and the valleys, *sulci*. The cortex is traditionally divided into four lobes: *frontal, parietal, occipital*, and *temporal*. The frontal lobe is particularly well developed in humans (although dolphins aren't too bad either), and is thought to be particularly important for planning actions, motor initiation, working memory, and speech production. The parietal lobe has a representation of the body's surface in the somatosensory cortex, as well as participating in spatial perception (see Chapter 9). The occipital lobe contains the main cortical area for vision. Portions of the temporal lobe deal with hearing, highly processed visual information, and visual–spatial memory. Of course, ascribing functions to specific cortical areas is not entirely accurate, as there are significant connections between lobes, as well as functional differences between the same lobes in each hemisphere.

As one example of how information is processed between lobes, Ungerleider and Mishkin (1982) postulated that there are two main streams of cortical processing in the monkey (which, as a primate, has cortical lobes which are similar to the human lobes). The 'what' stream allows identification of a viewed object, and courses through the occipital, parietal, and frontal lobes. The 'where' stream processes the location of objects via a more ventral (closer to the bottom of the brain) pathway from the occipital to the temporal lobes. In humans, the loss of connections between cortical regions (cortico-cortical connections) in Alzheimer's disease may underlie problems with perceptual integration (e.g. Mapstone *et al.* 2006).

The remainder of the brain can be considered from different perspectives. From a gross anatomy perspective, just below the cerebrum (the part of the brain with the cerebral cortex) is the *cerebellum* and the *brain stem*. The cerebellum contributes to coordination of movement, and is the site of convergence for learning of some

A neuroanatomy primer *(Continued)*

forms of classical conditioning (see Thompson 1986). Intriguingly, the cerebellum has as many neurons as the cerebral cortex.

Just in front of the cerebellum, and again below the cerebrum, is the brain stem. It is divided into three regions: *midbrain, pons,* and *medulla oblongata* (see Barr and Kiernan (1988) for a full description). In the brain stem there are a number of critical groups of neurons—called nuclei—that control basic functions such as breathing and arousal. Twelve pairs of *cranial nerves* issue from the brain stem, and these comprise motor outputs and sensory inputs from the head, face, and upper shoulders.

Another way of describing the anatomy of the brain is based on how it develops. An excellent description of this is found in *Brain Architecture* by Larry Swanson (2003). Briefly, the proliferating cells in the embryo give rise to a neural plate, which in turn folds upon itself to form a neural tube. The top bit of the tube gives rise to the forebrain, including most of the structures of the cerebrum—the cerebral cortex, limbic system, basal ganglia, thalamus, and hypothalamus. The next bit of the tube gives rise to the midbrain portion of the brain stem, and the bit below this gives rise to the hindbrain—the pons and medulla.

The top of the neural tube further develops into two bumps. The top-most bump will go on to form the *telencephalon*—the cerebral hemispheres. The bump below this will make the *diencephalon*, which gives rise to the thalamus and hypothalamus. The thalamus processes incoming sensory information, for example vision, before passing it on to the cortex. It also contains higher-order neuronal groups (called nuclei), which enable coordination of information between cortical regions (see Sherman and Guillery 2006). The hypothalamus contains nuclei that are critical for basic functions—sleeping, eating, temperature regulation—and regulate the release of many hormones.

These developmental distinctions are occasionally referred to in the neuroscience literature. For example, the term 'diencephalic anterograde amnesia' refers to a memory impairment produced by damage to the anterior thalamus and mammillary bodies (see Vann and Aggleton (2004) for an excellent review of this anatomy). This type of amnesia is often associated with Korsakoff's syndrome, a brain pathology associated with chronic alcoholism and an associated deficit in vitamin B1 (thiamine) intake. An interesting feature of Korsakoff's amnesia is the tendency for patients to confabulate—make up memories—to fill voids in their recall of the past.

From the perspective of brain areas involved in spatial cognition, the main brain regions that we will consider lie within the forebrain. These include cortical areas such as the parietal cortex (Chapter 9), and the entorhinal cortex (Chapters 7 and 8). They also include many structures within the limbic system—a set of interconnected brain structures, largely subcortical—that are involved in learning, memory, emotion, and spatial cognition. These include the hippocampus, amygdala, nucleus accumbens, septum, anterior thalamus, and mammillary bodies.

A neuroanatomy primer

One brain circuit that is particularly central to memory and spatial cognition is the *Papez circuit*. This is a set of pathways that include connections between the hippocampus, mammillary bodies, anterior thalamus, cingulate gyrus, parahippocampus gyrus, and entorhinal cortex.

In this chapter we focus on the hippocampus—one of the brain regions removed in patient H.M. In humans, the hippocampus lies tucked within the cortex of the temporal lobe, near the bottom of the brain. In the rat it is proportionally larger and extends from near the top (dorsal surface) of the brain to the bottom (ventral surface) (see Fig. 6.1). O'Keefe and Nadel (1978) state that the differences in the relative size of the hippocampus between humans and other animals are due to the expansion of the neocortex in humans.

A complete description of the anatomy of the hippocampus and its afferents (inputs) and efferents (outputs) is beyond the scope of this work, and the interested reader is referred to the clear review by David Amaral and Pierre Lavenex in *The Hippocampus Book* (2007). Here I provide only a brief overview of this structure.

Essentially, different cortical regions provide inputs to the hippocampus via cortical areas adjacent to the hippocampus itself. Specifically, the frontal, parietal, and temporal cortices project to the *perirhinal* and *parahippocampal (postrhinal* in the rat) cortices (Fig. 6.2; for reviews see Squire and Zola-Morgan 1991; Burwell 2000). These, in turn, project to the *entorhinal cortex*, forming two-thirds of the cortical input to this structure (Insausti *et al.* 1987). The entorhinal cortex (EC) is the primary cortical input to the hippocampus, and this is in the form of collections of axons from neurons in layer II, termed the *perforant path*.

From here, we can consider the organization of the hippocampus proper as described by Amaral and Lavenex (the hippocampal formation refers to the hippocampus and the adjacent structures of the entorhinal cortex, dentate gyrus, presubiculum, and parasubiculum). The axons of the perforant path synapse on the granule cells of the dentate gyrus. These, in turn, send excitatory projections (termed *mossy fibres*) to the CA3 cell layer. CA3 neurons project to one another, and also project (via *Schaffer collaterals*) to the CA1 cell layer. CA1 neurons send excitatory projections to the subiculum. The subiculum, in turn, projects to the deep layers of the entorhinal cortex.

In addition to this 'indirect' path from the entorhinal cortex to the hippocampus, there is evidence of a direct projection from the entorhinal cortex to the CA1 cell layer (Fig. 6.3; Brun *et al.* 2002; 2008).

The detail of the hippocampal cell organization is of interest from a cognitive mapping perspective, in that neurons in many of the structures I've mentioned encode spatial information. It's likely that the hippocampus is part of a larger cortical- and subcortical spatial information processing stream that underlies the ability to recognize one's location, direction, and locomoter movements within a given space.

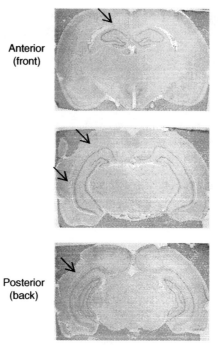

Anterior
(front)

Posterior
(back)

Fig. 6.1 Coronal (frontal) sections of the rat brain showing the hippocampus (arrows) at three different levels, from the front of the brain to the back. (See also Plate 1.)

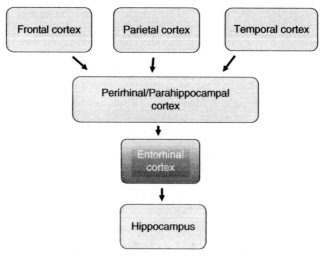

Fig. 6.2 Convergence of cortical inputs to the hippocampus (after Squire and Zola-Morgan 1991).

The basic hippocampal circuit

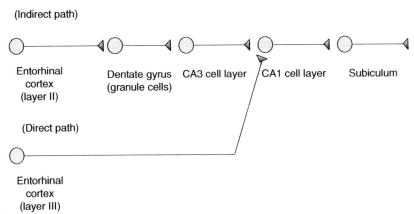

Fig. 6.3 Work by Brun *et al.* (2002; 2008) has demonstrated that there are two pathways for information flow through the hippocampus. The 'direct' pathway comprises projections from neurons in layer III of the entorhinal cortex directly to the CA1 cell layer within the hippocampus. The 'indirect' pathway originates in layer II of the entorhinal cortex, and projects to the CA1 cell layer via the dentate gyrus and CA3 cell layer.

image of a shape based on the reflection in a mirror. Such gradual improvements in motor-based performance are *non-declarative* memories, although (at least for H.M.) they occur in the absence of any conscious knowledge of the learning experience (Squire 1987). Subsequent work has indicated that memory for specific events within one's life—*episodic memories*—are particularly sensitive to damage in some of the brain regions removed in H.M.

An interesting addition to this story is that damage to the hippocampus in childhood results in considerably fewer day-to-day difficulties than are apparent in H.M. Vargha-Khadem and colleagues (1997) described a young man by the name of Jon, who, despite growing up without a full hippocampus, was able to go to normal schools and learn new information. Jon can't remember specific events that have happened to him, so there must be a way in which the brain can still form declarative memories in the absence of a hippocampus. A subsequent study with H.M. has also shown that he has learned some information—the names of some famous personalities—since his operation (O'Kane *et al.* 2004).

A third impact of H.M.'s intriguing memory problems is that basic researchers became interested in the brain regions removed in H.M.'s surgery, and particularly the hippocampus. As I will describe in the remainder of this chapter, studies of the hippocampus in experimental animals—primarily rats—have revealed its striking contribution to spatial cognition.

Attempts to produce anterograde amnesia in monkeys

Following the description of H.M.'s memory deficits, experimenters attempted to develop an animal model of anterograde amnesia by removing the hippocampus and the brain areas adjacent to it in non-human primates. Although many of these studies speak more to the neural bases of memory than to spatial cognition, they show how focus on the hippocampus has broadened to appreciate the contributions of adjacent cortical structures. Such a shift, as we will see in Chapters 7 and 8, is also apparent in considering the brain structures involved in cognitive mapping.

Efforts in monkeys have an interesting history. In an experiment conducted at the National Institute of Health, Mortimer Mishkin removed the hippocampus, the amygdala, or both in separate groups of monkeys (Mishkin 1978). Prior to these surgeries, the monkeys were trained on a task in which they were first presented with an object in the centre of a three-well tray. The object was removed from view and, after a delay of 10 seconds, it and a new object were presented at the other two wells on the tray. If the monkey chose the new object, it was given a peanut reward. This is the delayed non-matching to sample (DNMS) task. In Mishkin's study, only combined removal of the hippocampus and amygdala produced an impairment on this memory task. In other versions of the task, when the monkey was trained after surgery, removal of the hippocampus itself produced an impairment at longer delays (Alvarez *et al.* 1995). Impaired performance at long delays, in the presence of intact performance at short delays, suggests a difficulty in memory because impairments in other aspects of the task, such as the ability to discriminate between stimuli or understand the rules of the task, would affect performance at all delays.

A refinement in our understanding of the brain regions that are necessary for the memory assessed by the DNMS task was provided in an experiment by Elizabeth Murray and Mishkin (1998). They removed the hippocampus and amygdala by injecting ibotenic acid, a neurotoxin that works via glutamate receptors, and kills neurons by exciting them to death (termed an excitotoxic lesion).Importantly, this toxin is relatively specific for neurons, and is said not to damage the axons that pass through the infused region. The ibotenic acid lesions of Mishkin and Murray were more focused on the hippocampus and amygdala than earlier lesions where the brain tissue was aspirated with a small sucking device. Aspiration lesions, Mishkin and Murray argued, damage the cortex overlying the hippocampus and amygdala, and also remove the fibres coming out of the perirhinal cortex as well as fibres going from the amygdala to the medial dorsal nucleus of the thalamus. They found that selective removal of the hippocampus and amygdala with ibotenic acid produced no memory impairment for the monkeys on the DNMS task. This was in contrast to the severe, delay-dependent impairment that followed removal of the rhinal cortex (the entorhinal and perirhinal cortex) overlying the hippocampus. In Mishkin and Murray's view, earlier findings of memory impairments following aspiration lesions of the hippocampus and amygdala were actually the result of damage to the cortex covering these structures—the entorhinal and perirhinal cortices (see also Zola-Morgan *et al.* 1993).

This reappraisal is consistent with a synthesis provided by Larry Squire. In his view (Squire and Zola-Morgan 1991; Squire 1992), the brain circuit underlying recognition memory involves the perirhinal cortex, the entorhinal cortex, and the hippocampus. The perirhinal cortex receives inputs from many different cortical areas (the frontal, parietal, and temporal cortices), and these are then fed forward to the entorhinal cortex and the hippocampus. Indeed, damage to all three of these brain regions occurred in patient H.M., and another severe amnesic, E.P. (Stefanacci *et al.* 2000).

The discovery of place cells in the hippocampus

As we've seen in Chapters 2 and 3, rats have been a model organism for assessing basic questions in the field of psychology. They are also central to the field of neuroscience, and in particular the field of behavioural neuroscience, where the goal is to establish the neural bases of behaviour. In rodents, removal of the hippocampus produces significant impairments in spatial learning and memory. However, it was the finding from electrophysiological recordings of individual neurons within the rodent hippocampus that led to one of the most influential views on the function of the hippocampus and the neural bases of spatial cognition.

In 1971, John O'Keefe and Jonathan Dostrovsky reported a striking finding in a short communication entitled 'The hippocampus as a spatial map. Preliminary evidence from unit activity in the freely-moving rat'. They observed that individual neurons within the hippocampus fired when a rat was in a specific location in its environment. These neurons 'responded solely or maximally when the rat was situated in a particular part of the testing platform facing in a particular direction' (p. 172).

In the first full paper on these neurons (O'Keefe 1976), individual cells were recorded as a rat traversed an elevated three-arm maze in a curtained enclosure. Two basic types of neurons were characterized: *place* units and *displace* units. Place units, commonly referred to as place cells, fired when the animal was in a particular location on the maze. The locations where individual cells fired—their place 'fields'—were distributed throughout the maze (though a somewhat greater number of fields were observed on the maze arm closest to the experimenter). These cells seemed not be driven by specific visual cues, as they continued to fire in the same location when the lights were switched off, or in dim red light. In addition, olfactory and tactile cues did not appear to drive the cells as either substituting a new maze arm or covering the existing arm with cardboard had no effect on most cells.Some cells appeared to be more active when the animal was facing one direction as opposed to another, although other cells were equally responsive to all directions. An example of a place cell is shown in Fig. 6.4.

A subset of the place cells—which O'Keefe termed *misplace* units—fired when the animal sniffed in a particular area following either the addition of a novel object or the removal of an expected object. A colourful example of this is a cell that had its best response when the rat encountered a toy rubber crocodile on a specific arm. The cell had little activity when the animal encountered

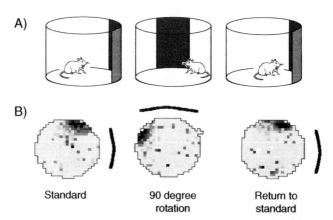

Standard   90 degree   Return to
                  rotation   standard

Fig. 6.4 Example of a hippocampal place cell. *A)* Schematic of a typical testing environment in which a rat moves about freely, searching for small food pellets, while its neurons are recorded. *B)* Overhead view of the cylinder floor, with the firing rate of an individual place cell plotted by darker shades of grey (the darker the shade, the higher the firing rate). The large portion of the floor with light grey shading represents areas that the animal has visited in a recording session, but where the cell did not fire. When the cue card within the cylinder (shown as a dark line outside the cylinder) was shifted by 90° in the animal's absence, the place field shifted by a corresponding amount when the animal returned to the environment. When the cue card was returned to its original position (return to standard) in the absence of the animal, the place field returned to its original position when the animal re-entered the environment.

Reproduced from Dudchenko, Goodridge, and Taube (1997a), *Experimental Brain Research* **115**: 375–380. Published by Springer-Verlag, and reprinted with permission.

other objects (a toy bear, sandpaper) on this maze arm, and did not respond to the crocodile when it was encountered on other arms. Thus, this misplace cell seemed to be maximally responsive not merely to a specific location, but to a combination of location and an additional stimulus.

Displace units fired when the animal was involved in 'spatial displacements', or movement in the environment independent of the animal's location. These cells are also known as theta cells (Ranck 1973), and typically fire in bursts synchronized to a particular phase of the theta EEG rhythm (described in the next section).

The discovery of place cells, coupled with a full review of the data on hippocampal lesions in the rodent, led John O'Keefe and Lynn Nadel to propose that the hippocampus served as a cognitive map, underpinning spatial cognition in rodents, and potentially provided the spatial substrate for episodic memory in humans (O'Keefe and Nadel 1978). As this work is central to thinking on the brain bases of spatial cognition, I will consider it in detail.

The Hippocampus as a Cognitive Map

The Hippocampus as a Cognitive Map begins with a history of thinking about space. Two views are contrasted. The first, as described by Isaac Newton,[1] is that space, in our everyday way of thinking of it, exists. That is, physical space exists independent of the objects within it, and it forms a unitary, continuous environment. There is an *absolute space*. As an alternative, space can be thought of in relative terms—objects may be defined relative to us or to one another. Things may be close together or far apart, depending on the perspective of the observer. A perhaps extreme view of this was taken by George Berkeley, who maintained that the world was a construction of our sensations, and our reflections on these sensations. Of course, at some level this is true. But the next step is more difficult: for Berkeley, reality doesn't exist independent of our sensations. Thus, from a spatial perspective, space is defined with regard to our freedom to move. If one can move their arm without encountering any external resistance, one would say that there's space for it to move. If resistance is encountered, one may say that there's something in the way. On this account, if one didn't have a physical body, there'd be no space, because space is the sensation of unrestricted movement. Our perception of space from different sense organs is learned from our interactions with movement.

---

[1] Isaac Newton's approach to science would be recognizable today. His treatise on the diffusion of light from a prism was written as a clear test of a specific hypothesis. There is, however, a suggestion that his habit of sleeping in the laboratory might have caused madness via mercury poisoning (*Newton's Madness: Further Tales of Clinical Neurology*, by Harold Klawans (1990)).

For example, we learn that the same object appears smaller at a distance than it does when before us because in the past we have walked to distant objects and found them to be the same.

In O'Keefe and Nadel's account, a return to the idea of absolute space is found in the work of Immanuel Kant. One of Kant's arguments for the existence of absolute space was that some objects—for example, left and right hands—possess all of the same features, yet are different because of the space that they occupy. Another argument is that space cannot be 'annihilated.' That is, we can conceive of an object, for example, a yellow sandstone building viewed from one's office window, with one or another of its features removed. We can imagine the building without its windows, or without its sandstone cladding. However, if we removed every feature, we'd still be left with the space that the building occupied. This feature of the object—its location (or former location)—still exists when all other features are removed. We can't imagine away space.

For Kant, spatial knowledge is something we're born with. We don't have to learn about space—it's not *empirical*, or *a posteriori*—in Kant's terms. It is *a priori*. It is also *synthetic*, in that the way we represent space informs how we perceive the world. Of course, not all agreed with this view, and one notable objector to the presence of a unitary absolute space was Williams James, author of the classic *Principles of Psychology* (1890). In his view (and that of others), space is a notion, reflecting our momentary focus of our attention. For Jean Piaget, as mentioned in the previous chapter, our ability to represent 3-D space isn't something we are born with, but rather something that develops. However, Piaget's view isn't a strictly empirical view. Rather, his view is that we're born with the precursors for perceiving space, and as we interact with our environment, our knowledge of objects and their properties are refined. Again, the development of spatial knowledge follows a sequence, and this moves from a topological representation, to a projective representation, and finally to a Euclidean notion.

The conclusions of O'Keefe and Nadel's review of the philosophical perspectives on space are that a unitary representation of absolute space exists and is found in the brain, and that it is not the product of experience or derived from relative space. It underlies our ability to perceive the world 'coherently.' This *locale* space corresponds to Kant's idea of absolute space, and the *locale system* in the brain encodes an allocentric representation of the world. In contrast, egocentric space is referred to as *taxon* space, and our sensory and motor systems work in this realm.

O'Keefe and Nadel next review behavioural evidence—such as the findings from Tolman that I considered in Chapter 2—for a cognitive map. They liken the locale system to map use, and the taxon system to following a route.

Routes are a series of precise, yet relatively inflexible instructions on how to get from A to B. For example, to get from my lab to the train station, I turn left after leaving the building, veer right through the pedestrian tunnel, go left on the street, and head down the stairs to Edinburgh Waverly train station. However, if you were unfamiliar with Edinburgh and were attempting to follow this route, you could easily get lost if you left out an instruction or missed a turn. Also, the instructions of how to get from A to B may not necessarily be meaningful when heading from B to A, as heading towards a landmark in one situation may be useful, whereas heading away from the same landmark may not constrain your alternative paths sufficiently. Maps, in contrast, don't specify a goal, and contain a great deal of information on the spatial relationships between locations. They can be used flexibly, and even if the environment changes a bit, they are still useful. A point not made by O'Keefe and Nadel in this regard, however, is that it is still possible to be lost with a map (as I described at the beginning of Chapter 4). You need to know where you are on the map. One can infer this, in many instances, from the terrain. Alternatively, a 'you are here' indicator solves the problem for building or city centre representations. For the hippocampal cognitive map, this isn't a problem as place cells provide the 'you are here' information. Indeed, it has been argued that since immediate location is all the hippocampus represents, it is unclear how destinations are represented (Morris 1990).

The map, place, or locale system resides in the hippocampus. It provides a representation of the animal's place, and is driven by combinations of external landmarks, or by a dead-reckoning system that informs the representation of the distance and direction in which the animal has moved. Subsequent experiments, reviewed later, have confirmed these views. The place representation remains intact if one or the other cue is removed from the environment, as long as the remaining cues are sufficient to specify locations. The animal's exploration builds up the place representation, and when there's a change or addition to the environment, a 'misplace' detector drives the animal to explore the alteration. In this way, the cognitive map is updated. If the animal attends to an object, it is included in the map.

The taxon system, outside the hippocampus, is akin to a route-based means of representation. It depends on the approach or avoidance of specific cues, and the associations with individual cues are strengthened with repeated exposure. In the place system, in contrast, associational strength does not increase dramatically once a cue has been added to the map. With repeated contact, spatial representations may shift from a place to a taxon representation, and in this way become the 'autonomous habits' that find us inadvertently driving to the office when we meant to go to the grocery store.

Anticipating contemporary views on the hippocampus and episodic memory, O'Keefe and Nadel hold that the hippocampal locale system represents 'the spatio-temporal context within which . . . knowledge is acquired' (p. 100). Loss of hippocampus would impair this type of memory, and impair exploration and place learning.

After reviewing the anatomy of the hippocampus, O'Keefe and Nadel consider the findings from electrophysiological recordings. First, they describe the 3–7 Hz *theta rhythm*, a prominent electrical signal seen on the EEG (electroencephalogram) when the rat is moving or actively exploring its environment. When sitting still, sleeping, eating, or drinking the theta rhythm (theta, for short) is not apparent, and large, irregular amplitude activity (LIA) may be apparent. A characteristic of LIA is the presence of a high-frequency 'ripple' recorded in the CA1 cell layer of the hippocampus; also, theta cells and complex spike cells may show a burst of activity coincident with an LIA spike. As will be described in the next chapter, it is currently thought that the theta rhythm and place cell activity together provide a better resolution of the animal's location, and a possible means of encoding and linking memories.

O'Keefe and Nadel next consider the basic properties of place cells. One of the 'rules' about place cell behaviour is that the location of a cell's place field is often anchored to spatial landmarks in the environment. O'Keefe and Conway (1978) showed this by recording place cells on a T-maze that was placed within a curtained enclosure. Within the enclosure there were different landmarks (a light, a fan, a buzzer, and a white card), and the rat's task was initially to run to a specific arm to get food, and later to visit different arms to get food. Importantly, the maze and the landmarks were together moved by 90° increments on different trials. Thus, the maze was always in the same location relative to the landmarks within the enclosure, but was in a different orientation relative to the environment outside the enclosure. What O'Keefe and Conway observed was that a given place field would be found on the same part of the maze even when the maze (and the surrounding landmarks) were in different orientations relative to the environment outside the curtain. It was as if the rat was fooled by the reorientation—or rotation, as it is sometimes referred to—of the maze and the extra-maze landmarks.

An elegant, subsequent study by Robert Muller and John Kubie (1987) showed this clearly. They recorded from place cells in a grey, cylindrical apparatus that had a single white 'cue' card taped to the wall, covering 100° of the wall's arc. Grey photographic backdrop paper served as the floor of this cylinder, and the paper could be changed frequently to minimize any odour cues left by the rat. The entire apparatus was curtained off from the remainder of the recording room, and the animal was tracked using a ceiling mounted

THE LESION REVIEW—UPDATED | 129

video camera. The experimenters tossed small food pellets into the cylinder, and the animals quickly learned to search the cylinder floor for the randomly scattered pellets. Once a place cell was identified in this apparatus, the authors assessed the stimulus control of the white card by first recording a 'standard' session with the cue card in its usual position, and then a rotation session where the cue card was shifted by 90° about the cylinder perimeter. In 14 of the 15 attempts, rotation of the white card led to a corresponding rotation of the place field (see Fig. 6.4). Return of the card to its initial position resulted in a return of the place field to its initial orientation. Thus, the cue card exerted stimulus control over the place fields—the fields were anchored to it. Removal of the cue card altogether, in most instances, did not change the shape or radial location of the place field, but did result in an apparently random shift in the angular position of the field. Thus, although the white card was sufficient to control the orientation of place fields, it was not necessary for their existence.

For O'Keefe and Nadel, the properties of place cells and their view of spatial representation were sufficient to propose a neural model of a spatial map. Some of the specifics of this model, particularly with respect to its anatomical location, have been superseded by subsequent discoveries (see Chapter 8), and will not be considered here. Essentially, their view was that specific 'taxon' views are combined to form a locale representation. A theta-like mechanism aids in the sequential encoding of stimuli encountered as the rat moves, and new information is encoded into the map by misplace cells in CA1. The direction of the rat's movement is encoded as well, and subsequent discoveries have shown that this occurs outside the hippocampus. (Interestingly, goal-directed navigation is envisioned as the simultaneous activation of the rat's current location and, for example, that part of the map encoding the location of food if the rat is hungry. A programming system then selects a motor programme that connects the two locations.)

The lesion review—updated

What follows in the *Cognitive Map* is a review of the experiments, up to January 1976, on the effects of hippocampus lesions on a variety of tasks. A full consideration of this older work and that in the ensuing decades of studies is beyond the scope of this book. Instead I will limit my review to the effects of hippocampus removal on the spatial tasks described in Chapter 3. Put briefly, animals without a hippocampus have difficulty learning the layout of their environments, and remembering where they have been. They have additional deficits, several of which point to a role for the hippocampus that extends beyond cognitive mapping. This is a point I'll return to near the end of the chapter.

Exploration

O'Keefe and Nadel first review studies in which hippocampectomized animals are impaired in exploring new objects added to a familiar environment. Such an impairment is predicted by the cognitive map theory, as it holds that the hippocampus detects mismatches in the animal's environment and these trigger exploration. Subsequent studies have used the spontaneous exploration of novel objects not to test the cognitive map view per se, but to test object recognition memory. In these situations, the animal is first habituated to a pair of identical objects. It is then presented with one of these objects and an unfamiliar object. Normal rats will preferentially explore the unfamiliar object, thus showing that they have a memory for the habituated object. In a number of studies, rats with damage to the hippocampus or fornix (the output fibers of the hippocampus) also spend more time exploring an unfamiliar object, and thus appear to retain intact object-recognition memory (for review see Mumby 2001). In others, impairments are observed (e.g. Clark *et al.* 2000; for review see Squire *et al.* 2007). One possibility is that the size of the hippocampus lesion is critical. If lesions are either incomplete, or extended beyond the hippocampus, impairments are observed. In contrast, complete, circumscribed lesions are not associated with an impairment (Ainge *et al.* 2006). In situations where the previously established spatial relationships between objects are altered, consistent deficits with hippocampus lesions are observed.

Alternation on the T-maze

The story with alternation on the T-maze is much clearer: the removal of the hippocampus abolishes performance. This has been observed in a number of studies (e.g. Racine and Kimble 1965; Rawlins and Olton 1982; Aggleton *et al.* 1986; Bannerman *et al.* 2002; but see Jarrard 1975), and Fig. 6.5 shows the data from a study I conducted (Dudchenko *et al.* 2000). In this version of the task, normal rats readily remembered the arm that they had entered on their first run on the maze, and chose the alternate arm on their second run. Rats without a hippocampus, however, failed to do this. This inability, of course, could reflect either a problem with representing or recognizing different spatial locations (in this case, arms of the T), or a memory impairment. Earlier studies (e.g. Cohen and LaRoche 1973) have also shown that rats without a hippocampus are impaired in acquiring a 'place' strategy on a T-maze, as described in Chapter 2. Rats with hippocampus lesions are also impaired at learning an alternation task on the 'Ш'-shaped maze used by Loren Frank and colleagues, though they eventually perform at nearly the same level as non-lesioned animals (Kim and Frank 2009).

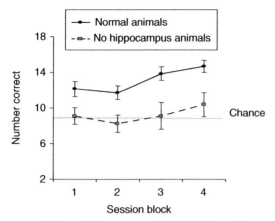

Fig. 6.5 Rats without a hippocampus (dashed line) perform at a chance level across several sessions of testing on a T-maze delayed alternation task. Normal animals, in contrast, perform significantly better. Each session block is made up of three testing sessions, and each session is made up of six trials.

Adapted from Dudchenko, Wood, and Eichenbaum (2000), *The Journal of Neuroscience*, **20**(8): 2964–2977. Copyright: Society for Neuroscience.

The radial arm maze

Olton *et al.* (1978) found that damage to the inputs or outputs to the hippocampus in rats impairs their ability to efficiently find food on the arms of the radial maze. Often, rats with this disruption of the hippocampus would enter a few maze arms and consume the food they found at the arm ends. Then, erroneously, they would repeat the same series of arm entries even though food was no longer available on these arms. In a subsequent study by Olton and Papas (1979), disruption of hippocampal projections produced an impairment that was interpreted in terms of a memory deficit, and not a spatial deficit. The authors trained rats on a 17-arm radial maze where the same 12 maze arms were never baited. The remaining arms were baited, and the rat's task was thus twofold: it had to remember which arms were baited and which weren't (a reference memory), and it had to remember, within a session, which of the baited arms it had already taken the food from (a working memory). Olton and Papas found that large lesions of the fimbria–fornix impaired the rats' working memory, but did not affect their reference memory. This result would appear to argue against a cognitive map view of hippocampus function and for a working memory view. However, subsequent experiments with more specific hippocampus lesions yield a conclusion that lies between these two views. Using ibotenic acid to selectively destroy the cells of the hippocampus

(Jarrard 1989), Leonard Jarrard and his colleagues showed that selective removal of the hippocampus impaired the rats' learning of a RAM task where a subset of the maze arms were never baited (as in the Olton and Papas experiment). These rats did, eventually, succeed in learning which arms were baited and which were not, but persisted in re-entering previously visited baited arms. However, rats with these types of lesions were not impaired in learning the same task when the arms were equipped with intra-maze cues. Thus, rats without a hippocampus were impaired in learning a spatial version of the RAM task (where maze arms were identified by their spatial relationships with extra-maze landmarks), but were not impaired on a non-spatial version of the maze. Intriguingly, if rats were trained on the spatial version of the maze task before the removal of the hippocampus, their impairment post-surgery was transient. This pattern of results suggests that the hippocampus is necessary for learning the spatial layout of an environment, but is not necessary for spatial performance once the environment is familiar (for an excellent review of these experiments see Jarrard (1993)).

The Morris water maze

In a classic paper, Morris *et al.* (1982) showed that rats without a hippocampus were impaired at finding a hidden platform when compared to control or cortically lesioned rats (see Fig. 6.6). Moreover, in test sessions where the rats were placed in the pool in the absence of the hidden platform, hippocampectomized rats showed no preference for the former location of the platform, whereas control and cortically lesioned animals showed a strong preference for this location. When tested with a platform that stuck out of the water, hippocampectomized rats performed at the same level as controls. Interestingly, even in this 'visible' platform task, control rats appeared to have learned something

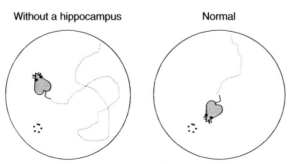

Without a hippocampus   Normal

Fig. 6.6 Rats without a hippocampus (left plot) search randomly for the submerged platform in a Morris water maze. In contrast, normal rats navigate directly to the hidden platform location after training.

about the spatial location of the platform, as they showed a preference for its location when it was removed from the pool on test trials. This suggested a Tolman-like predisposition to learn places, even when the escape platform was visible. Overall, the results of this experiment provided support for the cognitive map view, as rats without a hippocampus were impaired when the hidden platform could only be located based on its spatial relationship to extra-maze landmarks. They were not impaired when a taxon strategy, swimming to a visible platform, was used.

Subsequent experiments have refined these views. Morris *et al.* (1990) found that rats with ibotenic acid lesions restricted to the hippocampus were impaired at learning the location of a hidden platform in the water maze. However, if these rats were given additional training with both hidden and visible platform trials in the same position within the pool, they could learn the location of the hidden platform. Rats with combined hippocampus and subiculum lesions were also impaired on the initial learning of a hidden platform location, but did not benefit from additional training to the same extent. Animals that were trained on the maze prior to the removal of the hippocampus were equal to control animals in the number of times they swam across the hidden platform location (on test sessions without the platform), but were somewhat worse in terms of their preference for the general location of the hidden platform. This pattern of results suggests that the hippocampus may be necessary for navigating to a location, but other brain regions can, in some circumstances, allow the rat to recognize the goal location once it has arrived there.

Others have confirmed this finding. Whishaw and Jarrard (1995) showed that rats with either ibotenic acid lesions of the hippocampus, or electrolytic lesions of the fimbria–fornix, were significantly slower in learning the location of a hidden platform in the water maze. However, after 31 days of training, the lesioned animals showed a significant preference for the quadrant of the pool where the hidden platform was located. When the platform was moved to a new location, the lesioned animals, like the control animals, searched for it in its previous location. Thus, animals without a hippocampus or with disruption of the fimbria–fornix can learn the location of a hidden platform. However, rats without a hippocampus also exhibit a 'looping' pattern of swimming.

In another study Whishaw and Jarrard (1996) showed that rats with ibotenic acid lesions of the hippocampus could learn the location of a hidden platform following training with a visible platform. The lesioned animals could not, however, learn to find the platform if it was in a new position every day. Similar findings were observed in animals with fimbria–fornix lesions (Whishaw *et al.* 1995). One of the conclusions from these experiments is that structures other than the hippocampus must be sufficient for place learning.

Another is that rats with a damaged hippocampus can learn places, but are impaired at 'getting there.' Thus, place navigation may comprise two separable components: navigation to a location, and recognition of a location upon arrival.

Another interpretation of the impairments found in the water maze follow-ing removal of the hippocampus is offered by Day et al. (1999). They argue that rats without a hippocampus have difficulty with pliancy—the ability to change strategies. Whereas normal rats switch from an initial wall-following (thigmotaxic) search strategy to an extra-maze landmark-based place strategy when learning the water maze task, rats without a hippocampus are unable to do so. In Day et al.'s account, rats without a hippocampus should learn the water maze if the same strategy can be used throughout training. To achieve this, the authors trained rats without a hippocampus on a large submerged platform that filled most of the maze, and then successively smaller platforms. This was thought to increase the use of a place strategy from the outset, and, as predicted, rats without a hippocampus learned where the hidden platform was located. As mentioned earlier, this result suggests that gradual place learning is possible without a hippocampus.

It's also clear that different parts of the hippocampus play different roles in water maze learning and performance. Moser et al. (1995) found that rats with removal of 60–80% of the hippocampus could learn the platform location. Crucially, this was only seen when the 20–40% of remaining tissue included the dorsal (septal) portion of the hippocampus. If the dorsal hippocampus was removed, and the ventral hippocampus left intact, rats were impaired at learn-ing the platform location (see also Moser et al. 1993). Interestingly, if rats learned the platform location before removal of the ventral hippocampus, they were impaired at subsequent retrieval of this memory (Moser and Moser 1998). This suggests that under normal circumstances, the entire hippocampus is involved in encoding the hidden platform location, and the entire structure is required to retrieve this memory. However, a rat can still display new learning if its dorsal hippocampus is intact.

The sufficiency of the dorsal hippocampus for learning the hidden platform location, however, depends on whether the task is learned slowly (across days) or rapidly (within a day). In an elegant study, Bast et al. (2009) showed that only the intermediate hippocampus—the portion of the hippocampus excluding the dorsal and ventral poles—was necessary and sufficient for rats to show unimpaired learning of the hidden platform location when this location was changed daily. Animals with dorsal lesions were impaired on this working-memory version of the task, although they could learn the location of the hidden platform when it stayed in the same position across training days (the traditional, or 'reference-memory' version of the task). In the authors' view, the intermediate hippocampus is necessary for linking rapid spatial learning to behaviour. In contrast, for spatial learning that takes place over longer periods of time (e.g. across days), brain regions beyond the hippocampus become sufficient to maintain behaviour.

For the entorhinal cortex, the primary cortical input to the hippocampus, there is also evidence of a dorsal–ventral distinction. Although some previous studies suggested that removal of the entorhinal cortex has little effect on spatial learning (for review see Aggleton *et al.* 2000),[2] Steffenach *et al.* (2005) argued that these lesions may have missed a crucial portion of the entorhinal cortex. Specifically, the lesions done in earlier studies may have spared the dorso-lateral band of the entorhinal cortex, which projects to the dorsal hippocampus. (The remaining division of the entorhinal cortex is the ventro-medial band, which projects to the ventral hippocampus (Fyhn *et al.* 2004).) Steffenach *et al.* found that removal of the dorso-lateral band impaired the rats' ability to remember the location of a hidden platform that they'd learned prior to surgery. Removal of the ventro-medial band, in contrast, did not impair this recall. Interestingly, when trained on a new platform location after surgery, both lesioned groups were able to learn its location, although the dorso-laterally lesioned animals may have had a slight impairment. Lesions of the perirhinal and post-rhinal cortices did not impair recall of a pre-surgically trained platform location or the learning of a new location after surgery.

Edvard and May-Britt Moser have also developed an annular variant of the Morris water maze, where rats are confined to a circular path near the periphery of the maze (Fig. 6.7). A hidden platform is typically located in one position in the annulus, and rats appear to identify this location on the basis of extra-maze landmarks. Rats who have learned where the hidden platform is located, as in the traditional Morris maze, will tend to dwell in this location on probe sessions where the platform is unavailable. In addition, as the rats learn this maze, they tend to swim slower in the part of the annulus that usually contains the hidden platform. Hollup *et al.* (2001) showed that rats without a hippocampus were unable to learn the platform location in this task, and on trials where the hidden platform was removed, they showed no preference for its previous location. In this same study, rats that had learned where the

---

[2] Aggleton *et al.*'s review is clear and well-supported. Their essential point is that lesions to the individual cortical input structures to the hippocampus, the entorhinal, perirhinal, postrhinal, or retrosplenial cortices, rarely produce impairment on spatial tasks that are comparable to those following removal of the hippocampus. The reconciliation of this view is that traditional spatial tasks may tap multiple spatial abilities, and that these may arise from the different inputs which the hippocampus receives.

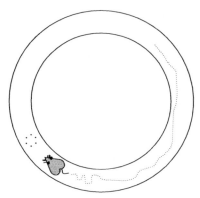

Fig. 6.7 An annular variant of the Morris water maze developed in the lab of Edvard and May-Britt Moser.

hidden platform was located prior to removal of the hippocampus were unable to retrieve this memory when tested after surgery. In a subsequent experiment (Brun *et al.* 2002), rats with damage restricted to the CA3 region of the hippocampus were able to learn the hidden platform location on this maze, but not on the traditional water maze. Brun *et al.* suggest that the main remaining part of the hippocampus circuit following removal of the CA3 region, the direct pathway from neurons in layer III of the entorhinal cortex to the CA1 region, is sufficient for rats to recognize the location of the hidden platform on the annular maze. However, when placed on an open water maze, rats must also navigate to the hidden platform from different locations within the pool (whereas in the annulus the rats' paths are constrained). On this view, the CA3 region is necessary for goal-dependent navigation, but is not necessary for recognition of spatial locations. This distinction between different components of water maze performance echoes that of the experiments with hippocampus disruption mentioned earlier. In this study, unlike the Whishaw studies above, rats were not overtrained on the task. One would predict that given sufficient overtraining, CA3 lesioned animals could also learn where the hidden platform was located.

Barnes maze

Studies using the Barnes maze have found that successful memory in this task likely involves the hippocampus. Barnes (1979) showed that performance on the maze correlated with how rapidly synaptic enhancement (LTP) decayed in the hippocampus. A related finding was observed in old mice, where poorer performance on the Barnes maze corresponded to a lower level of late-LTP in the hippocampus (Bach *et al.* 1999). In this study, older mice tended to search for the correct escape hole using a serial-search strategy, whereas young mice would run directly towards the correct hole, presumably on the basis of its spatial location. A similar reliance on a serial-search strategy as opposed to a spatial strategy was also observed in mice with genetically induced damage to the mammillary nuclei and mammillo-thalamic tract (Radyushkin *et al.* 2005). Irradiation of the hippocampus and the overlying cortex in mice also appears to produce an impairment in performance of the Barnes maze (Raber *et al.* 2004). With the exception of the Radyushkin *et al.* experiment, these studies imply that the hippocampus is necessary for performance of the Barnes maze task. The effects of direct disruptions of the hippocampus in this task have been assessed in the homing experiments described next.

Homing by path integration

The hippocampus appears to play a central role in the ability for rats to home. Much of the work establishing this conclusion was done in the lab of Ian Whishaw, at the University of Lethbridge, on mazes similar to the Barnes maze. In a 1998 paper, Whishaw and Maaswinkel showed that rats with fimbria–fornix lesions were able to return to a 'home' hole on an eight-hole Barnes-type maze after finding a food pellet on the maze surface. In this learning, the maze was in a room with many extra-maze cues, and the same home hole was used across days. The ability of the lesioned rats to find this home is consistent with the previously described findings from the Morris water maze task, as it again shows that rats without a hippocampus, or without its outputs, can recognize a location. However, when Whishaw and Maaswinkel tested rats from a new home location, the lesioned animals were unable to return to the new location, and perseverated in returning to the 'old' home hole. Rats without lesions initially returned to the old hole, but then ran to the new location. If the animals were blindfolded, the control animals accurately returned to the hole from which they began their homing journey. However, lesioned animals were unable to do so. In subsequent studies, removal of the hippocampus itself reduced the accuracy of blindfolded homing (Maaswinkel *et al.* 1999) and sighted, spontaneous homing in a novel environment (Wallace and Whishaw 2003).[3] Impairments on the Whishaw-type homing task have also been found

---

[3] There are two points worth noting about the Maaswinkel *et al.* (1999) study. First, although the hippocampectomized rats were more dispersed in their homing while blindfolded, their overall choices, like those of control animals with an intact hippocampus, were clustered around the correct hole. Thus, there was some evidence of a residual ability to home following hippocampal lesions, although rats with larger lesions were found to be less consistent in their homing directions. The second point is that, when initially blindfolded and tested from a novel home hole, hippocampectomized rats tended to

with lesions restricted to the dorsal hippocampus (Save *et al.* 2001). Together, these results suggest that disruption of the hippocampus or its outputs impair homing when visual landmarks are unavailable.[4]

Rats with a disrupted hippocampal output are also impaired on a task that resembles the triangle-completion problem (Chapter 4). Whishaw and Gorny (1999) trained rats on a Barnes-like maze to leave a home hole and follow a scented string to a food pellet. Upon finding the food, normal rats would gather it and return directly to the home hole. The string was configured in a straight line for some trials and in others as a polygon. In the latter, normal rats would 'complete' the polygon by returning directly to their home hole after gathering their food at the end of the string, even when blindfolded. Rats with fimbria–fornix lesions, however, were severely impaired at this homing task when blindfolded. Again, this is consistent with a central role for the hippocampus formation in homing.

Converging evidence suggests that homing also has a vestibular basis. First, an experiment by Wallace *et al.* (2002) showed that rats with vestibular lesions were unable to home in the dark, when presumably they rely on path integration. This impairment was not due to an overall inability to home, as the same rats could do so in the light, when extra-maze landmarks were available. Thus, both hippocampus disruption and vestibular lesions impair homing in the absence of visual landmarks. Second, inactivation of the vestibular system stops place cells from being place cells (Stackman *et al.* 2002; Russell *et al.* 2003). This is a significant finding, because the removal of other types of

----

return to the originally trained hole (and some hint of this is seen in the Whishaw and Maaswinkel 1998 study as well). This behaviour suggests that surface olfactory cues might have been used by the hippocampectomized rats when they were blindfolded.

[4] Alyan and McNaughton (1999) found, however, that removal of the hippocampus did not impair path integration. They argued that the fimbria–fornix lesions used in the Whishaw studies likely also disrupt projections between the anterior thalamus and the postsubiculum, which convey head direction information (Chapter 8). To test this, they removed the hippocampus in rats and then tested them on two putative path integration tasks. In the first, rats without a hippocampus were able to return to a start point on the periphery of a circular table after being led to the table's centre. In the second, the same rats were able to make a shortcut between two locations by digging through bedding underneath the locations when the previously trained, above-ground route was blocked. On the surface, these results would be at odds with those of the Whishaw studies. However, in the Maaswinkel *et al.* (1999) study, rats without a hippocampus did show significant homing. Their homing, however, was more dispersed than controls. Somewhat greater variability was also seen by Alyan and McNaughton in their shortcutting task, although this did not reach significance. So, their central point stands: it is possible that fimbria–fornix lesions are more disruptive to homing or path integration tasks because they disrupt the processing of directional spatial information.

sensory information—for example vision—does not disrupt place specific firing (O'Keefe 1976; Quirk *et al.* 1990; Save *et al.* 1998). Finally, electrical stimulation of the medial vestibular nucleus increases the firing of neurons (with the firing characteristics of place cells) in the hippocampus (Horii *et al.* 2004). Together, these findings suggest that homing by path integration requires the vestibular system, including its inputs to the hippocampus.

The use of environmental geometry (shape) for orientation

In Chapter 3, I reviewed behavioural data suggesting that animals can use the shape of the environment to find a goal. Does this ability depend on the hippocampus? The answer appears to be 'yes.' McGregor *et al.* (2004b) tested rats without a hippocampus on a rectangular water maze where the hidden platform was near one corner (or its rotational equivalent). Care was taken to exclude extra-maze cues, and the hippocampectomized rats failed to distinguish between the corners of the rectangle that contained the hidden platform and the corners that did not. This deficit was specific to the use of shape, as the same animals could learn the correct corners if, in a square environment, alternate walls were of different colours. In a second experiment, hippocampectomized rats were similarly impaired when tested with a rectangular array of identical objects in a circular pool. Again, the same rats could find the hidden platform corners if distinguishable objects were substituted for two of the identical objects. As the authors suggest, although the hippocampus was necessary to learn these shape tasks, it is unclear exactly how they were performed. For example, as an alternative to using the overall shape of the environment to find the platform, the rats could have used a simple response strategy (e.g. turn left at the short wall), could have recognized the local features of specific corners (e.g. the correct corner could be found by keeping the long wall to one's left and the short wall to one's right).

Some evidence in favour of the 'local feature' interpretation of these results was found by Pearce *et al.* (2004). In this study, as in the McGregor *et al.* experiment, rats without a hippocampus were impaired in learning the location of a hidden platform in a rectangular water maze when only the shape of the environment could be used. When subsequently trained on a kite-shaped maze that possessed a corner that was equivalent to the correct corner in the rectangle and a corner equivalent to an incorrect corner, control animals searched in the correct corner or the corner found by following the long wall by the correct corner. Rats without a hippocampus failed to discriminate between correct and incorrect corners. As additional experiments suggested that the task was solved by the use of local features, it may be that the hippocampus is necessary for the use of these. However, rats without a hippocampus were able to learn to find a hidden platform if it was placed at the apex (smallest angle corner) of a kite maze, so the impairment in local feature use following hippocampus lesions is not absolute (Jones *et al.* 2007).

Summary

Removal of the hippocampus or removal of its outputs via fimbria–fornix lesions produces impairments on the radial arm maze, T-maze delayed alternation, the Morris water maze, homing tasks on the Barnes maze, and the use of maze geometry or local features to find a goal site. The evidence for impairments following hippocampus removal in the exploration of novel objects is, however, far from unanimous.

Extension to humans

In the concluding chapters of the *Cognitive Map*, O'Keefe and Nadel extend the idea of a locale system to humans. For memory, they distinguish between memories of items that exist independent of their context (e.g. one's name)[5] and memories of things within their spatial and temporal context. The former, akin to the notion of semantic memory, is taxon memory. The latter is memory in the locale system. These memories, like the information on a map, can be used flexibly, and can be accessed indirectly. The ability to manipulate locale memories by re-ordering them or combining them in new ways may give rise to 'thinking, imagination, and creativity' (p. 385). For language, the underlying meaning of parts of a sentence—its 'deep' structure—can be thought of in map-like terms. This semantic (meaning) map is hypothesized to reside in the left hippocampus, whereas the allocentric spatial map resides in the right. This view is still contemporary. In a review of more recent neuropsychological and neuroimaging findings, Burgess *et al.* (2002) conclude that the right hippocampus is involved in allocentric spatial memory, and argue that the left hippocampus is involved in episodic and autobiographical memory.

The *Cognitive Map*, to use a British expression, does what is says on the tin. In it O'Keefe and Nadel posit that an allocentric, or locale, representation of the outside world exists in the hippocampus. They provide a model by which more stimulus-bound approach or avoidance type associations—taxon represenations—are combined to provide a flexible, map-like representation of the world. The encounter of new stimuli triggers exploration and the

---

[5] Curiously, in trying to come up with an example of a context-free, semantic memory, I have difficulty. If I think of a tree, I'm immediately transported to this huge hemlock that I tented under in Yosemite. Car tyre? I think of my old red Toyota.

incorporation of new information into the map. In humans, the notion of a stimulus-bound representation and a more flexible representation can be applied to memory and language. As we'll see in the next chapter, there is evidence for activity in the human hippocampus during navigation. Before moving to this, however, I will consider alternative views of the hippocampus and additional findings from H.M. and other patients with hippocampus damage.

Is cognitive mapping all the hippocampus does?

This chapter has emphasized the role of the hippocampus in spatial cognition. I've detailed this view because to understand why we get lost, we need to understand how the brain represents the outside world. In the *Cognitive Map*, O'Keefe and Nadel made a strong case for a flexible, map-like representation of space within the hippocampus. The integrity of this representation, as I will show, underlies our ability to learn the layout of new environments.

However, when we consider the function of the hippocampus, we also touch on the broader issue of the brain bases for memory. Thus, a different question is whether cognitive mapping is the *only* function performed by the hippocampus. This isn't central to the issue of wayfinding, but is important for those trying to bridge the gap between views of the hippocampus derived from experiments with rats to views derived from human amnesia.

The first point, of course, is that O'Keefe and Nadel themselves argue that the hippocampus is involved, in humans, in the flexible use of memories and the processing of language. However, O'Keefe (1999) argues that 'the processing and storage of spatial information is the primary and perhaps the exclusive role of the hippocampus in the rat' (p. 352). Thus, the issue is not whether the hippocampus underlies aspects of non-spatial cognition in humans, but rather whether there is a difference in the types of information represented in the rodent hippocampus as opposed to the human hippocampus.

A second tenet of the cognitive map theory is that this representation is located within the hippocampus. As we'll see in later chapters, subsequent discoveries have revealed strong allocentric encoding of head direction and location in the brain structures projecting to the hippocampus. It's possible that the hippocampus is a convergence site for allocentric spatial information and elements of the animals experience, together comprising the 'what, where, and when' of episodic memory.

A third point is that human imaging studies have provided support for a role of the hippocampus in navigation and spatial memory. I will review this evidence in the next chapter.

I've already mentioned the declarative/non-declarative distinction made by Larry Squire and colleagues. In their view, the hippocampus is necessary for acquiring and consolidating new memories for facts and events, be they spatial or non-spatial (e.g. Squire and Alvarez 1995). Long-term storage of memory occurs outside the hippocampus, and thus in hippocampus-dependent amnesia, memories that were formed before the hippocampus is compromised, are still intact. This is sometimes referred to as the 'standard model of memory consolidation'.

A related, but overarching view of memory and brain systems is offered by Howard Eichenbaum and Neil Cohen in their book *From Conditioning to Conscious Recollection* (2001). In it they argue that there isn't a specialized brain system for storing memories, or a specific part of the brain in which these are 'warehoused'. Instead, the same brain systems that process a type of information are also involved in its storage. Different types of information and memories depend on different neural systems. Broadly, declarative memories are sub-served by the hippocampus, parahippocampal regions, and their connections to the cortex. Procedural memories may be sub-served by basal ganglia, cerebellar, and motor outputs. Emotional memory depends on the amygdala and hypothalamus. For declarative memory, converging connections in the parahippocampal region from different cortical regions may be critical for maintaining representations of stimuli. The connections between the hippocampus and cortical areas allow the hippocampus to process the relations between stimuli. The emphasis here is on the flexible handling of memories. In a subsequent review, Eichenbaum (2004) provided evidence that this type of flexible processing includes the association of stimuli, actions, and the contexts in which they occur. It also includes the representation of sequences of events, and, again, the relations between stimuli which allow flexible memory expression. For Eichenbaum and colleagues, the rat hippocampus is not fundamentally different from that of the human in the types of memory it sub-serves. It processes spatial information, to be sure, but it also is essential for the representation of relations between stimuli, and their use in a flexible way. Evidence supporting this view is presented later.

Spatial information is likewise not privileged in the multiple trace theory (MTT) of Moris Moscovitch, Lynn Nadel, and colleagues (Moscovitch *et al.* 2005). In their view, the hippocampus is necessary for vivid, detail-laden memories. These may take the form not only of autobiographical memories, but also of rich spatial context memories. In contrast, the hippocampus is not the storage site for semantic memories—memories for facts and information (and even information like one's name)—that exist independent of episodic detail. Semantic memory can also include aspects of the spatial layout of familiar environments. Semantic memory, in Moscovitch *et al.*'s account, resides in neocortical regions. Evidence for this view comes from findings in human amnesia patients (see later) and experiments with rats (Winocur *et al.* 2005). The multiple trace theory is so named because it holds that memories are encoded in multiple connections between the hippocampus and the neocortex. Every time an event is experienced, it is encoded by the hippocampus and neocortex, but with often repeated, related traces, the cortical representations come to be sufficient to support memory without a hippocampus.

The distinction between multiple trace theory and the standard model of memory consolidation is that the former holds that the hippocampus is always necessary for the retrieval of rich, detailed memories, including episodic memories. In the standard model, the hippocampus is only necessary for a period of time in which consolidation occurs. The distinction between the multiple trace theory of the hippocampus and the cognitive map view is that in the former navigation and spatial memory for quite familiar environments is possible without a hippocampus. In the cognitive map view, the hippocampus is necessary for navigation and spatial cognition at all times.

The work of Richard Morris and colleagues has yielded a perspective on hippocampus function that spans multiple levels of analysis (e.g. Frey and Morris 1997; Morris and Frey 1997; Morris 2006). In their view, the hippocampus automatically encodes all events to which an animal attends. Of course, only a few of these encoded events find their way to longer-term storage, and Morris and colleagues have described a mechanism by which this may occur. Essentially, some synapses on a given hippocampal neuron are transiently potentiated when an animal encodes an event. Experimentally, this potentiation can be artificially induced by administering a brief series of electrical stimulations (LTP). The potentiated synapse is 'tagged' such that it attracts plasticity proteins synthesized in the cell nucleus or in the dendrites. If another encoding event occurs which stimulates the same neuron and causes the induction of plasticity proteins, then the potentiation at the tagged synapse will be strengthened. Alternatively, if the neuron is not stimulated and plasticity proteins are not produced, potentiated synapses will return to a baseline state after a few hours. So too, presumably, will encoded events fade from memory. This synaptic tagging is a cellular-level mechanism of the consolidation of memory. At a systems level, consolidation occurs as the hippocampus establishes an 'index' of the cortical regions that contain the more neurally eidetic representations of attended stimuli. Over a longer period of time, cortical regions will develop schemas—representations of the structures of repeatedly experienced information. Once acquired, these structures may allow rapid cortical learning of new information.

Other perspectives emphasize the connections of the hippocampus and its inputs and outputs. Aggleton and Brown (1999) hypothesize that recognition memory (knowing that a stimulus is familiar) and recall (remembering the stimulus/recollection) are sub-served by different neural circuits. Recognition memory critically depends on the perirhinal cortex and its projections to the medial dorsal thalamus. Recall depends on the hippocampal formation and its connections via the fornix to the anterior thalamic nuclei (and their return connections via the cingulum bundle) and the mammillary bodies. This circuitry is also critical for spatial memory in rodents. For Murray, Bussey, and Saksida (2007), the perirhinal cortex is essential for functions that differ from those of the hippocampus. Based on findings from their labs and others (e.g. Buckley and Gaffan 1997; Buckley *et al.* 2001), the perirhinal cortex is seen as necessary for visual discrimination of stimuli with overlapping features. It is also necessary for object memory. The hippocampus is not necessary for these types of visual discriminations, but is essential for spatial and scene memory. Similarly, for Buckley and Gaffan (2006), the function of the medial temporal lobe (the hippocampus, perirhinal, entorhinal and parahippocampal cortices) is not restricted to memory, but also involves perception. They suggest that structures beyond this region are also likely to underlie specific types of memory.

Another view of the hippocampus and memory is provided by David Redish in his book *Beyond the Cognitive Map* (1999). He suggests that the properties of place cells in the hippocampus provide not only a basis for spatial cognition, but also the starting point for episodic memory. Thus, the ability of place cells to 'recognize' familiar environments and to replay previously experienced sequences of place fields (as has been shown by Matthew Wilson and colleagues: Wilson and McNaughton 1994; Louie and Wilson 2001; Lee and Wilson 2002; Foster and Wilson 2006) may be the way in which the animal recreates and possibly consolidates representations of specific contexts.

Hippocampus lesions and non-spatial tasks

A complete review of this literature is its own book, and the interested reader is referred to Eichenbaum and Cohen (2001). Here I consider just a few examples. First, removal of the hippocampus produces impairments on trace classical conditioning, where the conditioned stimulus (CS) begins and ends before the onset of the un-conditioned stimulus (US) (Solomon *et al.* 1986). In contrast, rabbits without a hippocampus readily learn a CS–US association if the CS begins before the US, but they co-terminate. This is 'delay' conditioning. A similar pattern of impaired trace conditioning and intact delay conditioning has been found in human amnesic patients with hippocampus damage (Clark and Squire 1998). Thus, the hippocampus appears to be necessary to bridge the delay between the CS and the US in trace conditioning. However, trace conditioning is acquired more slowly than delay conditioning, and a more difficult form of delay conditioning is also impaired by removal of the hippo-campus (Beylin *et al.* 2001). Further, although rats without a hippocampus are impaired in trace conditioning and in conditioning with simultaneous presentation of the CS and US, they are not impaired when the two types of conditioning are combined (Bangasser *et al.* 2006). Thus, task difficulty may be a factor in whether a CS–US association can be made in the absence of a hippocampus.

The hippocampus is also necessary for the flexible use of relations between stimuli. For example, Dusek and Eichenbaum (1997) trained rats on a series of overlapping pairs of odour stimuli, and tested their ability to make an infer-ence about two stimuli that had not been presented together. The stimuli were bowls of sand scented with specific odour (e.g. paprika, coffee, etc.). For each pair of odours presented (A and B, B and C, etc.), one odour was always paired with the presence of a food reward (A+ B−; B+ C−; C+ D−; and D+ E−; '+' is the rewarded odour). Rats with fornix lesions or perirhinal and entorhinal cortex lesions performed these discriminations at the same level as control animals. When tested with a pair of familiar odours that hadn't been pitched against one another (odour B versus odour D), control animals readily made the correct transitive inference—that odour B came earlier in the sequence than odour D, and was therefore correct. In contrast, the lesioned animals were unable to make this inference. Thus, the outputs of the hippocampus and the perirhinal and entorhinal cortex are necessary for the flexible processing of stimulus relations. In other experiments, rats with hippocampus damage were impaired at recognizing the order in which odours were presented (Fortin *et al.* 2002), or selecting the correct odour in a pair based on a preceding set of specific odour pairs (Agster *et al.* 2002).

These and other examples (e.g. an impaired fear response to an artificial snake in hippocampectomized monkeys (Chudasama *et al.* 2008)) show that the hippocampus is essential for some aspects of non-spatial learning and memory, in addition to its well-established role in spatial cognition.

Does H.M. get lost? Evidence from neuropsychological studies with amnesiacs

The previous discussion notwithstanding, many of the studies reviewed in this chapter point to a significant contribution of the hippocampus to spatial navi-gation and memory. With this in mind, we can return to our start point, H.M. Does he get lost?

H.M. was asked to draw the floor plan of the house in which he lived on two occasions (Corkin 2002). H.M. had moved to this house 5 years after his operation, and had lived there with his parents. His drawing of the layout of the house was accurate. Thus, he had acquired this spatial information without a hippocampus. Corkin suggested that other brain regions, for example the parietal cortex and the spared portion of the cortex near the hippocampus, may enable some types of spatial memories to be formed. Indeed, H.M. showed evidence of learning a location of a hidden weight sensor (underneath a carpet) (Bohbot and Corkin 2007). However, his search strategies on some trials on this task suggested that he did not remember performing it previously, and he was also unable to learn a second sensor location. For Bohbot and Corkin, H.M.'s ability to learn the initial sensor location was ascribed to his intact parahippocampal cortices.

H.M. also had difficulties with other spatial tasks. For example, H.M. couldn't learn a table-top maze, either with a combination of vision and sound (Milner 1965), or by touch (Corkin 1965). Nor was he able to remember the spatial layout of 16 everyday objects placed on a table, although he couldn't remember seeing the objects in the first place (Smith and Milner 1981). One difficulty with these results is that it's not clear what types of spatial ability table-top tasks assess (Maguire *et al.* 1999). That is, a rat navigating in a maze or a human wayfinding in an environment may use different spatial capacities and neural systems than those involved in learning a table-top maze or the locations of objects within one's reach.

One approach to this difficulty is to have the study participant view the to-be-remembered information on the table top, and then move to the other side of the table before making their response. Using such a procedure, Holdstock *et al.* (2000) found that a 60-year-old woman with hippocampus damage, Y.R., was impaired at remembering the location on a test board where a small LED had been illuminated. Y.R. was considerably less impaired on this task when it was made more egocentric by having Y.R. stay in the same position throughout the test, and by presenting the to-be-remembered LED illumination in the dark.

Another patient with significant hippocampus damage, E.P., has been tested on his memory for where he grew up (Teng and Squire 1999). At the time of testing, E.P. was a 76-year-old, retired laboratory technician, and his hippocampus damage was due to a bout of viral encephalitis in 1992. E.P.'s anterograde memory impairment resembles that of H.M. (Stefenacci *et al.* 2000). When tested for his memory of his childhood neighbourhood, E.P. was able to respond as accurately as control subjects who lived in the area at the same time. Thus, his memory for the environment that he lived in prior to the onset of his amnesia was intact. However, when asked about the neighbourhood he has lived in since developing amnesia, he was unable to provide any response.

It's unclear why H.M. could form memories of the house he lived in after his operation, yet E.P. was unable to learn about the neighbourhood he lived in after becoming amnesic. For Teng and Squire, the pattern of intact pre-amnesia memory and impaired post-amnesia memory argues for a temporary role of the hippocampus in processing memory generally.

Findings from another patient, K.C., agree with the main findings with E.P., but also provide a qualification (Rosenbaum *et al.* 2000). Patient K.C. was a 49-year-old, who suffered a closed-head brain injury in a motorcycle accident. He had a significant reduction in hippocampus size, and also loss of parahippocampal cortex. Like E.P., K.C. had significant anterograde amnesia, and was unable to draw the layout of the library where he had worked after his injury. However, when tested for his memory of the neighbourhood in which he had been living for 40 years, he was able to draw the layout of the major streets, describe the correct route from one landmark to another, and correctly indicate the distance and direction between major landmarks. Although this suggests that he has intact older memories and an impaired ability to form new memories, there was one caveat. When tested for his recognition of landmarks (for example, houses) in his neighbourhood, K.C. was severely impaired. Given 48 photographs from his neighbourhood, he could only recognize 15, and could only indicate the location of 7 of these—in contrast, his brother recognized 46 landmarks, and his mother 45. Interestingly, the only landmarks he could remember were major ones like the school or shopping centre. For Rosenbaum *et al.* these results suggest that the hippocampus isn't necessary for all spatial memories, but is necessary for the fine-grain detail of cognitive maps.

Patient E.P. and K.C. also show similarities with patient T.T., a former London taxi driver with damage to the hippocampus (Maguire *et al.* 2006). T.T.'s pathology was the result of limbic encephalitis and an unusual immune response, and it involved damage to the hippocampus and general brain atrophy. T.T. had worked as a taxi driver for 37 years, but stopped working when he became ill. On a number of neuropsychological tests, T.T., like E.P., was impaired in recognition and delayed memory. However, when tested for his recognition of London landmarks and their spatial relationships, he performed at the same level as similarly experienced, control taxi drivers. On the surface, this result is consistent with the intact memory E.P. has for the neighbourhood in which he was raised. In addition, again like E.P., T.T. had moved to a new location after his illness, and his wife reported that he was unable to navigate and wayfind there despite repeated experience. However, when tested with active navigation through a virtual (game-based) representation of London, T.T. was impaired on a number of routes. These routes were characterized by not being main arteries, though they were apparently equally familiar to the control taxi drivers. Maguire *et al.*'s interpretation of these findings is that they are consistent with a diminished level of detail in previously learned information.

Patients who have had portions of their hippocampi and the adjacent regions removed also exhibit impaired spatial learning. In one study, Maguire *et al.* (1996) found that patients with either right or left temporal lobe removal (a surgery that is typically done, as in the case of H.M., to control seizures) were impaired at learning the spatial relationships between landmarks when viewing videos of two urban routes. With more viewing of the videos than control subjects, however, they were able to recognize scenes. Maguire *et al.* argue that the patients' impairment doesn't apply to all types of memories, just spatial ones. In a subsequent study, Spiers *et al.* (2001a) tested 17 patients with right temporal lobe partial removal and 13 patients with left temporal lobe partial removal on navigation and memory in a virtual town. The town was based on a computer game, and after the patients 'explored' the virtual town, they were asked to navigate between 10 different locations in the most direct way possible. In a subsequent task, the patients followed a route through the town and encountered different virtual characters who presented them with different objects. Patients with portions of their right temporal lobe removed were significantly impaired on the navigation task, and in their recognition memory for locations visited in the virtual town. In the second task, they were also impaired at remembering which objects they had previously seen, and which character presented them with a specific object. In contrast, patients with partial left temporal lobe removal were not impaired in navigation or location recognition. They were, however, impaired in remembering the order in which objects had been presented to them, and the context in which a given object had been presented. Thus, damage to the right temporal lobe (including the hippocampus and the parahippocampus) impaired navigation and object recognition, whereas damage to the left temporal lobe impaired aspects of episodic or context memory.

Individuals who sustained damage to the hippocampus early in life also have wayfinding and spatial memory difficulties. Vargha-Khadem *et al.* (1997) describe three such individuals, and observe that 'None . . . can reliably find their way in familiar surroundings, remember where objects are located, or remember where they have placed them' (p. 377). In other tests, one of these patients, Jon, was impaired at learning the layout of the virtual town described earlier, but showed intact memory for previously seen objects (Spiers *et al.* 2001b). In this same study Jon also showed episodic memory impairments, in that he had difficulty recognizing the individual who had presented him with

Anterior
(front)

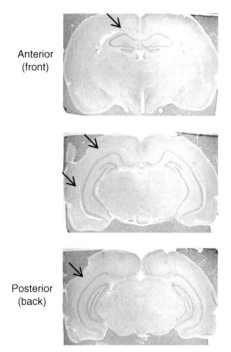

Posterior
(back)

Plate 1 Coronal (frontal) sections of the rat brain showing the hippocampus
(arrows) at three different levels, from the front of the brain to the back.
(See also Fig. 6.1.)

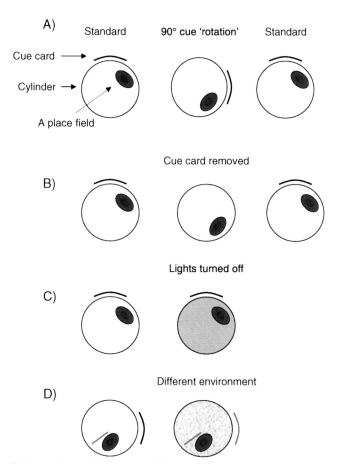

Plate 2 A) 90° rotation of a cue card within a cylindrical environment causes a corresponding shift in the location of the place fields of hippocampal place cells. B) Place fields are still evident after the removal of the cue card from the environment, although their angular location may shift. C) Place fields are usually maintained in darkness. D) Place fields can maintain their anchoring to a specific barrier, even across environments. (See also Fig. 7.1.)

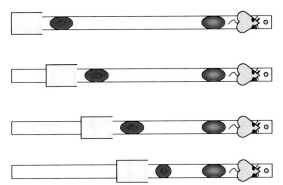

Plate 3 Gothard et al. (1996b) provided evidence that place cells are driven by path integration and by landmarks. Place fields that were active as a rat departed from a start box remained anchored to that start box, even when it was displaced. Thus, these cells appeared to encode the animal's distance from the start box. In contrast, place fields near the end of the linear track fired in the same location, regardless of the position of the start box. Thus, these fields appeared to be anchored to the end of the maze or to extra-maze landmarks. (See also Fig. 7.2.)

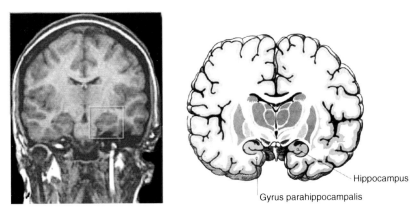

Hippocampus

Gyrus parahippocampalis

Plate 4 *Left:* Magnetic resonance image of the human brain at the level of the hippocampus. *Right:* Sketch of the human brain, cut at the level of the hippocampus, highlighting the hippocampus and the parahippocampal gyrus. (See also Fig. 7.5.)

Source: Wikipedia commons.

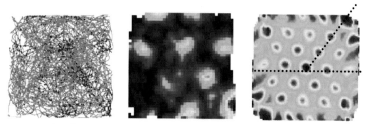

Plate 5 Example of a grid cell recorded in the medial entorhinal cortex. In the right plot, the path of the animal is shown in grey, and the spikes of the grid neuron are shown as dots. In the middle plot, the firing rate of this neuron is colour-coded, with higher firing rates represented as warmer colours. The 'gridness' of this grid cell is particularly evident when the firing rate map is correlated with itself, as shown in the right-most plot. The orientation of a grid field is the angle at which a line can be drawn through the grid sub-fields. Example courtesy of Dr James Ainge, University of St. Andrews. (See also Fig. 8.3.)

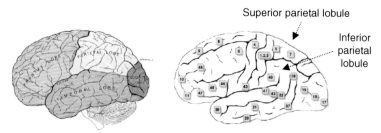

Plate 6 *Left:* The four lobes of the brain *Right:* Brodman's areas of the cortex. (See also Fig. 9.2.)

Source: Wikipedia commons (based on *Gray's Anatomy*).

an object (in the virtual game), where he received an object, or the order in which objects were presented. Interestingly, he was unimpaired at a test of recognition memory for photographs of scenes. For Spiers *et al.* these results suggest that the hippocampus is necessary for learning the layout of an environment via active navigation, but not for recognition of photos of scenes (which may depend on parahippocampal cortex; see Chapter 9), or for object recognition. Jon also showed impaired memory for a long list of outdoor scenes, but normal memory for faces (Bird *et al.* 2008). In Bird *et al.*'s account, this impairment argues against domain general views of hippocampus-dependent memory—where, for example, the hippocampus is necessary for recollection, as opposed to familiarity, or declarative memory as opposed to non-declarative memory. In its place, the impairments that Jon showed in this study, and elsewhere (Hartley *et al.* 2007), are consistent with the view that the hippocampus is preferentially involved in processing topographical information.

Path integration in humans with hippocampus damage

Human path integration following lesions to the temporal lobe, including the hippocampus, has been examined in three studies. In the first, Worsley *et al.* (2001) found that patients with right temporal lobe resections (partial removals) were impaired on a triangle completion task while blindfolded. These patients were able to walk the correct distance to the start point, but showed significant error in the direction they turned to return to this point. Right temporal lobe patients were also impaired at reproducing a two-legged route, again because they misjudged the angle of the turn between the two legs. Patients with left temporal lobe resections were unimpaired at either task. However, in a simpler version of the task where the experimenter turned the patient, and then the patient took two steps forward and attempted to reproduce this turn, no impairment was found. These results suggest that the right temporal lobe may be critical for maintaining directional orientation.

In a subsequent study, Philbeck *et al.* (2004) found that right temporal lobe resection patients were impaired at blindfolded walking to a previously viewed target. These patients tended to overshoot the distance to the target, whereas patients with left temporal lobe resections were unimpaired on this task. It's not entirely clear why Philbeck *et al.* observed an impairment in estimating distance, whereas Worsley *et al.* did not, but a possibility suggested by Philbeck *et al.* is that shorter distances were used in the triangle completion task (2.5 metres) compared to the target estimation task (5 metres).

In contrast to these findings, a third study on human path integration showed that damage to the hippocampus and entorhinal cortex did not impair performance. Schrager *et al.* (2008) compared path integration abilities in control subjects and two patients with damage to the hippocampus and entorhinal cortex, E.P and G.P., as well as three additional patients with damage restricted to the hippocampus. Subjects were blindfolded and wore earphones, and were led on short routes (average length: 4.5metres) with one or two turns. At the end of the route they stepped onto a platform and were asked to point in the direction of the route's start point. Both control subjects and patients pointed accurately to the start point, and the two groups did not differ. In another condition the participants were asked to estimate the distance they'd travelled. Here again no differences were observed. To test whether this task depends on path integration, in one condition the subjects were rotated slowly at the end of the route before they pointed to the start point. Both groups showed considerable and comparable error following this rotation. The only circumstance in which differences between the patients and the control subjects were observed was if a distraction task—mental navigation over 1 minute 10 seconds—was interposed between the completion of the route and the estimation of the route's start point direction. Here, the patients were significantly worse than the control subjects. For the authors, this pattern of results suggests that the hippocampus and the entorhinal cortex are not necessary for path integration. Rather, impairments are only seen when the duration of the task exceeds the time span of working memory.

These results provide a challenge to the view that the hippocampus is essential for path integration. Schrager *et al.*'s argument is that, in humans, other brain regions, such as the parietal cortex, may be essential for this ability. Rats, in contrast, may be more reliant on the hippocampus and entorhinal cortex for path integration. A reconciliation of these findings likely requires additional experimentation, although as I've suggested in footnotes 3 and 4, even the rodent studies aren't unanimous on the contribution of the hippo-campus to path integration. Of particular interest would be a comparison between patients with hippocampus/entorhinal cortex disruption and controls on a task where the controls are able to detect and compensate for a passive rotation. In the Schrager *et al.* study, neither control nor medial temporal lobe patients reliably compensated for the rotations given (possibly because of the speed or duration of the rotation).

Summary

When trying to identify the reasons for us getting lost, we need to consider how, under normal circumstances, we stay oriented. Experimental studies in rats have provided one of the most intriguing clues in this regard with the finding that place cells represent different locations within an environment. Together, these may comprise a cognitive map, thus substantiating Edward Tolman's earlier views.

Does such a map exist in humans? The influential case of patient H.M. was the starting point of much subsequent work. H.M. was profoundly impaired at acquiring new declarative memories—be they spatial or non-spatial. Subsequent studies with other hippocampal amnesics have shown that they retain memory for previously learned spatial environments (for example, a childhood neighbourhood), but have great difficulty learning the layouts of locations or the topography of an environment after the onset of their amnesia.

Do we get lost because our hippocampus misleads us? Possibly, and there is intriguing evidence that the cognitive map breaks down when no spatial information is available (Chapter 7). However, as I'll show in later chapters, the hippocampus is just one component of an interlinked system that provides orientation and recognition of environments. Thus, although there is strong evidence that the hippocampus is necessary for learning the layout of an environment, misorientation may be due to errors in neural representations upstream from this structure.

Chapter 7

Place cells and brain imaging

In a remarkable study by Hassabis *et al.* (2007), patients with damage to the hippocampus were asked to imagine new experiences. For example, they were asked to imagine, in as much detail as possible, being in a museum with many exhibits. The patients typically responded with few details, as given in the following excerpt:

> ... To be honest there's not a lot coming. [*Experimenter: Do you hear or smell anything?*] No, it's not very real. It's just not happening. My imagination isn't ... well, I'm not imagining it, let's put it that way. Normally you can picture it can't you? I'm not picturing anything at the moment. (p. 1727)

In contrast, control subjects provided much richer detail:

> ... It's a pillared hall and the floor is marble, the ceiling is domed and sculpted. There is a buzz about the place. I think there must be some special exhibition which I had not expected ... (p. 1727)

Hassabis *et al.* found that patients without a hippocampus had difficulty imagining future experiences. This raises the intriguing possibility that imagination and memory are functionally related (see also Addis *et al.* 2007). Of course, on reflection, imagined experiences must be constructed, at least in part, from previously experienced elements. But the finding that the same brain structure is critical for both may indicate that mental time travel, either to the past or to the future, is a single capacity.

From a spatial cognition standpoint, Hassabis *et al.* suggest that the inability to imagine new experiences in patients with a damaged hippocampus may coincide with a lack of spatial coherence in the imagined experience. That is, when patients attempted to imagine a future setting, they often produced fragmentary images, whereas control subjects imagined coherent environmental contexts. From a wayfinding perspective, these findings may imply that imagining one's destination is an important part of getting from A to B without becoming lost.

In this chapter I will review what is known about hippocampal place cells and present data which indicate that place cells in the hippocampus encode not only current locations, but also intended destinations. I will then consider the findings from human neuroimaging studies using spatial tasks. In dealing with the behaviour of place cells, it will be apparent that the same sources of spatial information that animals use for solving spatial tasks—extra-maze landmarks and path integration—also control place fields. Likewise, in humans, navigation based on these sources of information is associated with activation of the hippocampus. Together, these findings provide strong evidence for a brain system that allows recognition of locations.

Individual neurons within the hippocampus fire in specific places

In the previous chapter, I described the first findings of place cells in the hippocampus, and their control by visual landmarks in the environment. Here, I flush out this description with a review of what we know about this remarkable representation of space.

First, I'll note a small caveat. Almost all of the data on place cell properties described later are based on recordings from the dorsal hippocampus. Place cells are found in the intermediate and ventral hippocampus, and these have much larger place fields—up to 10 metres on a linear track for place cells in the ventral CA3 region (Jung et al. 1994; Maurer et al. 2005; Kjelstrup et al. 2008). It's likely that the larger place fields one observes when moving from the septal to the temporal poles of the hippocampus are the product of differences in spatially tuned neurons observed along the dorso-ventral axis of the entorhinal cortex (Chapter 8).

If you were to record from a place cell in the dorsal hippocampus as a rat moves around in a cylindrical environment as shown in the previous chapter (Fig. 6.4), you'd observe that the cell would fire whenever the rat's head was in a certain location in the environment. In this type of environment, it would likely do so independent of which direction the rat faced. If you were to record from other place cells at the same time, you'd find that they have receptive fields in different parts of the cylinder, and if you were to record from a sufficient number you'd find that the entire apparatus would be represented. This representation is not topographic—adjacent place cells within the hippocampus are as likely to have place fields far apart as they are to have fields next to one another (O'Keefe 1976; Redish et al. 2001).

If you were to pick your rat up and place it in a different environment—say a different maze or enclosure—you'd find that your original cell would likely have an unrelated place field, or it might stop firing. Other, previously silent place cells would begin firing. Even if the second environment was new to the animal, place fields would be evident nearly immediately (Hill 1978), although

10 to 20 minutes of exploration may be necessary for a stable representation to develop (Wilson and McNaughton 1993; see also Frank *et al.* 2004). If you were to record from several place cells simultaneously, you'd find that you could not necessarily predict how a given place cell responded to a change in environment based on the behaviour of other place cells (Kubie and Ranck 1983; Muller and Kubie 1987). This reshuffling of place fields in different environments is referred to as *remapping*. Its occurrence suggests that the hippocampus contains independent representations of each environment that the rat experiences.

In some circumstances the development of remapping requires experience with the environments in question. In a study by Lever *et al.* (2002), place cells were alternately recorded in a cylindrical environment and a square environment, each of which was centred within the same curtained enclosure in a lab room. When the animals were first placed in each environment, individual place cells would fire in corresponding locations in both. That is, instead of remapping between the cylinder and the square environment, the same map was evident. With repeated experience of the two environments across days, remapping began to occur. Interestingly, the amount of experience required before remapping appeared to differ between animals.

Another qualification of the remapping phenomenon is that it isn't always complete. Skaggs and McNaughton (1998) showed that when rats ran from one square box-like environment to another, identical environment, some place cells fired in the same relative locations in both boxes, whereas others did not. Thus, there was *partial remapping* of the place cell representation. This result suggests that place cells represent similarities between environments as well as their differences, and that different place cells are driven by different cues within an environment (as will be described later). Partial remapping was not observed in a subsequent study where rats shuttled between two parallel square environments, although full remapping emerged when these environments were placed in a different angular orientation to one another (Fuhs *et al.* 2005). It's not clear why partial remapping was seen in the Skaggs and McNaughton study, and not in this latter study.

Remapping has also been characterized in relation to changes in the firing rates of place cells. Leutgeb *et al.* (2005) showed that replacing one recording arena with another of a different colour or shape produced a change in the firing rates of the place cells, but no change in where they fired. This was termed *rate remapping*, and was particularly evident in CA3 place cells. However, when rats were taken from an arena in one room to a similar arena in a different room, the place cells changed both their firing rates and where they fired. This greater change was termed *global remapping*. Leutgeb *et al.*

suggest the rate of remapping may describe some of the modulation of place fields by ongoing behaviour that I will describe later. Global remapping appears to be a direct result of changes in the firing locations of another class of spatially tuned neurons found in a structure upstream from the hippocampus (Fyhn *et al.* 2007; see Chapter 8).

Visual landmarks exert stimulus control over place fields

In the previous chapter I mentioned early studies by John O'Keefe and Robert Muller, which showed that visual landmarks exert stimulus control

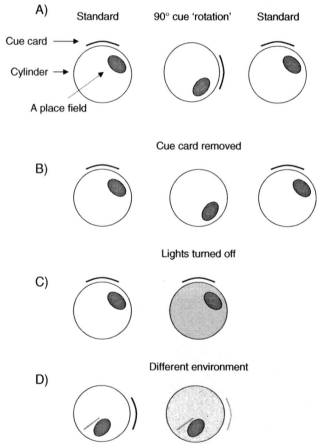

Fig. 7.1 A) 90° rotation of a cue card within a cylindrical environment causes a corresponding shift in the location of the place fields of hippocampal place cells. B) Place fields are still evident after the removal of the cue card from the environment, although their angular location may shift. C) Place fields are usually maintained in darkness. D) Place fields can maintain their anchoring to a specific barrier, even across environments. (See also Plate 2.)

over place fields (Fig. 7.1a). The establishment of this control requires NMDA (glutamatergic) receptor activation and the synthesis of new proteins (Kentros *et al.* 1998; Agnihotri *et al.* 2004). It's also important that the landmarks be either at or near the periphery of the environment. As an illustration of this, Cressant *et al.* (1997) found that if three landmarks (a black wooden cone, a white plastic cylinder, and a bottle of French wine) were arranged in a triangle near the centre of a recording cylinder, they did not exert stimulus control over place fields. However, if the same cues were placed against the cylinder walls, or were put next to one another in a line and positioned close to the cylinder walls, they exerted strong stimulus control. As we have seen in Chapter 3, gerbils can learn the location of a hidden food source by using landmarks in an open field, but Cressant *et al.* note that this learning requires many trials, whereas a task that requires the use of distal landmarks, such as the Morris water maze, can be learned in just a few trials. If place cells underlie spatial learning, then the Cressant *et al.* results imply that learning a location based on centrally placed landmarks would be much more difficult than learning the same location when these landmarks are placed at the periphery of the environment.

In an experiment where two cue cards, one white and one black, were present in the recording cylinder, Fenton *et al.* (2000a) showed that the cue card closer to a given place field exerted more stimulus control over it than an equivalent landmark farther away. To describe this finding, Fenton *et al.* (2000b) proposed that the shift in a given place field following the rotations of the two cue cards was a sum of the rotation vectors for each cue card, weighted by the distance of the field from each cue card. Hetherington and Shapiro (1997) have also shown that removal of a landmark near a place field caused a decrease in the firing rate and field area, whereas removal of a more distal landmark was associated with an increase in firing and field areas. Thus, even within an environment, there is some local modulation of place fields by nearby landmarks. These results parallel the findings of overshadowing in the Morris water maze with a landmark near the hidden platform (Chapter 3).

Similarly, I previously described behavioural findings in which initial learning of landmarks block subsequent learning of additional landmarks in the water maze or in an open field task. A study by Barry and Muller (2006) suggests that this blocking is likewise observed, to an extent, with place fields. If rats were initially exposed to a traditional recording cylinder with a single white cue card, and then a black cue card was added to the environment, the black one alone subsequently controlled place fields in only a subset of animals. In contrast, if animals were exposed to both cue cards from the start, the black cue card exerted much stronger stimulus control.

It also appears that different place cells encode different subsets of landmarks within an environment. For example, Gothard *et al.* (1996a) trained rats to find food in a spatial location near two distinct landmarks within a circular arena. The arena was curtained off from the remainder of the room, and five additional, extra-arena landmarks were placed at different positions around the curtain circumference. The rats' task was to leave a start box, navigate to the goal location defined by the two intra-arena landmarks, and return to the box, which was moved to a different position by the experimenters in the interim. On different trials the intra-arena landmarks were moved to different positions within the arena, and the rat's task was to navigate with respect to these landmarks, and not the extra-arena background landmarks. Although many place cells recorded during this task were anchored to the background landmarks (and thus may be considered 'traditional' place cells), others encoded locations near the intra-arena landmarks, or the start box. The latter place cells followed the movements of the intra-arena landmarks or the start box across trials. Thus, different place cells participated in different spatial reference frames, either encoding space relative to intra-arena landmarks, or encoding locations relative to the background landmarks.

One of the most convincing demonstrations of this effect was observed by James Knierim (2002). He trained rats to run a circular track that had different floor surfaces—rubber mat, sandpaper, carpet, and duct tape—on different portions of the track. The track itself was placed within a curtained enclosure, and different cues were hung on the curtain to serve as distal landmarks. After recording place cells as the rats ran approximately 15 laps around the track, the rat was removed from the environment. The circular track was then rotated in one direction, and the distal landmarks in the opposite direction, a manipulation termed a 'double-rotation' (Shapiro *et al.* 1997). Upon returning to the track, the place fields of some place cells shifted to agree with the circular track, whereas others, recorded at the same time, shifted to agree with the distal landmarks. Remarkably, some place fields split, and showed a field that agreed with the local cues on the track and a field that agreed with the distal cues. These results, coupled with other consistent findings (Shapiro *et al.* 1997; Tanila *et al.* 1997a; Zinyuk *et al.* 2000; Siegel *et al.* 2008), suggest that place cells may not be wholly cohesive, as would be expected if all cells were part of a strong attractor neural network (e.g. Samsonovich and McNaughton, 1997). Rather, inputs encoding external stimuli exert a strong influence over place fields, whereas the intrinsic connections between cells exert a weaker influence.

There are, however, differences in the coherence of place cells recorded in different regions of the hippocampus. In the same double-rotation type of experiment, Lee *et al.* (2004) found that CA3 place cells tend to behave coherently—that is, most simultaneously recorded cells shifted their place field to agree with one set of cues—often, but not exclusively, the local cues. CA1 place cells, in contrast, did not behave very coherently if the shift between the local and distal cues was more than 90°. This finding is consistent with the observation that CA3 neurons have an extensive set of connections with one another (recurrent collaterals or associational connections), whereas this is not the case for CA1 (for review see Amaral and Lavenex 2007). Lee *et al.* also raise the interesting possibility that the CA1 place cell network may 'listen' to its indirect pathway (inputs from the dentate gyrus—CA3) in some situations, and at other times may be driven by the direct pathway from the entorhinal cortex (see also Leutgeb *et al.* 2004). These latter inputs are sufficient to sustain normal place field activity (McNaughton *et al.* 1989; Mizumori *et al.* 1989; Brun *et al.* 2002).

Place fields are driven by path integration

Another principle of hippocampal place cell behaviour is that landmarks, although sufficient to control place fields, aren't necessary for normal place cell activity. The evidence for this conclusion comes from studies showing that place fields persist in the absence of visual information, and that they can ignore landmarks under certain circumstances. Evidence suggests that, in addition to vision, path integration is an important contributor to place cell firing.

Place fields are present even when visual landmarks are removed. For example, if one removes the cue card from the standard cylindrical environment, place cells continue to fire, although the angular positions of their fields shift (Fig. 7.1b; Muller and Kubie 1987). Muller and Kubie noted that there was some loss of 'crispness' when the cue card was removed, but clear place fields were usually apparent.

In the dark, place field stability was initially described by O'Keefe (1976), and subsequently confirmed by others (Hill and Best 1981; Quirk *et al.* 1990; Markus *et al.* 1994; Sharp *et al.* 1995). In the Quirk *et al.* experiment, rats ran around a recording cylinder for 8 minutes, and then, while the animals were still in the cylinder, the lights were turned off. After 8 minutes in the dark, the lights were turned back on for 8 minutes. The majority of place fields stayed in the same place in the dark, as shown in Fig. 7.1c. Additionally, stable place fields have been observed in blind rats (Save *et al.* 1998). These findings show that visual information is not necessary for normal place cell activity. Indeed, in darkness, odour cues (Save *et al.* 2000) or the slope of the floor of the environment can anchor place fields (Jeffery *et al.* 2006).

Other findings show that information in addition to visual landmarks is used by place fields. For example, in a spatially ambiguous environment, Sharp et al. (1990) found that the location of place fields depended on the direction the rat was brought into the enclosure. They first exposed a rat to a cylindrical environment with a single cue card. After a 16 minute recording session, they removed the rat from the cylinder and, after an additional session, added a second, identical cue card to the environment, 180° from the initial cue card. Under these circumstances, when the animal was returned to the cylinder, many place fields fired with respect to only one of the two cue cards, depending on the direction that the rat had been brought into the environment. Thus, where a place cell fired wasn't exclusively determined by the sensory properties of the cue card, but also by the direction in which the animal entered the environment. This said, a few place cells showed two firing fields in the presence of the two cue cards.

A more explicit test of visual and vestibular control over place fields was done in another study by Patricia Sharp and colleagues (1995). They recorded place cells in rats that foraged for scattered food pellets in a recording cylinder with eight alternating, black and white 45° stripes on the walls. The cylinder was constructed in such a way that the floor and the walls could be moved independently or together. When the walls and floor were rotated together slowly (below the rat's vestibular threshold) in the dark, the majority of place fields also rotated by the same amount. However, when the lights were on, and either the floor or the walls were rotated quickly (above the rat's vestibular threshold), the majority of place fields stayed in the same location. Thus, if the rat felt the floor move, its place fields compensated for this movement and remained in the same location. Likewise, if the rat's vestibular system indicated that the rat had not moved but the visual cues on the cylinder wall had, the place fields weren't fooled. If the rotation of the walls was small (45°) and done in the dark, the majority of the place fields rotated by a comparable amount. Together, these results suggest that vestibular information is an important contributor to place field stability, although landmarks may dominate when the mismatch between vestibular and visual information is small.

Comparable findings were observed in a study where the cue card was rotated in front of the animal. Recall that in the typical place field rotation experiment, the experimenter rotates the cue card when the animal is not in the cylinder. When the animal is subsequently returned, its place fields typically shift to maintain their same position relative to the cue card. However a different story emerges when the rats see the cue card being moved, as suggested by the Sharp et al. findings given earlier. Rotenberg and Muller (1997) rotated a cue card in the traditional recording cylinder by either 45° or 180°, both in the presence of the rat or after the rat had been removed. When the card was moved in the absence of the rat, on its return its place fields shifted to agree with the cue card, as is usually observed. However, when the cue card was shifted by 180° in the presence of the rat, its place fields did not shift (in almost every instance). Instead, the fields stayed in the same place within the cylinder. Thus, the cue card's control over place fields was not absolute, and this reinforces the fact that place cell firing doesn't simply encode sensory features of a landmark. Rather, place fields were sensitive to mismatches between the rat's movements and the movement of landmarks in the environment. That is, the animals 'knew' that their orientation within the environment hadn't changed—presumably by their inertial sense, but possibly because of olfactory or other uncontrolled cues in the environment—and their place cells ignored the cue card rotation. However, when the cue card was rotated by only 45°, the rats' place fields were typically fooled, and shifted by 45°. So, when there is a small mismatch between the cue card and the other source of orientation information available to the animal (path integration and/or uncontrolled cues), the place cell system goes with the cue card. If there's a big mismatch, the place fields go with the other sources of information. Results consistent with this conclusion have been observed by Knierim et al. (1998), Jeffery and O'Keefe (1999), and Hargreaves et al. (2007).

So, although visual landmarks can control place fields, other information—including the rat's presumed sense of its own movement (or lack of movement)—also appears critical. An important demonstration of these two influences was shown in a task first used by Gothard et al. (1996b). They trained rats to run on a linear track from a start box to a small food bowl at the end of the track and back. On different journeys, the start box was moved up the track by different amounts. What Gothard et al. found was that place fields near the box were 'anchored' to the box, and fired in the same place relative to the box wherever it was on the track. However, place fields that were farther away from the box generally fired on the same location on the track, regardless of where the box was positioned (Fig. 7.2). In the authors' account, place fields near the box were driven by the rat's integration of the distance it had travelled relative to the box, since the box was behind the rat as it ran to the end of the track. Place fields farther along the track, in contrast, were anchored to locations along the track (possibly in relation to fixed room cues). Thus, when the rat left its start box, its place fields were initially driven by path integration, but were then controlled by cues in the environment. Indeed, when this task was run in the dark, box-anchored fields were found farther from the box than when the task was run in the light (Gothard et al. 2001).[1] Further, this switch

---

[1] Gothard et al. (2001) also examined place fields of cells from the dentate gyrus (DG). Both DG and CA1 place cells behaved in a similar way—they were tied to the start box over

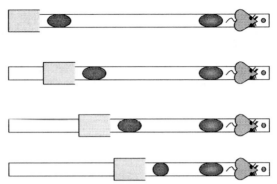

Fig. 7.2 Gothard *et al.* (1996b) provided evidence that place cells are driven by path integration and by landmarks. Place fields that were active as a rat departed from a start box remained anchored to that start box, even when it was displaced. Thus, these cells appeared to encode the animal's distance from the start box. In contrast, place fields near the end of the linear track fired in the same location, regardless of the position of the start box. Thus, these fields appeared to be anchored to the end of the maze or to extra-maze landmarks. (See also Plate 3.)

from path integration to room-bound place fields appears to occur at a constant time after leaving the start box for each rat, although the specific time differs between rats (Redish *et al.* 2000). It also occurs farther along the track in old rats compared to young rats, and correlates with an impairment in the use of external cues to identify a reward location (Rosenzweig *et al.* 2003). Overall, these results suggest that, within the same task, place fields can be controlled by path integration or by external landmarks.

Place cells encode boundaries

Another basic property of place cells is their sensitivity to barriers. For example, if one places a barrier in the middle of a cell's place field, the field almost disappears (Muller and Kubie 1987; Breese *et al.* 1989). Muller and Kubie showed that this effect was not simply due to a change in the local view near the field, as a transparent barrier had the same effect. Placing the same barrier outside a given cell's field had little effect.

a greater distance in the dark than in the light. This finding, the authors suggest, indicates that path integration is not likely to have occurred in CA3, the cell region between the DG and CA1. If this had been the case, differences in the behaviour of place cells in the DG and CA1 would have been expected. The observed results suggest that path integration occurs in brain structures upstream from the hippocampus, for example the entorhinal cortex. This prediction has been borne out by subsequent observations, and underpins McNaughton and colleagues' (2006) recent view of where path integration occurs.

A likely explanation for this effect is that place cells encode not just locations in an environment, but also the animal's ability to move through a location in the environment. Several findings support this explanation. First, Muller and Kubie (1989) found that place fields were best correlated with the animal's position 120 milliseconds in the future. That is, place cell firing doesn't represent where the animal actually is, but where it will be in a step or two (see also Battaglia *et al.* 2004). A study by Patricia Sharp (1999) found that anticipatory firing, although present in subicular neurons, only occurred in hippocampal cells when the rat was moving slowly. When moving quickly, the firing was best correlated with where the rat had just been. In addition, Foster *et al.* (1989) found that if a rat was kept from being able to move, its place cells stopped firing. However, if the animal was motionless but free to move, its place cells still fired in their respective fields. Thus, a barrier may inhibit place cell firing because it prevents the rat from moving through a given location.

Interestingly, place cells with fields near a barrier will encode this barrier even in a different environment. Rivard *et al.* (2004) identified place cells in rats as they foraged for food in a traditional cylindrical apparatus that also had a transparent, Plexiglas barrier in one position within the cylinder. The authors found that place cells firing near the barrier would shift position with the barrier if it was moved within the cylinder, despite the presence of a stable cue card. In addition, if the barrier was placed in another environment, some of the same place fields would remain anchored to it (see Fig. 7.1d), whereas place fields farther away from the barrier remapped. From these findings, Rivard *et al.* suggested that some place cells acted as object cells—encoding specific objects in the environment—whereas other cells behaved as more traditional place cells—encoding locations.

Of course, the walls of a given environment may be considered barriers, and place cells behave in a predictable way when the shape of the environment is changed. In a classic paper, O'Keefe and Burgess (1996) recorded from place cells in rectangles and squares, and found that place fields behaved as if they summed inputs from two or more walls. For example, a place field along one wall of a small square environment would appear to stretch when the square was made into a rectangle by extending two of its parallel walls. In O'Keefe and Burgess's model of this behaviour, place fields comprised the summed inputs of the distance of each field, represented by a Gaussian tuning curve, from each wall. Thus, as we have seen for spatial behaviour (Chapter 3), place fields are responsive to the geometry of the environment—and in this instance, in a predictable way.

A more general account of the effects of barriers is found in the 'boundary vector model' of place fields (Hartley *et al.* 2000). In this model, place cells receive inputs from boundary vector cells, which are tuned to boundaries at a specific distance and direction from the rat. The directional component of this input is likely based on the directionally tuned neurons described in the next chapter. By summing the inputs of boundary vector cells, place fields at a given location within an environment can be modelled, and these simulations closely match the observed findings of O'Keefe and Burgess.

Initial support for this model was presented in a review by Barry *et al.* (2006), and some of their findings are intriguing. For example, for a place cell with a field near one long wall of a rectangle, introduction of an additional barrier, parallel to the long wall and in the middle of the environment, caused the cell to develop a second field along the introduced wall. Also, gradual removal of the walls in the dark caused place fields to lose their place specificity. Finally, some cells in the dorsal subiculum appeared to fire as boundary-vector cells. These were described in more detail in a subsequent paper (Lever *et al.* 2009). The identification of boundary-vector cells in the subiculum, traditionally viewed as the output target of the hippocampus, suggests that the flow of information to the hippocampus may be more complex than previously thought. Lever *et al.* suggest that the subiculum may also serve as an *input* to the hippocampus, via connections with the pre- and parasubiculum, and their projections to the entorhinal cortex. Thus, as an alternative to Rivard *et al.*'s view that some place cells encode barriers whereas others encode locations, the boundary vector model suggests that all cells are driven by boundaries, although different cells are driven by different boundary vector inputs.[2]

Additional support for the boundary vector model comes from the identification of boundary or 'border' cells in the entorhinal cortex (EC) and the parasubiculum (Savelli *et al.* 2008; Solstad *et al.* 2008). Solstad *et al.* found that about 10% of the principal cells in EC and parasubiculum fired along one or more walls of a square enclosure. If the cell fired along a given wall of the square, it would continue to do so even if the wall was made longer (converting the square environment into a rectangular environment). If an additional border was inserted into the environment, parallel to the wall in which a given border cell fired, the cell would fire along the initial wall and the added border. Border cells would also fire if the border of the environment were a 60-centimetre drop, instead of a wall. The firing locations of border cells, like place cells, were controlled by a cue card in a cylindrical environment.

---

[2] Barry *et al.* (2006) also describe an addition to the boundary vector cell model that allows changes in place cells with repeated exposure to environments. This change allows the model to deal with 'slow remapping' changes that occur over days, as seen by Lever *et al.* (2002).

Place fields are modulated by behaviour

In the previous chapter I described how, in addition to cognitive mapping, the hippocampus is thought to be essential for declarative, relational, episodic, and detail-laden memories. Thus, it's not surprising that the representation of location provided by hippocampal place cells also reflects ongoing aspects of the animal's experience. Together, the findings that I describe below suggest that place fields may reflect the animal's experience in a location, and its anticipation of what lies ahead.

An early, qualitative study of hippocampal cells by James Ranck Jr. (1973) identified different complex-spike cells that fired when the rat sniffed, drank, approached a food pellet, and consumed it. At least one of these cells was described as occurring without a spatial correlate. Ranck referred to these cells as 'approach-consummate' cells, and their existence provides a hint that place cells may encode more than just location. Other cells appeared to fire in the locations in which water or food was or had previously been found. Ranck stated that these 'approach-consummate-mismatch' cells were likely to be the same as the place cells found by O'Keefe and Dostrovsky (1971).

Hippocampal cells with properties akin to those of Ranck's approach-consummate cells have been found in behavioural tasks run in operant chambers. Eichenbaum *et al.* (1987) found that the firing of some hippocampal cells encoded aspects of an odour discrimination task. For example, 'cue-sampling' neurons fired when the animal poked its nose into a port where odours were presented, and some of these cells fired more to odours that were paired with reinforcement than to those that were not. Other 'goal-approach' cells fired when the animal approached the odour port to begin a trial, or approached the reward cup to obtain reinforcement. In a subsequent experiment, Wiener *et al.* (1989) found traditional place cells when rats performed a spatial task in an operant chamber. However, some of the same cells also encoded aspects of an odour discrimination task run in the same environment (see also Otto and Eichenbaum 1992; Wood *et al.* 1999; Dudchenko *et al.* 2002). For Wiener *et al.* these results were consistent with a role for the hippocampus in processing the *relations* between independent stimuli.

Another example of the behavioural modulation of place cell firing is found in a study by Markus *et al.* (1995). They recorded place cells as rats foraged for chocolate pellets that were randomly dispersed on a circular platform. After 30 minutes of this, the tasked changed to one in which the chocolate pellets could only be found in one of four locations, separated by 90°, on the platform periphery. The rat was cued to each baited location by the experimenter (who tapped near it), and the locations were rewarded in order. The rats learned to run directly from one location to the next, and about one-third of the place cells recorded showed changes in the locations of their place fields. Thus, within an unchanged environment, a subset of place cells changed firing locations when the behavioural task changed, as in the Wiener *et al.* results described earlier (see also Oler and Markus 2000; Siegel *et al.* 2008).

Of course, it might be argued that the location of the food itself can serve as a landmark for place fields. In the Markus *et al.* experiment, however, one or more salient extra-maze landmarks were available in the recording environment, so reward location would potentially be 'blocked' by these pre-existing landmarks. Although there is some evidence that reward itself can serve as a cue when only a single polarizing landmark is available (Breese *et al.* 1989), in other circumstances moving the reward has no effect on the location of place fields (Speakman and O'Keefe 1990).[3] In other studies, increased place cell firing has been observed in locations where food is expected (Hölscher *et al.* 2003), and in locations where occupancy leads to the delivery of a food pellet (Hok *et al.* 2007). In this latter study, goal firing appeared as a weaker, additional place field in the goal location, whereas a traditional place field was observed elsewhere in the environment. Hok *et al.* suggest that place cells thus represent the current environment and the location of a goal.

A number of other studies, particularly those from the lab of Sam Deadwyler and Robert Hampson, have provided evidence that place cells encode aspects of ongoing behaviours (Hampson *et al.* 1993; Deadwyler *et al.* 1996; Hampson *et al.* 1999). Place cells also show task-related firing in fear conditioning (e.g. McEchron *et al.* 2003), and in freely moving rats this can occur within place fields (Moita *et al.* 2003). In the latter study, many theta cells also developed responsiveness to the stimulus, a series of white-noise pips that predicted shock. For Moita *et al.* the fact that responsiveness to the conditioned stimuli occurred within place fields suggests that the hippocampus encodes CS–US relationships occurring in a specific location.

In another intriguing experiment, Moita *et al.* (2004) found that fear conditioning changes the place cell representation of an environment. This change

---

[3] These contrasting results have puzzled me: why are place cells sensitive to the location of reward in one situation and not another? The examples in the Breese *et al.* paper seem convincing. One possibility is that, on the square platform used by Breese *et al.* the shape of the platform is a strong cue for orientation, and the cue card is relatively weak. A somewhat similar lack of cue control was described by Golob *et al.* (2001) for the spatially tuned neurons described in the next chapter. Data from Kobayashi *et al.* (1997) also showed that place cells did not change firing locations when animals switched from a random foraging task on a circular open field to a directed search task. However, the results are a bit ambiguous on this point, as some place fields shifted towards a reward site on a second directed search task.

was a partial remapping; some fields changed whereas others, recorded at the same time, did not. Thus, the rat's memory for what occurred in an environment changed its representation of that environment. This may, in some ways, be compatible with the partial remapping seen when animals walk into the second of two identical environments. There, place cells are presumably driven not just by the appearance of the environment but also by the rat's memory for just having come from a similar environment.

How can these observations of behavioural or task-related encoding in place cells be reconciled with the boundary encoding described in the previous section? Part of the answer, as argued by Kate Jeffery and colleagues, may be that boundary cells are driven by inputs that represent different properties of contexts. Anderson and Jeffery (2003), for example, found that place fields partially remapped when the colour and the smell of an environment were changed, even while the shape stayed the same. If place cells were solely driven by boundary cells, one would expect little change between environments of the same shape. The fact that place fields changed when the context changed, however, suggests that the context itself drives different subsets of boundary cells, which in turn cause the field to change its location relative to the environment's boundaries.[4] As place cells responded in different ways to manipulations of the colour and smell of the environment (e.g. some fields responded to changes in colour, but not smell, and vice versa), it appears that individual cells are driven by inputs representing different aspects of the environment, as opposed to its overall context (Jeffery et al. 2004). The partial remapping fear conditioning, described earlier, suggests that these aspects of the environment may also include the animal's prior experiences.

Place cells encode the animal's intended destination

A more recently established property of hippocampal place cells is their encoding of previous or anticipated locations. This is also referred to as *retrospective* and *prospective* firing. The essential finding is that some place fields fire only when a rat has just come from a specific location, or is about to go to a specific destination.

----

[4] Anderson and Jeffery (2003; see also Jeffery et al. 2004) also make an interesting point with regard to the cognitive mapping view of the hippocampus. They suggest that because of their sensitivity to changes in context, place cells likely do not provide an absolute map of space, but rather a representation of spatial context. Although this would be less useful for directly guiding navigation, it may provide a means for distinguishing environments that are different but have similar features. The finding that a learned spatial behaviour is the same across environments that produce remapping reinforces the idea that the hippocampal representation does not guide all spatially oriented behaviour (Jeffery et al. 2003).

Several authors have observed this conditional place cell firing (Frank *et al.* 2000; Wood *et al.* 2000; Ferbiteneau and Shapiro 2003; Bower *et al.* 2005; Smith and Mizumori 2006; Dayawansa *et al.* 2006; Lipton *et al.* 2007; Ainge *et al.* 2007a,b; Ji and Wilson 2008; Takahashi *et al.* 2009; but see Lenck-Santini *et al.* 2001; Hölscher *et al.* 2004). I describe here two examples of conditional place cell activity that I have been involved in, and a few additional findings.

In the first study (Wood *et al.* 2000), Dr Emma Wood and I trained rats to alternate left and right turns on a T-shaped maze. The maze differed from a traditional T-maze in that, at the end of the two arms of the T, a return arm led back to the base of the T. Thus the rats' task on starting at the base of the T was to run up the stem of the maze, and make a left or right turn. At the end of the T, a reward—a drop of sugar water—was available on the arm of the T that the rat had not chosen on its previous run. After consuming this reward, the rat continued down the return arm to the base of the maze, and then began another 'trial' by running up the centre stem again. Essentially, the rats ran a continuous loop with an overlapping segment—the central stem—that was common to both left and right journeys.

Our interest was in the behaviour of place cells with fields on this central stem (Fig. 7.3a). We wondered whether place cells would fire in different ways depending on where the rat was going (or where the rat had just been). The traditional view, in contrast, predicts that place cells should fire every time the rat runs through the cell's receptive field, regardless of its destination.

We found that a large subset of place cells with fields on the central stem of the maze fired in different ways on left versus right turn trials. Fig. 7.3b shows one example of such a place cell. Only the portion of the maze that was overlapping between the two types of trials—the central stem—is shown. Each of the overlaid grey lines indicates the path that the rat took. Individual spikes from a place cell are shown as dots. When the rat was on the central stem and about to turn left, this place cell fired a great deal (the average firing rate is shown in the far right figure). However, when the rat was on the central stem and about to turn right, this same cell fired only a few times. Thus, there was a significant difference in the cell's firing depending on which type of turn the rat was about to make (or, alternatively, which return stem the rat had just come from). This finding was also reported by Frank *et al.* 2000, and a subsequent study revealed that this conditional firing can represent either the rat's past location or its intended destination (Ferbiteneau and Shapiro 2003).[5]

---

[5] A remarkable subsequent finding using the continuous T-maze task of Wood *et al.* (2000) was that place fields gradually shift their locations in the direction that the rat is running (Lee *et al.* 2006a; see also Yu *et al.* 2006). Although Lee *et al.* offer a model of how this

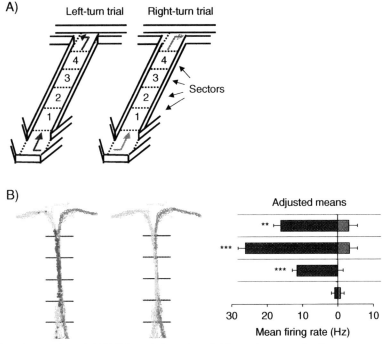

Fig. 7.3 Wood *et al.* (2000) found that place fields on the stem of a T-maze were modulated by the direction that the rat was about to turn (or had just recently turned). A) Place cells were identified on the stem of a continuous T-maze, and their fields were compared when on left-turn and right-turn trials. B) On left-turn trials, this place cell fired at a high rate (individual dots represent individual spikes; the paths of the rats are shown in grey). In right-turn trials, however, the same place cells fired at a very low rate. This difference in firing rate is evident when the mean firing rate for each portion of the central stem of the maze is considered (*right plot*).

Adapted from Wood, Dudchenko, Robitsek, and Eichenbaum (2000) *Neuron*, **27**: 623–633. Copyright: Cell Press.

In a second example of prospective firing, Dr James Ainge and I trained rats to run on a double Y-maze to find food (Ainge *et al.* 2007a). As shown in Fig. 7.4a, the rat started a trial at the base of the Y, and was then faced with a choice of going left or right. After it advanced in either direction, it then faced a second Y choice. At the ends of each of these choices was a small box, and two of the four boxes contained a reward (chocolate cereal loops, to which the rats were partial). After it consumed its reward, or entered a box that didn't

might occur, it's unclear what the significance of shifting place fields might be for the behaving animal.

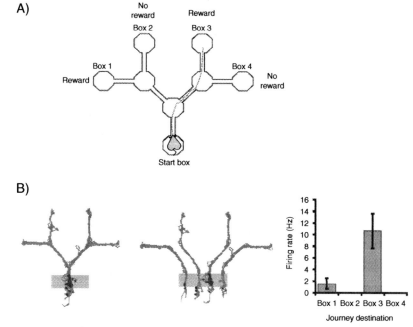

Fig. 7.4 Place fields reflect the animal's anticipation of a goal location. A) Rats were trained to find reward at the end of some arms, but not others, on a double Y-maze. B) A subset of the place cells recorded in this task fired at high rates only when the animal was about to travel to a specific goal location. In this example, a high firing rate was observed when the rat travelled to goal box 3, but not when it travelled to any of the remaining goal boxes. Individual dots represent individual spikes; the paths of the rats are shown in grey.

Adapted from Ainge, Tamosiunaite, Woergoetter, and Dudchenko (2007) *The Journal of Neuroscience* **27**(36): 9769–9779. Copyright: Society for Neuroscience.

contain reward, the rat was picked up by the experimenter and returned to the start box for another trial.

On the first few trials of each day, the rat chose one or the other box until it found a goal box that contained reward. Typically, it returned to this box on every repeated trial. After several trials, we moved the reward to a previously non-rewarded box. The rats initially re-entered the previously rewarded box, but soon chose alternative boxes until they found one containing reward. This box was rewarded for several trials, until the rewarded box was switched once again. At the beginning of every day different goal boxes contained reward, and again over sets of trials, the reward was switched between the boxes.

Our interest was initially in the behaviour of place cells at the choice points on the maze, but it quickly became apparent that the rats did not spend a great deal of time at these. Rather, the rats made a ballistic run from the start box to one of the rewarded goal boxes. When we examined place fields at the start box and along the maze, we found that a large percentage fired in different ways depending on the goal box the rat was heading to. An example is shown in Fig. 7.4b. Here again the overlaid grey paths indicate where the rats ran on all of the trials for a given day's session. The dots at the base of the Y are the spikes from one place cell recorded as the rat ran these trials. When we separated the trials by the four goal boxes the rat chose, we found that this cell, and others like it, fired primarily when the rat was going to only one of the goals. Thus, some place fields encoded not only the rat's current location (and we found a large percentage of traditional, non-conditional fields in this task as well), but also the rat's intended destination. This fits well with the finding that the hippocampus is necessary to imagine future situations, as described in the opening of this chapter, as the rats, at the beginning of the maze, may have anticipated their specific goal. It also fits with the finding that place cells in the human hippocampus, as described later, often fire with respect to an intended goal.

Additional findings complement these results. For example, Pastalkova *et al.* (2008) recorded place cells as rats ran on an alternation task similar to that of the Wood *et al.* study mentioned earlier. However, the maze also included a running wheel at the beginning of the central stem, and on every lap the rat had to run on the wheel for a short period before proceeding up the central stem. As in the Wood *et al.* study, a subset of place cells with fields on the central stem fired differentially when the rat was about to make either a right or left turn at the choice point. Remarkably, this differential activity was also seen on the running wheel *before* the rat began running up the central stem. The authors showed that a sequence of place cells was activated as the rat ran on the wheel, in the same way that a sequence of different place cells was activated when the rat ran up the central maze stem. Thus, it was as if the running wheel was part of the central stem. Importantly, this sequential activity on the running wheel was only seen when rats performed a memory task. When the running wheel was placed in the rat's cage, place cells active on the running wheel did not fire sequentially and instead individual cells were usually active for as long as the rat ran on the wheel. The differential activity on the maze likely participated in the rat's behaviour, as the firing on the central stem and running wheel predicted where the rats were going to go, even when they made mistakes.

A different and intriguing form of prospective place cell firing is described by Johnson and Redish (2007). They trained rats to run on a maze with multiple T-junctions, the last of which led to left and right return rails.

On each day, reward was provided on only one of the return rails, and the rat's task was to learn which turn would bring it to the food. An incorrect choice led to a rail without food, and a relatively long run (≥ 3 metres) through the maze again before the next opportunity for food. At the final T-junction, rats, particularly early in training, often paused and appeared to engage in vicarious trial-and-error (VTE) head movements. Ensembles of place cells recorded from the CA3 region of the hippocampus showed that, at this last choice point, the place representation for each choice arm was activated in turn, even though the animal had yet to enter either arm. It was as if the rat mentally travelled down each arm before making its actual choice. On the authors' view, these forward sweeps of place cell activity may have been the way in which the rat planned which way it was going and anticipated what it might find ahead. Recent studies have also provided evidence that place cells ensembles replay recently experienced routes during high-frequency oscillations ('ripples') in the hippocampal EEG (Karlsson and Frank 2009; Davidson *et al.* 2009).

The behaviour of place cells in old animals differs from that seen in young animals

Several studies have compared the properties of place cells in old animals to those of young animals. Although there is some evidence for a decrease in place field specificity in older animals (Barnes *et al.* 1983; Tanila *et al.* 1997c; Sava and Markus 2008), this is not observed in other situations (Markus *et al.* 1994; Mizumori *et al.* 1996). Reactivation of recently active place cells in sleep does not differ substantially between young and aged animals (Gerrard *et al.* 2001), nor does the ability to distinguish environments based on path integration (Wilson *et al.* 2005a).

There is evidence, however, that the link between place cells and the animal's environment is altered with old age. Barnes *et al.* (1997) tested this by recording from multiple place cells in both old and young rats. The rat's task was to run on a rectangular figure of 8 track. After running on the track, in one manipulation, rats were removed from the room for 1 hour. They were then returned to the room and track for a second recording session. For young animals, the place fields observed on the initial track run were nearly identical to those seen after being out of the room for an hour. In old rats, however, there were a number of instances where there was little correlation between the place field locations in the two track sessions. The authors suggest that, in these instances, the old rats selected the wrong cognitive map for the environment, possibly because the binding of their place cell representation to the room landmarks, via LTP, was deficient. Thus, the hippocampus in aged animals may have less capacity to recognize environments.

Other work has shown that the place cells in old rats are more anchored to distal than local landmarks, and are less likely to stop firing or form a new field following changes in the environment (Tanila *et al.* 1997a; 1997b). Similarly, Oler and Markus (2000) found that place cells in old rats were less likely to change with changes in behavioural tasks compared to middle-aged rats. Comparable findings were also observed when old rats were exposed to different shaped environments, and this inflexibility correlated with difficulties in Morris water maze learning (Wilson *et al.* 2003). In a subsequent study, Iain Wilson and colleagues (Wilson *et al.* 2004) found that place cells in old rats had less of a tendency to remap in a new environment, compared with those of young rats. However, with additional experience in a new environment, remapping occurred at a similar level between age groups. Interestingly, the place fields of aged rats in this study had less of a tendency to be controlled by the landmarks in the newly learned environment, and this lack of stimulus control correlated with poorer performance on a Morris water maze.

In examining the data from several previous experiments, Wilson *et al.* (2005b) found that the tendency for the place cells of old animals not to remap was particularly evident in cells from the CA3 sub-region of the hippocampus. Overall, these studies suggest that place cells in old rats are less sensitive to changes in the environment or behavioural contingencies.

Another difference in the place cells of young and old rats is related to the so-called Mehta effect. Mehta *et al.* (1997) observed that when rats repeatedly run through the same series of locations, place fields expand in the direction opposite to that in which the rat is running. Essentially, a given place cell starts firing slightly before the location of its original field evident in the initial maze laps. This property of place cells was predicted by Blum and Abbot (1996) in their model of place cell connectivity. They reasoned that if the same series of place cells were activated repeatedly—as would occur if the animal runs laps around a track, for example—then, if the cells synapse on one another, the connections between the cells would be strengthened (via Hebbian synaptic plasticity). This would cause a given cell to begin firing just before the animal enters the cell's original place field. The actual backward expansion of place fields observed by Mehta *et al.* resets between daily sessions, and appears to require LTP (Ekstrom *et al.* 2001; Mehta *et al.* 2000). In old rats, Chen *et al.* (1997) found that this backward expansion of place fields did not occur. The authors suggest that a deficit in LTP in aged animals may be responsible for this effect. Interestingly, the backward-expansion effect of receptive fields is seen in other types of neurons (Yu *et al.* 2006), and may reflect a general property of neurons with reciprocal connectivity and the capacity for synaptic plasticity.

Theta rhythm

There is a wealth of research on the generation of the theta rhythm and its function, and for a complete review the interested reader is directed to Buzáki (2005), O'Keefe (2007), and György Buzsáki's book entitled *Rhythms of the Brain* (2006). Here I'll mention a few salient findings. First, O'Keefe and Recce (1993) found that place cells fire in a specific part of the theta rhythm, and as the rat runs through a cell's place field, the firing occurs in progressively 'earlier' phases of the theta wave. This *phase precession* may more accurately identify the rat's location, as its location within a place field can be identified (in downstream brain structures, presumably) by where along the theta rhythm the cell fires. Interestingly, phase precession is also seen when rats run in a single location, on a running wheel, as long as the running is part of an ongoing working memory task (Pastalkova *et al.* 2008). As O'Keefe (2007) suggests, the theta rhythm is likely the way that groups of neurons work together. Its entrainment across different brain areas may also allow coordination of spatial working memory (Jones and Wilson 2005).

Theta rhythm also appears to be associated with human spatial learning and recall, at least in virtual environments. Kahana *et al.* (1999) recorded episodes of theta with electrodes placed near the brain surface in patients with intractable epilepsy. The purpose of the electrodes themselves was to identify where in the brain the epileptic activity originated. The patients learned to find their way through a series of virtual mazes with multiple T-junctions. When doing so, the patients exhibited episodes of theta rhythm, and there appeared to be more theta during retrieval than during learning of the maze.

This finding fits well with one hypothesized function of theta rhythm, the encoding and retrieval of episodic memories. As summarized by Michael Hasselmo (2005), encoding may occur at the trough of the theta rhythm (as measured at a specific area within the hippocampus) when the hippocampus receives a strong input from the entorhinal cortex and when LTP is more likely. Conversely, retrieval may occur at the peak of the theta rhythm, when the entorhinal cortex input is weaker, and when long-term depression may be seen. In another model, the conditional place field firing described earlier (and in the study mentioned in footnote 5), can be accounted for by interference between hippocampal theta rhythm and theta rhythm inputs from the entorhinal cortex that are gated by the animal's running speed (Hasselmo 2007). A somewhat different model by Buzáki (2005) holds that the theta rhythm is the way in which different ensembles of place cells, representing past, current, and anticipated locations, are linked. This linkage also may not simply be restricted to spatial location, but may also apply to episodic memories.

Place cells are found in the hippocampi of humans and other primates

A remarkable study by Ekstrom *et al.* (2003) found that neurons in the human hippocampus fire when people experience different locations. The authors recorded from patients with epilepsy who were implanted with electrodes to identify the source of their seizures. In previous work using this approach, human hippocampal neurons were shown to be responsive to pictures of objects, faces, and attributes of the faces including expression and familiarity (Fried *et al.* 1997). In the Ekstrom *et al.* study, patients played a computer game where they navigated, as a taxi driver, through a virtual town to pick up passengers and drop them off at specified locations. Twenty four percent of the neurons recorded in the hippocampus were place responsive, as were smaller percentages of cells (10% or less) in the parahippocampal region, the amygdala, and the frontal lobe. Some place-responsive cells were also goal cells—firing in a specific location when the patient attempted to reach a specific virtual destination. Cells that were responsive to specific views within the virtual environment were more common in the parahippocampal region.

The observation of place-by-goal cells in the human hippocampus may suggest that both the human and the rodent hippocampus encodes intended destination. However, in the Ainge *et al.* findings, goal encoding was typically in the form of a cell's firing when one goal was sought, and little or no firing when other goals were sought. In the Ekstrom *et al.* data, the firing appears to be in different locations when different goals were sought.

Neurons that may be analogous to the cells that responded to specific virtual views in humans have also been found in monkeys. For example, in rhesus macaque monkeys, some cells in the hippocampal formation show increases in activity when a stimulus is presented in a specific position on a computer screen during a matching-to-sample memory task (Cahusac *et al.* 1989; Rolls *et al.* 1989). In a subsequent study, this spatial tuning persisted even when the computer screen was moved to the left or right of the animal, suggesting that this class of cells responds to the position of a stimulus on the computer screen, and not the position of the screen relative to the animal (Feigenbaum and Rolls 1991). The authors of this study also found that some neurons in the hippocampus and adjacent cortical regions showed increased responses when the monkey fixated on small spots occurring in specific positions on a computer screen.

Subsequent experiments in the laboratory of Edmund Rolls have identified *spatial view* neurons. Rolls and O'Mara (1995) described neurons in the monkey hippocampus (or adjacent regions) that encoded specific views within the environment, independent of the animal's location within the environment. The authors attempted to show that these spatial view cells were controlled by the visual landmarks in the environment, like place cells in rats, by rotating the landmarks by 90°. Although there was some evidence of a rotation in one cell, the results weren't that strong—possibly because the monkey remained in the testing room, although it was darkened, during rotation of the landmarks. Turning off the lights caused some view cells to lose their view specificity. In a subsequent study, however, some spatial view cells were shown to maintain their view specific firing when views of the room landmarks were prevented by a curtain (Robertson *et al.* 1998). This result suggests that spatial view neurons can encode a position in space rather than a specific landmark view. Further observations showed that these cells don't encode eye position or head direction, but are specifically tuned to portions of the viewed environment 'out there' (Georges-François *et al.* 1999). Rolls *et al.* (2005) have also encountered neurons that fired differentially to different objects presented on a computer screen, to different locations in which objects were presented, and to specific objects only when they occur in a specific location. The authors suggest that these different properties of hippocampal formation neurons make them ideal for remembering the locations of objects in space.

Spatial view neurons in the monkey differ from rodent place cells in that the former encode where the monkey looks, whereas the latter encode the animal's actual location. According to one model, the differences between spatial view and place cells could be accounted for by considering the differences in the size of the visual receptive fields in monkeys and rats (de Araujo *et al.* 2001). However, as we've seen above, it is also clear that in the rodent non-visual inputs can maintain place-specific firing.

Cells in the monkey that more closely resemble place cells have been observed in other studies. For example, Ono *et al.* (1991; 1993) recorded from neurons in the hippocampus while monkeys were on a moveable apparatus, and found that some of these neurons fired when the monkey viewed stimuli presented in specific locations in the testing room. Other neurons fired more egocentrically— for example, they responded to a stimulus presented to the animal's right, regardless of the direction it was facing. Still other neurons showed place-like firing, or increased activity to aspects of a conditioning task, but only when the monkeys were in specific parts of the testing room. The authors also found neurons that fired when a stimulus was presented while the monkey was in a specific location and facing a particular direction in the room. Neurons with other correlates, for example cells that respond to the monkey's forward or backward movement, or to left or right turning, have also been observed in the hippocampus and the cortex adjacent to the hippocampus (O'Mara *et al.* 1994).

Additional examples of place-like activity were observed by Matsumura *et al.* (1999). They recorded from monkeys in a movable monkey 'cab' that the animal could control with a joystick. During these recordings, some neurons in the hippocampus and the underlying parahippocampal gyrus fired in a place-specific way in the experimental room. Many cells showed place fields that depended on the task that the monkey was performing, and more cells were active during the room navigation tasks than during performance of a computer task in a fixed location. The authors argue that the higher percentage of place-like cells that they observed relative to previous studies was due to the animals' ability to move about the room. In a subsequent re-analysis of this data, Hori *et al.* (2003) found a correspondence between lab space and the 2D ordering of the place fields, based on their statistical relationships. This, the authors argue, provides additional evidence that the hippocampus and parahippocampal gyrus represent allocentric space.

The human hippocampus and parahippocampal gyrus are active during navigation tasks

In the previous chapter I reviewed some of the findings from patients with damage to the hippocampus and temporal lobe which indicate that they have difficulty in learning the layouts of new environments. Presumably, these patients would readily become lost if left to their own devices in a new location. The neuroimaging data that I review below complement these neuropsychological findings, and reinforce the idea that the hippocampus and the cortical regions adjacent to it are active in wayfinding. These findings are considered in a roughly chronological order.

The parahippocampal gyrus

The parahippocampal gyrus is the cortical gyrus just below the hippocampus (see Fig. 7.5). Rostrally, towards the front of the brain and hippocampus, it is made up of the entorhinal and perirhinal cortices. Moving caudally, towards the back of the brain, the gyrus contains the parahippocampal cortex. As evident in MRI scans of the brain, the entorhinal and perirhinal cortices surround the anterior collateral sulcus, whereas farther back in the brain, this sulcus disappears and the posterior sulcus and surrounding parahippocampal cortex are visible (Bohbot *et al.* 1998).

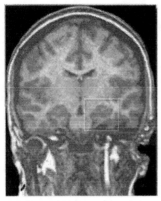 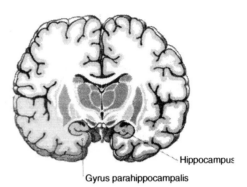

Hippocampus

Gyrus parahippocampalis

Fig. 7.5 *Left:* Magnetic resonance image of the human brain at the level of the hippocampus. *Right:* Sketch of the human brain, cut at the level of the hippocampus, highlighting the hippocampus and the parahippocampal gyrus. (See also Plate 4.)

Source: Wikipedia commons.

An initial functional magnetic resonance imaging (fMRI) study revealed that the parahippocampal gyrus was active when people learned the layout of a virtual maze, and when they subsequently navigated through this maze (Aguirre *et al.* 1996). As the authors suggest, the finding of activity in this brain region during spatial performance fits well with impairments observed after damage to this area. For example, Habib and Sirigu (1987) described four patients with parahippocampal gyrus damage who showed topographical disorientation. One patient, a 44-year-old officer in the French Air Force, suffered from a cerebral infarct that caused him to be unable to find his way to his hospital room. After he was discharged, he was able to find his way through familiar parts of Paris, where he lived, but had great difficulties finding his way on unfamiliar streets. Another patient, a 60-year-old housewife who had suffered from a stroke, lost her 'sense of direction'. She had great difficulty finding her way back to her hospital room after leaving it, and even 3 years after her discharge could not find her way in her neighbourhood. The remaining two patients also had difficulties in wayfinding, and all four had damage to the right parahippocampal gyrus due to blockage in the right posterior cerebral artery.

Additional evidence supports the relationship between this brain region and spatial memory. Bohbot *et al.* (1998) showed that patients with damage to the right parahippocampal cortex were impaired in remembering the location of objects in a room, the location of a hidden goal within a room after a 20 minute delay, and the layout of an abstract figure (the Rey–Osterrieth figure).

Patients with right hippocampus damage showed similar impairments, although they were not impaired in remembering the location of a hidden goal after a delay. In another study, patients in which the parahippocampal cortex and the perirhinal cortex had been removed on one side of the brain— as a treatment for epilepsy—were impaired at remembering the location of a briefly presented light flash presented on the other side of the visual field (Ploner *et al.* 2000). This impairment appeared to be due to the lack of parahippocampal cortex, as patients with perirhinal cortex removal alone were not impaired on the task.

A portion of the parahippocampal gyrus has also been implicated in the processing of views of locations. Epstein and Kanwisher (1998) identified the 'parahippocampal place area' (PPA), a portion of the parahippocampal gyrus that showed a large response to pictures of spatial scenes and little activity in response to pictures of houses or faces. This brain activation appeared to be driven by spatial stimuli because it occurred when participants viewed pictures of outdoor scenes, landscapes, rooms, and landmarks, but not when they viewed individual objects, multiple objects, or faces. In subsequent work, Epstein *et al.* (2007) provided evidence that the PPA and the retrosplenial regions perform somewhat different functions. The PPA was generally active when the subject viewed pictures of scenes, whereas activity in the retrosplenial regions, measured at the same time, varied depending on whether a scene was familiar and whether a spatial judgement was required. Thus, the PPA may encode local views of locations, whereas the retrosplenial region may allow orientation within an environment and navigation (Epstein 2008).

Activation of the right parahippocampal gyrus was also observed when people with a long-standing familiarity with a city (Toronto) were tested on their knowledge of the spatial relationships between the city's landmarks (Rosenbaum *et al.* 2004). Increased brain activity was also observed in the left retrosplenial cortex and left precuneus, as well as a portion of the right occipital lobe. When simply viewing familiar Toronto landmarks, increases in the activity in the parahippocampal gyrus, the left retrosplenial cortex, and portions of the occipital lobes were also evident. However, no significant increases in hippocampus activity were observed in spatial relationship tasks or in a landmark-viewing task. Based on these results, the authors suggest that some well-established spatial memories *do not* require the hippocampus.

In summary, there is neuropsychological and neuroimaging evidence which suggests that the cortical region just below the hippocampus—the parahippocampal gyrus—contributes to wayfinding, spatial memory, and the views of spatial scenes.

The hippocampus

Although the results from the Rosenbaum *et al.* study suggest that mental navigation through a highly familiar environment does not cause activation of the hippocampus, other work has shown activation of the hippocampus during virtual navigation. One example is a study by Maguire *et al.* (1998) where participants navigated through a virtual town, based on a computer game, while being scanned. Maguire *et al.* found that in the navigation tasks, with or without detours, there was a significant activation of the right hippocampus relative to an arrow-following task. Thus, when participants had to use a cognitive map of the virtual environment to navigate, as opposed to just following signs (arrows), the neural activity in the (right) hippocampus increased (see also Maguire *et al.* 1997). Moreover, for navigation without detours, more accurate performance was associated with increased activity in the right hippocampus and right inferior parietal cortex (as reflected by regional cerebral blood flow). The authors suggest that right parietal cortex activation may reflect the processing of body turns to orient towards a goal, and noted that this brain region was most active in tasks that involved movement. Two other findings from this study are of note. First, the left frontal cortex was more active when participants had to navigate around detours, and this may reflect the role of this brain area in planning and sequencing actions. Second, the speed of virtual travel through the environment was correlated with activity in the right caudate nucleus (a part of the basal ganglia).

Mellet *et al.* (2000) looked at brain activation, as measured by cerebral blood flow, when people recalled a route through a park that they had learned the day before. In a second study, a different group of study participants were asked to visualize the connection between two locations on a map they had learned earlier. Under both conditions, activity in the right hippocampus was observed. In addition, a set of cortical regions in the parietal and frontal lobes were activated. Increased activity was observed in the parahippocampal cortex for participants who recalled routes they'd experienced, but not in participants who recalled a map. Similarly, an fMRI study by Grön *et al.* (2000) found increased neural activity in a number of areas when participants tried to find their way out of a virtual maze. These brain areas included the right hippocampus, the right parahippocampal gyrus, and a portion of the parietal lobe, the superior parietal lobule. Differences between men and women included an activation of the left parahippocampal gyrus in men, and right front parietal areas in women.

Ground level route learning of a virtual convention centre, park, and market place was compared to overhead view survey learning of the same environments in a study by Shelton and Gabrieli (2002). A number of brain areas were active during the route learning, including regions in the frontal and parietal cortices, as well as the parahippocampal cortex and the posterior hippocampus in both hemispheres. People who learned these environments from an overhead view showed activity in a subset of these brain regions, but not in the hippocampus or parahippocampal cortex. To account for this finding, the authors suggest that route learning virtual experience may have provided more immersion for the participants, and the activation of the hippocampus and parahippocampal cortex may be due to the process of 'map-building' as one moves through the environment. The survey perspective may have required less effort to bind locations together as the layout was obvious from the overhead view.

Changes in the activity of different brain regions as people learned the layout of a virtual environment were also found by Wolbers and Büchel (2005). They found that as the accuracy in identifying the spatial relationships between landmarks encountered in a virtual maze increased, so did the activity in the retrosplenial cortex. For the hippocampus, activation was most prominent in test sessions where the greatest amount of learning took place.

Kumaran and Maguire (2005) sought to test the relational theory of hippocampus function (see Chapter 6) by comparing activation in a spatial task and a relational, non-spatial task. To do this, they assessed brain activity when people imagined themselves navigating between friends' homes or when they performed a task that assessed their friends' relationship with one another. The spatial navigation task produced significantly more brain activation in the posterior hippocampus, the parahippocampal gyri, the retrosplenial and the posterior parietal cortices. The same brain regions, with the exception of the hippocampus, were also more active when people imagined their friends' residences as opposed to imagining their friends' faces. This pattern of results, the authors argue, supports the view that the hippocampus is preferentially involved in spatial relational memory as opposed to relational memory in general.

In a thorough study of the brain areas underlying navigation, Spiers and Maguire (2006) examined the brains of London taxi drivers as they navigated through a virtual, game-based representation of London. The taxi drivers' task was to drive a virtual taxi to a destination specified, on audio, by a passenger. After brain scanning, the participants reviewed a video of their experience, and were asked to describe what they were thinking at different specific times in the task. Somewhat surprisingly, the hippocampus only showed an increase in activity when the taxi drivers planned their routes in response to the passenger's request. At the same time, increased activity was also seen in the left parahippocampus, the retrosplenial cortices, portions of the frontal lobes, and portions of the temporal lobes, amongst other areas. Retrosplenial cortex activation was also seen when the taxi drivers spontaneously planned routes, when they encountered various portions of the route, and when they viewed the environment.[6] Right hippocampus activation was found when the passengers made comments that had nothing to do with navigation. For the authors, these results suggest that the hippocampus may not show increased activity throughout navigation, but only at the beginning of the trip when one plans the route to a desired goal.

Evidence also suggests that the right hippocampus contributes to path integration. Wolbers *et al.* (2007) scanned individuals as they performed a virtual triangle completion task. They found that, for individual subjects, the trials associated with the most accurate path integration were associated with the greatest increase in activity in the right hippocampus. In addition, across individuals, those with more consistent responses had higher levels of hippocampal and medial prefrontal cortex activation. The finding that the hippocampus was active during a path integration task is consistent with findings that patients with right temporal lobe removals are impaired in path integrating, as described in the previous chapter.

A qualification of the role of the hippocampus in navigation comes from a study by Rosenbaum *et al.* (2007). They tested memory for a familiar neighbourhood in control subjects and in K.C., the patient described in the previous chapter who has substantial loss of hippocampus, among other regions, following a motorcycle accident. The tests included navigation from one location in the neighbourhood to another, distance judgements, and navigation when a detour was required. For both control subjects and K.C., no activation in the hippocampus was observed during these tests. The right hippocampus was activated when K.C. was tested for his recognition memory of specific houses in the neighbourhood, for which he was impaired, whereas no activation was seen in control subjects on the same task. Both control subjects and K.C. showed activation in the right parahippocampal cortex on a task where photographs of landmarks were used, although K.C.'s activation was more posterior than the control subjects. Right retrosplenial cortex, portions of the frontal lobe, and the left precuneus (see later) and extrastriate cortex were also active for both K.C. and the control subjects. These results suggest that, as in the

---

[6] Maguire (2001) reviewed both the neuroimaging and neuropsychological studies that provide evidence for a role of the retrosplenial cortex in spatial cognition. The data from patients suggests that damage to the right retrosplenial cortex produces disorientation, although recovery occurs over a month or two. Maguire suggests that the retrosplenial cortex may be a transition zone from egocentric representations to allocentric ones.

Spiers and Maguire study, the hippocampus may be more involved in planning routes, as opposed to executing a navigation challenge.

It's also possible that the hippocampus is not involved in tasks requiring short-term updating of one's position. Wolbers *et al.* (2008) found that the precuneus, a portion of the parietal lobe within the middle of the brain (within the longitudinal fissure), was involved in keeping track of the location of remembered landmarks after self-movement in a virtual environment. The hippocampus, in contrast, did not show effects in the task.

Intriguing work by Hassabis *et al.* (2009) has suggested that human hippocampus may exhibit some topography in its activation when individuals are located in different locations within a virtual room. They also observe that, across rooms, differences in activity in the parahippocampal gyrus (assessed by a multivariate pattern classification analysis) were sufficient to correctly distinguish these two locations. The results from the hippocampus are unexpected, for as described earlier in this chapter, there is evidence that the place fields are not topographically organized in the rodent (Redish *et al.* 2001).

There is also evidence that the CA1 region of the hippocampus is activated when one learns the layout of a virtual environment starting from several (virtual) locations, when compared to learning the layout starting repeatedly from a single location (Suthana *et al.* 2009). Parahippocampal cortex activation was also seen during learning the virtual environment in this study, and this activation occurred in both types of starting conditions.

The hippocampus versus the caudate nucleus

Several imaging studies have compared hippocampus and caudate nucleus activation during performance of spatial tasks and during non-spatial, response-based tasks. As the reader may recall from Chapter 2, early studies wrestled with the question of whether rats solve spatial mazes by learning to go to a specific place, or by learning to make a specific response. Subsequent experiments have shown that place learning requires the hippocampus, but that other brain areas, including the caudate nucleus, are sufficient to maintain a response strategy with continued training (Packard and McGaugh 1996; for review see White and McDonald 2002). In support of this distinction in humans, Iaria *et al.* (2003) found right hippocampus activation when people used a spatial strategy to solve a virtual eight-arm maze. In the same study, participants who used a non-spatial strategy, for example counting arms, showed activity increases in the caudate nucleus. (All subjects showed increased activity in other areas, including the posterior parietal cortex.)

Further support for this distinction was found in a study of navigation through virtual towns. Using fMRI, Hartley *et al.* (2003) compared the brain activation associated with taking novel shortcuts through a recently learned virtual environment to that associated with repeatedly following a familiar route through a different virtual city, or that associated with following a marked trail through a virtual environment. When people took novel shortcuts through an environment, they showed greater activity in the parahippocampal, retrosplenial, and posterior parietal cortices (among other areas), compared with when they followed a trail. Compared to following a familiar route through an environment, greater activation was seen with those making novel shortcuts in the lateral posterior parietal cortex, the retrosplenial cortex, and cerebellum, again amongst other regions. Interestingly, hippocampus activation was only revealed when the accuracy of performance was considered. On trials where people were more accurate in taking shortcuts, greater activation of the right hippocampus and right insula was observed. For individuals who showed more accurate navigation during shortcutting, greater activation was seen in the left hippocampus (and right, although this didn't reach significance). For those who were more accurate in the familiar route-finding task, greater activation was seen in the right caudate nucleus.

A different approach to the hippocampus versus caudate comparison was taken by Voermans *et al.* (2004). They compared patients with Huntington's disease, an inherited neurodegenerative condition in which the caudate nucleus is particularly disrupted, to control subjects. The idea behind this comparison was that patients with Huntington's disease might compensate for the dysfunction in their caudate nuclei by showing increased activity in the hippocampus during navigation through familiar virtual environments. When tested for their recognition of previously seen routes through these environments, control subjects had greater caudate activity than patients with Huntington's disease. However, Huntington's disease sufferers showed greater activity in the right hippocampus and right parahippocampal cortex. The authors argue that, in Huntington's disease, normal navigation with familiar routes is achieved by a compensatory increase in hippocampal and parahippocampal cortex activity.

Finally, the distinction between hippocampus-dependent learning and caudate-dependent learning is supported by a pair of studies by Doeller and Burgess (2008; Doeller *et al.* 2008). They looked at brain activation when study participants learned the location of various objects placed in a virtual environment. The task was structured in such a way that some objects maintained a fixed position relative to a landmark—virtual traffic cone—within the environment. Other objects were in a fixed position relative to virtual cliff boundaries of the environment. In the far distance, beyond the virtual cliffs, various mountains served as general orienting cues, although they weren't sufficient to define distances from the cliffs. What Doeller *et al.* observed was that when participants learned the location of objects relative to the landmark, the right dorsal striatum (including the caudate nucleus) was activated. When they learned the location of objects relative to the boundaries of the environment, the right posterior hippocampus was activated. These activations appeared to be independent of one another. Behaviourally, learning the location of the objects relative to the landmark as opposed to the boundaries appeared to be distinct. Landmark-based learning appeared to be associative, and could be subject to overshadowing and blocking. In contrast, boundary-based learning appeared to be 'incidental' or obligatory, and was not susceptible to blocking or overshadowing. This supports a basic distinction between associative learning and cognitive map-based learning.

Interim summary

Evidence of hippocampus activation during navigation has been found in a number of studies. In particular, the hippocampus appears to be more involved in tasks requiring spatial strategies, as opposed to those that do not.[7] The distinction between place versus response learning and its reliance on the hippocampus versus the caudate nucleus is also supported by human imaging studies. There is some evidence that the participation of the human hippocampus in wayfinding may depend in part on how much spatial information is being learned, the familiarity of the environment, or whether there is a need to plan a route to a goal. What's also clear from these studies is that the hippocampus is one of a set of brain regions reliably activated during navigation. In addition to the parahippocampal gyrus, these include the retrosplenial cortex and portions of the parietal cortex.

Portions of the hippocampus are enlarged in London taxi drivers

A different source of evidence implicating the human hippocampus in wayfinding comes from studies looking at its size. This work began with a remarkable study by Maguire *et al.* (2000) that examined the size of the hippocampus

---

[7] Other studies, it should be noted, have examined the activity of the human hippocampus in tasks without an explicit spatial component. To cite just two examples: Kirchhoff *et al.* (2000) found that the posterior hippocampus shows greater activation, as viewed with functional MRI, when encoding items (words and pictures) that are subsequently remembered, as opposed to those that are not. Stark and Squire (2000) found activity increases in the hippocampus when participants were tested for their recognition of previously presented words or objects.

in London taxi drivers and non-taxi driving control subjects. The motivation behind this study was, in part, the finding that the hippocampus is larger in birds that store food in different locations than those that do not (e.g. Krebs *et al.* 1989; Sherry *et al.* 1989). Interestingly, in birds that store food, the hippocampus shows seasonal variation in size that corresponds with memory demands (Smulders *et al.* 1995; 2000; for reviews see Clayton 1998; Smulders 2006). Maguire and colleagues asked a similar question of humans: do people who have more cognitive maps have a bigger hippocampus? London taxi drivers were chosen as they spend nearly 2 years learning the layout of the city—a process referred to as being on 'the knowledge'. What Maguire *et al.* found was that the posterior hippocampus of taxi drivers was significantly larger than non-taxi driving control subjects. Moreover, this difference didn't appear to be due to some pre-existing differences in the size of the hippocampus, as increases in the size of the right posterior hippocampus correlated with the length of time one had been a taxi driver. A somewhat overlooked finding in this study, perhaps, was that the anterior hippocampus in taxi drivers was smaller than that of controls, and this decrease in size was greater the longer one had been a taxi driver. Nonetheless, these findings suggest the size of the human hippocampus may vary depending on how much spatial knowledge one has or the frequency with which it is called upon.[8]

To further rule out the possibility that people with a larger posterior hippocampus—and possibly a facility for learning spatial information—are more likely to become taxi drivers than those with a smaller posterior hippocampus, Maguire *et al.* (2003) looked at the brains of non-taxi drivers. These were tested on their ability to learn the layout of a virtual town and their memory for recently presented environmental scenes. No correlation between these abilities and the size of the posterior hippocampus was found. Thus, variance in the size of this part of the hippocampus does not relate to the ability to learn one's way about a new environment, or to subsequently remember its layout. These findings also suggest that the changes found in the hippocampi of

---

[8] I am encouraged by this finding, in a general way: it suggests that we can change our brains with consistent effort. A similar notion was expressed by Santiago Ramón y Cajal, the father of neuroanatomy, in his book entitled *Advice For A Young Investigator* (Swanson and Swanson translation, 1999). The beginning scientist, Cajal advises, should immerse themselves in a problem, as only through a sustained period of concentrated effort are new discoveries made. By harnessing one's attention to a problem, changes in the brain occur: 'When one reflects on the ability that humans display for modifying and refining mental activity related to a problem under serious examination, it is difficult to avoid concluding that the brain is plastic and goes through a process of anatomical and functional differentiation, adapting itself progressively to the problem'. (p. 35).

London taxi drivers were due to the acquisition of large amounts of spatial knowledge, and not pre-existing differences.

Taxi drivers, of course, may differ from non-taxi drivers in many respects. To try and control for some of these, Maguire *et al.* (2006b) compared the brains of London taxi drivers to those of London bus drivers. These two groups may be expected to be more similar than the taxi drivers and non-taxi driving control subjects used in the previous experiment. For example, both taxi and bus drivers may be expected to have similar levels of stress related to driving and dealing with passengers, and both may experience similar amounts of self-motion associated with driving. A key difference between the two is the amount of spatial knowledge required. Bus drivers repeatedly deal with the same series of routes in specific portions of the city, whereas taxi drivers presumably have a much more varied and extensive driving range. Thus, taxi drivers require 2+ years of training, whereas bus driver training requires about 6 weeks. What Maguire *et al.* observed was that, as in the previous study, taxi drivers had a larger mid-posterior hippocampus, in this case both on the left and the right, in comparison to bus drivers. Similarly, the anterior hippocampi were smaller in taxi drivers than in bus drivers. In this new group of taxi drivers, the same correlations with the length of time one had been a taxi driver, and the increase in mid-posterior hippocampus size, and decrease in anterior hippocampus size, were observed. Interestingly, taxi drivers were better than bus drivers on a test of London landmark recognition, and on a test where the proximity between landmarks had to be judged. Taxi drivers were worse, however, when attempting to recall a previously presented nonsense figure. The authors suggest that a larger mid-posterior hippocampus may confer some advantage for the taxi drivers, for example in their ability to judge the spatial relationships between London landmarks. However, this advantage comes at the cost of a small anterior hippocampus, and a reduction in the ability to remember certain types of visual information.

Another alternative explanation for the enlarged posterior hippocampus found in taxi drivers is that such changes occur whenever a large body of information is acquired, regardless of its nature. To test this, Woollett *et al.* (2008) measured the size of the hippocampus and the remainder of the brain in medical doctors and age- and IQ-matched control subjects who had attended university. Medical doctors, like taxi drivers on 'the knowledge', have to learn a great deal of information in an intensive period of training. However, medical knowledge is not inherently spatial. Woollett *et al.* found that the size of the hippocampus did not differ between medical doctors and control subjects, and no correlation between the duration of medical experience and the size of the hippocampus was found. Thus, in the authors' interpretation, it is the acquisition of a large amount of spatial information, such as that which occurs when learning the layout of London, which produces an enlargement of the posterior hippocampus.

Summary

I began this chapter with a summary of the properties of place cells in the hippocampus. Since their discovery in the 1970s, a substantial amount of information has accrued on how place cells behave, yet our views on their function are still evolving. The basic 'rules' of how place cells behave include the following:

(1) different place cells fire in different places;

(2) firing fields are often anchored to visual landmarks in an environment, and presumably olfactory and tactile cues; but

(3) firing fields are also driven by path integration; and

(4) place fields remap in different environments, although this remapping may sometimes be partial.

Refinements in our initial views on place cells include the recognition that:

(1) different place cells may be anchored to different subsets of cues within an environment;

(2) place cells are often driven by borders in the environment;

(3) place cells firing can encode aspects on ongoing behavioural tasks; and

(4) place cells may also fire in anticipation of the travel to a goal location.

This last property may be a link to the findings of impaired spatial imagination in humans with hippocampus damage: the ability of place cells in the rat to anticipate goal locations may reflect a simpler version of our ability to envision future contexts.

Place cells appear to provide a mechanism for location recognition via their unique neural signature for different environments. It's tempting to speculate that the loss of place-specific firing seen in an environment without walls, in the dark, represents a complete breakdown of spatial orientation. This, perhaps, is true *disorientation*. It's not simply an incorrectly oriented cognitive map; it is a disintegrated map.

For humans, greater levels of hippocampus activity are seen in those who are more consistent in their path integration or more accurate in their ability to take shortcuts. In addition, those who rely on a large body of spatial knowledge have larger posterior hippocampi. In general, however, neuroimaging work has made it clear that a number of brain regions contribute to navigation. In addition to the hippocampus, accumulating evidence implicates the parahippocampal and retrosplenial cortices in scene recognition and in navigation, respectively. As I'll describe in the next chapter, the discoveries of spatially tuned neurons outside the hippocampus support the idea that the hippocampus is a component of an interconnected neural circuit whose function may be to keep us from getting lost.

Chapter 8

The neural basis for a sense of direction: head direction neurons

In a paper published in 1916, Joseph Peterson described his experience of an 'illusion of direction orientation'. In Chicago, Peterson was transferring from a tram going north to a tram going south. He boarded the southbound train, and on taking his seat became convinced that the tram was heading north instead of south. He perceived streets that he knew to go in one direction as going in the opposite direction. It was only when he got off the tram in a familiar area that he began to regain a correct sense of direction:

> . . . in the midst of numerous perfectly familiar objects and buildings I felt an 'unwinding sensation' in the head, a sort of vertigo, and presto! the illusion was gone. (p. 229)

From this experience, Peterson suggests that the spatial associations we have with familiar landmarks can correct our sense of direction if it has somehow gone awry. This suggestion illustrates a central theme of this book: we have an internal 'sense' of direction, based in specific parts of our brains, which is subject to error but can be corrected by familiar landmarks.

As we'll see in this chapter, Peterson's observations in 1916 fit well with the behaviour of a remarkable neural system in the mammalian brain discovered in the 1980s. I'll first describe the discovery of this neural system, the head direction cell system, then outline its anatomy, and then describe its properties and relation to spatial behaviour. Within this context I will also describe a remarkable third class of spatial neuron, the grid cell.

Head direction cells

On the 15th of January, 1984, Professor James B. Ranck Jr. was working alone in his laboratory in Brooklyn, New York. He was attempting to record, in a rat, the activity of individual neurons in the subiculum, a brain region which receives the outputs of the hippocampus. However, Professor Ranck made a fortunate error and inadvertently placed his electrodes in an adjacent structure called the postsubiculum (an input structure to the hippocampus; confusingly, this structure is also known as the *presubiculum*).

On that afternoon, Ranck encountered a neuron that fired every time the rat faced a specific direction. The firing of this neuron didn't depend on whether the rat had its head up or down, it just depended on the direction in which the head was pointed. When the animal's head was pointed in the 'preferred' direction of the neuron it fired and it did so over about a 90° range. In later recordings, Ranck found other 'head direction' neurons both in the same rat and in others. He carried one rat from one room to another, still attached to a long recording cable, and observed that its head direction cell continued firing in about the same direction. Ranck tested whether the direction in which individual cells fired was based on a magnetic sense by bringing a magnet into the room, but this had no effect. Coupled with an earlier video tape of a head direction cell recorded in the hippocampus, these were the first descriptions of neurons that may serve as a neural compass in the mammalian brain.[1]

Jeffrey Taube, Bob Muller, and James Ranck Jr. later provided a description of the basic properties of head direction neurons in two papers in the *The Journal of Neuroscience*. In the first of these (1990a), Taube and colleagues recorded from neurons in the postsubiculum of seven rats. The rats were placed, individually, in a grey cylinder environment in which they were free to run around and gather small food pellets that the experimenters tossed in. This is the same apparatus that had been used in earlier place cell experiments (see Chapter 6), and, as in these previous experiments, it contained a white cue card that served as the sole spatial landmark in the environment.

About 26% of the neurons that Taube *et al.* recorded from in the postsubiculum were head direction (HD) cells. Each HD cell fired in a specific direction, and the direction in which the maximum firing was observed was referred to as the cell's 'preferred direction'. The average range over which an HD cell would fire was approximately 84°. When a rat faced a direction outside the directional range of a given cell, the cell stopped firing almost entirely. A given cell would fire whenever the rat's head was pointing in the cell's preferred direction, regardless of the position of the rat's body. Also, it didn't matter where the rat was located within the cylinder—a given cell would always fire in the same direction (Fig. 8.1a). The cells were truly tuned to where the rat's head pointed.

The preferred direction of an HD cell is evident if one graphs the firing rate of a cell according to the different directions (0° to 360°) the rat faces (Fig. 8.1b). Of course, when one considers direction, 0° and 360° are the same thing, so another way of showing the directional tuning of an HD cell is

---

[1] This account is based on Ranck (2005).

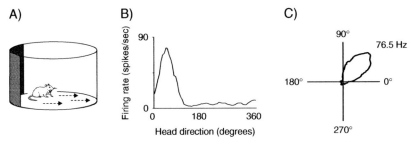

Fig. 8.1 *A)* A head direction neuron fires whenever the rat faces a specific direction within its environment. *B)* An individual head direction neuron will fire at a high rate when the rat faces the neuron's 'preferred firing direction', and is usually silent or nearly so when the rat faces other directions. *C)* The directional specificity of a head direction is evident when the firing of the neuron is plotted on a polar plot. The cell in this plot is the same as that shown in *B*.

a polar plot (Fig. 8.1c). Both of these figures are of the same cell, and this example illustrates the high firing rate associated with a specific preferred direction, the relatively narrow range of directions over which an HD cell fires, and the lack of activity observed when the rat faces directions away from the preferred firing direction.

In this first paper, Taube *et al.* observed that different HD cells fired in different directions, such that the entire 360° range appeared to be equally represented by different cells. Subsequent high-density recordings have confirmed this observation (Johnson *et al.* 2005).

In their second paper (1990b), Taube and colleagues addressed basic questions about these neurons. First, they found that the preferred firing directions of HD cells were anchored to the white card within the cylinder. That is, if a cell had an initial preferred firing direction at 100° in the cylinder, and then the experimenter took the rat out of the cylinder and shifted the white cue card by 90°, when the animal was returned to the cylinder the same HD cell would now exhibit a preferred direction of 190° (see Fig. 8.2).

But HD cells, like place cells, aren't simply visual cells. Although their firing directions were anchored to the cue card—the most salient, polarizing landmark in the environment—Taube *et al.* found that the cells continued firing in a directional manner even when the cue card was removed. In the absence of the cue card, the preferred directions of some cells changed, but all cells still fired in a directional manner. Subsequent work has shown that even if a rat is blindfolded and placed in a darkened environment, its HD cells will fire, albeit with a small amount of 'drift' in their firing directions (Goodridge *et al.* 1998). Under these conditions, HD cells appear to rely on olfactory or tactile

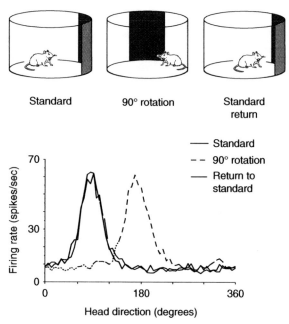

Fig. 8.2 Rotation of a cue card in a cylindrical environment (*top*) is associated with a corresponding shift in the preferred firing direction of individual head direction cells (*bottom*).

cues on the environment's floor or walls to maintain stable preferred firing directions.

Additional important findings in the second Taube *et al.* paper were as follows. When the authors recorded from two HD neurons with different preferred firing directions at the same time, they observed that the cells always behaved in the same way. For example, if one cell changed its firing direction by 50° after the cue card was removed from the cylinder, the second cell also changed its direction by 50°. The fact that all HD cells appeared tied to one another, although only one subset is active at any given moment, suggests that they behave as a continuous attractor neural network (Skaggs *et al.* 1995; Zhang 1996). Because of this, I'll sometimes refer to the 'orientation' of the HD cell system. This doesn't refer to which way around the neurons are in the brain, but rather to the overall directional reference of the HD ensemble, independent of which neurons happen to be active.

A final interesting observation was that when the rats were moved from the cylinder to an environment of a different shape, the preferred firing directions of the cells often changed dramatically. For example, if the cylinder was replaced with a rectangle—even with a cue card in a similar position if viewed from overhead—the majority of cells showed changes in firing direction of 78° or more. So, HD cells appear sensitive to the shape of the enclosure, in addition to using salient visual landmarks to anchor their firing directions.

A number of subsequent studies have elaborated on the basic properties of these neurons, and I'll consider these later. A detailed description of this system and its properties can also be found in Wiener and Taube (2005). However, before further consideration of HD cells, I'll describe a remarkable third type of spatially tuned neurons.

Grid cells

Grid cells are neurons that possess multiple place fields arranged in a triangular, tessellating array, or 'grid' (Fig. 8.3). Their discovery is potentially one of the most significant advances in our understanding of how the mammalian brain maps environments.

Although grid cells resemble place cells, albeit with multiple place fields, I have chosen to present them within the context of the head direction cell system for a number of reasons. Firstly, grid cells are found in some of the same brain areas as head direction cells. Secondly, some grid cells are themselves modulated by head direction, and thirdly, their coherent behaviour is more akin to the behaviour of head direction cells than of hippocampal place cells.

Grid cells weren't initially recognized as such. In an initial paper examining the firing properties of the neurons in the dorsal medial entorhinal cortex (dMEC), Fyhn *et al.* (2004) observed that cells there displayed multiple,

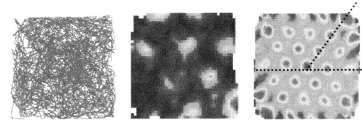

Fig. 8.3 Example of a grid cell recorded in the medial entorhinal cortex. In the right plot, the path of the animal is shown in grey, and the spikes of the grid neuron are shown as dots. In the middle plot, the firing rate of this neuron is colour-coded, with higher firing rates represented as warmer colours. The 'gridness' of this grid cell is particularly evident when the firing rate map is correlated with itself, as shown in the right-most plot. The orientation of a grid field is the angle at which a line can be drawn through the grid sub-fields. (Example courtesy of Dr James Ainge, University of St. Andrews.) (See also Plate 5.)

discrete firing fields. This part of the entorhinal cortex, the authors showed, projects to the dorsal hippocampus, and has been shown in previous work to receive inputs from visual and parietal regions. What was not recognized at the time, in part because of the size of the recording environments (although with the benefit of hindsight is apparent in the figures in this paper), was that the multiple fields of individual dMEC cells show a regular spacing. Subsequent work has shown that the same MEC cells can appear as a place-like cell in a small environment, and as a grid cell in a larger environment (Savelli *et al.* 2008).

The full characterization of grid cells appears in a paper entitled 'Microstructure of the spatial map in the entorhinal cortex' by Hafting *et al.* (2005). Using larger environments than in the Fyhn *et al.* study, the authors show that the multiple place fields of the dMEC cells form repeated, tessellating triangles. In this work the authors make several fundamental observations regarding these fields. Firstly, grid cells recorded in the same part of the dMEC have firing fields that are spaced by the same distance. They also have the same orientation, as defined as the angle formed by a camera-defined reference line and the nearest straight line that connects the grid fields (Fig. 8.3). Grid cells recorded in more ventral portions of the dMEC show larger firing fields and wider spacing between fields. This difference in grid field spacing appears to be due to differences in the below-threshold membrane potential oscillation rate of grid cells at different levels of the entorhinal cortex (Giocomo *et al.* 2007; Giocomo and Hasselmo 2008). Grid cells in different locations show different orientations, although these orientations don't appear to vary systematically from dorsal to ventral portions of the dMEC. Although grid cells recorded in the same area have the same spacing and orientation, the specific locations in which the fields are observed (their phases or vertices) differ between cells. Thus, with just a few grid cells, the entire environment is represented.

Other properties of grid cells are similar to those of place cells and head direction cells. For example, if one records from the same grid cell on two different occasions, the cell will fire in the same locations. Grid fields are also anchored to familiar landmarks in the environment, and displacement of landmarks at the periphery of the environment causes a corresponding rotation of the grids. In the dark, grid activity is maintained, although some shift in the vertices is observed relative to when the same cell is recorded in the light. In new environments, a given grid cell will continue to fire, although the orientation of the grid may change. Barry *et al.* (2007) have shown that grid fields can be 'squished' by recording in different sized environments, an effect that depends on the animal's familiarity with the environment.

Grid cells also appear to drive aspects of hippocampal place cell behaviour. Fyhn *et al.* (2007) found that changing the shape or location of a recording environment caused a shift in the vertices of grid cells and global remapping in CA3 place cells recorded at the same time. Changes in the colour of the recording environment were associated with rate remapping in place cells (changes in the firing rates, but not the location of the place fields), and no shift in the grid cells. Grid cells may also be the source of phase precession in the hippocampus, as phase precession is evident in grid cells even following inactivation of the hippocampus (Hafting *et al.* 2008). This inactivation, interestingly, appears to decrease the spatial specificity of the grid cell firing fields, although spatial firing is still evident.

The discovery of grid cells is arguably the most significant development in our understanding of the neural bases of spatial cognition since the discovery of place cells. In grid cells there is a relatively pure encoding of space, comparable in many respects, and coexisting, with head direction neurons. As suggested by several authors, the invariant representation of space provided by grid cells may underlie path integration (Hafting *et al.* 2005; Fuhs and Touretzky 2006; McNaughton *et al.* 2006; Fyhn *et al.* 2007).

The head direction/grid cell circuit

Following the initial description of postsubicular HD cells, researchers have found these cells, and now grid cells, in a number of interconnected brain regions. Fig. 8.4 is a summary diagram of where head direction, place, and grid cells have been identified. After their initial characterization in the postsubiculum, head direction cells were found in the anterior dorsal thalamus (Taube 1995), the lateral dorsal thalamus (Mizumori and Williams 1993), the retrosplenial cortex (Chen *et al.* 1994; Cho and Sharp 2001), the lateral mammillary nucleus (Blair *et al.* 1998; Stackman and Taube 1998), the dorsal tegmental nucleus (Sharp *et al.* 2001a; but see Bassett and Taube 2001), and the medial entorhinal cortex (MEC; Sargolini *et al.* 2006). There have also been reports of HD cells in the hippocampus (Leutgeb *et al.* 2000), although it is unclear whether these represent cells within the hippocampus, or fibres from, presumably, entorhinal cortex HD cells. To date, grid cells have been found in the dorsal medial entorhinal cortex (Hafting *et al.* 2005), the parasubiculum, and the postsubiculum (Boccara *et al.* 2008).

A series of experiments in the labs of Jeffrey Taube and Patricia Sharp have provided some idea of how information flows within this circuit. A detailed description of these can be found in Taube and Bassett (2003) and Taube (2007), but the take-home message is that the HD signal is thought to originate

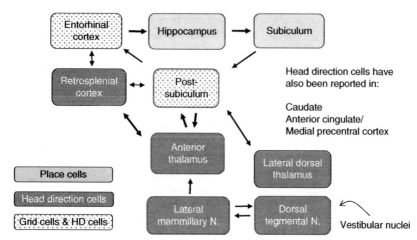

Fig. 8.4 Schematic of the brain regions containing place (light grey), head direction (dark grey), and grid cells (patterned grey). The regions containing grid cells also contain head direction cells. The essential circuit for the head direction cell system is the dorsal tegmental nucleus > lateral mammillary nucleus > anterior thalamus > postsubiculum. It's likely that this circuit also extends to the entorhinal cortex, where head direction cells are also observed.

in the connections between the dorsal tegmental nucleus and the lateral mammillary nucleus (Blair *et al.* 1998, 1999; Sharp *et al.* 2001b; Bassett *et al.* 2007; Sharp and Koester 2008; see also Bassett and Taube 2001). It then passes from the lateral mammillary nucleus (LMN) to the anterior dorsal thalamus (AD), and then to the postsubiculum (POS), and then the medial entorhinal cortex. Presumably, HD information is then passed on to the hippocampus.

Where does the head direction signal come from? The short answer is that the signal likely arises from the integration of head-turn information (angular head velocity signals) from the vestibular system. Lesioning the vestibular system abolishes directional firing in HD cells in the ATN (and presumably throughout the circuit) (Stackman and Taube 1997). The medial vestibular nucleus projects to the dorsal tegmental nucleus (DTN), which contains widely tuned HD cells, and HD cells that are modulated by angular velocity (Sharp *et al.* 2001a) as well as angular head velocity cells (Sharp *et al.* 2001a; Bassett and Taube 2001). It's also possible that other inputs to the DTN are critical (Sharp *et al.* 2001b; Bassett and Taube 2005). Sharp *et al.* (2001a) suggest that as the DTN neurons are inhibitory and widely tuned, they may sharpen the directional tuning of LMN neurons, and together the connections between the DTN and LMN serve as a stable attractor—path integration network (see also Song and Wang 2005). An important point of all this is that, if the HD signal is generated from some form of integration of vestibular information and the animal's own movement, there is the likelihood that it will be subject to cumulative error.

There are several observations to make about this circuitry. First, HD cells are found in a set of interconnected brain regions. These regions roughly correspond to the *Papez* circuit, a neural circuit elucidated by James Papez (1937) in rabbits. Papez described a neural pathway that travels from the hippocampus, through the fornix, to the mammillary bodies. From the mammillary bodies, the mammillothalamic tract projects to the anterior thalamus. From here projections go to the cingulate cortex, the parahippocampal cortex, and the hippocampus. Papez hypothesized that this circuit was critical for emotion.

A second observation is that the mammillary body projection to the anterior thalamus comprises two parallel circuits. As described by Vann and Aggleton (2004), both the medial and the lateral mammillary nuclei send projections through the mammillothalamic tract to the anterior thalamus, and clinical evidence suggests that the mammillary bodies and anterior thalamus may be critical for human episodic memory. However, the medial mammillary nucleus projects to the anterior medial and anterior ventral thalamus,[2] whereas the lateral mammillary nucleus projects to the anterior dorsal nucleus. The later pathway, as stated earlier, is a part of the HD cell circuit (both the lateral mammillary and anterior dorsal nuclei contain HD neurons). The former circuit appears to have a high concentration of neurons that fire in the theta rhythm. Theta cells are found in the medial mammillary nucleus, and 75% of the cells in the anterior ventral thalamic nuclei (to which the medial mammillary nucleus projects) are theta cells.

A third point is that mammillary nuclei projections may or may not be critical inputs for grid cells. In Burgess *et al.*'s (2007; Burgess 2008) model, speed-modulated head direction cells are inputs to velocity-controlled oscillators that combine to form grid fields.[3] Thus, head direction cell-like inputs may be necessary for grid cells. In Blair *et al.*'s (2007) model, grid cells are built from 'theta grids', possibly originating in the medial and supramammillary nuclei. Again, this may suggest that the mammillary nuclei are necessary for grid cells. However, if, as is assumed, place cells arise from grid cells (e.g. McNaughton *et al.* 2006) then removing the head direction input to the grid

---

[2] Yoganarasimha *et al.* (2006) provide some evidence of the presence of head direction cells in the anterior ventral nucleus of the thalamus.

[3] Empirical support for Burgess's model of how grid cells are formed has been provided by Jeewajee *et al.* (2008).

cell system should disrupt place cells. This isn't the case. Clear place fields are still found in the hippocampus following lesions of the mammillary body region (Sharp and Koester 2008). Place fields are also evident after removal of the postsubiculum (Calton *et al.* 2003). Thus, place cells in the hippocampus are still present when the HD input to the hippocampus is removed. This may imply that HD cells outside the DTN > postsubicular pathway are involved in grid cell formation, if such inputs are indeed necessary.

Finally, there are some differences in HD cells recorded in different brain areas. One relates to what is termed anticipatory firing, or the anticipatory time interval. First shown by Blair and Sharp (1995), this is when HD cells fire slightly in advance of the rat facing a specific direction. For example, HD neurons in the anterior dorsal thalamus fire about 25 milliseconds before the animal arrives in a given cell's preferred firing direction, whereas HD cells in the POS fire when the animal's head is actually in the preferred direction (see also Taube and Muller 1998). HD cells in the LMN have yet a longer anticipation—with estimates of 70 milliseconds (Stackman and Taube 1998) or 40 milliseconds (Blair *et al.* 1998). The directional range over which individual HD fires, also differs between brain regions. The most narrowly tuned cells are in the POS, with those of the AD being slightly wider, and those of the LMN and DTN being wider still.

Landmark control over HD cell firing

How do HD cells 'know' which direction the rat is facing? As mentioned earlier, one of the basic properties of HD cells is that their directional firing is anchored to visual landmarks, like a white cue card, in the environment. The stimulus control of this landmark can be strong, as shown by Goodridge and Taube (1995). They recorded HD cells in a cylinder with a cue card, and then took the rat out of the cylinder, removed the cue card, and cleaned the maze. They walked the animal around the cylinder a few times to misorient it, and then put it back in the now cue-less cylinder. In the cylinder, HD cells sometimes fired in a similar direction (< 30° different) to that shown when the cue card was present. On other occasions, there were larger changes in firing directions. Goodridge and Taube put the cue card back in the cylinder while the rat was still present. If the HD cells displayed a large change in firing direction in the absence of the cue card, the authors returned the cue card to its former position. If the HD cells had shown only a small change in firing direction when the cue card was removed, they replaced the card in a position 90° away from its initial position.

The essential finding from these manipulations was that the firing directions of HD cells shifted to agree with the position of the cue card when it was put back in the environment. If a HD cell's firing direction had shifted by a large amount when the cue card was removed, replacement of the card caused the cell to shift back to its original direction in most instances. If a HD cell's firing direction had shifted by a small amount in the absence of the cue card, replacing the cue card in a 90° shifted position caused a comparable shift in the cell's firing direction. This change, however, was somewhat less than the full 90° that would be expected if the cue card had exclusive control over the firing direction of the cells. One possibility is that in these under-rotation sessions, the rats had picked up on some other subtle cue in the environment (e.g. a newly laid scent-mark on the floor), and thus cue control by the card was not complete. Additional work has shown that distal landmarks exert much stronger stimulus control over HD cell firing directions compared to local cues (Zugaro et al. 2001; Yoganarasimha and Knierim 2005; Yoganarasimha et al. 2006).

A study by Zugaro et al. (2003) showed that the reorientation of HD cells to a cue card in a cylinder occurs rapidly. The authors recorded from HD cells in a cylinder with a cue card while rats drank from a port in the centre of the apparatus. The lights were then turned off and the cue card was moved by the experimenter. When the lights were turned back on, HD cells would reorient (in some instances) to the cue card, and would do so in about 80 milliseconds. For the authors, this rapid reorientation suggests that activation in the HD cell network may jump from cells with one preferred orientation to cells with a distal preferred orientation, without activating the cells with orientations between the two.

How is the stimulus control of landmarks over HD cell firing directions established? An experiment by Goodridge et al. (1998) examined this by recording HD cells when a new landmark—an unfamiliar cue card—was introduced to the recording environment (see Fig. 8.5). When the new card was attached to the wall of the recording environment, the ongoing firing direction of the HD cells, in most instances, did not change. This is important, because it shows that HD cells aren't simply driven by the sensory features of the cue card. After exposure to the card for up to 8 minutes, the rats were removed from the cylinder, and the cue card was shifted by 90°. Upon the rats' return to the cylinder, the cells' firing directions usually shifted by 90°. (Somewhat less consistent rotations in firing directions were observed by animals exposed to the cue card for only 1 minute.) This finding shows that the association between the firing directions of HD cells and a landmark in the environment is formed within minutes of exposure to the landmark. Thus, stimulus control over HD

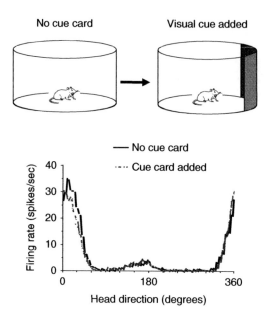

Fig. 8.5 Head direction cells are not sensory cells, but their firing direction can become anchored to a landmark with experience. Goodridge *et al.* (1998) demonstrated this by adding a novel cue card to a cylindrical environment in the presence of the rat. The cue card had no effect on the cell's ongoing firing direction (*bottom* plot). However, subsequent rotation of this cue card, in the absence of the animal, caused a corresponding shift in the cell's preferred firing direction. Thus, the cue card rapidly acquired stimulus control over the firing direction of this cell.

Adapted from: Goodridge, Dudchenko, Worboys, Golob, and Taube (1998) Cue control and head direction cells, *Behavioral Neuroscience*, **112**:749–761. Published by the American Psychological Association, and reprinted with permission.

cell directional firing is learned, and learned rapidly. Such a process, it may be speculated, is akin to our rapid ability to 'learn' what a specific environment looks like. We don't need too much exposure to the inside of someone's house, for example, to be able to recognize it again.

How does this learning take place? One theory is that local views and landmarks come to control the directional firing of HD cells by being consistently associated with their firing (McNaughton *et al.* 1991, 1996). For example, consider a rat that has been placed into a cylindrical environment with a cue card for the first time. Different HD cells would fire in different directions in this environment, but if they were stable, then every time the rat faced the cue card certain cells would fire. Every time it faced to the left of the cue card, other cells would fire, etc. As the animal spent more time in the environment, this consistent pairing of views of the cue card and the firing of specific cells would lead to a strengthened association between some type of local-view cells and the HD cells. This association would enable the landmark to correct for any internal error in the maintenance of HD cell firing directions arising from the integration of vestibular and self-movement information.

The prediction that follows from this view is that, if the rat's internal orientation is unstable, then its HD cells (and hippocampal place cells) would have difficulty becoming associated with the landmarks in an environment. That is, if a rat is misoriented before being placed in a cylinder with a cue card, then the animal's HD cells should be less likely to be anchored to the cue card. Just this result was observed by Knierim *et al.* (1995). In other studies, misorientation had less of an impact on cue control for HD cells (Dudchenko *et al.* 1997a), although it did disrupt the learning of spatial landmarks in some spatial tasks (Dudchenko *et al.* 1997b). Also, misorientation of the rat relative to the cue card weakens the stimulus control of the card over place fields if the cue card has previously been moved in front of the animal (Jeffery and O'Keefe 1999). So, it's likely that a stimulus's ability to serve as a spatial landmark depends on its consistent association with the internal orientations represented by HD, place and grid neurons.

On a lighter note, this raises an interesting question: if you were a waiter in a slowly revolving, sky-view restaurant (such as the Space Needle in Seattle, or the CN Tower in Toronto), would you have difficulty finding your way around the city after work? The stable inertial sense plus landmark association view of spatial learning would predict that the city landmarks viewed from the slowly moving restaurant would tend not to be associated with one's internal sense of orientation.

Path integration and head direction cells

Even from the initial experiments with HD cells it has been clear that they don't just rely on visual information for orientation. As mentioned earlier, Ranck showed that a HD cell would maintain its preferred direction if the rat was carried to a different room. This suggests that the head direction cell system is able to maintain a stable orientation across environments. In this section I consider evidence showing that the HD cell system maintains stable directional orientation based on an internal sense of movement.

Blair and Sharp (1996) looked at the relative strength of visual and internal cues in controlling the firing directions of HD cells. They recorded from HD cells in rats in a cylinder that had alternating black and white 45° stripes on the wall. Thus, unlike a cylinder with a single cue card, the striped cylinder was ambiguous—the rat couldn't really tell which direction was which. The walls and the floor of the cylinder were independently moveable. The authors tested the relative strength of visual and internal cues by rotating the walls of the environment in front of the rat. When they moved the walls by 90° relatively quickly, the majority of cells did not change their firing directions. When they moved the floor by 90° (again, with the rat present), there was no change in firing direction for any cell. So, if the rat saw that the walls had moved, or felt (with its vestibular system) that the floor had moved, its HD cells weren't fooled. However, when Blair and Sharp rotated both the walls and the floor very slowly over 90°, *all* cells shifted by 90°. In this instance, the rats (or at least their HD cells) did not notice the movement of the floor or the walls, and were fooled. The results were a bit more complicated when the rotations were done in the dark, but the take-home message is that both vestibular information and vision exert an influence on the firing direction of HD cells.

Knierim *et al.* (1998) also examined this issue with recordings of HD cells and hippocampal place cells. HD or place cells were recorded in a grey cylinder with a cue card, and then the cylinder, with the rat inside, was rotated relatively quickly by 45°, 135°, or 180°. If the cylinder was rotated by a relatively small amount (45°), then place cells and HD cells tended to maintain their orientation relative to the cylinder and cue card (that is, they too rotated by 45°). For the larger rotations, HD cells, and to a lesser extent place cells, were much less likely to follow the cylinder and cue card. Slow rotation (~0.5°/second) of the apparatus with the rat inside fooled both the place and HD cells in almost every instance. Thus, with small dissociations between the animal's internal sense of orientation and the outside world, the rats usually reoriented to the world (i.e., their HD cells and place cells remained anchored to the cylinder and cue card). With larger, fast rotations, the rat knew it had been rotated, and its place and HD cells tended not to follow the cue card, but adopted a different firing direction (for HD cells) or new place field (for place cells).

There are two additional interesting findings in this study. First, in a few of the 180° rotation sessions, the HD cells rotated to agree with the cue card, but not immediately. Their firing directions initially maintained their room-based firing direction following the rotation of the apparatus, but then drifted back into alignment with the now rotated cue card. Second, when HD cells were recorded in the dark on an open circular platform, their firing directions appeared to be largely stable (as in Goodridge *et al.* 1998). The firing directions could be induced to drift in the dark if the platform was rotated slowly. Under these circumstances, if the cells' firing directions changed by a relatively large amount (> 45°) relative to their pre-darkness orientation, they usually remained changed when the lights were turned on, despite the presence of extra-maze landmarks. In the cases where the HD cells reverted to the firing directions they'd exhibited before the darkness session, the drift in the darkness had usually been less than 45°. This result reinforces the message that if there is a small mismatch between the landmarks in the environment and the orientation of the rat's HD cell system, the HD cells will switch their firing directions to agree with the landmarks. If the mismatch is large, then HD cells are less likely to reorient to the landmarks.

Additional evidence that the head direction cell system reflects the animal's internal orientation is provided by Hargreaves *et al.* (2007). They recorded from place cells, head direction cells, and cells in the medial entorhinal cortex/parasubiculum. In one manipulation, animals were recorded in a square environment with a cue card. The rat was then placed in a covered bucket and rotated slowly by 90°. At the same time, the cue card was rotated in the opposite direction by 90°. For HD cells, rotation of the rat resulted in a corresponding rotation of preferred firing directions in the majority (6/9) instances. In two of the remaining three attempts, the firing directions did not rotate, but remained in the same orientation relative to the room. In the remaining attempt, the HD cells reoriented to the cue card. When this manipulation was attempted during place and parasubicular cell recording sessions, rotations in firing fields that corresponded to the rats' rotation were also found, although many instances of non-rotation were observed. Importantly, when the dominant response of an ensemble of place cells was identified, it agreed with that of simultaneously recorded HD cells or simultaneously recorded parasubicular cells. This shows that an interconnected system of spatially tuned neurons appears to behave coherently, and it may be that the head direction cell system sets the orientation of the place cell and grid cell systems (Jeffery *et al.* 1997; Yoganarasimha and Knierim 2005).

The maintenance of orientation across environments

A different way of looking at the role of path integration in controlling the orientation of the HD cell system is to look at HD cells when rats walk into a new environment. If the rat can't see its previous environment, what determines the orientation of the HD cell system in a new environment is, presumably, how well the animal is able to keep track of the direction it has travelled. Taube and Burton (1995) examined this by recording from HD neurons while rats travelled from a familiar cylindrical environment, through a novel passage way, into a rectangular environment that they hadn't seen before (Fig. 8.6).

What they found was that when rats walk into the new environment their HD cells maintained the firing directions seen in the familiar cylinder.

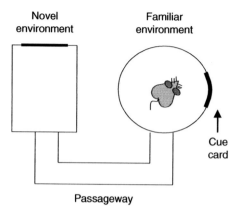

Fig. 8.6 Taube and Burton (1995) developed an apparatus to test how well head direction cells maintained their firing directions in a new environment. Rats were initially placed in a familiar, cylindrical environment. After several minutes in this portion of the apparatus a concealed doorway was opened, allowing passage to a novel environment.

The average shift in directions between the new environment and the cylinder was only 18°. This finding is important because it quantifies the ability of HD cells to maintain their preferred firing directions based on path integration. In a subsequent study, Stackman *et al.* (2003) found that if rats walked from the familiar cylinder to the novel rectangle in darkness, the average shift in firing directions was 28.8°. They also observed that if the animals didn't walk between the environments, but were instead passively wheeled between the two, the shift in firing directions was 69.5° (in the light) or 66.7° (in the dark). These results suggest that visual flow and the rat's own movements contribute to the ability of HD cells to maintain their orientation across environments.

A second major finding occurred in Taube and Burton's 'conflict' situation. The conflict was set up after the initial exploration of the rectangle from the familiar cylinder. The rats were removed from the cylinder, and the cue card was rotated by 90°. When the rats were put back in the cylinder (with the passage door to the rectangle closed), HD cell firing directions shifted to agree with the new position of the cue card. This shift was somewhat less than the full shift described previously for this type of rotation, likely because the doorway itself serves as a landmark. Nonetheless, a conflict arose when the door to the rectangle was subsequently opened. The rats' HD cells, having previously established a firing direction in the rectangle similar to that shown in the cylinder with the cue card in its initial position, now entered the alleyway to the rectangle with a different firing direction. What Taube and Burton found was that when the rats entered the alleyway leading to the rectangle, their HD cells shifted back to the firing direction established in the initial exploration of the rectangle. I will return to this observation later.

Brain regions underlying the ability to maintain orientation across environments

Golob and Taube (1999) tested the capacity of HD cells to maintain their firing directions across environments following removal of either the hippocampus or the portion of the parietal cortex overlying the hippocampus. The average shift in HD cell firing directions between the familiar cylinder and the novel rectangle, walking between the two as described earlier, was 46.5° for animals with parietal cortex lesions and 96.5° for animals with hippocampus lesions. Both of these shifts were significantly higher than the 17° average shift seen in the control, non-lesioned animals. These results suggest that the hippocampus (as we saw in Chapter 6) is necessary for path integration. The intermediate impairment in path integration following parietal cortex removal was confirmed in a subsequent experiment where large parietal cortex lesions produced a 42° average shift in HD cell firing directions between the cylinder and rectangle (Calton *et al.* 2008). In this same study, smaller parietal cortex lesions were associated with a 36° average shift, whereas control animals only showed a 19.5° average error between environments.

More dramatic impairments in path integration, as assessed by this task, have been found when the interpeduncular nucleus (IPN) is removed (Clark *et al.* 2009). The interest in this structure arises from its projections to the dorsal tegmental nucleus, which, as described previously, is thought to participate in the generation of the HD cell signal. Clark *et al.* hypothesized that the IPN receives motor information from the basal ganglia via the lateral habenula. What they found was that removing the IPN produced a 60° average shift in HD cell preferred firing directions when animals walked from a familiar cylinder to a novel rectangle. In another test, HD cells in IPN-lesioned animals drifted (gradually) by an average of 77.9° in the dark in a cylinder, whereas HD cells in control animals only drifted by 23.3°. These two findings appear to confirm the role of the IPN in providing an important path integration input to the HD cell system. However, there was another interesting consequence of these lesions: HD cells in animals without an IPN were controlled to a much weaker extent by a visual cue card. This lack of cue control was evident both when a cue card was rotated by 90° and when it was returned to its initial position. One possibility is that the HD cells in the lesioned animals drifted when the animals were outside of the cylinder.

Path integration versus landmarks in head direction cell orientation

Dr Larissa Zinyuk and I conducted an experiment that followed on from the results of the Taube and Burton study, and really drove home (for me, at least) the relative strength of familiar landmarks and path integration in controlling the HD cell system, and possibly the rat's sense of direction (Dudchenko and Zinyuk 2005).

We first exposed individual rats to a square environment, Box A, which contained distinctive landmarks (Fig. 8.7). The rat had never been in A before, and we recorded from its HD cells as it explored this environment for 15 minutes. Next, we put the rat into an opaque box and carried the box around our testing environment. The reason for doing this is that we didn't want the rat's HD cells to maintain the same firing direction when we placed it into the second environment, Box C. C was a square environment like A, but contained different landmarks. We allowed the rat to explore this environment for 15 minutes, and again recorded the firing direction of its HD cells.

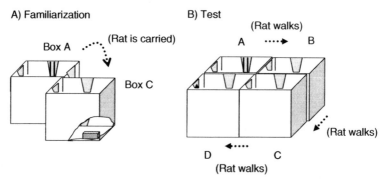

Fig. 8.7 Testing procedure for assessing the relative strength of landmarks and path integration in maintaining the preferred firing direction of head direction cells. The rat was first exposed to an unfamiliar environment, Box A, for 15 minutes. It was then carried by the experimenter, by an indirect route, to a second unfamiliar environment, Box C. Following this, the rat was replaced in Box A, and then allowed to walk from there, via a removable door, to Box B, an environment it had never seen before. In the same way, the rat was allowed to walk from Box B to Box C, and from there to Box D.

Reproduced from: Dudchenko and Zinyuk (2005) The formation of cognitive maps of adjacent environments: evidence from the head direction cell system. *Behavioral Neuroscience*, **119**, 1511–1523. Published by the American Psychological Association, and reprinted with permission.

After this exposure, we moved to the test phase of the experiment. Here, we took the rat out of Box C, put it in the opaque container, and again walked it around the apparatus a few times. We then replaced the rat in Box A. Now, if the rat recognize A, its HD cells should fire in the same direction as they had when the rat initially explored the environment—and this is what happened (Fig. 8.8). After 8 minutes in A we opened a door in the wall, and allowed the rat to enter Box B, a new environment that the rat had never seen before. Based on the results of Taube and Burton (1995), we expected the HD cells to

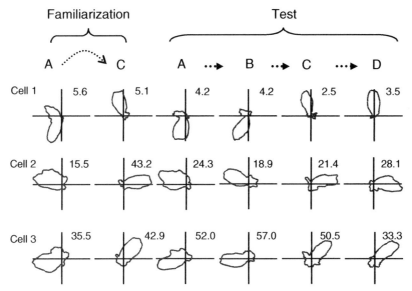

Fig. 8.8 Three simultaneously recorded head direction cells. When the rat was carried between Boxes A and C, these HD cells fired in different directions in the two environments (in the familiarization stage). When the rat was replaced in Box A, in the test stage, each cell resumed its previously established firing direction in Box A, indicating that the rat's HD cell system had recognized Box A. When the rat next walked into Box B, its HD cells maintained a similar preferred firing direction, indicating that the rat was able to maintain its orientation by the integration of self-movement cues. When the rat then entered Box C, the HD cells immediately switched firing directions to those established previously in Box C. This suggests that the landmarks in Box C exerted a stronger control over the cells' firing directions than the animal's path integration system. In Box D, the cells maintained the orientation evident in Box C, again suggesting that path integration operates to maintain orientation when entering a new environment.

Reproduced from: Dudchenko and Zinyuk (2005) The formation of cognitive maps of adjacent environments: evidence from the head direction cell system. *Behavioral Neuroscience*, **119**, 1511–1523. Published by the American Psychological Association, and reprinted with permission.

fire in a similar direction in B compared to A, and this is what we observed. Next we opened a doorway between Boxes B and C. The rat, of course, had seen C before. In Box C all HD cells immediately changed from the firing directions that they'd maintained from A to the directions previously established in C. After this, a doorway was opened between Box C and Box D, the latter being a second environment that the rat hadn't seen before. In D, the HD cells maintained a similar direction to Box C.

These results show three things. Firstly, the rat's HD cell system 'remembers' environments, because its HD cells fire in the same direction when the rat sees the same environment again. In this study, we controlled the amount of exposure to these environments, so this recognition memory occurs after just 15 minutes' exposure to a box.

Secondly, as shown by Taube and Burton (and earlier by Ranck), HD cells fire in the same direction even when the rat moves to another room. It may be speculated that this is how learning about the layout of an environment occurs: starting from a known orientation, the rat ventures farther and farther away, and each time establishes an association between its HD cell firing and new landmarks. These rapidly come to control the HD cell system, so that the animal is able to use landmarks in different locations to maintain a consistent orientation.

A third finding is that the stimulus control exerted by landmarks—even recently learned landmarks—can override the maintenance of directional orientation by path integration. This is interesting, and is consistent with Joseph Peterson's reorientation to familiar landmarks in Chicago. Can this switch in directional sense occur when there is a repeated conflict between landmarks and path integration?

To test this, Dr Zinyuk and I did another manipulation. Once we established the initial observation—maintenance of direction from A to B, switch in direction when entering C, maintenance of switched direction from C to D—we gave the rat repeated exposure to the conflict situation. Our question was: if every day you walk into room C and it is wrong, will you eventually stop reorienting in C?

In some, but not all rats, this is exactly what we observed. As shown in Fig. 8.9, by the third exposure to the four boxes, the HD cell in this example fired in a similar direction in all four environments. This occurred only when the rat walked between the four chambers; if the rat was picked up and placed in boxes A and C, its HD cells still showed different firing directions. So, in the same environment, the same HD cells fired in different directions, depending on how the animal entered the enclosure.

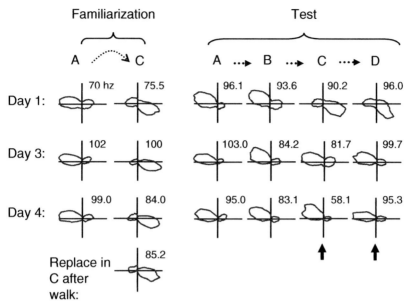

Fig. 8.9 With repeated exposure to the four-chamber apparatus, the switch in preferred firing directions between Boxes B and C eventually ceased, and a consistent firing direction was observed in all four environments. This consistency was only observed when the animal walked between environments; when it was carried between Boxes A and C, or replaced in C after the test (bottom plot), this cell resumed its 'C' firing direction. Thus, the same cell exhibited different firing directions in the same environment, depending on how it was transported to that environment.

Reproduced from: Dudchenko and Zinyuk (2005) The formation of cognitive maps of adjacent environments: evidence from the head direction cell system. *Behavioral Neuroscience*, **119**, 1511–1523. Published by the American Psychological Association, and reprinted with permission.

A final point on this experiment is that when the rats walked from their familiar environments into the new environments their HD cells maintained similar firing directions, *but with some error*. Moving from box A to box B, for example, caused an average shift in firing directions of 19.1°. Similarly, moving from Box C to Box D caused a shift of 21.5°. One can imagine that the cumulative effect of this error when exploring new environments may cause the animal's internal sense orientation to diverge from its true orientation. This account of misorientation is something I will return to in Chapter 10.

Do head direction cells guide spatial behaviour?

In this section I'll describe results from experiments that have tried to correlate the behaviour of HD cells with the spatial behaviour of the rat (cf. O'Keefe and Speakman 1987). Although it might seem obvious that the robust firing of HD cells guides navigation, it is not clear that this is true—at least in all situations.

The first evidence of a relationship between HD cell activity and spatial behaviour was provided by Mizumori and Williams (1993). They found that HD cells in the lateral dorsal thalamus recorded in two rats became more sharply tuned as the rats learned a radial arm maze task. This might be a bit surprising because one wouldn't expect the basic properties of HD cells—the range of direction over which they fire—to depend on how well a rat performs a given task. However, one possibility is that, early in training, the rats occasionally mistook one arm of the maze for the other. If firing occurred in the maze arms aligned with a cell's preferred firing direction, but also, on occasion, in other arms that the rats mistook for the former arms, the cell may appear to be firing in a less directional way. With experience on the maze, the rat may have seldom mistook one arm for another, and thus the directional firing represents just the cell's true directional range.

A direct attempt to correlate HD cells and behaviour was a study that I conducted in the lab of Jeffrey Taube (Dudchenko and Taube 1997). We recorded HD cells in the anterior thalamus or postsubiculum while the rat found a single baited arm on an eight arm radial maze. The maze was curtained off from the rest of the room with a set of black curtains, which together formed a circular environment in which the maze was centred. A white curtain occupying approximately 48° of the enclosure's circumference provided a landmark that the rat could use as a directional reference. We recorded from HD cells as the rat performed a series of trials on the maze, then removed the rat from the environment, moved the curtain by 90° or 180°, and then returned the rat to the maze for another series of trials. If the rat uses the white curtain as a reference for finding the reinforced maze arm, then following the movement of the curtain it should choose a maze arm that maintains the same spatial relationship with the curtain. Thus, if the curtain was moved by 180°, the rat should choose the arm 180° away from the initially correct arm.

An example of the results we obtained is shown in Fig. 8.10. In this example, the cue curtain was initially positioned by maze arm 2, and the rat found reinforcement at the end of arm 1. The rat chose arm 1 on six consecutive trials. The rat was then removed from the maze, and the curtain was shifted by 180°. When the rat was returned to the maze it chose arm 5 more often than any other arm. This arm was 180° away from arm 1, so the cue curtain appeared to

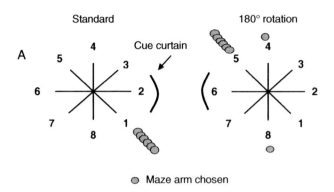

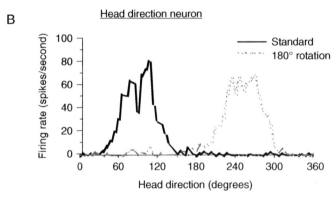

Fig. 8.10 A) Rats were trained to select the single rewarded arm on a radial arm maze, and in this example the rat reliably chose maze arm 1 (grey dots = choices). Next the cue curtain in the arena was rotated, in the absence of the animal, by 180°. On the animal's return to the maze, it reliably chose maze arm 5, the maze arm 180° away from its initial choices. Thus, the cue curtain exhibited stimulus control over the rat's maze arm choices. B) A head direction cell recording during these trials similarly showed a 180° shift in its preferred firing direction following rotation of the cue curtain. Thus, the rat's spatial behaviour and the behaviour of its head direction cells were correlated.

Reproduced from: Dudchenko and Taube (1997) Correlation between head-direction single unit activity and spatial behavior on a radial arm maze. *Behavioral Neuroscience*, **111**(1): 3–19. Published by the American Psychological Association, and reprinted with permission.

exert stimulus control over the rat's choices. In Fig. 8.10b, the firing direction of an HD cell recorded during these trials is shown. With the curtain in the standard position, the HD cell fired between 60 and 120°. Following the movement of the curtain, the firing direction of the cell changed by about 180°.

Thus, there was a correlation between the change in the rat's behaviour and the change in the firing direction of its HD cells following displacement of the cue curtain.

An important paper by Golob *et al.* (2001) showed, however, that this correlation does not extend to all situations. In one experiment, rats were trained to find reward in one corner of a square environment. Each of the four corners contained an opaque cup, but only one of the cups contained reward. A cue card was attached to one wall of the square and different corners were correct for different rats—although for each rat, the same corner was always correct.

Golob *et al.* recorded HD cells as the rats performed this task. In one manipulation, after recording in the square environment, the rats were placed in a rectangular environment. This environment was the same colour as the square and also contained a cue card (at one of the short ends) and a cup in each corner. In the rectangle, the rewarded corner was in the same position relative to the cue card. The question the authors asked was: would the rats generalize from the square to the rectangle, and choose the correct corner right away?

What they observed was that the rats did choose the same corner, relative to the cue card, in both environments. On the first trials in the rectangle the rats chose the correct corner on 75% of the trials. The striking observation, however, was the mismatch between the animals' behaviour and the behaviour of their HD cells. In 92% of the sessions the firing direction of the HD cells changed between the rectangle and the square. So, although the behaviour was largely the same between the two environments, the HD cells fired in quite different directions. Put another way, one couldn't predict which corner of the rectangle the rat was going to select based on its HD cells.

In a second experiment in this study, Golob *et al.* tried to find out whether the rats used the cue card, the apparatus walls and floor, or their internal sense of orientation to identify the corner of the environment that was consistently rewarded. They found that the rats could use an orientation based on information outside the square environment to find the correct corner. Indeed, when the rats were rotated slowly in a container outside the square, their performance was significantly impaired. This suggests that the animal's orientation outside the enclosure, perhaps dictated by HD cells, guides behaviour inside the enclosure (see also Gallistel 1990). This is consistent with the results of Jeffery *et al.* (1997), who found that slow rotation of the rat outside a rectangular recording chamber caused a corresponding rotation of their place fields within the chamber.

A third experiment in the Golob *et al.* study reinforced the results from the first experiment. In a rectangle, rats performed a match-to-sample task with the correct (reinforced) corner of the rectangle being the same on the sample and test phases of the trial. The essential result was that, in the test phase of the trial, the corner of the rectangle chosen by the rat could not be predicted on the basis of its HD cells. As an aside, in this last experiment the rats often chose both the correct corner of the rectangle and its rotational equivalent. This supports the earlier findings of a geometric module (Chapter 3).

The take-home message of the Golob *et al.* experiments is that changes in HD cell firing directions were not accompanied by changes in the rats' spatial behaviour. This contrasts with the correlation between the two observed in the Dudchenko and Taube study described earlier. What's the difference? My take on this is that there is a hierarchy of cues that the HD cell system is hard-wired to use. In an ambiguous environment like a cylinder, the cells will use the only available cue in the environment, the polarizing cue card. However, if the environment has distinguishing geometric features—such as corners—then the HD direction cells tend to orient to these, even if a cue card is present. Spatial behaviour and HD cell firing directions are likely to be controlled by the same landmark if it's the only one available—as in the Dudchenko and Taube study. However, in situations where multiple cues for orientation are available (for example, a cue card and the shape of the environment), rats can learn to use one type of cue to guide their behaviour, while at the same time other cues exert stimulus control over the HD cell system.

Another attempt to relate HD cells to spatial behaviour was reported by Muir and Taube (2004). They tested rats on the Tolman sun-burst maze (see Chapter 2), recording HD cells in a training configuration of the maze, and then on the multi-alley sun-burst configuration. Again, the idea behind the maze is that in running the training configuration repeatedly rats learn the direction of the reward, not just a sequence of responses. When given the opportunity, rats who know the direction of the reward should take a novel shortcut to it. For Muir and Taube, the assumption was that if HD cells guide behaviour, then any shift in firing direction between the training maze and the sun-burst maze would result in a corresponding shift in the direction of the maze arm selected on the sun-burst maze.

The results, however, didn't support the assumption: the rats' choices on the sun-burst maze were variable whereas the firing directions of their HD cells were constant. As the start boxes at the beginning of both the training and sun-burst mazes were identical, it is likely that the HD cells oriented to these on each maze. The variable performance on the sun-burst maze suggests that the rats either didn't have a strong idea of where the reinforcement was, or that they had a competing motivation to explore alternative arms. Either way, it's clear that the HD cells didn't drive the rats' choices on the sun-burst maze, and it's likely that some aspect of the maze's shape anchors the firing direction of the HD cells.

Head direction cells and homing behaviour

A way around this difficulty is to manipulate the HD cell system and look for corresponding changes in behaviour. Before describing efforts that Dr Matthijs van der Meer and I made in this regard, I will briefly describe two related studies that examined homing behaviour and the HD cell system.

Frohardt *et al.* (2002) recorded HD cells from the anterior dorsal thalamus in a task where the rats had to gather food from the centre of a circular platform, and then return to a home site on the periphery of the platform. The platform was curtained off from the remainder of the room, and a white cue curtain (occupying 30° of the surrounding black curtains) served as a landmark for the recording environment. At the edge of the platform there were eight evenly spaced doorways, only one of which led to the home box. The remaining doors were closed. The rat's task was to leave the home box, retrieve food from the centre of the platform, and then return to the home box via the correct doorway. The authors tested rats in darkness and following removal of the cue curtain, and the rats made few errors under these circumstances. When there were errors, they weren't accompanied by shifts in HD firing directions. Frohardt *et al.* also moved the home box to a different doorway (90° or 180° away from its previous initial position), and found that this caused a corresponding shift in the HD cell firing direction. In some instances, however, the shift in firing direction was less than the shift in the home box location. On these occasions, the rat made initial errors (doorway choices) that corresponded to the HD cell shifts. However, when the rats began to choose the correct doorway, the HD cells still fired in the same direction. So, the results provide a hint of a correspondence between HD cell orientation and homing behaviour, but also show that behaviour can vary when the HD cell firing directions are stable.

Additional evidence for a role of the HD cell system in homing behaviour is found in a lesion study by Frohard *et al.* (2006). They trained animals on the task described earlier, and found that removal of the DTN impaired the rats' ability to return to their home box. (In a later study, Bassett *et al.* (2007) showed that DTN lesions appear to abolish HD cell firing in the anterior thalamus. This, presumably, disrupts the entire HD cell circuit.) In the Frohard *et al.* study, DTN-lesioned animals mistakenly selected doorways all around the platform periphery. Removal of the anterior dorsal thalamus (ADN) in a different group of rats also impaired performance, although in this case the mistakes made were typically to doorways adjacent to the correct doorway. One caveat to these results is that the DTN and ADN impairments were observed both when animals were blindfolded and when they weren't. When blindfolded, the rats presumably relied on path integration to keep track of the direction of their home box. When not blindfolded, rats presumably used the cue curtain to identify the home box location. So, two issues emerging from this work are:

(1) why the DTN and ADN lesions didn't produce comparable impairments (given that they both contain HD cells and may be sequential relays in the HD circuit); and

(2) the nature of the impairments observed.

Using a somewhat different approach, Dr Matthijs van der Meer, Dr Emma Wood, and I attempted to predict the rats' homing behaviour by the behaviour of their HD cells. We used a homing task where the rat left a nest box at one of eight locations around the periphery of a large, circular table. The rat's task was to go to the centre of the table, fetch a food reward, and return with it to the home box. As in the Frohardt *et al.* studies, if the reward is large enough, rats tend to return to their home boxes to consume it (Whishaw and Dringenberg 1991). In our study, however, we attempted to manipulate the rat's sense of direction while the animal was in the centre of the maze. While the rat fetched its reward there, a large tube would emerge from the floor and restrict the rat to the maze centre. The centre floor rested on a rotation mechanism that allowed it to be rotated, mechanically, very slowly. We could thus rotate the animal by a given amount before the containing tube was lowered and the rat was free to return to the location it believed its home box to be in. If HD cells guide homing behaviour in this task, then changing the firing direction of the HD cells (by slow rotation of the rat in the maze centre) should cause a corresponding change in the rat's homing behaviour.

Fooling the rat's sense of direction proved to be surprisingly difficult. In earlier attempts (Dudchenko and Bruce 2005), rats were able to maintain their homing despite a great deal of effort to change their directional orientation. Nonetheless, it can be done, and the example shown in Fig. 8.11 is of an HD cell that changed its firing direction at the same time that the rat changed its homing direction (van der Meer *et al.* 2010). This result, though preliminary (and, of course, correlational), suggests that the HD cell system may guide directional homing in the rodent. As such, it may indicate that the HD cell system is particularly relevant for naturalistic navigation tasks, such as returning to a home site after a foraging episode.

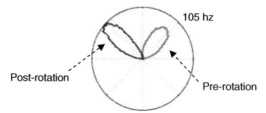

105 hz

Post-rotation

Pre-rotation

Fig. 8.11 van der Meer *et al.* (2010) found that on a circular homing platform, slow rotation of the animal while it retrieved a food morsel from the centre of the platform caused a corresponding rotation in the preferred firing direction of its head direction cells.

Reproduced from: van der Meer, Richmond, Braga, Wood, and Dudchenko (2010) Evidence for the use of an internal sense of direction in homing, *Behavioral Neuroscience*, **124:** 164–169. Published by the American Psychological Association, and reprinted with permission.

Unresolved questions

As our consideration of the HD cell system draws to a close I wish to raise a few questions about it. The first is a circuitry question: where in the brain does head direction and landmark information converge? That is, we know that landmarks exert stimulus control over the firing direction of HD cells, and we presume that the head direction signal itself is generated within the connections early in the HD cell circuit, but we don't know where these two meet. An obvious contender would be the hippocampus, but Golob and Taube (1997) showed that HD cells are still present in animals without a hippocampus and, remarkably, these cells readily form associations with landmarks in new environments. This result suggests that the rapid association between landmarks and the head direction signal must take place outside the hippocampus.

One possible location for the convergence site is the postsubiculum—the brain area in which HD cells were first described. Lesions of the postsubiculum severely disrupt the ability of landmarks to anchor the firing direction of HD cells in the anterior thalamus (Goodridge and Taube 1997). Interestingly, these lesions also disrupt the stimulus control of landmarks over the place fields of hippocampal place cells (Calton *et al.* 2003). So, HD cells and place cells are still present after removal of the postsubiculum, but their association with landmarks is broken. If the postsubiculum is critical for landmark learning, one would predict that inactivating it while the rat was exposed to new landmarks would prevent the rat's HD and place cells from becoming anchored to these landmarks.

A second, more general question is: do humans have HD and grid cells? Recent neuroimaging work has provided indirect evidence for grid cells in humans (Doeller *et al.* 2010). For HD cells, however, this evidence has yet to be obtained. HD cells have been recorded in the rhesus macaque monkey (Robertson *et al.* 1999), and, being a primate, their brains look much more like ours than the rat's. HD cells have also been recorded in mice (Khabbaz *et al.* 2000) and chinchillas (Muir and Taube 2002), so they are found in a variety of mammals, and may comprise a basic neural circuit of the mammalian brain. Finally, the brain areas in which HD cells are found are also found in humans, and damage to these brain regions produces difficulties in spatial cognition, as I will describe in the next chapter. So, there is good reason to expect that the HD neural system exists in humans.

Summary

The head direction cell system may be the neural substrate for our sense of direction. Unlike a magnetic compass, HD cell orientation is rapidly established relative to salient, distal landmarks. When exploring new environments or in the dark, directional orientation can be maintained, although drift may occur. This ability to maintain orientation independent of landmarks is likely based on integration of angular self-motion information.[4] Presumably, grid cells provide a substrate for linear path integration, although the two systems are likely to be interrelated.

I opened this chapter with the account of Joseph Paterson's misorientation following a tram journey. Based on the findings that I've described earlier, we can speculate on the nature of this misorientation. It's possible that, as Paterson was passively displaced on the tram, there was either drift in the activity of his head direction network, or a failure of the network to compensate for changes in the tram's direction. Upon leaving the tram and encountering familiar streets and landmarks, activity in his head direction system was reset to reflect a previously established association with these cues. Once re-established, his illusion of directional orientation disappeared.

---

[4] Kubie and Fenton (2009) provide a model in which mammalian navigation is based on representations of path vectors—the direction and distance of the goal relative to the individual. A path vector is based on the summation of path segments with head direction accumulator cells. These are hypothetical cells that are individually tuned to different head directions, but also increase their firing the further the animal travels in a cell's preferred direction.

Chapter 9

Alzheimer's disease, the parietal lobe, and topographical disorientation

So common is the association [between parietal cortex damage and spatial difficulties] that the clinical occurrence of marked disorder of spatial thought should, at the bedside, lead to the strong suspicion of a lesion in the hinder part of the brain, and more precisely of the territory linking the parietal, occipital and temporal lobe. (p. 355)
Macdonald Critchley (1953)

In the most literal sense, the space in which I roam, delimited by the physical boundaries within which I live my life, has grown very small. It's not just that I can no longer drive, save to those two or three places where the route is etched into memory; it's also because I have lost the ability to navigate in unfamiliar places, and some places that were once familiar seem like foreign terrain. I am often lost in space, unsure of where I am and how to get to where I need to go . . .
Grayboys and Zheutlin (2008)

A key piece of evidence that, in our brains, there exists a dedicated neural circuitry for wayfinding, is the observation that certain kinds of brain damage produces deficits in this ability. In this chapter I'll consider three neurological topics: Alzheimer's disease, parietal lobe damage, and topographical disorientation. For Alzheimer's disease, I will argue that problems with wayfinding and spatial cognition are not just a product of overall cognitive decline, but are a specific deficit in their own right. Moreover, the brain areas that undergo the earliest damage in this disease are the same as those which, in rodents, contain head direction and grid cells. For the parietal lobe, neurological evidence suggests that its dysfunction leads to a number of agnosias (lack of knowledge), including problems with wayfinding. These difficulties in turn comprise a portion of the syndrome known as topographical disorientation—an inability to find one's way when moving from one place to another.

The story of Alois Alzheimer

Alois Alzheimer was a German psychiatrist in the nineteenth century, who identified changes in the brain that produce the form of dementia that bears his name. Alzheimer was a student of Emil Kraepelin, one of the founders of psychiatry. Kraepelin provided one of the first systematic accounts of psychiatric disorders in his *Compendium of Psychiatry*. Ultimately, he argued, there were three main forms of psychiatric disorder: dementia-praecox, manic-depression, and paranoia. Although these may have overlapping symptoms, they were the product of distinct pathologies, which in turn had different causes (Bentall 2003). The problem with this, at the time revolutionary view, was that there was little evidence to support it (Shenk 2001).

It was in this context that Alzheimer encountered a patient by the name of Frau D. She presented with memory difficulties, feelings of jealousy towards her husband, and personality changes (Finger 1994). Frau D. also had difficulty finding her way about her house. At one point, her memory deteriorated to the point that she had difficulty recalling the spelling of her own name.

After Frau D.'s death, Dr Alzheimer examined her brain and found that it was considerably shrunken (atrophied). Under the microscope, two types of pathology were observed. In the first, bundles of fibres within neurons—neurofibrillary tangles—were evident. The second, found throughout the cortex, was sclerotic plaques. These are the two pathological hallmarks of Alzheimer's disease. We now know that plaques are made up of a protein called beta-amyloid, and the soluble form of this protein is seen by many to be the cause of Alzheimer's disease (for review see Masters and Beyreuther 2006). Alternatively, beta-amyloid may be involved be in the body's response to the disease (Soscia *et al.* 2010).

For Alzheimer and Kraepelin, the demonstration of clear pathological changes in the brain in a patient with dementia provided support for their view that psychosis had a physiological basis. Although there is still debate on whether this view holds for all forms of psychosis (see Bentall 2003), there is no argument about Alzheimer's disease: it is a degenerative brain disease whose early symptoms are memory impairments and difficulties in way finding.

Spatial difficulties in Alzheimer's disease

People with Alzheimer's disease (AD) often have difficulty recognizing places and finding their way in new locations. In home interviews with carers, 41% of Alzheimer's patients were described as having difficulty finding their way in their neighbourhoods, and 30% of AD patients were described as having difficulty finding their way within their homes (Ballard *et al.* 1991). In another study, 54% of the AD patients at a dementia clinic were described as having problems recognizing locations and finding their way, and for 25% of the patients this disorientation was one of the early symptoms of the disease (Pai and Jacobs 2004). Indeed, disorientation is often one of the first symptoms noticed by the family members of persons with AD (Taussig and Mack 1992). As we will consider later, almost all patients with Alzheimer's disease get lost when they are asked to reproduce a route that they've just experienced, whereas no young or middle-aged subjects do so, and only just over one-third of older adults do so (Monacelli *et al.* 2003).

Impairments in spatial cognition are evident in the classification of the severity of the disease. One way in which this is done is the Global Deterioration Scale. This is a descriptive scale developed by Reisberg *et al.* (1982) where the symptoms of primary degenerative dementia are classified at seven different levels of severity. The first three levels are considered 'pre-dementia', but even in these, difficulties with spatial cognition are evident. In the first level, there are no cognitive deficits, but in level 2, 'Age Associated Memory Impairment', patients report problems with memory, and this includes forgetting where one has placed objects. In level 3, 'Mild Cognitive Impairment', clear-cut cognitive deficits are observed, and one of the first of these is getting lost when travelling to a new location. Levels 4 to 7 are considered dementia stages, and in level 4, 'Mild Dementia', patients may still know where they are and what time it is, but they may have difficulties with travel. In level 5, 'Moderate Dementia', there are severe problems with memory and patients may frequently have difficulty recognizing where they are. In level 6, 'Moderate Severe Dementia', patients require assistance getting around, although they are sometimes able to travel to familiar locations. Generally, people at this stage are unaware of their immediate surroundings and also, for example, the time of year. In the final level, 'Severe Dementia', verbal abilities and the ability to walk are lost.

This progression illustrates not only the stark erosion of cognitive abilities in general, but also the decline in the ability to remember the location of objects and to wayfind. One example of this is found in a recent documentary entitled *The Forgetting: A Portrait of Alzheimer's* (2003). In it, a woman with the inherited form of Alzheimer's disease describes the experience of driving her car to pick up her children at school and being unable to remember the school's location. Such a difficulty suggests that even navigation in familiar environments can be compromised in AD.

Studies with Alzheimer's disease patients

A number of studies have shown that losing one's way is a clear difficulty associated with Alzheimer's disease. For example, de Leon *et al.* (1984) interviewed hospital staff about the navigation abilities of 21 Alzheimer's disease patients. Staff members were asked whether a given patient got lost within the hospital, whether the patient needed help, independent of physical aid, to get from one place to another, whether there were times when the patient was unable to navigate on their own, and whether the patient responded to street and traffic signals when outside. If the answers to three or more of these questions were 'yes', the patient was considered to be a 'wanderer'—a patient with significant difficulties in navigation. The authors also tested the patients on a number of tasks that are sensitive to parietal cortex damage, and found that 'wanderers' were significantly worse on these tasks than those who weren't classified as having impairments in navigation. This result, the authors suggest, may indicate that wandering in Alzheimer's disease patients is indicative of a parietal lobe-impaired subgroup.

In a subsequent study, Henderson *et al.* (1989) interviewed caregivers about the spatial abilities of 28 patients with probable Alzheimer's disease. Thirty-nine percent of these patients displayed symptoms of spatial disorientation (wandering, getting lost indoors, getting lost in familiar outdoor locations, and being unable to recognize familiar environments) three or more times a week. Part of this impairment could be predicted based on deficits in memory and difficulties with drawing or copying clocks or models of houses. These drawing difficulties, according to the authors, again suggest impaired posterior parietal lobe function.

In another study AD patients were impaired at learning the spatial layout of a new environment. Liu *et al.* (1991) tested 15 patients with probable Alzheimer's disease and 15 control subjects on a variety of perceptual tasks, as well as on their knowledge of the spatial layout of their home, and their ability to learn the layout of a new location (a series of five rooms within the testing building). The AD patients were either of stage 3 (mild cognitive impairment) or 4 (mild dementia) on the Global Deterioration Scale. AD patients were able to lead the experimenter through their homes, and thus showed intact spatial orientation within a highly familiar environment. However, when asked to navigate within an environment that they'd only experienced three times (having been led through by the experimenter), they were significantly worse than control subjects (who had no difficulty with this). Thus, AD patients at this stage of the disease exhibited considerable difficulty in learning the layout of new locations.

Passini *et al.* (2000) approached the spatial difficulties of AD patients from the perspective of nursing home design. The authors sought information on how well patients with advanced AD were able to find their way to specific rooms within a Canadian nursing home. From interviews with the staff of the home, it was evident that new AD patients had difficulty learning the layout of the home:

> New patients seem to have more difficulties getting around. Problems are evident when having to find their rooms and when having to distinguish one wing of the layout from the other. They may simply walk to the end of the corridor and may have to be redirected by staff. Learning seems to be slow and the adaptation to the new setting may take months. (p. 694)

Patients also exhibited distress when disoriented within the home:

> When lost, patients exhibit a variety of behaviors expressing anxiety, confusion, and even panic. Some will resort to mutism whereas others will talk non-stop. Some will walk excessively, incapable of saying that they are lost. It appears that these wayfinding difficulties vary within a typical day. They seem to be accentuated in the late afternoon ('sundowning'). Aimless wandering also increases during this period. (p. 694)

In assessing the AD patients' way finding abilities, Passini *et al.* found that four of the six patients tested had problems finding their own bedrooms. On a floor with more advanced cases, more than two-thirds of the patients had problems recognizing the doors to their rooms. Other tasks were better preserved: four of the six patients were able to go from their room to the living room independently, and an additional patient was able to do so with some help from the experimenter. The authors conclude that patients with AD are impaired in cognitive mapping and planning complex routes. Their recommendations include increasing the distinctiveness of individual rooms, increasing the architectural richness of the environment, and allowing visual access to different spaces so that reorientation can be easily established.

Although direct assessments of spatial learning and wayfinding reveal impairments in AD, the results of some paper and pencil type spatial tasks can be more difficult to interpret. One such task is the 'Standardised Road-Map Test of Direction Sense', or the Money test, developed by Money *et al.* (1976). In the test, the subject is presented with a schematic street map of a portion of a city with the route of an imaginary traveller shown as a dashed line.

The subject's task is to follow the route and at each intersection indicate which turn the traveller must take. Thus, the subject must not only have an intact sense of egocentric (left–right) space, but also be able to mentally rotate their perspective, as the route turns back towards itself. Rainville *et al.* (2002) found that AD patients were impaired on this task, even when the map was reoriented for the subject at each choice point. This suggests that AD patients had a difficulty in distinguishing left–right space, and thus were unable to accurately indicate which direction the traveller went. However, the authors also found that AD patients could tell their left from their right, with respect to themselves and to others. Although the authors argue that both a difficulty in mental rotation and an impairment in selective spatial attention may contribute to impaired performance of the Money test, one possibility is that processing 2D spatial representations (such as maps and photos)[1] may contribute to the impairments of AD patients.

In another experiment, Monacelli *et al.* (2003) tested 14 AD patients on their ability to recall a route through a lobby at a hospital. The patients were pushed in a wheelchair over a 1000 foot route that took about 4 minutes. After doing the route once, their memory for it was tested in several ways. First, they began the route again and were asked at 10 different points whether they should be wheeled left, right, or straight ahead to continue the original route. Patients who made one or more mistakes were classified as being 'lost'. Although some patients had seen the lobby before the experiment began, their results did not differ from those who had not.

After retracing the route, the patients were asked to recall as many objects or landmarks that they'd encountered on the route as they could in 1 minute. They were then seated at the beginning of the route and shown pictures of objects or landmarks that were found along the route. The patients' task was to point in the direction of the object or landmark pictured, thus showing their ability to remember where things were located. Patients were later asked to draw the route over which they'd been taken, and to name any objects or landmarks they found helpful on their second trip through the route. Their memory for views along the route was tested by having them identify pictures

---

[1] A student under my supervision, Ms. Jessica Lee, tested the recognition memory of residents at a local nursing home, several of whom suffered from moderately severe dementia. Ms. Lee took photographs of locations within the home—for example, doorways and stairs—and then subsequently asked residents whether they recognized these locations. Whereas the staff at the home recognized every photo, the residents did not recognize many. In a subsequent test, they were able to recognize objects (for example, a cup), but not photos of the same objects. This pattern of results, though based on a small number of residents, suggests difficulties in recognition of 2D representations (see Fig. 9.1).

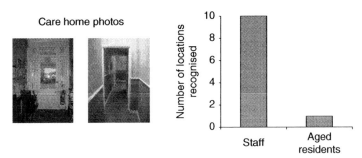

Fig. 9.1 Care home residents with dementia and their staff caretakers were tested on their ability to recognize photographs of the home. The staff members recognized all of the photographs from within the building. The residents of the home, however, recognized very few of these photographs.

that were taken from the route, as well as placing photographs of route locations on a drawn outline of the hospital lobby. Finally, patients were asked to view short video clips of segments of the route and to mark on the map where the segment began, and the direction in which the person recording the video was travelling. The scores from these different tests were added together for a single 'spatial orientation' measure.

The results were clear. Patients with Alzheimer's disease were significantly worse than young and middle-aged subjects on every test. Ninety-three percent of the AD patients were 'lost'—making one or more mistakes about the direction to take when redoing the route—whereas none of the young or middle-aged subjects made mistakes, and only 38% of the old-aged subjects did so. The subtests that were most strongly related to the overall spatial orientation measure were the tests assessing the patients' ability to place photographs or video clips of route scenes on a map, and to point in the direction of a pictured object or landmark from the starting point in the route. These navigation impairments in AD patients were replicated in a subsequent study (Kavcic *et al.* 2006).

A similar approach to these studies was used by deIpolyi *et al.* (2007). They took AD patients and patients with mild cognitive impairment (MCI) on an unfamiliar route through a hospital clinic. Patients were asked to pay attention to locations and landmarks along the route, because they would later be asked questions about them. The route included six turns, and when the patients were subsequently tested for their memory of the route, they had to indicate which direction to turn at each of these junctions. About 50% of the AD patients were described as getting 'lost on route', in that they made one or more mistakes in turning. When tested on the route in reverse, 75% of the AD patients were lost. In contrast, only 8% of the age-matched control subjects were lost on the route going in the forward direction, and none of the control subjects made errors when the route was done in reverse. The MCI patients showed impairments on this task as well, although their performance was better than the AD patients. Importantly, patients who got lost did not differ from patients who did not on other tests of memory, suggesting that the spatial difficulties were not just a general feature of impaired memory. Indeed, on other measures of spatial ability AD patients also showed deficiencies. They were worse than controls at maintaining their sense of direction while on the route. They were also impaired at drawing a map of the route, at correctly matching photographs of locations to locations on a map of the route, and at identifying the correct order of locations along the route in photographs. Structural MRI scans showed that patients who were lost on the route showed decreases in the size of their right posterior hippocampus and inferior parietal lobule. The larger the decrease in these brain regions, the greater the impairment in matching photographs of locations with map positions. These results, together with the DeLeon *et al.* findings described earlier, point to a contribution of the parietal lobe to the wayfinding difficulties found in AD patients.

Kalová *et al.* (2005) tested the spatial abilities of patients with the early symptoms of AD on tasks that resembled a Morris water maze. In a computer task, patients were asked to 'navigate', with the computer mouse, to a hidden goal location in a 2D circular arena. Patients were also tested in a real world version of this task where they had to walk to a hidden target location in a circular arena. On both tests, when the target location could only be identified by its spatial relationship to two spatial landmarks, AD patients were impaired. This finding, the authors suggest, reflects an impairment in the use of allocentric spatial information by patients with Alzheimer's disease. However, as the landmarks and the hidden location were in a different position (but still in register with one another) on every trial, it is also possible that a lack of viewpoint spatial flexibility contributes to these impairments (see Burgess *et al.* 2006, below). The patients of Kalová *et al.* were also impaired at remembering a sequence of locations, both in the 2D arena and in the real world arena.

Rosenbaum *et al.* (2005) tested the navigational and spatial memory abilities of an 80-year-old former Toronto taxi driver with AD, S.B. Brain scans revealed that S.B. had substantial hippocampus loss, as well as additional cortical and basal ganglia loss. S.B. was readily able to indicate the location of Toronto landmarks, judge the distances and directions between them, and describe alternate routes between pairs of landmarks if the most direct route was blocked. Thus, his topographical memory for a well-learned environment—he'd been a taxi driver for 30 years, and then a courier for 15 more—was still viable. However, when presented with photographs of Toronto landmarks, he was unable to distinguish true landmarks from unknown landmarks. Also, S.B. was unable to learn a new route when tested in a hospital building, and couldn't navigate accurately in the retirement home in which he'd been living for 6 months. Rosenbaum *et al.* concluded that S.B.'s pattern of spared and impaired abilities suggest a dissociation between the brain areas necessary for navigation and the areas necessary for recognition of landmarks. Strikingly, S.B.'s capacity for navigation with regard to an old cognitive map was intact, despite substantial hippocampus loss. Thus, according to the authors, way-finding difficulties in AD may not represent an inability to navigate per se, but rather an impairment in recognizing familiar landmarks and learning new environments. This may be an example of combined *landmark agnosia* and *anterograde disorientation*, conditions that I'll describe in more detail later in this chapter.

Although they did not specify the type of dementia that their subjects suffered from, Sheehan *et al.* (2006) found that, when accompanied on a 30 minute walk in a familiar location, 6 of 13 dementia sufferers reported problems in knowing where they were. Five of the thirteen dementia sufferers got lost on the walk, whereas none of the ten age-matched controls did so.

Difficulty with navigation in a familiar environment was also described in a case study of patient C.F., a 65-year-old writer with possible early-stage AD (Burgess *et al.* 2006). This patient showed intact verbal memory and recognition memory for famous London and world landmarks. However, despite knowing London well, she had begun to get lost when travelling there, and had difficulties knowing how to get from one location to another within the city. She also had difficulty describing the route from her house to a nearby restaurant that she had visited regularly over 10 years. In a virtual navigation task, C.F. was impaired at finding her way between locations in a previously explored virtual town. She also was impaired at remembering the location of objects in a virtual town square when the test view differed from the initial view. Burgess *et al.* suggest that these impairments reflect a difficulty in allocentric spatial memory, and may be due to pathology in the hippocampus, the perirhinal cortex, or retrosplenial cortex. An intriguing aspect of this impairment is that it occurred in the absence of impaired memory for non-spatial information.

A progression in spatial difficulties in a patient with probable AD was described by Grossi *et al.* (2007). Their patient, S.G., was a 56-year-old man who had problems navigating in unfamiliar environments. Initially, he performed normally on story recall tasks and had no difficulties in speaking.

S.G. did, however, have difficulties with visual–spatial tasks, and was impaired on the Corsi span task, as well as copying a complex figure. Six months after his first assessment, he reported getting lost while walking in familiar locations. In subsequent testing 6 months after this, S.G. was able to recognize pictures of locations in his hometown, Naples, but was unable to describe the spatial relationships between these locations. Eventually, S.G. was unable to find his way within his own home, and only succeeded in doing so by trial and error. Subsequent to this, the patient showed a general decline in memory and orientation, and difficulties with speech. The authors suggest that S.G.'s case may be an example of an AD variant where the neural systems underlying navigation are affected earlier and more prominently than those underlying other cognitive capacities.

A factor which may contribute to the spatial difficulties associated with AD is impaired visual perception, particularly the perception of visual flow. O'Brien *et al.* (2001), for example, tested the ability of AD patients to discriminate the apparent motion created by white dots moving on a large screen. Although the patients could discriminate between the 'flow' of dots moving either to the left or right on the screen, a subset were significantly impaired at discriminations where the dots moved outward or inwards. This radial flow contributes to the perception that one is moving in a specific direction, and thus a deficit in this perception may contribute to difficulties in keeping track of one's own movements. In a subsequent study, impairment in the perception of optic flow was correlated with impairment in a visual attention task, and it was suggested that AD patients might require a longer view of a visual stimulus pattern to successfully perceive it (Kavcic and Duffy 2003). Further, impaired perception of radial optic flow in AD patients and in older subjects predicted their performance on navigation tests, as did visual contrast sensitivity and an EEG response to the onset of radial optic flow (Kavcic *et al.* 2006). AD patients, as well as older subjects, had difficulties in perceiving their heading when viewing the passage of a series of objects—file cabinets—on a screen (Mapstone *et al.* 2006).

With static images, AD patients may also show perceptual loss. Lee *et al.* (2006b) found that AD patients were impaired at detecting differences in simultaneously presented views of virtual spatial scenes. Patients with semantic dementia, where perirhinal cortex damage is more prominent than in AD, were unimpaired at this task, but were impaired on a difficult face discrimination task.

Interim summary

Deficits in way finding are common in AD. AD sufferers have particular difficulty in learning the layout of new environments, and thus may be unable to find their way within a wing of a hospital or care home. Difficulties in other aspects of spatial cognition may or may not be as evident, and this variability, I suggest, may be due to the stage of the disease or variability in the brain regions affected. These difficulties include impaired recognition of familiar landmarks (impaired in patient S.B., but intact in patient C.F.), impaired judgement of routes, and possibly inflexible object-location memory. Additional work also suggests that AD patients, like individuals with hippocampus damage, are impaired at discriminating spatial scenes.

The diseased brain: is Alzheimer's a head direction cell disease?

In AD there is a progressive loss of synapses (the connections between neurons), neurons, and brain mass. At the same time, there is an accumulation of the neuropathologic hallmarks of the disease, amyloid plaques and neurofibrillary tangles, within the brain. However, post-mortem assessment of the brains of people who had suffered from AD has revealed a clear pattern of brain damage. Imaging studies in patients has shown that some of this damage occurs before the first obvious symptoms of the disease (e.g. Fox *et al.* 2001). A brief consideration of this pattern of brain damage reveals that many of the brain regions which are crucial for spatial cognition and wayfinding are particularly affected by this disease.

In a thorough study by Braak and Braak (1991) the brains of Alzheimer's patients were examined to see where in the brain amyloid deposits and neurofibrillary changes (neurofibrillary tangles and neuropil threads) are found. For amyloid, there was considerable variability in its distribution between individuals. Based on this, only three stages of amyloid depositions could be identified. In Stage A, low amounts of amyloid are observed in the cortex near the bottom of the brain, and no amyloid is found in the hippocampus. In Stage B, medium amounts of amyloid are found throughout the cortex, with the exception of primary sensory and motor cortices. The hippocampus in this stage exhibits only a mild deposition of amyloid. Finally, in Stage C, almost all areas of the cortex have dense amounts of amyloid.

More distinct staging of the progress of brain changes with AD was possible when the distribution of neurofibrillary changes were considered. Neurofibrillary tangles (NFTs) are an accumulation of a specific protein associated with microtubules (small conduits for transport within a neuron), and their presence within a neuron is indicative of a neuron that is dying. Neuropil threads are parts of neurons—often dendrites—that may come from neurons with NFTs. Using the distribution of these, together referred to as neurofibrillary changes, Braak and Braak identified six stages of AD:

> Stage 1: In stage 1 NFTs are evident in what the authors describe as the 'transentorhinal region'. This is the cortical region next to the entorhinal

cortex, and appears to correspond to the perirhinal cortex and the lateral portion of the parahippocampal gyrus (Van Hoesen *et al.* 2000). Occasional NFTs are also observed in the nucleus basalis (the origin of neurons that release acetylcholine in the cortex) and in the anterodorsal nucleus of the thalamus.

Stage 2: In this stage more NFTs are found in the transentorhinal region, and some are observed in the CA1 cell layer of the hippocampus and in the subiculum.

Stage 3: Neurofibrillary changes are observed in both transentorhinal region and entorhinal cortex in this stage. There is also some involvement in CA1, and small-to-moderate involvement of the anterodorsal thalamic nucleus. In this stage there is still little evidence of changes in the remainder of the cortex.

Stage 4: This stage is characterized by severe involvement of the transentorhinal region. There are numerous NFTs in CA1 cell layer of the hippocampus, and the anterodorsal thalamic nucleus is 'densely filled' with neurofibrillary changes.

Stage 5: In this stage nearly all of the hippocampal formation exhibits neurofibrillary changes. There is severe involvement in cortical association areas, and even in cases with less severe cortical changes, damage to the retrosplenial region and the portions of the temporal and occipital lobes is observed. In this stage, the anterodorsal thalamic nucleus shows a substantial loss of neurons.

Stage 6: In this stage there is a substantial loss of neurons in the entorhinal cortex. The hippocampal formation is 'infested' with NFTs, and the thalamic damage extends to the antero-ventral and reticular nucleus. All cortical association areas show severe pathology.

This description of the progression of brain damage is consistent with other descriptions of the course of AD. For example, Fox *et al.* (2001) did repeated MRI brain scans of people who were at a high risk of developing the inherited form of AD.[2] Fox *et al.* found that the brain volume of those who developed AD began decreasing up to 5 years before their diagnosis with this condition.

---

[2] The inherited form of the disease is associated with 'early onset' Alzheimer's, and occurs in people under the age of 65. It accounts for 10% or less of the total incidence of Alzheimer's; the cause of the remaining 90%, referred to as the sporadic form, is unknown. For the inherited form of Alzheimer's there is a 50% chance that an individual offspring will inherent the gene that causes the disease. Thus far, three genetic faults have been shown to cause the inherited form of the disease.

Damage was evident in the medial temporal lobe, inferolateral temporal lobe, parietal lobe, and posterior cingulate. The authors argue that the pattern of damage that they observe with MRI scans agrees with the patterns of neuronal damage seen by Braak and Braak, although the brain volume losses likely occur after (and presumably as a consequence of) these neuronal losses.

The specificity of the disease for the entorhinal cortex and the adjacent tranentorhinal region has also been observed in a study examining the number of neurons in the entorhinal cortex in AD. Gómez-Isla et al. (1996) found that in the brains of those with the mildest detectable symptoms of AD, there was already a 32% loss of entorhinal cortex neurons relative to the control subjects without the disease. In severe AD, the number of entorhinal cortex neurons in layer II (the neurons that project to the hippocampus) decreased by approximately 90%. Gómez-Isla et al. conclude that loss of neurons in entorhinal cortex layer II is not seen in normal aging, but is rather a hallmark of early and progressive brain damage in AD.

In addition to the entorhinal cortex, the retrosplenial cortex may be affected early in the course of AD. Nestor et al. (2003) examined the brain activity of people with mild cognitive impairment, as defined by clear difficulties on a set of memory tests. They used a scanning technique (a radioactively labelled glucose compound visualized by Positron Emission Tomography) that enabled them to see which brain areas were most active when the individuals were in a normal, resting state. Ten patients were scanned, and in all patients the retrosplenial cortex was less metabolically active when compared to the brains of healthy, age-matched control subjects. In 7 of the 10 subjects, the retrosplenial cortex was the brain region that differed most significantly from the control group. Nestor et al. suggest that the retrosplenial cortex is one of the earliest cortical areas where decreased metabolic activity is observed in AD.

The striking thing about these findings—damage early in AD to the entorhinal cortex, anterior dorsal thalamus, and retrosplenial cortex—is that each of these areas, in the rodent brain, contains head direction neurons. In addition, damage to the hippocampus (Stage 4 of Braak and Braak's description) is also prominent. If the encoding of heading direction is a fundamental function of the mammalian brain, we may hypothesize that deficits in wayfinding and navigation in AD are in part due to damage to the head direction cell circuit.

The parietal cortex and spatial cognition

In AD, as I've described, there is significant pathology in the brain regions that in rodents and non-human primates contain head direction neurons. In addition, there is evidence that patients who have a tendency to get lost also have parietal cortex atrophy, or symptoms of parietal dysfunction. In the second part of this chapter, I will consider the role of the parietal cortex in wayfinding.

An exhaustive review of the literature on the parietal cortex is beyond the scope of this book.[3] In its place, I will outline briefly the anatomy and physiology of the region, and then focus on a description of the spatial deficits associated with damage to this brain region. These neuropsychological findings show that parietal lobe damage causes difficulties in wayfinding, visual attention, and spatial perception.[4]

Overview of parietal lobe anatomy

The excellent summaries of Andersen (1987) and Stein (1991) provide a helpful introduction to the complexity of parietal lobe anatomy (Fig. 9.2). Briefly, the parietal lobe lies behind the frontal lobe, and the demarcation between the two is the central sulcus. The first gyrus of the parietal lobe, adjacent to the central sulcus, contains the primary somatosensory cortex. Herein is a representation of the body surface, with the most sensitive portions of the body having larger cortical receptive fields. Behind this lies the posterior

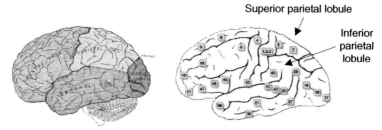

Fig. 9.2 *Left:* The four lobes of the brain *Right:* Brodman's areas of the cortex. (See also Plate 6.)

Source: Wikipedia commons (based on *Gray's Anatomy*).

---

[3] The interested reader is referred to *The parietal lobes*, edited by Siegel, Anderson, Freund, and Spencer (2003).

[4] I have focused on the role of the parietal lobe in spatial cognition and attention here, but doubtless it plays a role in many other capacities. As an example, a recent review by Cabeza *et al.* (2008) extended the parietal visual–spatial neglect syndrome to attention and memory functions. In attention, the dorsal parietal cortex is seen as being involved in effortful, goal driven, 'top-down' direction of attention. The ventral parietal cortex, in contrast, captures attention in response to behaviourally relevant or unexpected stimuli. Similarly, in memory, the dorsal parietal cortex is involved in directing attention during goal-directed retrieval efforts, whereas the ventral parietal cortex captures attention in a more automatic way in response to memories or memory cues.

parietal cortex. Broadly, this can be divided into a top portion and a bottom portion, referred to as superior parietal lobule and the inferior parietal lobule, respectively. The dividing line between the two is the intraparietal sulcus. On the cortical scheme of Brodman,[5] the superior parietal lobule in humans contains areas 5 and 7. The inferior parietal lobule contains areas 39 and 40 (see Fig. 9.2, right). In monkeys, the regions are defined slightly differently, although functionally the superior/inferior distinction appears to hold. The portion of the inferior parietal lobule (IPL) that lies towards the front of the brain (area PF) has neurons that respond to somatosensory stimuli. The region of the IPL that lies towards the back of the brain (area PG) contains neurons that are involved in visual saccades, in visual object motion, and in encoding the position of the eyes (Fig. 9.3). Within the intraparietal sulcus lies the lateral intraparietal area (LIP), a region that projects to brain areas involved in visual saccades. The primary thalamic input to the inferior parietal lobe is from the pulvinar nucleus, lesions to which produce attentional impairments. The general scheme of the parietal cortex is that it receives a variety of sensory and motivational inputs and links them to outputs that control the motor response of the organism.

Physiology

From a physiological standpoint, a great deal is known about the properties of neurons within the inferior parietal lobe. As reviewed by Andersen (1987, 1997), pioneering studies in the monkey by Vernon Mountcastle and his students have identified visual–sensory and visual–motor encoding in IPL neurons. For example, some IPL neurons fire specifically when the monkey, with its head in a fixed position, gazes in a particular direction. These may be

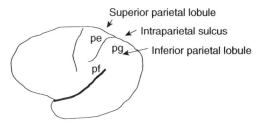

Fig. 9.3 A schematic of the regions of the parietal lobe in the monkey brain.

[5] Kobinian Brodman was a German researcher who, in 1909, proposed a division of the human cerebral cortex into 52 areas, based on the organization of the neurons within each area.

considered 'eye-position' cells. A subsequent study found the complement of this—parietal neurons that are tuned to a specific gaze direction with the eyes centreed in their orbits—but with the monkey's head facing a specific direction (Brotchie *et al.* 1995). Other cells are active when the monkey visually tracks a moving stimulus in a specific direction. Some IPL cells are active when the monkey makes purposeful visual saccades, suggesting a motor role, although many of these same cells are responsive to visual stimuli, suggesting that they also have a sensory role. Cells that are responsive to visual stimuli may also show attention effects—greater responsiveness to a stimulus within the cell's receptive field if it is the target of a saccade.

IPL cells in one subregion, area 7a, respond to a visual stimulus moving in a specific direction while the monkeys fixate at a specific point. Some of these cells are tuned to stimulus movement either towards or away from the fixation point. Cells in area 7a also show tuning to stimuli presented when the animal faces a specific direction, and as this area projects to the parahippocampal gyrus and presubiculum, they may contribute to the representations of location and direction described in previous chapters (Snyder *et al.* 1998).

Cells in the medial superior temporal area (MST, a portion of area PG), encode visual stimulus motion, rotation, change in size, and motion of the animal. As some of these cells compensate for eye movements during the presentation of optic-flow stimuli, they may provide a means for the animal to maintain a stable heading (Bradley *et al.* 1996). Indeed, the monkey's perception of its heading correlates with the activity of MST neurons, and these show similar responses to visual and vestibular displacement (Gu *et al.* 2008).

Together, studies looking at the properties of neurons in the monkey inferior parietal lobe provide evidence that this brain region is involved in processing visual information, although it is not simply a sensory or a motor command region. Rather, the inferior parietal lobe integrates retina and eye positions to define spatial locations relative to the animal's head, and, in the MST, to maintain a self-motion based heading during different forms of optic flow and vestibular inputs. As a population, IPL neurons may give rise to a body-centred representation of space (Brotchie *et al.* 1995).

In rodents, neurons recorded from the parietal lobe appear to encode motor–kinaesthetic portions of a trained route. For example, Nitz (2006) found that parietal cortex neurons encoded portions of a route, particularly turns, straight runs, and the start and end points. A given parietal cell often encoded more than one aspect of the route. When rats ran a route that included both a left and right turn, and then ran back along the same route, parietal cells encoded common aspects of the two routes, for example, the right turns. These neurons were not, however, akin to hippocampal place cells. Parietal cell 'fields' would increase in size when the size of the route was increased, whereas place cells maintained a similar place field size, or remapped.

Consequences of damage

From a wayfinding perspective, the clinical and neuropsychological studies of patients with parietal region dysfunction are of particular interest. Early case studies identified two conditions associated with damage to the parietal cortex, *Balint* and *Gerstmann* syndromes (Stein 1991). The first of these is named after Reszo Balint, and is characterized by an impaired visual guidance of movement, an inability to pay attention to more than one thing at a time, and a shift in attention towards the patient's right side. In its initial characterization, these symptoms were ascribed to bilateral parietal lobe damage. For Gerstmann syndrome, there is debate about whether it reflects a single clinical entity, but its symptoms include an inability to distinguish one's fingers (finger agnosia), an inability to write (dysgraphia) or manipulate numbers (dyscalculia), and left–right confusion. This syndrome is associated with damage to the left parietal lobe.

A classic account of this brain region is *The Parietal Lobes*, written by Dr Macdonald Critchley, a noted British neurologist. In this 1953 work, Critchley devotes a chapter to 'Disorders of Spatial Thought'. In it he states that patients with parietal disease, as he refers to it, are unable to visualize spatial scenes. They may be unable to describe the layout of their neighbourhood, or may even fail to recognize the outside or inside of buildings where they live or work. A second deficit is a lack of 'sense of orientation in space' or a 'homing instinct'. This shows up as an impairment in wayfinding and a tendency to get lost. Critchley notes that, for parietal lobe patients, 'the symptom of losing oneself often constitutes a conspicuous feature in the case-history' (p. 337). In one case, for example, a patient with bilateral parietal–occipital tumours was unable to visualize his house or his bedroom, and was disoriented in the town where he'd been living for 15 years. In another, a patient with a right parietal–occipital tumour had a tendency to walk past her house when attempting to go home. When in the hospital, this patient was frequently lost, and could only tell her bed apart from others if she left one of her possessions on it. Another patient with a right parietal–occipital tumour tended to get lost on the estate in which he lived, and was unable to find his way in his home when it was dark. This patient is also described as having forgotten his sense of direction.

Other symptoms of parietal lobe damage include what is referred to as *contralateral neglect*. This refers to an inattention to objects and space on the side of the body opposite to the brain damage. Typically, damage to the right parietal lobe results in neglect of stimuli on the patient's left. Critchley presents

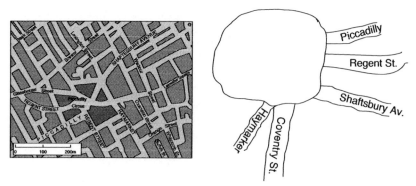

Fig. 9.4 An example of contralateral neglect in a patient with right parietal lobe damage (after Critchley 1953). The patient fails to represent streets converging in Piccadilly Circus from the left.

Source: Image of Piccadilly Circus from Wikipedia Commons.

several examples of the drawings made by such patients. They appear to be particularly challenged when asked to draw maps or the layout of buildings. For example, the drawing in Fig. 9.4 shows the attempt of a patient with right parietal damage to draw the layout of Piccadilly Circus, a well-known location for those living in London. As is evident in this figure, the streets entering at the left are not shown. Similar omission or distortions are seen when patients are asked to draw maps of a familiar country. Here the patient may omit the western part of the country, or mistakenly place cities towards the east. Patients with spatial neglect will not be aware that the drawings are incomplete. Remarkably, this neglect can even extend to one's own body, and patients may deny that a part of their body, for example their left arm, belongs to them. For example, a 36-year-old woman who suffered a left parietal wound in an air raid described her experience as follows 'All the right side feels as if it doesn't belong to me. When I move my right hand I don't feel I'm moving my hand myself, although it goes' (Brain 1941, p. 249). In this same work, Brain describes patients with right parietal–occipital damage who get lost within their homes because they ignore left hand turns or doorways.

A colourful example of contralateral neglect is given by Bisiach and Luzzatti (1978), from the University of Milan. They asked two stroke patients to describe the view from the Piazza del Duomo in Milan from different perspectives. For each patient, the stroke had produced damage to the right hemisphere, including portions of the temporal and parietal lobes. When imagining the first perspective, facing the cathedral in the middle of the Piazza, both patients only described buildings and shops found on the right of the square, and not on the left. However, when asked to imagine themselves on the steps of the cathedral facing the opposite direction the patients were able to describe the previously neglected buildings, but were unable to describe buildings and shops that were on the left. Thus, the patients knew the entire layout of the square, but because of their left-side neglect, could only access a portion of this memory based on their egocentric perspective.

In addition to contralateral neglect, Critchley describes other tasks that may be difficult for those with parietal lobe damage. They may have difficulty drawing, from memory, objects that have several features, for example a bicycle or a human profile. They may have difficulty completing a shape-matching task on a horizontal shape board, neglecting to add the shapes to the left-most portion of the board. Even a simple puzzle made from cutting a picture into quarters is a significant challenge for those with impaired spatial abilities. Reading a clock face can prove difficult. Studies in monkeys show that visual guidance of limb movement—for example, picking up a piece of food—can be impaired by parietal lobe lesions (for review see Glickstein 2003). Damage to the parietal lobe, in humans, is also associated with difficulties identifying objects by manipulating them in the hand ('active touch'), as well as problems with posture and hand force control (see Freund 2003).

A well-argued paper by McFie and Zangwill (1960) distinguished between the consequences of damage to the right and left parietal lobes. In the eight cases of left parietal damage they described, almost every patient was impaired on visual-constructive tasks such as copying drawings or block designs, or arranging matches to make specific shapes. Several patients also had difficulties telling their right from their left, and most showed a general intellectual decline. In contrast, patients with right parietal lobe lesions, described in earlier papers, showed a different pattern of impairments. Right parietal lobe patients did not have left–right difficulties. However, right parietal lobe patients often showed unilateral neglect, difficulties in dressing, and a loss of topographical abilities. This loss was rarely seen in left parietal lobe patients. Thus, patients with damage to the left parietal lobe often show *constructional apraxia*—difficulties in manipulating things and putting them together, but not because of difficulties in spatial perception. Patients with right parietal lobe damage may also show difficulties in putting things together, but this reflects a difficulty in understanding the spatial relationships between elements of a stimulus. Again, they also have a tendency to get lost and show other spatial impairments, and thus a cardinal feature of this brain damage may be a *spatial agnosia*.

In the next section I'll consider more recent neuropsychological findings on the spatial deficits resulting from damage to the parietal and other regions.

Before doing so, however, I wish to mention one circumstance where AD and parietal dysfunction may intersect. This is in a syndrome referred to as *posterior cortical atrophy* (Tang-Wai *et al.* 2004). As the name implies, the hallmark of this syndrome is damage to the parietal and/or occipital lobes. This can be due to a number of causes, with AD as the leading cause. Its symptoms include visual difficulties and Balint's syndrome, amongst others. In many cases topographical disorientation or environmental disorientation is observed. Interestingly, patients with this condition have a good awareness of their difficulties, and appear to have much less of a memory impairment compared with typical cases of AD (Tang-Wai *et al.* 2004; McMonagle *et al.* 2006).

Topographical disorientation

In the neurological and neuropsychological literature there are many case studies of patients who have difficulties finding their way in large-scale space as a result of brain injury. In what follows I describe examples of these within the useful framework provided by Aguirre and D'Esposito (1999). They argue that there are four types of topographical disorientation: *egocentric disorientation, heading disorientation, landmark agnosia,* and *anterograde disorientation.*[6]

Egocentric disorientation

Egocentric disorientation is a difficulty in locating objects relative to one's self, and is associated with damage to the parietal lobe. Patients with this type of disorientation may be able to recognize and point to visible landmarks, but are lost when their eyes are closed, and have difficulties in imagining or describing routes. A recent example of egocentric disorientation was provided by Wilson *et al.* (2005c). They described M.U., a 46-year-old man with bilateral damage to the occipito–parietal cortices. His verbal IQ was normal, but he was unable to read full words, and could not write. On the Corsi block test, a tabletop spatial working memory test where the patient watches the experimenter point to a series of blocks and then attempts to point to the same series of blocks themselves, M.U. was unable to copy even one block. With his eyes open, M.U. could point to different places in his apartment, for example, his bedroom. However, with his eyes closed, he was unable to do so. He had great difficulties with routes:

> ... he cannot describe routes, even those he travels regularly. He cannot tell someone how to get to the day centre he attended twice a week for several years (he was taken by a specially-adapted car), or to the college where he attends a special education class.

---

[6] A full history of topographic disorientation can be found in Barrash (1998).

In attempting to describe routes he provides little or no detail on distances and directions. (pp. 551–552)

However, when Wilson *et al.* tested M.U. for his recognition of landmarks in photos of Cambridge, England (where he has lived for a large portion of his life), he correctly identified every landmark tested. On a verbal test of knowledge for the relative distances between locations within Cambridge, M.U. was also unimpaired. Thus, M.U. has intact landmark recognition memory, and possesses some representation of the distances between landmarks.

When tested on how he would travel between locations, however, M.U. showed a severe impairment. He was presented with photos of two landmarks and asked to indicate which direction he would have to turn if he faced the first landmark and wished to go to the second. In a verbal test, MU was unable to describe the route from one landmark to the second. Thus, despite being able to recognize landmarks, he was unable to translate this information into the left and right turns that comprise a route.

A similar inability to use landmark information to guide one's route was found in a patient described by Cammalleri *et al.* (1996). Their patient, a 53-year-old town clerk who had lived in a village near Palermo, Italy, experienced a transient 'topographical amnesia'. The patient described his experience in the following way: 'At the end of my workday, I was returning home when suddenly, even though I could recognize the place in which I was walking and the various shops and cafes on the street, I could not continue on my way because I no longer knew which way to go, whether to go forward or backward, or to turn to the right or to the left . . .' (p. 322). This disorientation passed, but tests by Cammalleri *et al.* suggested that it was due to a blood vessel tumour between the cingulate and retrosplenial cortices.

Heading disorientation

The second class of topographical disorientation, heading disorientation, refers to a loss of the ability to use landmarks to determine one's direction. This, it may be speculated, can be a consequence of damage to the head direction cell system. One example of heading disorientation as a result a haemorrhage in the left retrosplenial cortex is as follows:

On the evening of December 11th, 2000, a 55-year-old right-handed man with a history of hypertension, who had been working as a taxicab driver in Kyoto City for 10 years, suddenly lost his knowledge of the route to his house while returning home after work. He could recognize buildings and the landscape and therefore understand where he was, but the landmarks that he recognized did not provoke directional information about any other places with respect to those landmarks. Consequently, he

> could not determine which direction to proceed to go home. He telephoned his wife
> and successfully returned home by her instructions. (Ino *et al.* 2007; p. 248)

This patient also had significant difficulties in remembering how to get to
the lavatory from his hospital room, was unable to draw the layout of his
house, and was unable to remember previously presented words if distracted.
Thus, there was not only a clear lack of a directional sense, but also disruption
in learning new routes and in recalling familiar spatial representations. The
damage that this man sustained may not have been restricted to the retrosplenial cortex, as there was some evidence of left parietal abnormalities as well.

The retrosplenial cortex has also been implicated in the three cases of heading disorientation described by Takahashi *et al.* (1997). The experience of
Patient 1, a 54-year-old man, was described as follows:

> On March 22, 1989, he suddenly lost his way home, where he was going on foot.
> The buildings in front of him were familiar to him, so he could recognise them right
> away. However, he did not know which direction his house was from there. . . On
> March 24, he set out to drive his car to the hospital. Although he knew the route from
> his house to the hospital, on that day he found it hard to determine in which direction
> the hospital lay, and consequently, he lost his way several times. (p. 465)

This patient's loss of directional sense appeared to be due to a cerebral
haemorrhage that damaged the right retrosplenial cortex and the inferior
precuneus.

Takahashi *et al.*'s second patient was a taxi driver in Kawasaki who lost his
'understanding' of the route to his destination while driving. He recognized his
location, but was unable to figure out which direction he needed to go. This
patient also suffered from a cerebral haemorrhage, which appeared to damage
the right retrosplenial cortex and the inferior precuneus. Similarly, the third
patient, a 61-year-old man, lost his sense of direction while driving and had the
misfortune of running into a parked car. When hospitalized, he was unable to
remember the locations of the wards, or to find his way back to his room from
the restrooms. His impairment also appeared to be due to a cerebral haemorrhage that affected the subcortical white matter from the right retrosplenial
cortex to the medial parietal lobe.

The distinction between heading disorientation and egocentric disorientation appears a bit blurred in the patients of Takahashi *et al.* Although they
show an impaired sense of direction, they also were impaired in describing
what routes they'd take from one location to another. Similarly, a 31-year-old
male patient described by Maeshima *et al.* (2001) headed in the wrong
direction when he left the hospital room, his office, or his home, after a left
retrosplenial haematoma. These impairments appear to fit also under the

heading of egocentric disorientation. Additionally, the patients of Takahashi *et al.* were impaired in learning the layout of the hospital interior where they stayed, a symptom of anterograde disorientation.

Another example of overlap between heading disorientation and egocentric disorientation is described by Whitty and Newcombe (1973). They review the case history of a patient described in the papers of Professor R.C. Oldfield. The 28-year-old patient developed a right occipito–parietal abscess (a fluid-filled swelling). This was drained and removed, but damage to the right hemisphere was apparently sustained. This damage resulted in a variety of difficulties in perception and spatial orientation. In particular, the patient didn't appear to have an overall sense of orientation, and could only navigate by memorizing specific details of the environment. He was described as getting 'no help from a sense of direction' (p. 472), and having to stop and recognize a feature of a landmark before continuing on his way. Ten years after his initial examination, the patient was able to cycle to work by relying on detailed cues encountered along the route. If these were obscured by darkness or fog he became lost. Likewise, on unfamiliar routes, he was unable to find his way. Thirty years after his initial examination the patient spent a week in a new hospital for tests and was unable to find his way on the ward. At night, he'd get lost going from his room to the bathroom and back.

Landmark agnosia

This form of topographical disorientation presents as an inability to recognize environments. Patients may retain the ability to draw maps and describe familiar environments, and so retain some spatial knowledge. They are also able to perceive their environments. However, recognition of the large-scale landmarks is disrupted. Aguirre and D'Esposito suggest that the medial portion of the occipital lobe, and possibly the parahippocampal gyrus, may be central to the recognition of landmarks. This fits well with the demonstrations of parahippocampal activation in navigation described in Chapter 7.

Martin Farrell (1996) reviewed several case studies of topographical disorientation that may fit the description of landmark agnosia. He distinguishes between the inability to recognize landmarks and the inability to recall their spatial location. This may map partially to Ungerleider and Mishkin's (1982) distinction between a ventral visual pathway that identifies objects, and a dorsal visual stream that identifies their location. Farrell describes several examples of patients who can't recognize places or landmarks, for example the rooms of their houses, but are nonetheless able to correctly draw maps. This suggests an impaired ability for landmark recognition, with an intact ability to recognize the spatial relationships between landmarks. However, the converse pattern of impairment—an impaired ability to specify spatial relationships and an intact ability to recognize landmarks—is rarer.[7] In these cases, according to Farrell, the ability to recognize landmarks is based on a 'piecemeal' recognition of features, or is restricted to very specific stimuli. On this account, the identity of landmarks and their spatial relations may not be handled separately in the brain, but may both be subserved by the ventral visual stream. The dorsal stream, in turn, may be involved in egocentric orientation. In particular, tasks that require the subject to mentally reorient themselves, such as the Money 'Road-Map' test, are impaired in some patients with damage to dorsal stream/parietal cortex.

Examples of landmark agnosia are also described by Landis *et al.* (1986). In their study, four patients are described who had either right hemisphere or bilateral damage to the medial parietal, occipital, or temporal–occipital lobes. One patient, an unemployed 54-year-old man, developed wayfinding problems in familiar environments:

> ... he began to have difficulty finding his way to and from the neighbourhood grocery store. On several occasions his sister found him walking up and down the street looking for their apartment. He stated that he could 'logically' figure out the correct building but could not recognize it... On more distant trips, he often ended up on the wrong side of town and had to call his sister to fetch him.(p. 133)

A second patient, a 58-year-old woman, became disoriented when travelling to work on a streetcar. She was unable to recognize her surroundings, although she was in a familiar location, and when she got off the streetcar she felt lost. She also found the apartment that she'd lived in for 20 years unfamiliar. These, and the remaining patients, had lost their ability to recognize previously familiar environments, although their general memory was intact (see also Hécaen *et al.* 1980). Landis *et al.* term this an 'environmental agnosia'.

Takahashi and Kawamura (2002) present additional examples of landmark agnosia, and suggest that brain area producing it is distinct from the area associated with prosopagnosia—the inability to recognize faces. The description of one of their cases is as follows:

> On September 12, 1986, a 69-year-old right-handed man was riding his bicycle to visit a place a few kilometres from his home. As he approached his destination, he suddenly

---

[7] One patient with this pattern of deficits was described by Hanley and Davies (1995). Their patient, Mr Smith, was able to find his way from the hospital to his home by using a route strategy based on specific landmarks, e.g. 'turn right at the graveyard'. In tests of his knowledge for spatial relationships, he was unable to correctly place locations, for example cutout shapes of different continents on a map, or the rooms within his house. He regularly was lost within his home, often making an incorrect turn at a stairway landing.

became unable to recognise where he was. Although he had visited the area several times before, and was familiar with the scenery around it to some extent, at the time of the incident, he felt that he had never seen the scenery before. . . During his [subsequent] stay in the hospital, he was frequently found to be lost and unable to remember where he was coming from or going to (for example, from the laboratory to his room). (p. 719)

Although this patient lost his recognition of an environment and was unable to recognize locations in the hospital, he was able to recognize pictures of his house and pictures of locations near his house. He was also able to draw maps of the region around his house. An MRI scan revealed that he had suffered damage to the right parahippocampus gyrus and the right fusiform gyrus.

Some of Takahashi and Kawamura's other patients, however, displayed more severe landmark agnosia. For example, Patient 3 would get lost in his house and claimed that the buildings near his house weren't familiar. This patient was able to tell the difference between buildings (even if he didn't recognize them), and was able to draw a map of his home neighbourhood. This patient's brain injury, as evidenced by MRI, was in the right parahippocampus, and the lingual and fusiform gyri, as well as the cuneus. This patient and the others with landmark agnosia had damage that extended slightly in front of the damage seen in prosopagnosics. Thus, landmark agnosics had damage to the parahippocampus, as well as portions of the lingual and fusifrom gyri. Patients with prosopagnosia alone appeared to have damage centred on the lingual and fusiform gyri, without parahippocampal involvement.

A patient with both prosopagnosia and landmark agnosia is described by Rainville et al. (2005). Their patient, F.G., was a 71-year-old former bank employee from the town of Orange, in France. As might be expected based on Takahashi and Kawamura's patients, F.G.'s brain damage includes atrophy of the right fusiform gyrus and the right parahippocampal cortex, as well as lesser damage to the hippocampus bilaterally. When presented with ten photos of landmarks from his hometown, F.G. was only able to identify three. He appeared to do so because the identified photos had distinguishable features. In comparison, age-matched control subjects correctly identified 10/10 landmarks from their hometown. However, F.G. was able to describe routes between locations in Orange, and was able to reproduce a 1.2 mile route through the town set by the experimenters. He did this by using street names and names visible on buildings (e.g. a café). When given the same test in an unfamiliar neighbourhood in Marseille, F.G. performed at a chance level. At 21 choice points along the route, he was as likely to go the incorrect way as the correct way. Thus, F.G. was able to navigate in a familiar environment, based on a strategy of recognizing street names, and some representation of the spatial relations between these locations.

Interestingly, when subsequently asked to point in the direction of the end of the route from different points along it, F.G. was as accurate as control subjects. In subsequent testing on a triangle completion task while blindfolded, F.G. again performed at a level comparable to that previously reported in unimpaired individuals. Thus, although F.G. could not recognize landmarks, he was able to maintain a sense of direction and distance, presumably by path integration. This suggests that the brain systems underlying landmark agnosia and heading disorientation may be separable.

Anterograde disorientation

The parahippocampus is also implicated in the learning of new spatial information, and the inability to do so has been referred to as anterograde disorientation. Here again the distinction between categories of topographical disorientation may not be absolute, as patients with landmark agnosia may also be unable to learn new landmarks. An example of such a combination of difficulties is the patient S.B., described earlier in the chapter. In pure anterograde disorientation, however, patients are able to recognize previously experienced locations, but can't learn new ones. Evidence in support of this impairment is found in the cases described by Habib and Sirigu (1987), Bohbot et al. (1998), and Ploner et al. (2000), summarized in Chapter 7.

In a larger-scale study, Barrash et al. (2000) tested 127 patients with brain injury on their ability to learn a route within a medical centre. Forty five of the patients had damage to 'target' brain areas thought to be critical for route learning, and they were compared to the 82 'control' patients, whose brain damage was elsewhere. The patients were led by the experimenter, individually, over a route that included main hallways and back hallways of the medical centre. After this the patient's task was to lead the experimenter back over the same route on three test trials, with the experimenter correcting any errors made by the patient. Eighty-two percent of the patients with damage to the target brain areas were impaired at learning the route, whereas only 33% of the control patients had difficulties. The brain regions most consistently associated with impaired route learning included the medial occipito–temporal region, the posterior parahippocampal gyrus, and the right hippocampus. Surprisingly, only about half of the patients with posterior parietal lobe damage were impaired on the task. A possible reason for this, the authors suggest, is that the parietal lobe may be more associated with learning spatial layouts as opposed to routes. Although this is not consistent with Aquirre and D'Esposito's view that parietal lobe damage produces egocentric disorientation, it's possible that route learning is impaired by damage either to a critical portion of the parietal region or to damage that extends beyond the parietal cortex into occipital regions.

Finally, a case worth noting as an example of anterograde disorientation is that of a 41-year-old sailboat skipper described by Turriziani *et al.* (2003). This patient had significant atrophy of the hippocampus, as well as moderate atrophy in the frontal, parietal, and portions of the temporal lobe. Although he had some general memory problems, his primary difficulty was in finding his way in unfamiliar environments. When tested, this patient could recognize previously presented words or pictures, but was significantly impaired at recalling the location on the page in which these appeared. He was also impaired at learning a tabletop maze task, although he could do so if the maze was equipped with visual cues. The patient had intact memory, however, for previously learned landmarks. Thus, he was able to identify pictures of famous buildings and the location of major European cities on a map, as well as the routes between locations within Rome (where he was tested). This patient thus appeared to have a particularly prominent difficulty in learning new spatial information, possibly as a consequence of his hippocampal damage.

Summary

In the current chapter I've considered the spatial difficulties associated with AD, the function of the parietal lobe, and examples of different types of topographical disorientation. For AD patients, learning the layout of new environments is often impaired, and difficulties in route finding, recognizing familiar landmarks, and using flexible object-location memory may also be observed. For patients with parietal lobe disruption, wayfinding and awareness of egocentrically defined space may be disrupted. This is consistent with the findings from neuronal recording studies in monkeys, where neurons within the parietal lobe have been shown to encode conjunctive representations of the eye and head position, and to potentially track heading during visual motion (in MST). For patients with topographical disorientation, deficits in egocentric-route knowledge, landmark recognition, a direction sense, and the ability to acquire new spatial knowledge may be observed.

We can link these neurological conditions to the basic research in rodents described in previous chapters. First, for AD, the pattern of initial pathology shows a striking overlap with the head direction cell circuit. This includes pathology to the entorhinal cortex, where both grid cells and head direction cells are found, and the anterior dorsal thalamus and retrosplenial cortex. Damage to these regions, together with the hippocampus, represents a devastation of the neural circuit known to represent head direction, path integration, and current location.

For the parietal lobe, it appears that it and the head direction—grid cell—place cell circuit work together to underlie wayfinding. Indeed, in rodents, lesions of either the entorhinal cortex or the parietal cortex impair homing (Parron and Save 2004; for review see Calton and Taube 2009). Whitlock *et al.* (2008) have argued that the former system provides an allocentric representation of space that is converted by the parietal lobe to an egocentrically based representation that can be used for movements in space. The authors note that it isn't entirely clear how the head direction—grid—place information gets to parietal regions, but there are several possibilities. The first is a direct projection from a portion of the medial entorhinal cortex to the posterior parietal cortex (PPC), although this projection is small. A second possibility is a projection from the medial entorhinal cortex to an intermediate area, which in turn projects to the PPC. Likely candidates for this intermediate, based on their connectivity, include the postrhinal, medial prefrontal, and retrosplenial cortices. The retrosplenial cortex appears to be a particularly interesting candidate, as it contains head direction cells, is active in virtual wayfinding tasks, and is associated with an impaired directional sense and topographical disorientation following its dysfunction. This fits well with the recent views of Calton and Taube (2009), who propose that head direction and place signals are forwarded to the PPC via the retrosplenial cortex, and that the PPC uses this and additional information to plan routes.

From a topographical disorientation perspective, the link between landmarks and the direction system may be central to heading disorientation. Specifically, in rodents, damage to the postsubiculum disrupts the ability of salient visual landmarks to anchor the firing direction of head direction cells and the place fields of place cells in the hippocampus. In the same way, in humans, the retrosplenial cortex, which is connected with the postsubiculum, is implicated in the loss of the ability to anchor the direction sense. It may be that one or both of these brain regions is the site at which an internal sense of direction, generated by the head direction cell system and possibly working with the grid cell system, converges with a representation of landmarks from the outside world to provide knowledge of which direction to travel based on familiar landmarks.

Although heading disorientation may rely on the head direction cell system, other forms of topographical disorientation may be the result of damage beyond the head direction circuit. Specifically, landmark agnosia appears to be the result of damage to the parahippocampal cortex. As illustrated by patient F.G., landmark agnosia can exist alongside an intact ability to keep track of one's direction. Thus, different aspects of wayfinding may require different neural circuits.

Finally, the idea that topographical disorientation can have different causes implies that we can get lost in different ways. First, when in a previously experienced environment, we must recognize it as such. Patients with land-mark agnosia are unable to do so, despite being able to perceive landmarks themselves. Next, if we recognize an environment, we must then be able to use the landmarks therein to calculate in which direction to head next. Perhaps closely related to this, we must translate this orientation into a route that we can use. Patients with heading disorientation appear unable to orient their sense of direction based on familiar landmarks, and patients with egocentric disorientation appear unable to orient themselves to decide in which egocentric direction to proceed.

Chapter 10

Why we get lost

The manner in which the sense of direction is sometimes suddenly disarranged in very old and feeble persons, and the feeling of strong distress which, as I know, has been experienced by persons when they have suddenly found out that they have been proceeding in a wholly unexpected and wrong direction, leads to the suspicion that some part of the brain is specialised for the function of direction.
Charles Darwin, 1873

The speculation that I will conclude this book with is that Charles Darwin was correct: parts of the mammalian brain, and even of the human brain, *are* specialized for maintaining spatial orientation. These underlie misorientation and disorientation, the two basic ways in which we lose our way.

Misorientation is the problem that William Naismith experienced at the top of the Scottish mountain in the mist (Chapter 1). It reflects a sense of direction that is no longer anchored to the external world. Under normal circumstances, this sense of direction, presumably provided by the head direction cell network, is something that we are not aware of. However, it is subject to error: in unfamiliar or ambiguous environments—fog, darkness, or unfamiliar woods—the orientation provided by this system may drift. Indirect evidence of this drift is based on the observation that, in the rodent, head direction cells show error when the rat walks into a new environment (Fig. 10.1). I propose that this error accumulates as an animal moves through environments that lack distinguishing landmarks, yielding a sense of direction that becomes 'turned around' (Fig. 10.2).

A second type of misorientation may occur when the head direction cell system fails to detect changes in our direction of movement. Humans veer when they attempt to walk in a straight line without vision. We may think that we are walking in a straight line, but there is small amount of error in the direction of each step. In the absence of large mismatches between our perceived

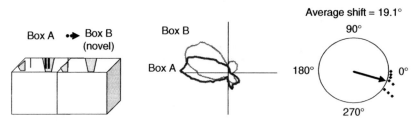

Fig. 10.1 When an animal walks into a new environment, the firing directions of its head direction cells are similar, but exhibit about 19° of error (Dudchenko and Zinyuk 2005).

heading and visual landmarks, the head direction cell network may not be alerted to these small changes in direction. Ultimately, we may walk in circles because our head direction network is insensitive to gradual changes in heading direction.

In familiar environments, the head direction, grid, and place cell systems can be re-set by salient landmarks. This re-setting is adaptive, as in most instances the landmarks we would choose to use as orientation cues—mountains, large buildings, etc.—don't change position. Thus, we rarely feel misoriented in familiar locations, and indeed exposure to familiar landmarks can provoke an unpleasant reorientation if our sense of direction has deviated from a previously established directional reference.

Misorientation, it may be speculated, may also entail the incorrect orientation of grid cell fields (at least for organisms possessing this type

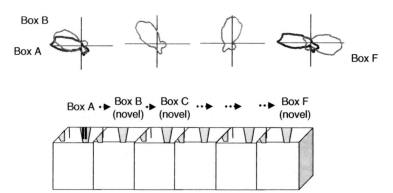

Fig. 10.2 If the small amount of error found when an animal moves into a single new environment is compounded as the animal enters multiple environments, the preferred firing directions of its head direction neurons may show increasing divergence from their initial orientation. In this way, the mammalian sense of direction may get 'turned around' in unfamiliar or ambiguous environments.

of neural representation). This mistaken orientation, presumably, would be due to head direction cell inputs to the grid cell network.

Disorientation is a breakdown in the cognitive map (Chapter 4). If, as some work indicates (Chapter 7), the place fields of place cells begin to disintegrate in dark, borderless environments, we may speculate that the grid cell network creating these fields also breaks down. This raises the interesting question of whether boundary cells also underlie grid cell fields.[1] With a complete lack of external reference, the likely way in which an organism represents the distances between objects and environmental borders—grid and border cell fields—may become unstable. Such instability would yield a profound inability for self-localization, possibly akin to the spatial disorientation that occurs when one is lost in a dark cave. Under these circumstances, it is possible that head direction cells, as part of a continuous neural network, retain their directional firing. Such a finding would suggest a neural dissociation between the representation of distance and direction.

Under normal circumstances, of course, our spatial representation systems keep us oriented. How such a process occurs in the human brain is not fully known. But we can offer an account based on what we know from other mammals. Rats, for example, may derive their initial orientation from their nest site. From this, they may make short excursions to and from the nest, within the range of their ability to integrate distance and direction changes from self-motion and vestibular feedback. Their internal system of orientation—particularly the head direction cell network—is primed to associate ongoing directional firing with stable, distal landmarks in the environment. These landmarks become sufficient to correct the system so that it is no longer driven solely by its internal connections. As the animal locomotes further from the nest, landmarks serve as anchoring points for the maintenance of orientation. When familiar landmarks are not available— for example, when a rat enters a portion of a maze that has not been visited previously—its capacity for path integration again allows a temporary continuity of orientation. This is quickly cemented by an association with any new landmarks encountered. In this way, the map grows.

After passive displacement—for example being picked up and carried to another environment by an experimenter—the continuity of orientation based on the integration of self-movement and vestibular cues may be interrupted.

---

[1] Ultimately, it's not entirely clear that the cognitive map is quite how it was initially imagined. Grid cells and place cells may merely encode distance from local boundaries and not the overall location within a contiguous space (Derdikman *et al.* 2009; Spiers *et al.* 2009).

Under these circumstances, the directional system may provide an incompletely updated orientation, or display a new orientation. In this other environment, however, the internal orientation landmark association process may begin again. Depending on the extent of the passive displacement, independent maps of different environments can develop. Such a process may be akin to our representation of regions that we travel to only by subway. We might have a good internal map of the above-ground region at a specific subway stop, but this may be independent of our representations of the areas above other stops because our link between these locations has only occurred following passive displacement.

Changes in how we represent space over the life-span

In childhood, our representations of space are restricted to our own perspectives. We can't imagine how the same scene looks to someone standing in a different location. To an extent, this lack of flexibility may make it difficult to infer the position of one's self relative to other landmarks. In terms of getting lost, of course, a lack of attention to landmarks and one's overall surroundings may compound the difficulty of maintaining orientation.

As we develop, our ways of representing the world become qualitatively different. We can envision locations independent of our position within them. We can link local views to form coherent wholes.

In aging, it is possible that the fidelity of our spatial systems degrades. Extrapolating from the results of place cell studies, our ability to reliably bring up the same cognitive map may be impaired. In addition, the flexibility of our maps in terms of incorporating new information may be diminished. From a path integration perspective, our ability to track our own movements and to integrate the distance and direction in which we have travelled may be less accurate than that of a young adult. Thus, the inputs to the head direction system may be less crisp, or the system itself may be functionally less able to respond accurately to given inputs. It is also possible that the ability for landmarks to become associated with our neural representations of space diminishes. Thus, the brain regions which bind the perception of a landmark or set of landmarks to a given directional reference may become somewhat less *bindy*. That is to say, the neural plasticity underlying landmark learning may decrease in the aged brain relative to that of the young adult.

In pathological states, and particularly in Alzheimer's disease, we know that there is damage to the brain regions which, in other mammals, contain head direction cells. This pathology may produce an inability to find one's way and, coupled with a disruption to the hippocampus and its inputs, a lack of familiarity with previously encountered locations.

Limitations

Much of this book, necessarily, has dwelt on results obtained from animals other than humans, and particularly on those obtained in rats. From a behavioural perspective, this work has yielded concepts such as the distinction between response and place learning, the cognitive map, the distinction between intramaze and extramaze landmarks, and homing by path integration. From a neuroscience perspective, experimental work in rats has elucidated the role of the hippocampus in spatial learning, and revealed the presence of place cells, head direction cells, grid cells, and border cells.

A clear difficulty with the assertion that the head direction cell system underlies *our* sense of direction is the lack of direct evidence for such a representation. No one has recorded a head direction or grid cell in a human. It's also clear that in humans, brain regions beyond those identified in the rodent as possessing spatially tuned neurons, for example the parahippoc- ampal gyrus, are active in the recognition of locations.

But the indirect evidence of a head direction system in humans is compelling. First, the human brain shares the plan of all vertebrates. In particular, the brain structures in which head direction neurons are found (dorsal tegmental nucleus, lateral mammillary nucleus, anterior dorsal thalamus, postsubiculum, entorhinal cortex, and retrosplenial cortex) are all identifiable in the human brain. Second, head direction neurons have been found in the postsubiculum of the rhesus monkey—and the primate brain is even more similar in structure to the human brain than the rodent. Finally, in the hippocampus, recordings in humans (and non-human primates) have revealed individual neurons that resemble place neurons in the rodent. As place neurons and head direction neurons share many properties, it's reason- able to think that the same types of inputs participate in their production. In this view, we get lost because our head direction cell network points us in the wrong direction.

References

Aadland, J., Beatty, W.W., and Maki, R.H. (1985) Spatial memory of children and adults assessed in the radial maze. *Developmental Psychobiology;* **18**: 163–172.

Abel, T., Nguyen, P.V., Barad, M., Deuel, T.A.S., Kandel, E.R., and Bourtchouladze, R. (1997) Genetic demonstration of a role for PKA in the late phase of LTP and in hippocampus-based long-term memory. *Cell;* **88**: 615–626.

Acredolo, L.P., Pick, H.L.J., and Olsen, M.G. (1975) Environmental differentiation and familiarity as determinants of children's memory for spatial location. *Developmental Psychology;* **11**: 495–501.

Addis, D.R., Wong, A.T., and Schacter, D.L. (2007) Remembering the past and imagining the future: common and distinct neural substrates during event construction and elaboration. *Neuropsychologia;* **45**: 1363–1377.

Aggleton, J.P., Hunt, P.R., and Rawlins, J.N. (1986) The effects of hippocampal lesions upon spatial and non-spatial tests of working memory. *Behavioural Brain Research;* **19**: 133–146.

Aggleton, J.P. and Brown, M.W. (1999) Episodic memory, amnesia, and the hippocampal–anterior thalamic axis. *Behavioral and Brain Sciences;* **22**(3): 425–444; discussion 444–489.

Aggleton, J.P., Vann, S.D., Oswald, C.J., and Good, M. (2000) Identifying cortical inputs to the rat hippocampus that subserve allocentric spatial processes: a simple problem with a complex answer. *Hippocampus;* **10**: 466–474.

Agnihotri, N.T., Hawkins, R.D., Kandel, E.R., and Kentros, C. (2004) The long-term stability of new hippocampal place fields requires new protein synthesis. *Proceedings of the National Academy of Sciences USA;* **101**: 3656–3661.

Agster, K.L., Fortin, N.J., and Eichenbaum, H. (2002) The hippocampus and disambiguation of overlapping sequences. *The Journal of Neuroscience;* **22**(13): 5760–5768.

Aguirre, G.K., Detre, J.A., Alsop, D.C., and D'Esposito, M. (1996) The parahippocampus subserves topographic learning in man. *Cerebral Cortex;* **6**: 823–829.

Aguirre, G.K. and D'Esposito, M. (1999) Topographical disorientation: a synthesis and taxonomy. *Brain;* **122**: 1613–1628.

Ainge, J.A., Heron-Maxwell, C., Theofilas, P., Wright, P., de Hoz, L., and Wood, E.R. (2006) The role of the hippocampus in object recognition in rats: examination of the influence of task parameters and lesion size. *Behavioral Brain Research;* **167**: 183–195.

Ainge, J.A., Tamosiunaite, M., Woergoetter, F., and Dudchenko, P.A. (2007a) Hippocampal CA1 place cells encode intended destination on a maze with multiple choice points. *The Journal of Neuroscience;* **27**: 9769–9779.

Ainge, J.A., van der Meer, M.A.A., Langston, R.F., and Wood, E.R. (2007b) Exploring the role of context-dependent hippocampal activity in spatial alternation behavior *Hippocampus;* **17**: 988–1002.

Allen, G.L., Kirasic, K.C., Dobson, S.H., Long, R.G., and Beck, S. (1996) Predicting environmental learning from spatial abilities: an indirect route. *Intelligence;* **22:** 327–355.

Allen, G.L. (1999) Spatial abilities, cognitive maps, and wayfinding. In: *Wayfinding Behaviour: Cognitive Mapping and Other Spatial Processes,* (ed. Golledge, R.N.), pp. 46–80. The Johns Hopkins University Press, Baltimore.

Alvarez, P., Zola-Morgan, S., and Squire, L.R. (1995) Damage limited to the Hippocampal region produces long-lasting memory impairment in monkeys. *Journal of Neuroscience;* **15:** 3796–3807.

Alyan, S. and McNaughton, B.L. (1999) Hippocampectomized rats are capable of homing by path integration. *Behavioral Neuroscience;* **113:** 19–31.

Amaral, D. and Lavenex, P. (2007) Hippocampal neuroanatomy. In: *The Hippocampus book,* (ed. Anderson, P., Morris, R., Amaral, D., Bliss, T., O'Keefe, J.), pp. 37–114. Oxford University Press, Inc., New York.

Andersen, R.A. (1987) Inferior parietal lobule function in spatial perception and visuomotor integration. In *Handbook for Physiology,* (ed. Plum, F. and Mountcastle, V.B.), pp. 483–518, Rockville, MD: American Physiological Society.

Andersen, R.A. (1997) Multimodal representation of space in the posterior parietal cortex and its use in planning movements. *Annual Reviews in Neuroscience;* **20:** 303–330.

Anderson, M.I. and Jeffery, K.J. (2003) Heterogeneous modulation of place cell firing changes in context. *The Journal of Neuroscience;* **23:** 8827–8835.

Bach, M.E., Barad, M., Son H, *et al.* (1999) Age-related defects in spatial memory are correlated with defects in the late phase of hippocampal long-term potentiation *in vitro* and are attenuated by drugs that enhance the cAMP signalling pathway. *Proceedings of the National Academy of Sciences of the United States of America;* **96:** 5280–5285.

Brain, W.R. (1941) Visual disorientation with special reference to lesions of the right cerebral hemisphere. *Brain;* **64:** 244–272.

Baker, R.R. (1980) Goal orientation by blindfolded humans after long-distance displacement: possible involvement of a magnetic sense. *Science;* **210:** 555–557.

Baker, R.R. (1987) Human navigation and magnetoreception: the Manchester experiments do replicate. *Animal Behavior;* **35:** 691–704.

Ballard, C.G., Mohan, R.N.C., Bannister, C., Handy, S., and Patel, A. (1991) Wandering in dementia sufferers. *International Journal of Geriatric Psychiatry;* **6:** 611–614.

Bangasser, D.A., Waxler, D.E., Santollo, J., and Shors, T.J. (2006) Trace conditioning and the hippocampus: the importance of contiguity. *The Journal of Neuroscience;* **26:** 8702–8706.

Bannerman, D.M., Deacon, R.M.J., Offen, S., Friswell, J., Grubb, M., and Rawlins, J.N.P. (2002) Double dissociation of function within the hippocampus: spatial memory and hypneophagia. *Behavioral Neuroscience;* **116:** 884–901.

Barnes, C.A. (1979) Memory deficits associated with senescence: a neurophysiological and behavioral study in the rat. *Journal of Comparative and Physiological Psychology;* **93:** 74–104.

Barnes, C.A., McNaughton, B.L., and O'Keefe, J. (1983) Loss of place specificity in hippocampal complex spike cells of senescent rat. *Neurobiology of Aging;* **4:** 113–119.

Barnes, C.A., Nadel, L., and Honig, W.K. (1980) Spatial memory deficit in senescent rats. *Canadian Journal of Psychology;* **34:** 29–39.

Barnes, C.A., Suster, M.S., Shen, J., and McNaughton, B.L. (1997) Multistability of cognitive maps in the hippocampus of old rats. *Nature;* **388:** 272–275.

Barr, M.L. and Kiernan, J.A. (1988) *The Human Nervous System: Anatomical Viewpoint,* 5th edition. Lippincott Publishing, New York.

Barrash, J. (1998) A historical review of topographical disorientation and its neuroanatomical correlates. *Journal of Clinical and Experimental Neuropsychology;* **20:** 807–827.

Barrash, J., Damasio, H., Adolphs, R., and Tranel, D. (2000) The neuroanatomical correlates of route learning impairment. *Neuropsychologia;* **38:** 820–836.

Barry, J.M. and Muller, R.U. (2006) Does blocking occur for stimulus control over place cells? Society for Neuroscience Abstract (574.19) Atlanta, GA.

Barry, C., Lever, C., Hayman, R., *et al.* (2006) The boundary vector cell model of place cell firing and spatial memory. *Reviews in the Neurosciences;* **17**(1–2): 71–79.

Barry, C., Hayman, R., Burgess, N., and Jeffery, K.J. (2007) Experience-dependent rescaling of entorhinal grids. *Nature Neuroscience;* **10:** 682–684.

Bast, T., Wilson, I.A., Witter, M.P., and Morris, R.G.M. (2009) From rapid place learning to behavioral performance: a key role for the intermediate hippocampus. *PLoS Biology;* 7(4): e1000089. doi:10.1371/journal.pbio.1000089.

Bassett, J.P. and Taube, J.S. (2001) Neural correlates for angular head velocity in the rat dorsal tegmental nucleus. *Journal of Neuroscience;* **21:** 5740–5751.

Bassett, J.P. and Taube, J.S. (2005) Head direction signal generation: ascending and descending information streams. In: *Head Direction Cells and the Neural Mechanism of Spatial Orientation,* (ed. Wiener, S.I., and Taube, J.S.), pp. 83–109. MIT, Cambridge, MA.

Bassett, J.P., Tullman, M.L., and Taube, J.S. (2007) Lesions of the tegmentomammillary circuit in the head direction system disrupt the head direction signal in the anterior thalamus. *The Journal of Neuroscience;* **27:** 7564–7577.

Battaglia, F.P., Sutherland, G.R., and McNaughton, B.L. (2004) Local sensory cues and place cell directionality: additional evidence of prospective coding in the hippocampus. *The Journal of Neuroscience;* **24:** 4541–4550.

Benhamou, S. and Poucet, B. (1998) Landmark use by navigating rats *(Rattus novergicus):* contrasting geometric and featural information. *Journal of Comparative Psychology;* **112:** 317–322.

Bentall, R.P. (2003) *Madness Explained: Psychosis and Human Nature.* Penguin Books Ltd., London.

Berlyne, D.E. (1950) Novelty and curiosity as determinants of exploratory behaviour. *British Journal of Psychology;* **41:** 68–80.

Berntson, G.G., Cacioppo, J.T., and Quigley, K.S. (1991) Autonomic determinism: the modes of autonomic control, the doctrine of autonomic space, and the laws of autonomic constraint. *Psychological Review;* **98:** 459–487.

Berntson, G.G., Cacioppo, J.T., Quigley, K.S., and Fabro, V.T. (1994) Autonomic space and psychophysiological response. *Psychophysiology;* **31**(1): 44–61.

Berthöz, A., Amorim, M-A., Glasauer, S., Grasso, R., Takei, Y., and Viaud-Delmon, I. (1999) Dissociation between distance and direction during locomoter navigation. In: *Wayfinding Behavior: Cognitive Mapping and Other Spatial Processes,* (ed. Golledge, R.G.), pp. 328–348. The Johns Hopkins University Press, Baltimore.

Beylin, A.V., Gandhi, C.C., Wood, G.E., Talk, A.C., Matzel, L.D., and Shors, T.J. (2001) The role of the hippocampus in trace conditioning: temporal discontinuity or task difficulty? *Neurobiology of Learning and Memory;* **76:** 447–461.

Biegler, R. and Morris, R.G. (1999) Blocking in the spatial domain with arrays of discrete landmarks. *Journal of Experimental Psychology: Animal Behavior Processes;* **25:** 334–351.

Binet, A. (1894) Reverse illusions of orientation. *The Psychological Review;* **1:** 337–350.

Bird, C.M., Vargha-Khadem, F., and Burgess, N. (2008) Impaired memory for scenes but not faces in developmental hippocampal amnesia: a case study. *Neuropsychologia;* **46:** 1050–1059.

Bisiach, E. and Luzzatti, C. (1978) Unilateral neglect of representational space. *Cortex;* **14:** 129–133.

Blair, H.T. and Sharp, P.E. (1995) Anticipatory head direction signals in anterior thalamus: evidence for a thalamocortical circuit that integrates angular head motion to compute head direction. *The Journal of Neuroscience;* **15:** 6260–6270.

Blair, H.T. and Sharp, P.E. (1996) Visual and vestibular influences on head-direction cells in the anterior thalamus of the rat. *Behavioral Neuroscience;* **110:** 643–660.

Blair, H.T., Cho, J., and Sharp, P.E. (1998) Role of the lateral mammillary nucleus in the rat head direction circuit: a combined single unit recording and lesion study. *Neuron;* **21:** 1387–1397.

Blair, H.T., Cho, J., and Sharp, P.E. (1999) The anterior thalamic head-direction signal is abolished by bilateral but not unilateral lesions of the lateral mammillary nucleus. *The Journal of Neuroscience;* **19:** 6673–6683.

Blair, H.T., Welday, A.C., and Zhang, K. (2007) Scale-invariant memory representations emerge from moiré interference between grid fields that produce theta oscillations: a computational model. *The Journal of Neuroscience;* **27:** 3211–3229.

Bliss, T., Collingridge, G., and Morris, R. (2007) Synaptic plasticity in the hippocampus. In: *The Hippocampus Book.* Oxford University Press, Oxford.

Blodgett, H.G. (1929) The effect of the introduction of reward upon maze performance of rats. *University of California Publications in Psychology;* **4**(8): 114–133.

Blodgett, H.G. and McCutchan, K. (1947) Place versus response learning in the simple T-maze. *Journal of Experimental Psychology;* **37:** 412–422.

Blum, K.I. and Abbott, L.F. (1996) A model of spatial map formation in the hippocampus of the rat. *Neural Computation;* **8**(1): 85–93.

Boccara, C.N., Sargolini, F., Hult-Thoresen, V.M., Witter, M.P., Moser, E.I., and Moser, M-B. (2008) Laminar analysis of grid cells in presubiculum and parasubiculum. *Society for Neuroscience Annual meeting,* 94.1, Washington, D.C.

Bohbot, V.D., Kalina, M., Stepankova, K., Spackova, N., Petrides, M., and Nadel, L. (1998) Spatial memory deficits in patients with lesions to the right hippocampus and to the right parahippocampal cortex. *Neuropsychologia;* **36:** 1217–1238.

Bohbot, V.D. and Corkin, S. (2007) Posterior parahippocampal place learning in H.M. *Hippocampus;* **17:** 863–872.

Böök, A. and Gärling, T. (1981) Maintenance of orientation during locomotion in unfamiliar environments. *Journal of Experimental Psychology: Human Perception and Performance;* **7:** 995–1006.

Bovet, J. (1994) Homing in humans: a different look. *Behavioural Processes;* **32:** 197–208.

Bower, M.R., Euston, D.R., and McNaughton, B.L. (2005) Sequential-context-dependent hippocampal activity is not necessary to learn sequences with repeated elements. *The Journal of Neuroscience;* **25:** 1313–1323.

Boyadjian, A., Marin, L., and Danion, F. (1999) Veering in human locomotion: the role of the effectors. *Neuroscience Letters;* **265:** 21–24.

Braak, H. and Braak, E. (2001) Neuropathological stageing of Alzheimer-related changes. *Acta Neuropathologica;* **82:** 239–259.

Bradley, D.C., Maxwell, M., Andersen, R.A., Banks, M.S., and Shenoy, K.V. (1996) Mechanisms of heading perception in primate visual cortex. *Science;* **273:** 1544–1547.

Breese, C.R., Hampson, R.E., and Deadwyler, S.A. (1989) Hippocampal place cells: stereotypy and plasticity. *Journal of Neuroscience;* **9:** 1097–1111.

Brotchie, P.R., Andersen, R.A., Snyder, L.H., and Goodman, S.J. (1995) Head position signals used by parietal neurons to encode locations of visual stimuli. *Nature;* **375:** 232–235.

Brun, V.H., Otnæss, M.K., Molden, S., *et al.* (2002) Place cells and place recognition maintained by direct entorhinal–hippocampal circuitry. *Science;* **296:** 2243–2246.

Brun, V.H., Leutgeb, S., Wu, H.Q., *et al.* (2008) Impaired spatial representation in CA1 after lesion of direct input from entorhinal cortex. *Neuron;* **57:** 290–302.

Buckley, M.J. and Gaffan, D. (1997) Impairment of visual object-discrimination learning after perirhinal cortex ablation. *Behavioral Neuroscience;* **111:** 467–475.

Buckley, M.J., Booth, M.C., Rolls, E.T., and Gaffan, D. (2001) Selective perceptual impairments after perirhinal cortex ablation. *The Journal of Neuroscience;* **21:** 9824–9836.

Buckley, M.J. and Gaffan, D. (2006) Perirhinal cortical contributions to object perception. *Trends in Cognitive Sciences;* **10:** 100–107.

Buresova, O. and Bures, J. (1982) Radial maze as a tool for assessing the effect of drugs on the working memory of rats. *Psychopharmacology;* **77:** 268–271.

Burgess, N., Maguire, E.A., and O'Keefe, J. (2002) The human hippocampus and spatial and episodic memory. *Neuron;* **35:** 625–641.

Burgess, N. (2006) Spatial memory: how egocentric and allocentric combine. *Trends in Cognitive Sciences;* **10:** 551–557.

Burgess, N., Trinkler, I., King, J., Kennedy, A., and Cipolotti, L. (2006) Impaired allocentric spatial memory underlying topographical disorientation. *Reviews in the Neurosciences;* **17:** 239–251.

Burgess, N., Barry, C., and O'Keefe, J. (2007) An oscillatory interference model of grid cell firing. *Hippocampus;* **17:** 801–812.

Burgess, N. (2008) Grid cells and theta as oscillatory interference: theory and predictions. *Hippocampus;* **18:** 1157–1174.

Burwell, R.D. (2000) The parahippocampal region: corticocortical connectivity. *Annals of the New York Academy of Sciences;* **911:** 25–42.

Butt, U.B. (2002) Response in Canadian *Geographic Survey* 'Lost in the woods'.http://www.canadiangeographic.ca/surveys/lost/comments.asp.

Buzáki, G. (2005) Theta rhythm of navigation: link between path integration and landmark navigation, episodic and semantic memory. *Hippocampus;* **15:** 827–840.

Buzáki, G. (2006) *Rhythms of the Brain.* Oxford University Press, Oxford.

Cabeza, R., Ciaramelli, E., Olson, I.R., and Moscovitch, M. (2008) The parietal cortex and episodic memory: an attentional account. *Nature Reviews Neuroscience;* **9:** 613–625.

Cahusac, P.M., Miyashita, Y., and Rolls, E.T. (1989) Responses of hippocampal formation neurons in the monkey related to delayed spatial response and object-place memory tasks. *Behavioural Brain Research;* **33:** 229–240.

Calton, J.L., Stackman, R.W., Goodridge, J.P., Archey, W.B., Dudchenko, P.A., and Taube, J.S. (2003) Hippocampal place cell instability after lesions of the head direction cell network. *The Journal of Neuroscience;* **23:** 9719–9731.

Calton, J.L., Turner, C.S., Cyrenne De-Laine, M., Lee, B.R., and Taube, J.S. (2008) Landmark control and updating of self-movement cues are largely maintained in head direction cells after lesions of the posterior parietal cortex. *Behavioral Neuroscience;* **122:** 827–840.

Calton, J.L. and Taube, J.S. (2009) Where am I and how will I get there from here? A role for posterior parietal cortex in the integration of spatial information and route planning. *Neurobiology of Learning and Memory;* **91:** 186–196.

Cammalleri, R., Gangitano, M., D'Amelio, M., Raieli, V., Raimondo, D., and Camarda, R. (1996) Transient topographical amnesia and cingulated cortex damage: a case report. *Neuropsychologia;* **34**(4): 321–326.

Campbell, R.N. (1999) *The Munroist's Companion.* Scottish Mountaineering Trust.

Cartwright, B.A. and Collett, T.S. (1983) Landmark learning in bees: experiments and models. *Journal of Comparative Physiology;* **151:** 521–543.

Carr, H.A. and Watson, J.B. (1908) Orientation in the white rat. *Journal of Comparative Neurology and Psychology;* **18:** 27–44.

Carr, H. (1917) Maze studies with the white rat. *Journal of Animal Behavior;* **7:** 259–306.

Chamizo, V.D., Manteiga, R.D., Rodrigo, T., and Mackintosh, N.J. (2006) Competition between landmarks in spatial learning: the role of proximity to the goal. *Behavioural Processes;* **71:** 59–65.

Chapuis, N. and Varlet, C. (1987) Shortcuts by dogs in natural surroundings. *Quarterly Journal of Experimental Psychology;* **35B:** 49–64.

Chen, L.L., Lin, L.H., Green, E.J., Barnes, C.A., and McNaughton, B.L. (1994) Head-direction cells in the rat posterior cortex. I. Anatomical distribution and behavioral modulation. *Experimental Brain Research;* **101:** 8–23.

Chen, J., Barnes, C.A., McNaughton, B.L., Skaggs, W.E., and Weaver, K.L. (1997) The effect of aging on experience-dependent plasticity of hippocampal place cells. *The Journal of Neuroscience;* **17:** 6769–6782.

Cheng, K. (1986) A purely geometric module in the rat's spatial representation. *Cognition;* **23:** 149–178.

Cheng, K. and Gallistel, C.R. (2005) Shape parameters explain data from spatial transformations: comment on Pearce *et al.* (2005) and Tommasi and Polli (2004) *Journal of Experimental Psychology: Animal Behavior Processes;* **31:** 254–259.

Cheng, K. and Newcombe, N.S. (2005) Is there a geometric module for spatial orientation? Squaring theory and evidence. *Psychonomic Bulletin and Review;* **12**(1): 1–23.

Cho, J. and Sharp, P.E. (2001) Head direction, place, and movement correlates for cells in the rat retrosplenial cortex. *Behavioral Neuroscience;* **115:** 3–25.

Chudasama, Y., Wright, K.S., and Murray, E.A. (2008) Hippocampal lesions in rhesus monkeys disrupt emotional responses by not reinforcer devaluation effects. *Biological Psychiatry;* **63:** 1084–1091.

Clark, R.E. and Squire, L.R. (1998) Classical conditioning and brain systems: the role of awareness. *Science;* **280:** 77–81.

Clark, R.E., Zola, S.M., and Squire, L.R. (2000) Impaired recognition memory in rats after damage to the hippocampus. *The Journal of Neuroscience;* **20:** 8853–8860.

Clark, R.E., Broadbent, N.J., and Squire, L.R. (2005a) Hippocampus and remote spatial memory in rats. *Hippocampus;* **15:** 260–272.

Clark, R.E., Broadbent, N.J., and Squire, L.R. (2005b) Impaired remote spatial memory after hippocampal lesions despite extensive training beginning early in life. *Hippocampus;* **15:** 340–346.

Clark, R.E., Broadbent, N.J., and Squire, L.R. (2007) The hippocampus and spatial memory: findings with a novel modification of the water maze. *The Journal of Neuroscience;* **27:** 6647–6654.

Clark, B.J., Sarma, A., and Taube, J.S. (2009) Head direction instability in the anterior dorsal thalamus after lesions of the interpeduncular nucleus. *The Journal of Neuroscience;* **29:** 493–507.

Clayton, N.S. (1998) Memory and the hippocampus in food-storing birds: a comparative approach. *Neuropharmacology;* **37:** 441–452.

Cohen, J.S. and LaRoche, J.P. (1973) Effect of a physical barrier on response preservation in hippocampal lesioned rats. *Physiology and Behavior;* **10:** 485–490.

Collett, T.S., Cartwright, B.A., and Smith, B.A. (1986) Landmark learning and visuo-spatial memories in gerbils. *Journal of Comparative Physiology A;* **158:** 835–851.

Corkin, S. (1965) Tactually-guided maze learning in man: effects of unilateral cortical excisions and bilateral hippocampal lesions. *Neuropsychologica;* **3:** 339–351.

Corkin, S. (1984) Lasting consequences of bilateral medial temporal lobectomy: clinical course and experimental findings in H.M. *Seminars in Neurology;* **4:** 249–259.

Corkin, S., Amaral, D.G., Gonzalez, R.G., Johnson, K.A., and Hyman, B.T. (1997) H.M.'s medial temporal lobe lesion: findings from magnetic resonance imaging. *The Journal of Neuroscience;* **17:** 3964–3979.

Corkin, S. (2002) What's new with the amnesic patient H.M.? *Nature Reviews Neuroscience;* **3:** 153–160.

Cornell, E.H. and Heth, C.D. (1983) Spatial cognition: gathering strategies used by preschool children. *Journal of Experimental Child Psychology;* **35:** 93–110.

Cornell, E.H., Heth, C.D., and Broda, L.S. (1989) Children's wayfinding: response to instructions to use environmental landmarks. *Developmental Psychology;* **25:** 755–764.

Cornell, E.H., Sorenson, A., and Mio, T. (2003) Human sense of direction and wayfinding. *Annals of the Association of American Geographers;* **93:** 399–425.

Cornell, E.H. and Heth, C.D. (2004) Memories of travel: dead reckoning within the cognitive map. In *Human Spatial Memory: Remembering Where* (ed. Allen, G.) Lawrence Erlbaum Associates, New Jersey.

Cousins, J.H., Siegel, A.W., Maxwell, S.E. (1983) Way finding and cognitive mapping in large-scale environments: a test of a developmental model. *Journal of Experimental Child Psychology;* **35:** 1–20.

Cressant, A., Muller, R.U., and Poucet, B. (1997) Failure of centrally placed objects to control the firing fields of hippocampal place cells. *The Journal of Neuroscience;* **17:** 2531–2542.

Cratty, B.J. (1965) *Perceptual Thresholds of Non-visual Locomotion (Part 1)* University of California, Los Angeles, CA.

Cratty, B.J. and Williams, H.G. (1966) *Perceptual Thresholds of Non-visual Locomotion, Part 2.* University of California, Los Angeles.

Critchley, M. (1953) *The Parietal Lobes.* Hafner Publishing Company, London.

Dashiell, J.F. (1930) Direction orientation in maze running by the white rat. *Comparative Psychology Monographs;* **7:** 1–72.

Darwin, C.R. (1873) Origin of certain instincts. *Nature;* **7:** 417–418.

Davidson, T.J., Kloosterman, F., and Wilson, M.A. (2009) Hippocampal replay of extended experience. *Neuron;* **63:** 497–507.

Day, H.D. and Goins, V.J. (1997) Veering in women: inconsistency of forward and backward progression. *Perceptual and Motor Skills;* **85:** 587–596.

Day, L.B., Weisend, M., Sutherland, R.J., and Schallert, T. (1999) The hippocampus is not necessary for a place response but may be necessary for pliancy. *Behavioral Neuroscience;* **113:** 914–924.

Dayawansa, S., Kobayashi, T., Hori, E., *et al.* (2006) Conjunctive effects of reward and behavioral episodes on hippocampal place-differential neurons of rats on a mobile treadmill. *Hippocampus;* **16:** 586–595.

de Araujo, I.E., Rolls, E.T., and Stringer, S.M. (2001) A view model which accounts for the spatial fields of hippocampal primate spatial view cells and rat place cells. *Hippocampus;* **11:** 699–706.

de Leon, M.J., Potegal, M., and Gurland, B. (1984) Wandering and parietal signs in senile dementia of Alzheimer's type. *Neuropsychobiology;* **11:** 155–157.

Deadwyler, S.A., Bunn, T., and Hampson, R.E. (1996) Hippocampal ensemble activity during spatial delayed-nonmatch-to-sample performance in rats. *Journal of Neuroscience;* **16:** 354–372.

DeLoache, J.S. and Brown, A.L. (1983) Very young children's memory for the location of objects in a large-scale environment. *Child Development;* **54:** 888–897.

deIpolyi, A.R., Rankin, K.P., Mucke, L., Miller, B.L., and Gorno-Tempini, M.L. (2007) Spatial cognition and the human navigation network in AD and MCI. *Neurology;* **69:** 986–997.

Dember, W.N. and Fowler, H. (1958) Spontaneous alternation behavior. *Psychological Bulletin;* **55:** 412–428.

Derdikman, D., Whitlock, J.R., Tsao, A., *et al.* (2009) Fragmentation of grid cell maps in a multicompartment environment. *Nature Neuroscience;* **12:** 1325–1332.

Dix, S.L. and Aggleton, J.P. (1999) Extending the spontaneous preference test of recognition: evidence of object-location and object-context recognition. *Behavioural Brain Research;* **99:** 191–200.

Doeller, C.F., Barry, C., and Burgess, N. (2010) Evidence for grid cells in a human memory network. *Nature;* **463:** 657–661.

Doeller, C.F. and Burgess, N. (2008) Distinct error-correcting and incidental learning of location relative to landmarks and boundaries. *Proceedings of the National Academy of Sciences;* **105:** 5909–5914.

Doeller, C.F., King, J.A., and Burgess, N. (2008) Parallel striatal and hippocampal systems for landmarks and boundaries in spatial memory. *Proceedings of the National Academy of Sciences;* **105:** 5915–5920.

Douglas, R.J. (1966) Cues for spontaneous alternation. *Journal of Comparative and Physiological Psychology;* **64:** 171–183.

Douglas, R.J., Mitchell, D., and Kentala, D. (1972) Spontaneous alternation as a function of maze configuration. *Psychonomic Science;* **27:** 285–286.

Dudchenko, P.A. and Taube, J.S. (1997) Correlation between head direction cell activity and spatial behavior on a radial arm maze. *Behavioral Neuroscience;* **111:** 3–19.

Dudchenko, P.A., Goodridge, J.P., and Taube, J.S. (1997a) The effects of disorientation on visual landmark control of head direction cell orientation. *Experimental Brain Research;* **115:** 375–380.

Dudchenko, P.A., Goodridge, J.P., Seiterle, D.A., and Taube, J.S. (1997b) Effects of repeated disorientation on the acquisition of spatial tasks in rats: dissociation between the appetitive radial arm maze and aversive water maze. *Journal of Experimental Psychology: Animal Behavior Processes;* **23:** 194–210.

Dudchenko, P.A., Wood, E.R., and Eichenbaum, H. (2000) Neurotoxic hippocampal lesions have no effect on odor span and little effect on odor recognition memory but produce significant impairments on spatial span, recognition, and alternation. *The Journal of Neuroscience;* **20:** 2964–2977.

Dudchenko, P.A. (2001) How do animals actually solve the T-maze? *Behavioral Neuroscience;* **115:** 850–860.

Dudchenko, P.A. and Davidson, M. (2002) Rats use a sense of direction to alternate on T-mazes located in adjacent rooms. *Animal Cognition;* **5:** 115–118.

Dudchenko, P.A., Wood, E.R., and Eichenbaum, H. (2002) Non-spatial correlates of hippocampal activity. In *The Neural Basis of Navigation: Evidence from Single Cell Recordings* (ed. Sharp, P.E.) Kluwell Academic Publishers, Norwell, MA.

Dudchenko, P.A. and Bruce, C. (2005) Navigation without landmarks: can rats use a sense of direction to return to a home site? *Connection Science;* **17:** 107–125.

Dudchenko, P.A. and Zinyuk, L.E. (2005) The formation of cognitive maps of adjacent environments: evidence from the head direction cell system. *Behavioral Neuroscience;* **119:** 1511–1523.

Dusek, J.A. and Eichenbaum, H. (1997) The hippocampus and memory for orderly stimulus relations. *Proceedings of the National Academy of Sciences of the United States of America;* **94:** 7109–7114.

Eichenbaum, H., Kuperstein, M., Fagan, A., and Nagode, J. (1987) Cue-sampling and goal-approach correlates of hippocampal unit activity in rats performing an odor-discrimination task. *The Journal of Neuroscience;* **7:** 716–732.

Eichenbaum, H., Stewart, C., and Morris, R.G. (1990) Hippocampal representation in place learning. *Journal of Neuroscience;* **10:** 3531–3542.

Eichenbaum, H. and Cohen, N.J. (2001) *From Conditioning to Conscious Recollection: Memory Systems of the Brain.* Oxford University Press, Oxford.

Eichenbaum, H. (2004) Hippocampus: cognitive processes and neural representations that underlie declarative memory. *Neuron;* **44:** 109–120.

Ekstrom, A.D., Meltzer, J., McNaughton, B.L., and Barnes, C.A. (2001) NMDA receptor antagonism blocks experience-dependent expansion of hippocampal 'place fields'. *Neuron;* **31:** 631–638.

Ekstrom, A.D., Kahana, M.J., Caplan, J.B., *et al.* (2003) Cellular networks underlying human spatial navigation. *Nature;* **425:** 184–188.

Elliot, D. (1986) Continuous visual information may be important after all: a failure to replicate Thompson (1983) *Journal of Experimental Psychology: Human Perception and Performance;* **12:** 388–391.

Ennaceur, A. and Delacour, J. (1988) A new one-trial test for neurobiological studies of memory in rats. 1: Behavioral data. *Behavioural Brain Research;* **37:** 47–59.

Epstein, R.A. and Kanwisher, N. (1998) A cortical representation of the local environment. *Nature;* **392:** 598–601.

Epstein, R.A., Parker, W.E., and Feiler, A.M. (2007) Where am I now? Distinct roles for parahippocampal and retrosplenial cortices in place recognition. *The Journal of Neuroscience;* **27:** 6141–6169.

Epstein, R.A. (2008) Parahippocampal and retrosplenial contributions to human spatial navigation. *Trends in Cognitive Sciences;* **12:** 388–396.

Etienne, A.S. (1980) The orientation of the golden hamster to its nest-site after the elimination of various sensory cues. *Experientia;* **36:** 1048–1050.

Etienne, A.S., Maurer, R., Saucy, F., and Teroni, E. (1986) Short-distance homing in the golden hamster after a passive outward journey. *Animal Behavior;* **39:** 696–715.

Etienne, A.S., Maurer, R., and Saucy, F. (1988) Limitations in the assessment of path dependent information. *Behaviour;* **106:** 81–111.

Etienne, A.S., Berlie, J., Georgakopoulos, J., and Maurer, R. (1998a) Role of dead reckoning in navigation. In *Spatial Representation In Animals* (ed. Healy, S.), pp. 54–68. Oxford University Press, Oxford.

Etienne, A.S., Maurer, R., Berlie, J., *et al.* (1998b) Navigation through vector addition. *Nature;* **396:** 161–164.

Etienne, A.S., Boulens, V., Maurer, R., Rowe, T., and Siegrist, C. (2000) A brief view of known landmarks reorientates path integration in hamsters. *Naturwissenschaften;* **87:** 494–498.

Farrell, M.J. (1996) Topographical disorientation. *Neurocase;* **2:** 509–520.

Feigenbaum, J.D. and Rolls, E.T. (1991) Allocentric and egocentric spatial information processing in the hippocampal formation of the behaving primate. *Psychobiology;* **19:** 21–40.

Fenton, A.A., Arolfo, M.P., Nerad, L., and Bures, J. (1994) Place navigation in the Morris water maze under minimum and redundant extra-maze cue conditions. *Behavioral and Neural Biology;* **62:** 178–189.

Fenton, A.A., Csizmadia, G., and Muller, R.U. (2000a) Conjoint control of hippocampal place cell firing by two visual stimuli. I. The effects of moving the stimuli on firing field positions. *Journal of General Physiology;* **116:** 191–209.

Fenton, A.A., Csizmadia, G., and Muller, R.U. (2000b) Conjoint control of hippocampal place cell firing by two visual stimuli. II. A vector-field theory that predicts modifications of the representation of the environment. *Journal of General Physiology;* **116:** 211–221.

Ferbiteneau, J. and Shapiro, M.L. (2003) Prospective and retrospective memory coding in the hippocampus. *Neuron;* **40:** 1227–1239.

Fildes, B.N., O'Loughlin, B.J., and Bradshaw, J.L. (1984) Human orientation with restricted sensory information: no evidence for magnetic sensitivity. *Perception;* **13:** 229–236.

Finger, S. (1994) *Origins of Neuroscience.* Oxford University Press, New York.

Foo, P., Warren, W.H., Duchon, A., and Tarr MJ (2005) Do humans integrate routes into a cognitive map? Map- versus landmark-based navigation of novel shortcuts. *Journal of Experimental Psychology: Learning, Memory, and Cognition;* **31:** 195–215.

Foo, P., Duchon, A., Warren W.H. Jr, and Tarr, M.J. (2007) Humans do not switch between path knowledge and landmarks when learning a new environment. *Psychological Research;* **71:** 240–251.

Foreman, N., Arber, M., and Savage, J. (1984) Spatial memory in preschool infants. *Developmental Psychobiology;* **17:** 129–137.

Foreman, N., Warry, R., and Murray, P. (1990) Development of reference and working spatial memory in preschool children. *The Journal of General Psychology;* **117:** 267–276.

Foreman, N. and Ermakova, I. (1998) The radial arm maze: twenty years on. In *A Handbook of Spatial Research Paradigms and Methodologies 2,*(ed. Foreman, N. and Gillett, R.), pp. 87–144. Psychology Press, Hove.

Fortin, N.J., Agster, K.L., and Eichenbaum, H.B. (2002) Critical role of the hippocampus in memory for sequences of events. *Nature Neuroscience;* **5:** 458–462.

Foster, T.C., Castro, C.A., and McNaughton, B.L. (1989) Spatial selectivity of rat hippocampal neurons: dependence on preparedness for movement. *Science;* **244:** 1580–1582.

Foster, D.J. and Wilson, M.A. (2006) Reverse replay of behavioural sequences in hippocampal place cells during the awake state. *Nature;* **440:** 680–683.

Fox, N.C., Crum, W.R., Scahill, R.I., Stevens, J.M., Janssen, J.C., and Rossor, M.N. (2001) Imaging of onset and progression of Alzheimer's disease with voxel-compression mapping of serial magnetic resonance images. *The Lancet;* **358:** 201–205.

Frank, L.M., Brown, E.N., and Wilson, M.A. (2000) Trajectory encoding in the hippocampus and entorhinal cortex. *Neuron;* **27:** 169–178.

Frank, L.M., Stanley, G.B., and Brown, E.N. (2004) Hippocampal plasticity across multiple days of exposure to novel environments. *The Journal of Neuroscience;* **24:** 7681–7689.

Freund, H-J. (2003) Somatosensory and motor disturbances in patients with parietal lobe lesions. In *The Parietal Lobes,* (ed. Siegel, A.M., Andersen, R.A., Freund, H-J., and Spencer, D.D.), pp. 179–194. Lippincott, Williams and Wilkins, Philadelphia.

Frey, U. and Morris, R.G. (1997) Synaptic tagging and long-term potentiation. *Nature;* **385:** 533–536.

Fried, I., Macdonald, K.A., and Wilson, C.L. (1997) Single neuron activity in human hippocampus and amygdala during recognition of faces and objects. *Neuron;* **18:** 753–765.

Frohard, R.J., Bassett, J.P., and Taube, J.S. (2006) Path integration and lesions within the head direction cell circuit: comparison between the roles of the anterodorsal thalamus and dorsal tegmental nucleus. *Behavioral Neuroscience;* **120:** 135–149.

Frohardt, R.J., Marcroft, J.L., and Taube, J.S. (2002) Do head direction cells guide spatial navigation in rats?: An electrophysiological investigation in a path integration task. *Society for Neuroscience Abstracts;* **28:** 584.1.

Fuhs, M.C., VanRhoads, S.R., Casale, A.E., McNaughton, B.L., and Touretzky, D.S. (2005) Influence of path integration versus environmental orientation on place cell remapping between visually identical environments. *Journal of Neurophysiology;* **94:** 2603–2616.

Fuhs, M.C. and Touretzky, D.S. (2006) A spin glass model of path integration in rat medial entorhinal cortex. *The Journal of Neuroscience;* **26:** 4266–4276.

Fukusima, S.S., Loomis, J.M., and Da Silva, J.A. (1997) Visual perception of egocentric distance as assessed by triangulation. *Journal of Experimental Psychology: Human Perception and Performance;* **23:** 86–100.

Futter, J.E. and Aggleton, J.P. (2006) How rats perform spatial working memory tasks: limitations in the use of egocentric and idiothetic working memory. *The Quarterly Journal of Experimental Psychology;* **59:** 77–99.

Fyhn, M., Molden, S., Witter, M.P., Moser, E.I., and Moser, M-B. (2004) Spatial representation in the entorhinal cortex. *Science;* **305:** 1258–1264.

Fyhn, M., Hafting, T., Treves, A., Moser, M-B., and Moser, E.I. (2007) Hippocampal remapping and grid realignment in entorhinal cortex. *Nature;* **446:** 190–194.

Gallistel, C.R. (1990) *The Organisation of Learning.* MIT Press, Cambridge, MA.

Garrad-Cole, F., Lew, A.R., Bremner, J.G., and Whitaker, C. (2001) Use of cue configuration geometry for spatial orientation in human infants (Homo sapiens) *Journal of Comparative Psychology;* **115:** 317–320.

Gatty, H. (1958) *Nature is Your Guide: How to Find Your Way On Land and Sea By Observing Nature.* Collins Press, London.

Georges-François, P., Rolls, E.T., and Robertson, R.G. (1999) Spatial view cells in the primate hippocampus: allocentric view not head direction or eye position or place. *Cerebral Cortex;* **9:** 197–212.

Gerrard, J.L., Kudrimoti, H., McNaughton, B.L., and Barnes, C.A. (2001) Reactivation of hippocampal ensemble activity patterns in the aging rat. *Behavioral Neuroscience;* **115:** 1180–1192.

Gibson, B.M., Shettleworth, S.J., and McDonald, R.J. (2001) Finding a goal on dry land and in the water: differential effects of disorientation on spatial learning. *Behavioural Brain Research;* **123:** 103–111.

Giocomo, L.M., Zilli, E.A., Fransén, E., and Hasselmo, M.E. (2007) Temporal frequency of subthreshold oscillation scales with entorhinal grid cell field spacing. *Science;* **315:** 1719–1722.

Giocomo, L.M. and Hasselmo, M.E. (2008) Time constants of h current in layer II stellate cells differ along the dorsal to ventral axis of medial entorhinal cortex. *The Journal of Neuroscience;* **28:** 9414–9425.

Glasauer, S., Amorim, M-A., Vitte, E., and Berthoz, A. (1994) Goal-directed linear locomotion in normal and labyrinthine-defective subjects. *Experimental Brain Research;* **98:** 323–335.

Glasauer, S., Amorim, M.A., Bloomberg, J.J., *et al.*(1995) Spatial orientation during locomotion following space flight. *Acta Astronautica;* **36:** 423–431.

Glickstein, M. (2003) Subcortical projections of the parietal lobe. In *The Parietal Lobes,* (ed. Siegel, A.M., Andersen, R.A., Freund, H-J., and Spencer, D.D.), pp. 43–56. Lippincott, Williams and Wilkins, Philadelphia.

Golledge, R.G., Gale, N., Pellegrino, J.W., and Doherty, S. (1992) Spatial knowledge acquisition by children: route learning and relational distances. *Annals of the Association of American Geographers;* **82:** 223–244.

Golob, E.J. and Taube, J.S. (1997) Head direction cells and episodic spatial information in rats without a hippocampus. *Proceedings of the National Academy of Sciences, U.S.A.;* **94:** 7645–7650.

Golob, E.J. and Taube, J.S. (1999) Head direction cells in rats with hippocampal or overlying neocortical lesions: evidence for impaired angular path integration. *The Journal of Neuroscience;* **19:** 7198–7211.

Golob, E.J., Stackman, R.W., Wong, A.C., and Taube, J.S. (2001) On the behavioral significance of head direction cells: neural and behavioral dynamics during spatial memory tasks. *Behavioral Neuroscience;* **115:** 285–304.

Golob, E.J. and Taube, J.S. (2002) Differences between appetitive and aversive reinforcement on reorientation in a spatial working memory task. *Behavioral Brain Research;* **136:** 309–316.

Gómez-Isla, T., Price, J.L., McKeel, D.W.Jr, Morris, J.C., Growdon, J.H., and Hyman, B.T. (1996) Profound loss of layer II entorhinal cortex neurons occurs in very mild Alzheimer's disease. *The Journal of Neuroscience;* **16:** 4491–4500.

Goodridge, J.P. and Taube, J.S. (1995) Preferential use of the landmark navigational system by head direction cells in rats. *Behavioral Neuroscience;* **109:** 49–61.

Goodridge, J.P. and Taube, J.S. (1997) Interaction between the postsubiculum and anterior thalamus in the generation of head direction cell activity. *Journal of Neuroscience;* **17:** 9315–9330.

Goodridge, J.P., Dudchenko, P.A., Worboys, K.A., Golob, E.J., and Taube, J.S. (1998) Cue control and head direction cells. *Behavioral Neuroscience;* **112:** 749–761.

Gothard, K.M., Skaggs, W.E., Moore, K.M., and McNaughton, B.L. (1996a) Binding of hippocampal CA1 neural activity to multiple reference frames in a landmark-based navigation task. *The Journal of Neuroscience;* **16:** 823–835.

Gothard, K.M., Skaggs, W.E., and McNaughton, B.L. (1996b) Dynamics of mismatch correction in the hippocampal ensemble code for space: interaction between path integration and environmental cues. *The Journal of Neuroscience;* **16:** 8027–8040.

Gothard, K.M., Hoffman, K.L., Battaglia, F.P., and McNaughton, B.L. (2001) Dentate gyrus and CA1 ensemble activity during spatial reference frame shifts in the presence and absence of visual input. *The Journal of Neuroscience;* **21:** 7284–7292.

Gould, J.L. and Able, K.P. (1981) Human homing: an elusive phenomenon. *Science;* **212:** 1061–1063.

Gouteux, S. and Spelke, E.S. (2001) Children's use of geometry and landmarks to reorient in an open space. *Cognition;* **81:** 119–148.

Gouteux, S., Thinus-Blanc, C., and Vauclair, J. (2001a) Rhesus monkeys use geometric and nongeometric information during a reorientation task. *Journal of Experimental Psychology: General;* **130:** 505–519.

Gouteux, S., Vauclair, J., and Thinus-Blanc, C. (2001b) Reorientation in a small-scale environment by 3-, 4-, and 5-year-old children. *Cognitive Development;* **16:** 853–869.

Graham, M., Good, M.A., McGregor, A., and Pearce, J.M. (2006) Spatial learning based on the shape of environment is influenced by properties of the objects forming the shape. *Journal of Experimental Psychology: Animal Behavior Processes;* **32:** 44–59.

Grayboys, T. and Zheutlin, P. (2008) *Life in the Balance, A Physician's Memoir of Life, Love, and Loss with Parkinson's Disease and Dementia.* Union Square Press, New York/London.

Griffin, A.S. and Etienne, A.S. (1998) Updating the path integrator through a visual fix. *Psychobiology;* **26:** 240–248.

Grön, G., Wunderlich, A.P., Spitzer, M., Tomczak, R., and Riepe, M.W. (2000) Brain activation during human navigation: gender-different neural networks as substrate of performance. *Nature Neuroscience;* **3:** 404–408.

Grossi, D., Fasanaro, A.M., Cecere, R., Salzano, S., and Trojano, L. (2007) Progressive topographical disorientation: a case of focal Alzheimer's disease. *Neurological Science;* **28:** 107–110.

Gu, Y., Angelaki, D.E., and DeAngelis, G.C. (2008) Neural correlates of multisensory cue integration in macaque MSTd. *Nature Neuroscience;* **11:** 1201–1210.

Guth, D. and LaDuke, R. (1994) The veering tendency of blind pedestrians: an analysis of the problem and literature review. *Journal of Visual Impairment and Blindness;* **88:** 391–400.

Guth, D. and LaDuke, R. (1995) Veering by blind pedestrians: individual differences and their implications for instruction. *Journal of Visual Impairment and Blindness;* **89:** 28–37.

Habib, M. and Sirigu, A. (1987) Pure topographic disorientation: a definition and anatomical basis. *Cortex;* **23:** 73–85.

Hafting, T., Fyhn, M., Molden, S., Moser, M-B., and Moser, E.I. (2005) Microstructure of a spatial map in the entorhinal cortex. *Nature;* **436:** 801–806.

Hafting, T., Fyhn, M., Bonnevie, T., Moser, M., and Moser, E.I. (2008) Hippocampus-independent phase precession in entorhinal grid cells. *Nature;* **453:** 1248–1253.

Hamilton, D.A., Rosenfelt, C.S., and Whishaw, I.Q. (2004) Sequential control of navigation by locale and taxon cues in the Morris water task. *Behavioural Brain Research;* **154:** 385–397.

Hampson, R.E., Heyser, C.J., and Deadwyler, S.A. (1993) Hippocampal cell firing correlates of delayed-match-to-sample performance in the rat. *Behavioral Neuroscience;* **107:** 715–739.

Hampson, R.E., Simeral, J.D., and Deadwyler, S.A. (1999) Distribution of spatial and nonspatial information in dorsal hippocampus. *Nature;* **402:** 610–614.

Hanley, J.R. and Davies, A.D.M. (1995) Lost in your own house. In *Broken Memories: Case Studies in Memory Impairment,* (ed. Cambell, R. and Conway, M.A.) Blackwell Publishers Ltd, Oxford.

Hargreaves, E.L., Yoganarasimha, D., and Knierim, J.J. (2007) Cohesiveness of spatial and directional representations recorded from neural ensembles in the anterior thalamus, parasubiculum, medial entorhinal cortex, and hippocampus. *Hippocampus;* **17:** 826–841.

Harrison, F.E., Reiserer, R.S., Tomarken, A.J., and McDonald, M.P. (2006) Spatial and nonspatial escape strategies in the Barnes maze. *Learning and Memory;* **13:** 809–819.

Hart, R.A. and Moore, G.T. (1973) The development of spatial cognition: a review. In *Image and Environment: Cognitive Mapping and Spatial Behaviour,* (ed. Downs, R.M. and Stea, D.), pp. 246–288. Aldive Publishing Co., Chicago.

Hartley, T., Burgess, N., Lever, C., Cacucci, F., and O'Keefe, J. (2000) Modelling place fields in terms of the cortical inputs to the hippocampus. *Hippocampus;* **10:** 369–379.

Hartley, T., Maguire, E.A., Spiers, H.J., and Burgess, N. (2003) The well-worn route and the path less traveled: distinct neural bases of route following and wayfinding in humans. *Neuron;* **37:** 877–888.

Hartley, T., Bird, C.M., Chan, D., *et al.* (2007) The hippocampus is required for short-term topographical memory in humans. *Hippocampus;* **17:** 34–48.

Hassabis, D., Kumaran, D., Vann, S.D., and Maguire, E.A. (2007) Patients with hippocampal amnesia cannot imagine new experiences. *Proceedings of the National Academy of Sciences of the United States of America;* **104:** 1726–1731.

Hassabis, D., Chu, C., Rees, G., Weiskopf, N., Molyneux, P.D., and Maguire, E.A. (2009) Decoding neuronal ensembles in the human hippocampus. *Current Biology;* **19:** 1–9.

Hasselmo, M.E. (2005) What is the function of hippocampal theta rhythm? – linking behavioral data to phasic properties of field potential and unit recording data. *Hippocampus;* **15:** 936–949.

Hasselmo, M.E. (2007) Arc length coding by interference of theta frequency oscillations may underlie context-dependent hippocampal unit data and episodic memory function. *Learning and Memory;* **14:** 782–794.

Hayward, A., McGregor, A., Good, M.A., and Pearce, J.M. (2003) Absence of overshadowing and blocking between landmarks and the geometrical cues provided by the shape of the test arena. *The Quarterly Journal of Experimental Psychology;* **56B:** 114–126.

Hazen, N.L., Lockman, J.J., and Pick, H.L.J. (1978) The development of children's representations of large-scale environments. *Child Development;* **49:** 623–636.

Hebb, D.O. (1949) *The Organisation of Behavior.* Wiley, New York.

Hécaen, H., Tzortzis, C., and Rondot, R. (1980) Loss of topographic memory with learning deficits. *Cortex;* **16:** 525–542.

Henderson, V.W., Mack, W., and Williams, B.W. (1989) Spatial disorientation in Alzheimer's disease. *Archives of Neurology;* **46:** 391–394.

Herman, J.F. and Siegel, A.W. (1978) The development of cognitive mapping of the large-scale environment. *Journal of Experimental Child Psychology;* **26:** 389–406.

Herman, J.F., Blomquist, S.L., and Klein, C.A. (1987) Children's and adults' cognitive maps of very large unfamiliar environments. *British Journal of Developmental Psychology;* **5:** 61–72.

Hermer, L. and Spelke, E.S. (1994) A geometric process for spatial reorientation in young children. *Nature;* **370:** 57–59.

Hermer, L. (1997) Internally coherent spatial memories in a mammal. *Neuroreport;* **8:** 1743–1747.

Hermer-Vazquez, L., Spelke, E., and Katsnelson, A.S. (1999) Sources of flexibility in human cognition: dual-task studies of space and language. *Cognitive Psychology;* **39:** 3–36.

Hermer-Vazquez, L., Moffet, A., and Munkholm, P. (2001) Language, space, and the development of cognitive flexibility in humans: the case of two spatial memory tasks. *Cognition;* **79:** 263–281.

Hetherington, P. and Shapiro, M.L. (1997) Hippocampal place fields are altered by the removal of single visual cues in a distance-dependant manner. *Behavioral Neuroscience;* **111:** 20–34.

Hill, A.J. (1978) First occurrence of hippocampal spatial firing in a new environment. *Experimental Neurology;* **62:** 282–297.

Hill, A.J. and Best, P.J. (1981) Effects of deafness and blindness on the spatial correlates of hippocampal unit activity in the rat. *Experimental Neurology;* 74: 204–217.

Hill, K.A. (1998) *Lost Person Behavior.* National SAR Secretariat, Ottawa.

Hok, V., Lenck-Santini, P-P., Roux, S., Save, E., Muller, R.U., and Poucet, B. (2007) Goal-related activity in hippocampal place cells. *The Journal of Neuroscience;* 27: 472–482.

Holdstock, J.S., Mayes, A.R., Cezayri, E., Isaac, C.L., Aggleton, J.P., and Roberts, N. (2000) A comparison of egocentric and allocentric spatial memory in a patient with selective hippocampal damage. *Neuropsychologia;* 38: 410–425.

Hollup, S.A., Kjelstrup, K.G., Hoff, J., Moser, M.B., and Moser, E.I. (2001) Impaired recognition of the goal location during spatial navigation in rats with hippocampal lesions. *The Journal of Neuroscience;* 21: 4505–4513.

Hölscher, C., Jacob, W., and Mallot, H.A. (2003) Reward modulates neuronal activity in the hippocampus of the rat. *Behavioural Brain Research;* 142: 181–191.

Hölscher, C., Jacob, W., and Mallot, H.A. (2004) Learned association of allocentric and egocentric information in the hippocampus. *Experimental Brain Research;* 158: 233–240.

Hori, E., Tabuchi, E., Matsumura, N., *et al.* (2003) Representation of place by monkey hippocampal neurons in real and virtual translocation. *Hippocampus;* 13: 190–196.

Horii, A., Russell, N.A., Smith, P.F., Darlington, C.L., and Bilkey, D.K. (2004) Vestibular influences on CA1 neurons in the rat hippocampus: an electrophysiological study in vivo. *Experimental Brain Research;* 155: 245–250.

Hothersall, D. (2004) *History of Psychology.* McGraw-Hill, New York.

Hull, C.L. (1943) *Principles of Behavior.* Appleton-Century-Crofts, New York.

Hull, C.L. (1951) *Essentials of Behavior.* Yale University Press, New Haven.

Hull, C.L. (1952) *A Behavioral System.* Yale University Press, New Haven.

Hund, A.M. and Nazarczuk, S.N. (2009) The effect of sense of direction and training experience on wayfinding efficiency. *Journal of Environmental Psychology;* 29: 151–159.

Hupbach, A. and Nadel, L. (2005) Reorientation in a rhombic environment: no evidence for an encapsulated geometric module. *Cognitive Development;* 20: 279–302.

Huttenlocher, J., Newcombe, N., and Sandberg, E.H. (1994) The coding of spatial location in young children. *Cognitive Psychology;* 27: 115–147.

Huttenlocher, J. and Vasilyeva, M. (2003) How toddlers represent enclosed spaces. *Cognitive Science;* 27: 749–766.

Iaria, G., Petrides, M., Dagher, A., Pike, B., and Bohbot, V. (2003) Cognitive strategies dependent on the hippocampus and caudate nucleus in human navigation: variability and change with practice. *The Journal of Neuroscience;* 23: 5945–5952.

Ino, T., Doi, T., Hirose, S., Kimura, T., Ito, J., and Fukuyama, H. (2007) Directional disorientation following left retrosplenial hemorrhage: a case report with fMRI studies. *Cortex;* 43: 248–254.

Insausti, R., Amaral, D.G., and Cowan, W.M. (1987) The entorhinal cortex of the monkey: II. Cortical afferents. *Journal of Comparative Neurology;* 264: 356–395.

Jarrard, L.E. (1975) Role of interference in retention by rats with hippocampal lesions. *Journal of Comparative and Physiological Psychology;* 89: 400–408.

Jarrard, L.E. (1989) On the use of ibotenic acid to lesion selectively different components of the hippocampal formation. *Journal of Neuroscience Methods;* 29: 251–259.

Jarrard, L.E. (1993) On the role of the hippocampus in learning and memory in the rat. *Behavioral and Neural Biology;* **60:** 9–26.

Jeewajee, A., Barry, C., O'Keefe, J., and Burgess, N. (2008) Grid cells and theta as oscillatory interference: electrophysiological data from freely moving rats. *Hippocampus;* **18:** 1175–1185.

Jeffery, K.J., Donnett, J.G., Burgess, N., and O'Keefe, J. M. (1997) Directional control of hippocampal place fields. *Experimental Brain Research;* **117:** 131–142.

Jeffery, K.J. and O'Keefe, J.M. (1999) Learned interaction of visual and idiothetic cues in the control of place field orientation. *Experimental Brain Research;* **127:** 151–161.

Jeffery, K.J., Gilbert, A., Burton, S. and Strudwick, A. (2003) Preserved performance in a hippocampal-dependent spatial task despite complete place cell remapping. *Hippocampus;* **13:** 175–189.

Jeffery, K.J., Anderson, M.I., Hayman, R., and Chakraborty, S. (2004) A proposed architecture for the neural representation of spatial context. *Neuroscience and Biobehavioral Reviews;* **28:** 201–218.

Jeffery, K.J., Anand, R.L., and Anderson, M.I. (2006) A role for terrain slope in orienting hippocampal place fields. *Experimental Brain Research;* **169:** 218–225.

Ji, D. and Wilson, M.A. (2008) Firing rate dynamics in the hippocampus induced by trajectory learning. *The Journal of Neuroscience;* **28:** 4679–4689.

Johnson, A., Seeland, K., and Redish, A.D. (2005) Reconstruction of the postsubiculum head direction signal from neural ensembles. *Hippocampus;* **15:** 86–96.

Johnson, A. and Redish, A.D. (2007) Neural ensembles in CA3 transiently encode paths forward of the animal at a decision point. *The Journal of Neuroscience;* **27:** 12176–12189.

Jones, M.W. and Wilson, M.A. (2005) Theta rhythms coordinate hippocampal-prefrontal interactions in a spatial memory task. *PLoS Biology;* **3:** 2187–2199.

Jones, P.M., Pearce, J.M., Davies, V.J., Good, M.A., and McGregor, A. (2007) Impaired processing of local geometric features during navigation in a watermaze following hippocampal lesions in rats. *Behavioral Neuroscience;* **121:** 1258–1271.

Jonsson, E. (2002) *Inner Navigation.* Scribner, New York.

Jung, M.W., Wiener, S.I., and McNaughton, B.L. (1994) Comparison of spatial firing characteristics of units in dorsal and ventral hippocampus of rats. *The Journal of Neuroscience;* **14:** 7347–7356.

Kahana, M.J., Sekuler, R., Caplan, J.B., Kirschen, M., and Madsen, J.R. (1999) Human theta oscillations exhibit task dependence during virtual maze navigation. *Nature;* **399:** 781–784.

Kallie, C.S., Schrater, P.R., and Legge, G.E. (2007) Variability in stepping direction explains the veering behavior of blind walkers. *Journal of Experimental Psychology: Human Perception and Performance;* **33:** 183–200.

Kalová, E., Vleck, K., Jarolímová, E., and Bures, J. (2005) Allothetic orientation and sequential ordering of places is impaired in early stages of Alzheimer's disease: corresponding results in real space tests and computer tests. *Behavioural Brain Research;* **159:** 175–186.

Kamil, A.C. and Jones, J.E. (1997) The seed-storing corvid Clark's nutcracker learns geometric relationships among landmarks. *Nature;* **390:** 276–279.

Kamin, L.J. (1968) Attention-like processes in classical conditioning. In *Miami Symposium on The Prediction of Behavior: Aversive Stimulation* (ed. Jones, M.), pp. 9–33. University of Miami Press, USA.

Kandel, E.R. (2006) *In Search of Memory - The Emergence of a New Science of Mind.* WW Norton and Company, New York, NY.

Karlsson, M.P. and Frank, L.M. (2009) Awake replay of remote experiences in the hippocampus. *Nature Neuroscience;* **12:** 913–918.

Kavcic, V. and Duffy, C.J. (2003) Attentional dynamics and visual perception: mechanisms of spatial disorientation in Alzheimer's disease. *Brain;* **126:** 1173–1181.

Kavcic, V., Fernandez, R., Logan, D., and Duffy, C.J. (2006) Neuropsychological and perceptual correlates of navigational impairment in Alzheimer's disease. *Brain;* **129:** 736–746.

Kearns, M.J., Warren, W.H., Duchon, A.P., and Tarr, M.J. (2002) Path integration from optic flow and body senses in a homing task. *Perception;* **31:** 349–374.

Kentros, C., Hargreaves, E., Hawkins, R.D., Kandel, E.R., Shapiro, M., and Muller, R.U. (1998) Abolition of long-term stability of new hippocampal place cell maps by NMDA receptor blockade. *Science;* **280:** 2121–2126.

Khabbaz, A., Feel, M.S., Tsien, J.Z., and Tank, D.W. (2000) A compact converging-electrode microdrive for recording head direction cells in mice. *Society for Neuroscience Abstracts;* **26:** 984.

Kim, S.M. and Frank, L.M. (2009) Hippocampal lesions impair rapid learning of a continuous spatial alternation task. *PLoS One;* **4:** e5494.

Kinnaman, A.J. (1902) Mental life of two Macacus Rhesus monkeys in captivity. - II. *The American Journal of Psychology;* **13:** 173–218.

Kirchhoff, B.A., Wagner, A.D., Maril, A., and Stern, C.E. (2000) Prefrontal-temporal circuitry for episodic encoding and subsequent memory. *Journal of Neuroscience;* **20:** 6173–6180.

Kjelstrup, K.B., Solstad, T., Brun, V.H., *et al.* (2008) Finite scale of spatial representation in the hippocampus. *Science;* **321:** 140–143.

Klatzky, R.L., Loomis, J.M., Golledge, R.G., Cicinelli, J.G., Doherty, S., and Pellegrino, J.W. (1990) Acquisition of route and survey knowledge in the absence of vision. *Journal of Motor Behavior;* **22:** 19–43.

Klawans, H.L. (1990) *Newton's Madness: Further Tales of Clinical Neurology.* Harper and Row Publishers.

Kobayashi, T., Nishijo, H., Fukuda, M., Bures, J., and Ono, T. (1997) Task-dependent representations in rat hippocampal place neurons. *Journal of Neurophysiology;* **78:** 597–613.

Kozlowski, L.T. and Bryant, K.J. (1977) Sense of direction, spatial orientation, and cognitive maps. *Journal of Experimental Psychology: Human Perception and Performance;* **3:** 590–598.

Knierim, J.J., Kudrimoti, H.S., and McNaughton, B.L. (1995) Place cells, head direction cells, and the learning of landmark stability. *The Journal of Neuroscience;* **15:** 1648–1659.

Knierim, J.J., Kudrimoti, H.S., and McNaughton, B.L. (1998) Interactions between idiothetic cues and external landmarks in the control of place cells and head direction cells. *Journal of Neurophysiology;* **80:** 425–446.

Knierim, J.J. (2002) Dynamic interactions between local surface cues, distal landmarks, and intrinsic circuitry in hippocampal place cells. *The Journal of Neuroscience;* **22:** 6254–6264.

Krebs, J.R., Sherry, D.F., Healy, S.D., Perry, V.H., and Vaccarino, A.L. (1989) Hippocampal specialization of food-storing birds. *Proceedings of the National Academy of Sciences USA;* **86:** 1388–1392.

Krechevsky, I. (1932) The genesis of 'hypotheses' in rats. *University of California Publications in Psychology;* **6:** 45–64.

Kubie, J.L. and Ranck, J.B.Jr. (1983) Sensory-behavioral correlates in individual hippocampus neurons in three situations: space and context. In *Neurobiology of the Hippocampus,* (ed. Seifert, W.), pp. 433–447. Academic Press, New York.

Kubie, J.L. and Fenton, A.A. (2009) Heading-vector navigation based on head-direction cells and path integration. *Hippocampus;* **19:** 456–479.

Kumaran, D. and Maguire, E.A. (2005) The human hippocampus: cognitive maps or relational memory? *The Journal of Neuroscience;* **25:** 7254–7259.

Landau, B., Gleitman, H., and Spelke, E. (1981) Spatial knowledge and geometric representation in a child blind from birth. *Science;* **213:** 1275–1278.

Landau, B., Spelke, E., and Gleitman, H. (1984) Spatial knowledge in a young blind child. *Cognition;* **16:** 225–260.

Landis, T., Cummings, J.L., Benson, D.F., and Palmer, E.P. (1986) Loss of topographic familiarity an environmental agnosia. *Archives of Neurology;* **43:** 132–136.

Lashley, K.S. (1929) *Brain Mechanisms of Intelligence: A Quantitative Study of Injuries to the Brain.* Chicago University Press, Chicago.

Learmonth, A.E., Newcombe, N.S., and Huttenlocher, J. (2001) Toddlers' use of metric information and landmarks to reorient. *Journal of Experimental Child Psychology;* **80:** 225–244.

Learmonth, A.E., Nadel, L., and Newcombe, N.S. (2002) Children's use of landmarks: implications for modularity theory. *Psychological Science;* **13:** 337–341.

Lee, A.C.H., Buckley, M.J., Gaffan, D., Emery, T., Hodges, J.H., and Graham, K.S. (2006b) Differentiating the roles of the hippocampus and perirhinal cortex in processes beyond long-term declarative memory: a double dissociation in dementia. *The Journal of Neuroscience;* **26:** 5198–5203.

Lee, A.K. and Wilson, M.A. (2002) Memory for sequential experience in the hippocampus during slow wave sleep. *Neuron;* **36:** 1183–1194.

Lee, I., Yoganarasimha, D., Rao, G., and Knierim, J.J. (2004) Comparison of population coherence of place cells in hippocampal subfields CA1 and CA3. *Nature;* **430:** 456–459.

Lee, I., Griffin, A.L., Zilli, E.A., Eichenbaum, H., and Hasselmo, M.E. (2006a) Gradual translocation of spatial correlates of neuronal firing in the hippocampus toward prospective reward locations. *Neuron;* **51:** 639–650.

Lehnung, M., Leplow, B., Friege, L., Herzog, A., Ferstl, R., and Mehdorn, M. (1998) Development of spatial memory and spatial orientation in preschoolers and primary school children. *British Journal of Psychology;* **89:** 463–480.

Lehnung, M., Leplow, B., Haaland, V.O., Mehdorn, M., and Ferstl, R. (2003) Pointing accuracy in children is dependent on age, sex and experience. *Journal of Environmental Psychology;* **23:** 419–425.

Lenck-Santini, P-P., Save, E., and Poucet, B. (2001) Place-cell firing does not depend on the direction of turn in a Y-maze alternation task. *European Journal of Neuroscience;* **13:** 1055–1058.

Leuba, J.H. and Fain, V. (1929) Note on orientation in the white rat. *Journal of Comparative Psychology;* **9:** 239–244.

Leutgeb, S., Ragozzino, K.E., and Mizumori, S.J. (2000) Convergence of head direction and place information in the CA1 region of hippocampus. *Neuroscience;* **100:** 11–19.

Leutgeb, S., Leutgeb, J.K., Treves, A., Moser, M-B., and Moser, E.I. (2004) Distinct ensemble codes in hippocampal areas CA3 and CA1. *Science;* **305:** 1295–1298.

Leutgeb, S., Leutgeb, J.K., Barnes, C.A., Moser, E.I., McNaughton, B.L., and Moser, M-B. (2005) Independent codes for spatial and episodic memory in hippocampal neuronal ensembles. *Science;* **309:** 619–623.

Lever, C., Wills, T., Cacucci, F., Burgess, N., and O'Keefe, J. (2002) Long-term plasticity in hippocampal place-cell representation of environmental geometry. *Nature;* **416:** 90–94.

Lever, C., Burton, S., Jeewajee, A., O'Keefe, J., and Burgess, N. (2009) Boundary vector cells in the subiculum of the hippocampal formation. *The Journal of Neuroscience;* **29:** 9771–9777.

Levi, P. (1979) *If This Is A Man / The Truce.* Penguin Books, London.

Lew, A.R., Foster, K.A., Bremner, J.G., Slavin, S., and Green, M. (2005) Detection of geometric, but not topological, spatial transformations in 6- to 12-month-old infants in a visual exploration paradigm. *Developmental Psychobiology;* **47:** 31–42.

Lewis, D. (1994) *We, the Navigators.* University of Hawai'i Press, Honolulu.

Liben, L.S. (1988) Conceptual issues in the development of spatial cognition. In *Spatial Cognition: Brain Bases and Development* (ed. Stiles-Davis, J., Kritchevsky, M., and Bellugi, U.) Lawrence Erlbaum Associates, Hillsdale.

Lipton, P.A., White, J.A., and Eichenbaum, H. (2007) Disambiguation of overlapping experiences by neurons in the medial entorhinal cortex. *The Journal of Neuroscience;* **27:** 5787–5795.

Liu, L., Gauthier, L., and Gauthier, S. (1991) Spatial disorientation in persons with early senile dementia of the Alzheimer Type. *The American Journal of Occupational Therapy;* **45:** 67–74.

Loomis, J.M., Klatzky, R.L., Golledge, R.G., Cicinelli, J.G., Pellegrino, J.W., and Fry, P.A. (1993) Nonvisual navigation by blind and sighted: assessment of path integration ability. *Journal of Experimental Psychology: General;* **122:** 73–91.

Loomis, J.M., Klatzky, R.L., Golledge, R.G., and Philbeck, J.W. (1999) Human navigation by path integration. In *Wayfinding Behavior: Cognitive Mapping and Other Spatial Processes* (ed. Golledge, R.G.), pp. 125–151. The Johns Hopkins University Press, Baltimore.

Lorenz, C.A. and Neisser, U. (1986) Ecological and psychometric dimensions of spatial ability (Rep. No. 10) Atlanta: Emory Cognition Project, Emory University.

Louie, K. and Wilson, M.A. (2001) Temporally structured replay of awake hippocampal ensemble activity during rapid eye movement sleep. *Neuron;* **29:** 145–156.

Lund, F.H. (1930) Physical asymmetries and disorientation. *American Journal of Psychology;* **42:** 51–62.

Maaswinkel, H. and Whishaw, I.Q. (1999) Homing with locale, taxon, and dead reckoning strategies by foraging rats: sensory hierarchy in spatial navigation. *Behavioural Brain Research;* **99:** 143–152.

Maaswinkel, H., Jarrard, L.E., and Whishaw, I.Q. (1999) Hippocampectomized rats are impaired in homing by path integration. *Hippocampus;* **9:** 553–561.

Mackintosh, N.J. (2002) Do not ask whether they have a cognitive map, but how they find their way about. *Psicologica;* **23:** 165–185.

Maeshima, S., Ozaki, F., Masuo, O., Yamaga, H., Okita, R., and Moriwaki, H. (2001) Memory impairment and spatial disorientation following a left retrosplenial lesion. *Journal of Clinical Neuroscience;* **8:** 450–451.

Maguire, E.A., Burke, T., Phillips, J., and Staunton, H. (1996) Topographical disorientation following unilateral temporal lobe lesions in humans. *Neuropsychologia;* **34:** 993–1001.

Maguire, E.A., Frackowiak, R.S., and Frith, C.D. (1997) Recalling routes around London: activation of the right hippocampus in taxi drivers. *The Journal of Neuroscience;* **17:** 7103–7110.

Maguire, E.A., Burgess, N., Donnett, J.G., Frackowiak, R.S., Frith, C.D., and O'Keefe, J. (1998) Knowing where and getting there: a human navigation network. *Science;* **280:** 921–924.

Maguire, E.A., Burgess, N., and O'Keefe, J. (1999) Human spatial navigation: cognitive maps, sexual dimorphism, and neural substrates. *Current Opinion in Neurobiology;* **9:** 171–177.

Maguire, E.A., Gadian, D.G., Johnsrude, I.S., *et al.* (2000) Navigation-related structural change in the hippocampi of taxi drivers. *Proceedings of the National Academy of Science USA;* **97:** 4398–4403.

Maguire, E.A. (2001) The retrosplenial contribution to human navigation: a review of lesion and neuroimaging findings. *Scandinavian Journal of Psychology;* **42:** 225–238.

Maguire, E.A., Spiers, H.J., Good, C.D., Hartley, T., Frackowiak, R.S.J., and Burgess, N. (2003) Navigation expertise and the human hippocampus: a structural brain imaging analysis. *Hippocampus;* **13:** 250–259.

Maguire, E.A., Nannery, R., and Spiers, H.J. (2006a) Navigation around London by a taxi driver with bilateral hippocampal lesions. *Brain;* **129:** 2849–2907.

Maguire, E.A., Woollett, K., and Spiers, H.J. (2006b) London taxi drivers and bus drivers: a structural MRI and neuropsychological analysis. *Hippocampus;* **16:** 1091–1101.

Mapstone, M., Logan, D., and Duffy, C.J. (2006) Cue integration for the perception and control of self-movement in ageing and Alzheimer's disease. *Brain;* **129:** 2931–2944.

Masters, C.L. and Beyreuther, K. (2006) Alzheimer's centennial legacy: prospects for rational therapeutic intervention targeting the Aß amyloid pathway. *Brain;* **129:** 2823–2839.

Margules, J. and Gallistel, C.R. (1988) Heading in the rat: determination by environmental shape. *Animal Learning and Behavior;* **16:** 404–410.

Martin, G.M., Harley, C.W., Smith, A.R., Hoyles, E.S., and Hynes, C.A. (1997) Spatial disorientation blocks reliable goal location on a plus maze but does not prevent goal location in the Morris maze. *Journal of Experimental Psychology: Animal Behavior Processes;* **23:** 183–193.

Martin, S.J., de Hoz, L., and Morris, R.G. (2005) Retrograde amnesia: neither partial nor complete hippocampal lesions in rats result in preferential sparing of remote spatial memory, even after reminding. *Neuropsychologia;* **43:** 609–624.

Markus, E.J., Barnes, C.A., McNaughton, B.L., Gladden, V.L., and Skaggs, W.E. (1994) Spatial information content and reliability of hippocampal CA1 neurons: effects of visual input. *Hippocampus;* **4:** 410–421.

Markus, E.J., Qin, Y.L., Leonard, B., Skaggs, W.E., McNaughton, B.L., and Barnes, C.A. (1995) Interactions between location and task affect the spatial and directional firing of hippocampal neurons. *The Journal of Neuroscience;* **15**: 7079–7094.

Matsumura, N., Nishijo, H., Tamura, R., Eifuku, S., Endo, S., and Ono, T. (1999) Spatial- and task-dependent neuronal responses during real and virtual translocation in the monkey hippocampal formation. *The Journal of Neuroscience;* **19**: 2381–2393.

Matthews, B.L., Ryu, J.H., and Bockaneck, C. (1989) Vestibular contribution to spatial orientation. *Acta Otolaryngol (Stockh);* **Suppl. 468**: 149–154.

Maurer, R. and Derivaz, V. (2000) Rats in a transparent Morris water maze use elemental and configural geometry of landmarks as well as distance to the pool wall. *Spatial Cognition and Computation;* **2**: 135–156.

Maurer, A.P., VanRhoads, S.R., Sutherland, G.R., Lipa, P., and McNaughton, B.L. (2005) Self-motion and the origin of differential spatial scaling along the septo-temporal axis of the hippocampus. *Hippocampus;* **15**: 841–852.

McEchron, M.D., Tseng, W., and Disterhoft, J.F. (2003) Single neurons in CA1 hippocampus encode trace interval duration during trace heart rate (fear) conditioning in rabbit. *The Journal of Neuroscience;* **23**: 1535–1547.

McFie, J. and Zangwill, O.L. (1960) Visual-constructive disabilities associated with lesions of the left cerebral hemisphere. *Brain;* **83**: 243–260.

McGregor, A., Good, M.A., and Pearce, J.M. (2004a) Absence of an interaction between navigational strategies based on local and distal landmarks. *Journal of Experimental Psychology: Animal Behavior Processes;* **30**: 34–44.

McGregor, A., Hayward, A.J., Pearce, J.M., and Good, M.A. (2004b) Hippocampal lesions disrupt navigation based on the shape of the environment. *Behavioral Neuroscience;* **118**: 1011–1021.

McGregor, A., Jones, P.M., Good, M.A., and Pearce, J.M. (2006) Further evidence that rats rely on local rather than global spatial information to locate a hidden goal: reply to Cheng and Gallistel (2005) *Journal of Experimental Psychology: Animal Behavior Processes;* **32**: 314–321.

McMonagle, P., Deering, F., Berliner, Y., and Kertesz, A. (2006) The cognitive profile of posterior cortical atrophy. *Neurology;* **66**: 331–338.

McNaughton, B.L., Barnes, C.A., Meltzer, J., and Sutherland, R.J. (1989) Hippocampal granule cells are necessary for normal spatial learning but not for spatially-selective pyramidal cell discharge. *Experimental Brain Research;* **76**: 485–496.

McNaughton, B.L., Chen, L.L., and Markus, E.J. (1991) 'Dead Reckoning,' landmark learning, and the sense of direction: a neurophysiological and computational hypothesis. *Journal of Cognitive Neuroscience;* **3**: 190–201.

McNaughton, B.L., Barnes, C.A., Gerrard, J.L., *et al.* (1996) Deciphering the hippocampal polyglot: the hippocampus as a path integration system. *Journal of Experimental Biology;* **199 (Pt 1)**: 173–185.

McNaughton, B.L., Battaglia, F.P., Jensen, O., Moser, E.I., and Moser, M-B. (2006) Path integration and the neural basis of the 'cognitive map'. *Nature Reviews Neuroscience;* **7**: 663–678.

Mehta, M.R., Barnes, C.A., and McNaughton, B.L. (1997) Experience-dependent, asymmetric expansion of hippocampal place fields. *Proceedings of the National Academy of Sciences of the United States of America;* **94**: 8918–8921.

Mehta, M.R., Quirk, M.C., and Wilson, M.A. (2000) Experience-dependent asymmetric shape of hippocampal receptive fields. *Neuron;* **25:** 707–715.

Mellet, E., Bricogne, S., Tzurio-Mazoyer, N., *et al.* (2000) Neural correlates of topographic mental exploration: the impact of route versus survey perspective learning. *NeuroImage;* **12:** 588–600.

Millar, S. (1999) Veering re-visited: noise and posture cues in walking without sight. *Perception;* **28:** 785–790.

Milner, B. (1965) Visually-guided maze learning in man: effects of bilateral hippocampal, bilateral frontal, and unilateral cerebral lesions. *Neuropsychologica;* **3:** 317–338.

Mishkin, M. (1978) Memory in monkeys severely impaired by combined but not separate removal of amygdale and hippocampus. *Nature;* **273:** 297–298.

Mittelstaedt, M-L. and Mittelstaedt, H. (1980) Homing by path integration in a mammal. *Naturewissenschaften;* **67:** 566–567.

Mittelstaedt, H. and Mittelstaedt, M-L. (1982) Homing by path integration. In *Avian Navigation,* (eds. Papi, F. and Wallraff, H.G.), pp: 290–297. Springer-Verlag, Berlin.

Mizumori, S.J., McNaughton, B.L., Barnes, C.A., and Fox, K.B. (1989) Preserved spatial coding in hippocampal CA1 pyramidal cells during reversible suppression of CA3c output: evidence for pattern completion in hippocampus. *The Journal of Neuroscience;* **9:** 3915–3928.

Mizumori, S.J. and Williams, J.D. (1993) Directionally selective mnemonic properties of neurons in the lateral dorsal nucleus of the thalamus of rats. *The Journal of Neuroscience;* **13:** 4015–4028.

Mizumori, S.J., Lavoie, A.M., and Kalyani, A. (1996) Redistribution of spatial representation in the hippocampus of aged rats performing a spatial memory task. *Behavioral Neuroscience;* **110:** 1006–1016.

Moghaddam, M. and Bures, J. (1996) Contribution of egocentric spatial memory to place navigation of rats in the Morris water maze. *Behavioural Brain Research;* **78:** 121–129.

Moita, M.A.P., Rosis, S., Zhou, Y., LeDoux, J.E., and Blair, H.T. (2003) Hippocampal place cells acquire location-specific responses to the conditioned stimulus during auditory fear conditioning. *Neuron;* **37:** 485–497.

Moita, M.A.P., Rosis, S., Zhou, Y., LeDoux, J.E., and Blair, H.T. (2004) Putting fear in its place: remapping of hippocampal place cells during fear conditioning. *The Journal of Neuroscience;* **24:** 7015–7023.

Monacelli, A.M., Cushman, L.A., Kavcic, V., and Duffy, C.J. (2003) Spatial disorientation in Alzheimer's disease: the remembrance of things passed. *Neurology;* **61:** 1491–1497.

Money, J., Alexander, D., and Walker, H.T. (1976) *A Standardised Road-Map Test of Direction Sense.* Johns Hopkins University Press, Baltimore.

Mora, C.V., Davison, M., Wild, J.M., and Walker, M.M. (2004) Magnetoreception and its trigeminal mediation in the homing pigeon. *Nature;* **432:** 508–511.

Morris, R.G. (1981) Spatial localization does not require the presence of local cues. *Learning and Motivation;* **12:** 239–260.

Morris, R.G., Garrud, P., Rawlins, J.N., and O'Keefe, J. (1982) Place navigation impaired in rats with hippocampal lesions. *Nature;* **297:** 681–683.

Morris, R.G. (1984) Developments of a water-maze procedure for studying spatial learning in the rat. *Journal of Neuroscience Methods;* **11:** 47–60.

Morris, R.G. (1990) Does the hippocampus play a disproportionate role in spatial memory? *Discussions in Neuroscience;* **VI:** 39–45.

Morris, R.G., Schenk, F., Tweedie, F., and Jarrard, L.E. (1990) Ibotenate lesions of hippocampus and/or subiculum: dissociating components of allocentric spatial learning. *European Journal of Neuroscience;* **2:** 1016–1028.

Morris, R.G. and Frey, U. (1997) Hippocampal synaptic plasticity: role in spatial learning or the automatic recording of attended experience? *Philosophical Transactions of the Royal Society of London. Series B: Biological Sciences;* **352:** 1489–1503.

Morris, R.G. (2006) Elements of a neurobiological theory of hippocampal function: the role of synaptic plasticity, synaptic tagging and schemas. *European Journal of Neuroscience;* **23:** 2829–2846.

Morrongiello, B.A., Timney, B., Humphrey, K., Anderson, S., and Skory, C. (1995) Spatial knowledge in blind and sighted children. *Journal of Experimental Child Psychology;* **59:** 211–233.

Moscovitch, M., Rosenbaum, R.S., Gilboa, A., *et al.* (2005) Functional neuroanatomy of remote episodic, semantic and spatial memory: a unified account based on multiple trace theory. *Journal of Anatomy;* **207:** 35–66.

Moser, E.I., Moser, M-B., and Andersen, P. (1993) Spatial learning impairment parallels the magnitude of dorsal hippocampal lesions, but is hardly present following ventral lesions. *The Journal of Neuroscience;* **13:** 3916–3925.

Moser, M.B., Moser, E.I., Forrest, E., Andersen, P., and Morris, R.G. (1995) Spatial learning with a minislab in the dorsal hippocampus. *Proceedings of the National Academy of Sciences of the United States of America;* **92:** 9697–9701.

Moser, M-B. and Moser, E.I. (1998) Distributed encoding and retrieval of spatial memory in the hippocampus. *The Journal of Neuroscience;* **18:** 7535–7542.

Muir, G.M. and Taube, J.S. (2002) Firing properties of head direction cells, place cells and theta cells in the freely-moving chinchilla. *Society for Neuroscience Abstracts;* 584.4. Orlando, Florida.

Muir, G.M. and Taube, J.S. (2004) Head direction cell activity and behavior in a navigation task requiring a cognitive mapping strategy. *Behavioural Brain Research;* **153:** 249–253.

Muller, R.U. and Kubie, J.L. (1987) The effects of changes in the environment on the spatial firing of hippocampal complex-spike cells. *The Journal of Neuroscience;* **7:** 1951–1968.

Muller, R.U. and Kubie, J.L. (1989) The firing of hippocampal place cells predicts the future position of freely moving rats. *The Journal of Neuroscience;* **9:** 4101–4110.

Mumby, D.G. (2001) Perspectives on object-recognition memory following hippocampal damage: lessons from studies in rats. *Behavioural Brain Research;* **127:** 159–181.

Munn, N.L. (1950) *Handbook of Psychological Research on the Rat.* Houghton Mifflin Company, Boston.

Murray, E.A. (1996) What have ablation studies told us about the neural substrates of stimulus memory? *Seminars in the Neurosciences;* **8:** 13–22.

Murray, E.A. and Mishkin, M. (1998) Object recognition and location memory in monkeys with excitotoxic lesions of the amygdale and hippocampus. *The Journal of Neuroscience;* **18:** 6568–6582.

Murray, E.A., Bussey, T.J., and Saksida, L.M. (2007) Visual perception and memory: a new view of medial temporal lobe function in primates and rodents. *Annual Review of Neuroscience;* **30:** 99–122.

Nestor, P.J., Fryer, T.D., Ikeda, M., and Hodges, J.R. (2003) Retrosplenial cortex (BA 29/30) hypometabolism in mild cognitive impairment (prodromal Alzheimer's disease) *European Journal of Neuroscience;* **18:** 2663–2667.

Newcombe, N. (1988) The paradox of proximity in early spatial representation. *British Journal of Developmental Psychology;* **6:** 376–378.

Newcombe, N., Huttenlocher, J., Drummey, A.B., and Wiley, J.G. (1998) The development of spatial location coding: place learning and dead reckoning in the second and third years. *Cognitive Development;* **13:** 185–200.

Nitz, D.A. (2006) Tracking route progression in the posterior parietal cortex. *Neuron;* **49:** 747–756.

O'Brien, H.L., Tetewsky, S.J., Avery, L.M., Cushman, L.A., Makous, W., and Duffy, C.J. (2001) Visual mechanisms of spatial disorientation in Alzheimer's disease. *Cerebral Cortex;* **11:** 1083–1092.

O'Kane, G., Kensinger, E.A., and Corkin, S. (2004) Evidence for semantic learning in profound amnesia: an investigation with patient H.M. *Hippocampus;* **14:** 417–425.

O'Keefe, J. and Dostrovsky, J. (1971) The hippocampus as a spatial map. Preliminary evidence from unit activity in the freely moving rat. *Brain Research;* **34:** 171–175.

O'Keefe, J. (1976) Place units in the hippocampus of the freely moving rat. *Experimental Neurology;* **51:** 78–109.

O'Keefe, J. and Conway, D.H. (1978) Hippocampal place units in the freely moving rat: why they fire where they fire. *Experimental Brain Research;* **31:** 573–590.

O'Keefe, J. and Nadel, L. (1978) *The Hippocampus as a Cognitive Map.* Oxford University Press, New York.

O'Keefe, J. and Speakman, A. (1987) Single unit activity in the rat hippocampus during a spatial memory task. *Experimental Brain Research;* **68:** 1–27.

O'Keefe, J. and Recce, M.L. (1993) Phase relationship between hippocampal place units and the EEG theta rhythm. *Hippocampus;* **3:** 317–330.

O'Keefe, J. and Burgess, N. (1996) Geometric determinants of the place fields of hippocampal neurons. *Nature;* **381:** 425–428.

O'Keefe, J. (1999) Do hippocampal pyramidal cells signal non-spatial as well as spatial information? *Hippocampus;* **9:** 352–364.

O'Keefe, J. (2007) Hippocampal neuroanatomy. In *The Hippocampus Book*, (ed. Anderson, P., Morris, R., Amaral, D., Bliss, T., O'Keefe, J.), pp. 475–548. Oxford University Press, Inc., New York.

Oler, J.A. and Markus, E.J. (2000) Age-related deficits in the ability to encode contextual change: a place cell analysis. *Hippocampus;* **10:** 338–350.

Olton, D.S. and Samuelson, R.J. (1976) Remembrance of places passed: spatial memory in rats. *Journal of Experimental Psychology: Animal Behavior Processes;* **2:** 97–116.

Olton, D.S., Collison, C., and Werz, M.A. (1977) Spatial memory and radial arm maze performance of rats. *Learning and Motivation;* **8:** 289–314.

Olton, D.S., Walker, J.A., and Gage, F.H. (1978) Hippocampal connections and spatial discrimination. *Brain Research;* **139:** 295–308.

Olton, D.S. and Papas, B.C. (1979) Spatial memory and hippocampal function. *Neuropsychologia;* **17:** 669–682.

Olton, D.S. (1992) Tolman's cognitive analyses: predecessor of current approaches in psychology. *Journal of Experimental Psychology: General;* **121:** 427–428.

O'Mara, S.M., Rolls, E.T., Berthoz, A., and Kesner, R.P. (1994) Neurons responding to whole-body motion in the primate hippocampus. *The Journal of Neuroscience;* **14:** 6511–6523.

Ono, T., Nakamura, K., Fukuda, M., and Tamura, R. (1991) Place recognition responses of neurons in monkey hippocampus. *Neuroscience Letters;* **121:** 194–198.

Ono, T., Nakamura, K., Nishijo, H., and Eifuku, S. (1993) Monkey hippocampal neurons related to spatial and nonspatial functions. *Journal of Neurophysiology;* **70:** 1516–1529.

Otto, T. and Eichenbaum, H. (1992) Neuronal activity in the hippocampus during delayed non-match to sample performance in rats: evidence for hippocampal processing in recognition memory. *Hippocampus;* **2:** 323–334.

Pai, M-C. and Jacobs, W.J. (2004) Topographic disorientation in community-residing patients with Alzheimer's disease. *International Journal of Geriatric Psychiatry;* **19:** 250–255.

Packard, M.G. and McGaugh. J.L. (1996) Inactivation of hippocampus or caudate nucleus with lidocaine differently affects expression of place and response learning. *Neurobiology of Learning and Memory;* **65:** 65–72.

Papez, J.W. (1937) A proposed mechanism of emotion. *Archives of Neurology and Psychiatry;* **38:** 725–743.

Paquet, N., Rainville, C., Lajoie, Y., and Tremblay, F. (2007) Reproducibility of distance and direction errors associated with forward, backward, and sideways walking in the context of blind navigation. *Perception;* **36:** 525–536.

Parron, C. and Save, E. (2004) Evidence for entorhinal and parietal cortices involvement in path integration in the rat. *Experimental Brain Research;* **159:** 349–359.

Passini, R., Pigot, H., Rainville, C., and Tetreault, M-H. (2000) Wayfinding in a nursing home for advanced dementia of the Alzheimer's type. *Environment and Behavior;* **32:** 684–710.

Pastalkova, E., Itskov, V., Amarasingham, A., and Buzáki, G. (2008) Internally generated cell assembly sequences in the rat hippocampus. *Science;* **321:** 1322–1327.

Paterson, A. and Zangwill, O.L. (1945) A case of topographical disorientation associated with a unilateral cerebral lesion. *Brain;* **68:** 188–212.

Pearce, J.M., Ward-Robinson, J., Good, M., Fussell, C., and Aydin, A. (2001) Influence of a beacon on spatial learning based on the shape of the test environment. *Journal of Experimental Psychology: Animal Behavior Processes;* **27:** 329–344.

Pearce, J.M., Good, M.A., Jones, P.M., and McGregor, A. (2004) Transfer of spatial behavior between different environments: implications for theories of spatial learning and for the role of the hippocampus in spatial learning. *Journal of Experimental Psychology: Animal Behavior Processes;* **30:** 135–147.

Pearce, J.M., Graham, M., Good, M.A., Jones, P.M., and McGregor, A. (2006) Potentiation, overshadowing, and blocking of spatial learning based on the shape of the environment. *Journal of Experimental Psychology: Animal Behavior Processes;* **32:** 201–214.

Péruch, P., Borel, L., Magnan, J., and Lacour, M. (2005) Direction and distance deficits in path integration after unilateral vestibular loss depend on task complexity. *Cognitive Brain Research;* **25:** 862–872.

Peterson, J. (1916) Illusions of direction orientation. *The Journal of Philosophy and Scientific Methods;* **13:** 225–236.

Philbeck, J.W., Behrmann, M., Levy, L., Potolicchio, S.J., and Caputy, A.J. (2004) Path integration deficits during linear locomotion after human medial temporal lobectomy. *Journal of Cognitive Neuroscience;* **16:** 510–520.

Piaget, J. and Inhelder, B. (1948/1963) *The Child's Conception of Space.* Routledge and Kegan Paul Ltd, London.

Piaget, J., Inhelder, B., and Szeminska, A. (1960) *The Child's Conception of Geometry.* Routledge and Kegan Paul Ltd, London.

Ploner, C.J., Gaymard, B.M., Rivaud-Péchoux, S., *et al.* (2000) Lesions affecting the parahippocampal cortex yield spatial memory deficits in humans. *Cerebral Cortex;* **10:** 1211–1216.

Poucet, B., Chapuis, N., Durut, M., and Thinus-Blanc, C. (1986) A study of exploratory behavior as an index of spatial knowledge in hamsters. *Learning and Behavior;* **14:** 93–100.

Prados, J. and Tobalon, J.B. (1998) Locating an invisible goal in a water maze requires at least two landmarks. *Psychobiology;* **26:** 42–48.

Presson, C.C. (1987) The development of landmarks in spatial memory: the role of differential experience. *Journal of Experimental Child Psychology;* **44:** 317–334.

Quirk, G.J., Muller, R.U., and Kubie, J.L. (1990) The firing of hippocampal place cells in the dark depends on the rat's recent experience. *The Journal of Neuroscience;* **10:** 2008–2017.

Raber, J., Rola, R., LeFevour, A., *et al.* (2004) Radiation-induced cognitive impairments are associated with changes in indicators of hippocampal neurogenesis. *Radiation Research;* **162:** 39–47.

Racine, R.L. and Kimble, D.P. (1965) Hippocampal lesions and delayed alternation in the rat. *Psychonomic Science;* **3:** 285–286.

Radyushkin, K., Anokhin, K., Meyer, B.I., Jiang, Q., Alvarez-Bolado, G., and Gruss, P. (2005) Genetic ablation of the mammillary bodies in the Foxb1 mutant mouse leads to selective deficit of spatial working memory. *European Journal of Neuroscience;* **21:** 219–229.

Rainville, C., Marchand, R., and Passini, R. (2002) Performance of patients with a dementia of the Alzheimer type in the Standardized Road-Map Test of Direction Sense. *Neuropsychologia;* **40:** 567–573.

Rainville, C., Joubert, S., Felician, O., Chabanne, V., Ceccaldi, M., and Péruch, P. (2005) Wayfinding in familiar and unfamiliar environments in a case of progressive topographical agnosia. *Neurocase;* **11:** 297–309.

Ranck, J.B.Jr. (1973) Studies on single neurons in dorsal hippocampal formation and septum in unrestrained rats. I. Behavioral correlates and firing repertoires. *Experimental Neurology;* **41:** 461–531.

Ranck, J.B.Jr. (2005) History of the discovery of head direction cells. In *Head Direction Cells and the Neural Mechanisms of Spatial Orientation,* (ed. Wiener, S.I. and Taube, J.S.) MIT Press, London.

Rawlins, J.N. and Olton, D.S. (1982) The septo-hippocampal system and cognitive mapping. *Behavioural Brain Research;* **5:** 331–358.

Redish, A.D. (1999) *Beyond the Cognitive Map*. MIT Press, Cambridge, Massachusetts.

Redish, A.D., Rosenzweig, E.S., Bohanick, J.D., McNaughton, B.L., and Barnes, C.A. (2000) Dynamics of hippocampal ensemble activity realignment: time versus space. *The Journal of Neuroscience;* **20:** 9298–9309.

Redish, A.D., Battaglia, F.P., Chawla, M.K., *et al.* (2001) Independence of firing correlates of anatomically proximate hippocampal pyramidal cells. *The Journal of Neuroscience;* **21:** RC134.

Reisberg, B., Ferris, S.H., de Leon, M.J., and Crook, T. (1982) The global deterioration scale for assessment of primary degenerative dementia. *American Journal of Psychiatry;* **139:** 1136–1139.

Restle, F. (1957) Discrimination of cues in mazes: a resolution of the 'place-vs-response' question. *The Psychological Review;* **64:** 217–228.

Richman, C.L., Dember, W.N., and Kim, P. (1986) Spontaneous alternation behavior in animals: a review. *Current Psychological Research and Reviews;* **5:** 358–391.

Riecke, B.E., van Heen, H.A.H.C., and Bulthoff, H.B. (2002) Visual homing is possible without landmarks: a path integration study in virtual reality. *Presence: Teleoperators and Virtual Environments;* **11:** 443–473.

Riesser, J.J., Ashmead, D.H., Talor, C.R., and Youngquist, G.A. (1990) Visual perception and the guidance of locomotion without vision to previously seen targets. *Perception;* **19:** 675–689.

Riesser, J.J. and Rider, E.A. (1991) Young children's spatial orientation with respect to multiple targets when walking without vision. *Developmental Psychology;* **27:** 97–107.

Ritchie, B.F. (1947) Studies in spatial learning. III. Two paths to the same location and two paths to two different locations. *Journal of Experimental Psychology;* **37:** 25–38.

Ritchie, B.F. (1948) Studies in spatial learning. VI. Place orientation and direction orientation. *Journal of Experimental Psychology;* **38:** 659–669.

Ritchie, B.F., Aeschliman, B., and Pierce, P. (1950) Studies in spatial learning VIII. Place performance and the acquisition of place dispositions. *Journal of Comparative and Physiological Psychology;* **43:** 73–85.

Ritchie, B.F., Hay, A., and Hare, R. (1951) Studies in spatial learning: IX. A dispositional analysis of response-performance. *Journal of Comparative and Physiological Psychology;* **44:** 442–449.

Rivard, B., Li, Y., Lenck-Santini, P.P., Poucet, B., and Muller, R.U. (2004) Representation of objects in space by two classes of hippocampal pyramidal cells. *Journal of General Physiology;* **124:** 9–25.

Robertson, R.G., Rolls, E.T., and Georges-François, P. (1998) Spatial view cells in the primate hippocampus: effects of removal of view details. *Journal of Neurophysiology;* **79:** 1145–1156.

Robertson, R.G., Rolls, E.T., Georges- François, P., and Panzeri, S. (1999) Head direction cells in the primate pre-subiculum. *Hippocampus;* **9:** 206–219.

Rolls, E.T., Miyashita, Y., Cahusac, P.M., *et al.* (1989) Hippocampal neurons in the monkey with activity related to the place in which a stimulus is shown. *The Journal of Neuroscience;* **9:** 1835–1845.

Rolls, E.T. and O'Mara, S.M. (1995) View-responsive neurons in the primate hippocampal complex. *Hippocampus;* **5:** 409–424.

Rolls, E.T., Xiang, J., and Franco, L. (2005) Object, space, and object–space representations in the primate hippocampus. *Journal of Neurophysiology;* **94:** 833–844.

Rosenbaum, R.S., Priselac, S., Köhler, S., *et al.* (2000) Remote spatial memory in an amnesic person with extensive bilateral hippocampal lesions. *Nature Neuroscience;* **13:** 1044–1048.

Rosenbaum, R.S., Ziegler, M., Winocur, G., Grady, C.L., and Moscovitch, M. (2004) 'I have often walked down this street before': fMRI studies on the hippocampus and other structures during mental navigation of an old environment. *Hippocampus;* **14:** 826–835.

Rosenbaum, R.S., Gao, F., Richards, B., Black, S.E., and Moscovitch, M. (2005) 'Where to?' Remote memory for spatial relations and landmark identity in former taxi drivers with Alzheimer's disease and encephalitis. *Journal of Cognitive Neuroscience;* **17:** 446–462.

Rosenbaum, R.S., Winocur, G., Grady, C.L., Ziegler, M., and Moscovitch, M. (2007) Memory for familiar environments learned in the remote past: fMRI studies of healthy people and an amnesic person with extensive bilateral hippocampal lesions. *Hippocampus;* **17:** 1241–1251.

Rosenzweig, E.S., Redish, A.D., McNaughton, B.L., and Barnes, C.A. (2003) Hippocampal map realignment and spatial learning. *Nature Neuroscience;* **6:** 609–615.

Rotenberg, A. and Muller, R.U. (1997) Variable place-cell coupling to a continuously viewed stimulus: evidence that the hippocampus acts as a perceptual system. *Philosophical Transactions of the Royal Society of London. Series B: Biological Sciences;* **352:** 1505–1513.

Russell, N.A., Horii, A., Smith, P.F., Darlington, C.L., and Bilkey, D.K. (2003) Long-term effects of permanent vestibular lesions on hippocampal spatial firing. *The Journal of Neuroscience;* **23:** 6490–6498.

Samsonovich, A. and McNaughton, B.L. (1997) Path integration and cognitive mapping in a continuous attractor neural network model. *The Journal of Neuroscience;* **17:** 5900–5920.

Sargolini, F., Fyhn, M., Hafting, T., *et al.* (2006) Conjunctive representation of position, direction, and velocity in entorhinal cortex. *Science;* **312:** 758–762.

Sava, S. and Markus, E.J. (2008) Activation of the medial septum reverses age-related hippocampal encoding deficits: a place field analysis. *The Journal of Neuroscience;* **28:** 1841–1853.

Save, E., Cressant, A., Thinus-Blanc, C., and Poucet, B. (1998) Spatial firing of hippocampal place cells in blind rats. *The Journal of Neuroscience;* **18:** 1818–1826.

Save, E., Nerad, L., and Poucet, B. (2000) Contributions of multiple sensory information to place field stability in hippocampal place cells. *Hippocampus;* **10:** 64–76.

Save, E., Guazzelli, A., and Poucet, B. (2001) Dissociation of the effects of bilateral lesions of the dorsal hippocampus and parietal cortex on path integration in the rat. *Behavioral Neuroscience;* **115:** 1212–1223.

Savelli, F., Yoganarasimha, D., and Knierim, J.J. (2008) Influence of boundary removal on the spatial representation of the medial entorhinal cortex. *Hippocampus;* **18:** 1270–1282.

Schaeffer, A.A. (1928) Spiral movements in men. *Journal of Morphology;* **45:** 293–298.

Séguinot, V., Maurer, R., and Etienne, A.S. (1993) Dead reckoning in a small mammal: the evaluation of distance. *Journal of Comparative Physiology A;* **173:** 103–113.

Shapiro, M.L., Kennedy, P.J., and Febinteanu, J. (2006) Representing episodes in the mammalian brain. *Current Opinion in Neurobiology;* **16:** 701–709.

Shapiro, M.L., Tanila, H., and Eichenbaum, H. (1997) Cues that hippocampal place cells encode: dynamic and hierarchical representation of local and distal stimuli. *Hippocampus;* **7:** 624–642.

Sharp, P.E., Kubie, J.L., and Muller, R.U. (1990) Firing properties of hippocampal neurons in a visually symmetrical environment: contributions of multiple sensory cues and mnemonic processes. *The Journal of Neuroscience;* **10:** 3093–3105.

Sharp, P.E., Blair, H.T., Etkin, D., and Tzanetos, D.B. (1995) Influences of vestibular and visual motion information on the spatial firing patterns of hippocampal place cells. *The Journal of Neuroscience;* **15:** 173–189.

Sharp, P.E. (1999) Comparison of the timing of hippocampal and subicular signals: implications for path integration. *Hippocampus;* **9:** 158–172.

Sharp, P.E., Tinkelman, A., and Cho, J. (2001a) Angular velocity and head direction signals recorded from the dorsal tegmental nucleus of Gudden in the rat: implications for path integration in the head direction cell circuit. *Behavioral Neuroscience;* **115:** 571–588.

Sharp, P.E., Blair, H.T., and Cho, J. (2001b) The anatomical and computational basis of the rat head-direction cell signal. *Trends in Neurosciences;* **24:** 289–294.

Sharp, P.E. and Koester, K. (2008) Lesions of the mammillary body region severely disrupt the cortical head direction, but not place cell signal. *Hippocampus;* **18:** 766–784.

Shelton, A.L. and Gabrieli, J.D. (2002) Neural correlates of encoding space from route and survey perspectives. *The Journal of Neuroscience;* **22:** 2711–2717.

Shenk, D. (2001) *The Forgetting.* HarperCollins Publishers, London.

Sherman, S.M. and Guillery, R.W. (2006) *Exploring the Thalamus and Its Role in Cortical Function.* The MIT Press, Cambridge, MA.

Sherry, D.F., Vaccarino, A.L., Buckenham, K., and Herz, R.S. (1989) The hippocampal complex of food-storing birds. *Brain, Behavior and Evolution;* **34:** 308–317.

Shettleworth, S.J. and Sutton, J.E. (2005) Multiple systems for spatial learning: dead reckoning and beacon homing in rats. *Journal of Experimental Psychology: Animal Behavior Processes;* **31:** 125–141.

Sholl, M.J. (1988) The relation between sense of direction and mental geographic updating. *Intelligence;* **12:** 299–314.

Sholl, M.J. (1989) The relation between horizontality and rod-and-frame and vestibular navigation performance. *Journal of Experimental Psychology: Learning, Memory, and Cognition;* **15:** 110–125.

Schrager, Y., Kirwan, C.B., and Squire, L.R. (2008) Neural basis of the cognitive map: path integration does not require hippocampus or entorhinal cortex. *Proceedings of the National Academy of Sciences;* **105:** 12034–12038.

Sheehan, B., Burton, E., and Mitchell, L. (2006) Outdoor wayfinding in dementia. *Dementia;* **5:** 271–281.

Siegel, A.M., Andersen, R.A., Freund, H-J., and Spencer, D.D. (2003) *The Parietal Lobes (Advances in Neurology, volume 93)* Lippincott Williams and Wilkins, Philadelphia.

Siegel, A.W. and White, S.H. (1975) The development of spatial representations of large-scale environments. *Advances in Child Development and Behavior;* **10:** 9–55.

Siegel, J.L., Neunuebel, J.P., and Knierim, J.J. (2008) Dominance of proximal coordinate frame in determining the locations of hippocampal place cell activity during navigation. *Journal of Neurophysiology;* **99:** 60–76.

Skaggs, W.E., Knierim, J.J., Kudrimoti, H.S., and McNaughton, B.L. (1995) A model of the neural basis of the rat's sense of direction. *Advances in Neural Information Processing Systems;* **7:** 173–180.

Skaggs, W.E. and McNaughton, B.L. (1998) Spatial firing properties of hippocampal CA1 populations in an environment containing two visually identical regions. *The Journal of Neuroscience;* **18:** 8455–8466.

Small, W.S. (1901) Experimental study of the mental processes of the rat. II. *American Journal of Psychology;* **12:** 206–239.

Smith, D.M. and Mizumori, S.J.Y. (2006) Learning-related development of context-specific neuronal responses to places and events: the hippocampal role in context processing. *The Journal of Neuroscience;* **26:** 3154–3163.

Smith, M.L. and Milner, B. (1981) The role of the right hippocampus in the recall of spatial location. *Neuropsychologia;* **19:** 781–793.

Smulders, T.V., Sasson, A.D., and DeVoogd, T.J. (1995) Seasonal variation in hippocampal volume in a food-storing bird, the black-capped chickadee. *Journal of Neurobiology;* **27:** 15–25.

Smulders, T.V., Shiflett, M.W., Sperling, A.J., and DeVoogd, T.J. (2000) Seasonal changes in neuron numbers in the hippocampal formation of a food-hoarding bird: the black-capped chickadee. *Journal of Neurobiology;* **44:** 414–422.

Smulders, T.V. (2006) A multi-disciplinary approach to understanding hippocampal function in food-hoarding birds. *Reviews in Neuroscience;* **17:** 53–69.

Snyder, L.H., Grieve, K.L., Brotchie, P., and Andersen, R.A. (1998) Separate body- and world-referenced representations of visual space in parietal cortex. *Nature;* **394:** 887–891.

Solomon, P.R., Vander-Schaaf, E.R., Thompson, R.F., and Weisz, D.J. (1986) Hippocampus and trace conditioning of the rabbit's classically conditioned nictating membrane response. *Behavioral Neuroscience;* **100:** 729–744.

Song, P. and Wang, X-J. (2005) Angular path integration by moving 'hill of activity': a spiking neuron model without recurrent excitation of the head-direction system. *The Journal of Neuroscience;* **25:** 1002–1014.

Solstad, T., Boccara, C.N., Kropff, E., Moser, M.B., and Moser, E.I. (2008) Representation of geometric borders in the entorhinal cortex. *Science;* **322:** 1865–1868.

Soscia, S.J. Kirby, J.E. Washicosky, K.J.Tucker, S.M., *et al.* (2010) The Alzheimer's disease-associated amyloid beta-protein is an anti-microbial peptide. *PLoS One;* **5:** e9505.

Souman, J.L., Frissen, I., Sreenivasa, M.N., and Ernst, M.O. (2009) Walking straight into circles. *Current Biology;* **19:** 1–5.

Speakman, A., and O'Keefe, J. (1990) Hippocampal complex spike cells do not change their place fields if the goal is moved within a cue controlled environment. *European Journal of Neuroscience;* **2:** 544–555.

Spiers, H.J., Burgess, N., Maguire, E.A., *et al.* (2001a) Unilateral temporal lobectomy patients show lateralized topographical and episodic memory deficits in a virtual town. *Brain;* **124:** 2476–2489.

Spiers, H.J., Burgess, N., Hartley, T., Vargha-Khadem, F., and O'Keefe, J. (2001bt) Bilateral hippocampal pathology impairs topographical and episodic memory but not visual pattern matching. *Hippocampus;* **11:** 715–725.

Spiers, H.J. and Maguire, E.A. (2006) Thoughts, behaviour, and brain dynamics during navigation in the real world. *NeuroImage;* **31:** 1826–1840.

Spiers, H.J., Jovaleki , A., and Jeffery, K.J. (2009) The hippocampal place code: multiple fragments or one big map? *Society for Neuroscience Abstracts;* 101.28. Chicago, USA.

Squire, L.R. (1987) *Memory and Brain.* Oxford University Press, New York.

Squire, L.R. and Zola-Morgan, S. (1991) The medial temporal lobe memory system. *Science;* **253:** 1380–1386.

Squire, L.R. (1992) Memory and the hippocampus: a synthesis from findings with rats, monkeys, and humans. *Psychological Review;* **99:** 195–231.

Squire, L.R. and Alvarez, P. (1995) Retrograde amnesia and memory consolidation: a neurobiological perspective. *Current Opinion in Neurobiology;* **5:** 169–177.

Squire, L.R. and Kandel, E.R. (1999) *Memory: From Mind to Molecules.* Scientific American Library, New York.

Squire, L.R. and Bayley, P.J. (2007) The neuroscience of remote memory. *Current Opinion in Neurobiology;* **17:** 185–196.

Squire, L.R., Wixted, J.T., and Clark, R.E. (2007) Recognition memory and the medial temporal lobe: a new perspective. *Nature Reviews Neuroscience;* **8:** 872–883.

Stackman, R.W. and Taube, J.S. (1997) Firing properties of head direction cells in the rat anterior thalamic nucleus: dependence on vestibular input. *The Journal of Neuroscience;* **17:** 4349–4358.

Stackman, R.W. and Taube, J.S. (1998) Firing properties of rat lateral mammillary single units: head direction, head pitch, and angular head velocity. *The Journal of Neuroscience;* **18:** 9020–9037.

Stackman, R.W., Clark, A.S., and Taube, J.S. (2002) Hippocampal spatial representations require vestibular input. *Hippocampus;* **12:** 291–303.

Stackman, R.W., Golob, E.J., Bassett, J.P., and Taube, J.S. (2003) Passive transport disrupts directional path integration by rat head direction cells. *Journal of Neurophysiology;* **90:** 2862–2874.

Standing, L. (1973) Learning 10,000 pictures. *Quarterly Journal of Experimental Psychology;* **25:** 207–222.

Stark, C.E.L. and Squire, L.R. (2000) Functional magnetic resonance imaging (fMRI) activity in the hippocampal region during recognition memory. *Journal of Neuroscience;* **20:** 7776–7781.

Stefanacci, L., Buffalo, E.A., Schmolk, H., and Squire, L.R. (2000) Profound amnesia after damage to the medial temporal lobe: a neuroanatomical and neuropsychological profile of patient E.P. *The Journal of Neuroscience;* **20:** 7024–7036.

Steffenach, H-A., Witter, M.P., Moser, M-B., and Moser, E.I. (2005) Spatial memory in the rat requires the dorsolateral band of the entorhinal cortex. *Neuron;* **45:** 301–313.

Stein, J.F. (1991) Space and the parietal association areas. In *The Brain and Space,* (ed. Pallard, J.), pp. 185–222. Oxford University Press, Oxford.

Suthana, N.A., Ekstrom, A.D., Moshirvaziri, S., Knowlton, B., and Bookheimer, S.Y. (2009) Human hippocampal CA1 involvement during allocentric encoding of spatial information. *The Journal of Neuroscience;* **29:** 10512–10519.

Suzuki, S., Augerinos, G., and Black, A.H. (1980) Stimulus control of spatial behavior on the eight-arm maze in rats. *Learning and Motivation;* **11:** 1–18.

Swanson, L.W. (2003) *Brain Architecture Understanding the Basic Plan.* Oxford University Press, New York.

Syrotuck, W.G. (2000) *Analysis of Lost Person Behavior.* Barkleigh Productions, Inc., Mechanicsburg.

Takahashi, M., Lauwereyns, J., Sakurai, Y., and Tsukada, M. (2009) A code for spatial alternation during fixation in rat hippocampal CA1 neurons. *Journal of Neurophysiology;* **102:** 556–567.

Takahashi, N., Kawamura, M., Shiota, J., Kasahata, N., and Hirayama, K. (1997) Pure topographic disorientation due to right retrosplenial lesion. *Neurology;* **49:** 464–469.

Takahashi, N. and Kawamura, M. (2002) Pure topographical disorientation – the anatomical basis of landmark agnosia. *Cortex;* **38:** 717–725.

Tang-Wai, D.F., Graff-Radford, N.R., Boeve, B.F., *et al.* (2004) Clinical, genetic, and neuropathologic characteristics of posterior cortical atrophy. *Neurology;* **63:** 1168–1174.

Tanila, H., Shapiro, M.L., and Eichenbaum, H. (1997a) Discordance of spatial representation in ensembles of hippocampal place cells. *Hippocampus;* **7:** 613–623.

Tanila, H., Shapiro, M., Gallagher, M., and Eichenbaum, H. (1997b) Brain aging: changes in the nature of information coding by the hippocampus. *The Journal of Neuroscience;* **17:** 5155–5166.

Tanila, H., Sipila, P., Shapiro, M., and Eichenbaum, H. (1997c) Brain aging: impaired coding of novel environmental cues. *The Journal of Neuroscience;* **17:** 5167–5174.

Taube, J.S., Muller, R.U., and Ranck, J.B. (1990a) Head-direction cells recorded from the postsubiculum in freely moving rats. I. Description and quantitative analysis. *Journal of Neuroscience;* **10:** 420–435.

Taube, J.S., Muller, R.U., and Ranck, J.B. (1990b) Head-direction cells recorded from the postsubiculum in freely moving rats. II. Effects of environmental manipulations. *Journal of Neuroscience;* **10:** 436–447.

Taube, J.S. (1995) Head direction cells recorded in the anterior thalamic nuclei of freely moving rats. *The Journal of Neuroscience;* **15:** 70–86.

Taube, J.S. and Burton, H.L. (1995) Head direction cell activity monitored in a novel environment and during a cue conflict situation. *Journal of Neurophysiology;* **74:** 1953–1971.

Taube, J.S. and Muller, R.U. (1998) Comparisons of head direction cell activity in the postsubiculum and anterior thalamus of freely moving rats. *Hippocampus;* **8:** 87–108.

Taube, J.S. and Bassett, J.P. (2003) Persistent neural activity in head direction cells. *Cerebral Cortex;* **13:** 1162–1172.

Taube, J.S. (2007) The head direction signal: origins and sensory-motor integration. *Annual Review of Neuroscience;* **30:** 181–207.

Taussig, I.M. and Mack, W.J. (1992) Caregivers' observations and report of early symptoms of Alzheimer's disease. *American Journal of Alzheimer's Disease and Other Dementias;* **7:** 28–34.

Teng, E. and Squire, L.R. (1999) Memory for places learned long ago is intact after hippocampal damage. *Nature;* **400:** 675–677.

Thinus-Blanc, C., Bouzouba, L., Chaix, K., Chapuis, N., Durup, M., and Poucet, B. (1987) A study of spatial parameters encoded during exploration in hamsters. *Journal of Experimental Psychology: Animal Behavior Processes;* **26:** 43–57.

Thinus-Blanc, C. (1996) *Animal Spatial Cognition: Behavioural and Brain Approach.* World Scientific, Singapore.

Thomson, J.A. (1983) Is continuous visual monitoring necessary in visually guided locomotion? *Journal of Experimental Psychology: Human Perception and Performance;* **9:** 427–443.

Thomson, J.A. (1986) Intermittent versus continuous visual control: a reply to Elliott. *Journal of Experimental Psychology: Human Perception and Performance;* **12:** 392–393.

Thompson, R.F. (1986) The neurobiology of learning and memory. *Science;* **233:,** 941–947.

Thorne, B.M. and Henley, T.B. (2005) *Connections in the History and Systems of Psychology.* Houghton Mifflin Company, New York.

Tolman, E.C. (1938) Determiners of behavior at a choice point. *Psychological Review;* **45:** 1–41.

Tolman, E.C. (1948) Cognitive maps in rats and men. *Psychological Review;* **55:** 189–208.

Tolman, E.C. and Gleitman, H. (1949) Studies in spatial learning: VII. Place and response learning under different degrees of motivation. *Journal of Experimental Psychology;* **39:** 653–659.

Tolman, E.C., Ritchie, B.F., and Kalish, D. (1946a) Studies in spatial learning: I. Orientation and the short-cut. *Journal of Experimental Psychology;* **36:** 13–24.

Tolman, E.C., Ritchie, B.F., and Kalish, D. (1946b) Studies in spatial learning. II. Place learning versus response learning. *Journal of Experimental Psychology;* **3:** 221–229.

Tolman, E.C., Ritchie, B.F., and Kalish, D. (1947a) Studies in spatial learning. IV. The transfer of place learning to other starting paths. *Journal of Experimental Psychology;* **37:** 39–47.

Tolman, E.C., Ritchie, B.F., and Kalish, D. (1947b) Studies in spatial learning. V. Response learning vs. place learning by the non-correction method. *Journal of Experimental Psychology;* **37:** 285–292.

Tommasi, L. and Polli, C. (2004) Representation of two geometric features of the environment in the domestic chick *(Gallus gallus) Animal Cognition;* **7:** 53–59.

Turriziani, P., Carlesimo, G.A., Perri, R., Tomaiuolo, F., and Caltagirone, C. (2003) Loss of spatial learning in a patient with topographical disorientation in new environments. *Journal of Neurology, Neurosurgery, and Psychiatry;* **74:** 61–69.

Ungerleider, L.G. and Mishkin, M. (1982) Two cortical visual systems. In *Analysis of Visual Behavior,* (ed. Ingle, D.J., Goodale, M.A., and Mansfield, R.J.W.) The MIT Press, Cambridge, Massachusetts.

Uttal, D.H. (2000) Seeing the big picture: map use and the development of spatial cognition. *Developmental Science;* **3:** 247–264.

van der Meer, M.A.A., Braga, R., Richmond, Z., Dudchenko, P.A., and Wood, E.R. (2010) Evidence for the use of an internal sense of direction in homing. *Behavioral Neuroscience;* **124:** 164–169.

Van Hoesen, G.W., Augustinack, J.C., Dierking, J., Redman, S.J., and Thangavel, R. (2000) The parahippocampal gyrus in Alzheimer's disease clinical and preclinical neuroanatomical correlates. *Annals of the New York Academy of Sciences;* **911:** 254–274.

Vander Wall, S.B. (1982) An experimental analysis of cache recovery in Clark's nutcracker. *Animal Behavior;* **30:** 84–94.

Vann, S.D. and Aggleton, J.P. (2004) The mammillary bodies: two memory systems in one? *Nature Reviews Neuroscience;* **5**: 35–44.

Vargha-Khadem, F., Gadian, D.G., Watkins, K.E., Connelly, A., Van Paesschen, W., and Mishkin, M. (1997) Differential effects of early hippocampal pathology on episodic and semantic memory. *Science;* **277**: 376–380.

Voermans, N.C., Peterson, K.M., Daudey, L., *et al.* (2004) Interaction between the human hippocampus and the caudate nucleus during route recognition. *Neuron;* **43**: 427–435.

Voyer, D., Voyer, S., and Bryden, M.P. (1995) Magnitude of sex differences in spatial abilities: a meta-analysis and consideration of critical variables. *Psychological Bulletin;* **117**: 250–270.

Vuillerme, N., Nougier, V., and Camicioli, R. (2002) Veering in human locomotion: modulatory effect of attention. *Neuroscience Letters;* **331**: 175–178.

Wall, P.L., Botly, L.C., Black, C.K., and Shettleworth, S.J. (2004) The geometric module in the rat: independence of shape and feature learning in a food finding task. *Learning and Behavior;* **32**: 289–298.

Wallace, D.G., Hines, D.J., Pellis, S.M., and Whishaw, I.Q. (2002) Vestibular information is required for dead reckoning in the rat. *The Journal of Neuroscience;* **22**: 10009–10017.

Wallace, D.G. and Whishaw, I.Q. (2003) NMDA lesions of Ammon's horn and the dentate gyrus disrupt the direct and temporally paced homing displayed by rats exploring a novel environment: evidence for a role of the hippocampus in dead reckoning. *European Journal of Neuroscience;* **18**: 513–523.

Waller, D. and Hodgson, E. (2006) Transient and enduring spatial representations under disorientation and self-rotation. *Journal of Experimental Psychology: Learning, Memory, and Cognition;* **32**: 867–882.

Wang, R.F., Hermer, L., Spelke, E.S. (1999) Mechanisms of reorientation and object localization by children: a comparison with rats. *Behavioral Neuroscience;* **113**: 475–485.

Wang, R.F. and Spelke, E.S. (2000) Updating egocentric representations in human navigation. *Cognition;* **77**: 215–250.

Wang, R.F. and Spelke, E.S. (2002) Human spatial representation: insight from animals. *Trends in Cognitive Sciences;* **6**: 376–382.

Watson, J.B. (1907) Kinaesthetic and organic sensations: their role in the reaction of the white rat to the maze. *Psychological Review (Monograph Supplements);* **8**(2): 1–100.

Watson, J.B. (1913) Psychology as the behaviorist views it. *Psychological Review;* **20**: 158–177.

Westby, G.W.M. and Partridge, K.J. (1986) Human homing: still no evidence despite geomagnetic controls. *Journal of Experimental Biology;* **120**: 325–331.

Whishaw, I.Q. and Dringenberg, H.C. (1991) Food carrying in the rat (Rattus norvegicus): influence of distance, effort, predatory odor, food size, and food availability support optimal foraging theory. *Psychobiology;* **18**: 251–261.

Whishaw, I.Q. and Jarrard, L.E. (1995) Similarities vs. differences in place learning and circadian activity in rats after fimbria–fornix section or ibotenate removal of hippocampal cells. *Hippocampus;* **5**: 595–604.

Whishaw, I.Q., Cassel, J.C., and Jarrard, L.E. (1995) Rats with fimbria–fornix lesions display a place response in a swimming pool: a dissociation between getting there and knowing where. *The Journal of Neuroscience;* **15**: 5779–5788.

Whishaw, I.Q. and Jarrard, L.E. (1996) Evidence for extrahippocampal involvement in place learning and hippocampal involvement in path integration. *Hippocampus;* **6:** 513–524.

Whishaw, I.Q. and Maaswinkel, H. (1998) Rats with fimbria–fornix lesions are impaired in path integration: a role for the hippocampus in 'sense of direction'. *The Journal of Neuroscience;* **18:** 3050–3058.

Whishaw, I.Q. and Gorny, B. (1999) Path integration absent in scent-tracking fimbria–fornix rats: evidence for hippocampal involvement in 'sense of direction' and 'sense of distance' using self-movement cues. *The Journal of Neuroscience;* **19:** 4662–4673.

Whishaw, I.Q., Hines, D.J., and Wallace, D.G. (2001) Dead reckoning (path integration) requires the hippocampal formation: evidence from spontaneous exploration and spatial learning tasks in light (allothetic) and dark (idiothetic) tests. *Behavioural Brain Research;* **127:** 49–69.

White, N. and McDonald, R.J. (2002) Multiple parallel memory systems in the brain of the rat. *Neurobiology of Learning and Memory;* **77:** 125–184.

Whitlock, J.R., Sutherland, R.J., Witter, M.P., Moser, M-B., and Moser, E.I. (2008) Navigating from hippocampus to parietal cortex. *Proceedings of the National Academy of Sciences of the United States of America;* **105:** 14755–14762.

Whitty, C.W.M. and Newcombe, F. (1973) R.C. Oldfield's study of visual and topographic disturbances in a right occipito–parietal lesion of 30 years duration. *Neuropsychologia;* **11:** 471–475.

Wiener, J.M. and Mallot, H.A. (2006) Path complexity does not impair visual path integration. *Spatial Cognition and Computation;* **6:** 333–346.

Wiener, J.M., Büchner, S.J., Hölscher, C. (2009) Towards a taxonomy of wayfinding tasks: a knowledge-based approach. *Spatial Cognition and Computation;* **9:** 152–165.

Wiener, S.I., Paul, C.A., and Eichenbaum, H. (1989) Spatial and behavioral correlates of hippocampal neuronal activity. *The Journal of Neuroscience;* **9:** 2737–2763.

Wiener, S.I. and Taube, J.S. (2005) *Head Direction Cells and the Neural Mechanisms of Spatial Orientation.* MIT Press, London.

Wilson, B.A., Berry, E., Gracey, F., *et al.* (2005c) Egocentric disorientation following bilateral parietal lobe damage. *Cortex,* **41:** 547–554.

Wilson, I.A., Ikonen, S., McMahan, R.W., Gallagher, M., Eichenbaum, H., and Tanila, H. (2003) Place cell rigidity correlates with impaired spatial learning in aged rats. *Neurobiology of Aging;* **24:** 297–305.

Wilson, I.A., Ikonen, S., Gureviciene, I., *et al.* (2004) Cognitive aging and the hippocampus: how old rats represent new environments. *The Journal of Neuroscience;* **24:** 3870–3878.

Wilson, I.A., Ikonen, S., Gurevicius, K., *et al.* (2005a) Place cells of aged rats in two visually identical compartments. *Neurobiology of Aging;* **26:** 1099–1106.

Wilson, I.A., Ikonen, S., Gallagher, M., Eichenbaum, H., and Tanila, H. (2005b) Age-associated alterations of hippocampal place cells are subregion specific. *The Journal of Neuroscience;* **25:** 6877–6886.

Wilson, M.A. and McNaughton, B.L. (1993) Dynamics of the hippocampal ensemble code for space. *Science;* **261:**1055–1058.

Wilson, M.A. and McNaughton, B.L. (1994) Reactivation of hippocampal ensemble memories during sleep. *Science;* **265:** 676–679.

Wiltschko, W. and Wiltschko, R. (2005) Magnetic orientation and magnetoreception in birds and other animals. *Journal of Comparative Physiology A;* **191**: 675–693.

Winocur, G., Moscovitch, M., Fogel, S., Rosenbaum, R.S., and Sekeres, M. (2005) Preserved spatial memory after hippocampal lesions: effects of extensive experience in a complex environment. *Nature Neuroscience;* **8**: 273–275.

Wolbers, T. and Büchel, C. (2005) Dissociable retrosplenial and hippocampal contributions to successful formation of survey representations. *The Journal of Neuroscience;* **25**: 3333–3340.

Wolbers, T., Wiener, J.M., Mallot, H.A., and Büchel, C. (2007) Differential recruitment of the hippocampus, medial prefrontal cortex, and the human motion complex during path integration in humans. *The Journal of Neuroscience;* **27**: 9408–9416.

Wolbers, T., Hegarty, M., Büchel, C., and Loomis, J.M. (2008) Spatial updating: how the brain keeps track of changing object locations during observer motion. *Nature Neuroscience;* **11**: 1223–1230.

Wood, E.R., Dudchenko, P.A., and Eichenbaum, H. (1999) The global record of memory in hippocampal neuronal activity. *Nature;* **397**: 613–616.

Wood, E.R., Dudchenko, P.A., Robitsek, R.J., and Eichenbaum, H. (2000) Hippocampal neurons encode information about different types of memory episodes occurring in the same location. *Neuron;* **27**: 623–633.

Woodworth, R.S. and Schlosberg, H. (1954) *Experimental Psychology* (revised edition) Methuen and Co. Ltd, London.

Woollett, K., Glensman, J., and Maguire, E.A. (2008) Non-spatial expertise and hippocampal gray matter volume in humans. *Hippocampus;* **18**: 981–984.

Worchel, P. (1951) Space perception and orientation in the blind. *Psychological Monographs: General and Applied;* **65**: 1–27.

Worchel, P. (1952) The role of vestibular organs in spatial orientation. *Journal of Experimental Psychology;* **44**: 4–10.

Worsley, C.L., Recce, M., Spiers, H.J., Marley, J., Polkey, C.E., and Morris, R.G. (2001) Path integration following temporal lobectomy in humans. *Neuropsychologia;* **39**: 452–464.

Yoganarasimha, D. and Knierim, J.J. (2005) Coupling between place cells and head direction cells during relative translations and rotations of distal landmarks. *Experimental Brain Research;* **160**: 344–359.

Yoganarasimha, D., Yu, X., and Knierim, J.J. (2006) Head direction cell representations maintain internal coherence during conflicting proximal and distal cue rotations: comparison with hippocampal place cells. *The Journal of Neuroscience;* **26**: 622–631.

Young, G.S., Choleris, E., and Kirkland, J.B. (2006) Use of salient and non-salient visuospatial cues by rats in the Morris Water Maze. *Physiology and Behavior;* **87**: 794–799.

Young, P.T. (1950) *Motivation of Behavior: the Fundamental Determinants of Human and Animal Activity.* John Wiley, New York.

Yu, X., Yoganarasimha, D., and Knierim, J.J. (2006) Backward shift of head direction turning curves of the anterior thalamus: comparison with CA1 place fields. *Neuron;* **52**: 717–729.

Zhang, K. (1996) Representation of spatial orientation by the intrinsic dynamics of the head-direction ensemble: a theory. *The Journal of Neuroscience;* **16**: 2112–2126.

Zinyuk, L., Kubik, S., Kaminsky, Y., Fenton, A.A., and Bures, J. (2000) Understanding hippocampal activity by using purposeful behavior: place navigation induces place cell discharge in both task-relevant and task-irrelevant spatial reference frames. *Proceedings of the National Academy of Sciences of the United States of America;* **97:** 3771–3776.

Zoladek, L. and Roberts, W.A. (1978) The sensory basis of spatial memory in the rat. *Animal Learning and Behavior;* **6:** 77–81.

Zola-Morgan, S., Squire, L.R., Clower, R.P., and Rempel, N.L. (1993) Damage to the perirhinal cortex exacerbates memory impairment following lesions to the hippocampal formation. *The Journal of Neuroscience;* **13:** 251–265.

Zugaro, M.B., Berthoz, A., and Wiener, S.I. (2001) Background, but not foreground, spatial cues are taken as references for head direction responses by rat anterodorsal thalamus neurons. *The Journal of Neuroscience;* **21:** RC154.

Zugaro, M.B., Arleo, A., Berthoz, A., and Wiener, S.I. (2003) Rapid spatial reorientation and head direction cells. *The Journal of Neuroscience;* **23:** 3478–3482.

Index

absolute space 125–6
agnosia
  finger 237
  landmark 229, 240, 243–6
  spatial 239
Allen, Gary 66
allocentric space 6, 88
alternation 36–7
  role of hippocampus 130–1
Alzheimer, Alois 222–3
Alzheimer's disease 221–33
  head direction cells in 231–3
  patient studies 224–31
  spatial difficulties 223–4
Amaral, David, *The Hippocampus Book* 119
amnesia 116–22
  anterograde 116, 122–3
  and getting lost 145–9
  retrograde 116
amygdala 175
animals
  locale space 129–40
  place cells 172–4
  primates *see* primates
  rats *see* rats
  triangle completion tasks 79
anterograde amnesia 116
  monkeys 122–3
anterograde disorientation 229, 240, 246–7
approach-consummate cells 165
autonomic nervous system 116
autonomous habits 127

Baker, Robin 83
Balint, Reszo 237
Balint syndrome 237, 240
Barnes, Carol 46
Barnes maze 46–7
  role of hippocampus 136–7
basal ganglia 118
behavioural modulation of place fields 165–7
behaviourism 9–11
  objective approach to 10–11
Berthöz, Alain 80
beta-amyloid 222
Binet, Alfred 3, 5
blind people
  circling/veering 70–2
  spatial abilities 98–102

triangle completion task 76–9
blood-brain barrier 117
border cells 164
boundary encoding 162–4
brain damage 4
brain imaging 153–89
brain stem 117
Brodman, Kobinian 235
Brodman's areas 234
Buzsáki, György, *Rhythms of the Brain* 174

caudate nucleus 180, 183–5
central nervous system 116
cerebellum 117
cerebral cortex 118
Cheng, Ken 57
children
  blind 98–102
  concept of geometry 96–7
  disorientation 102–7
  distance and direction 98–100
  getting lost 93
  inability to envision perspective 96
  language ability 104–5
  mini-maps 97–8
  projective space 94–6
  spatial cognition 93–114
  spatial working memory 111–13
  topological space 94
  wayfinding 107–11
cingulate cortex 199
circling behaviour 67–73
Clark's Nutcracker 35–6
cognitive mapping 27–9, 141–4
Cohen, Neil, *From Conditioning to Conscious Recollection* 142
constructional apraxia 239
contralateral neglect 237–8
Corsi block test 240
Corsi span task 230
cranial nerves 118
Critchley, Macdonald 237
cue-sampling cells 165

Darwin, Charles 251
Dashiell's maze 19–20
dead reckoning 49
Deadwyler, Sam 166
declarative memory 121

delay conditioning 144–5
dementia *see* Alzheimer's disease
diencephalon 118
disorientation 1–2, 92, 188, 253
    anterograde 229, 240, 246–7
    in children 102–7
    ecocentric 240–1
    egocentric 240
    heading 240, 241–3
disorientation effect 90
distance estimation 73–5
    children 98–100
dorsal medial entorhinal cortex 195
dorsal tegmental nucleus 197, 198
Dostrovsky, Jonathan 123
dysgraphia 237

EEG 128
egocentric disorientation 240–1
egocentric space 6, 87–90
Eichenbaum, Howard, *From Conditioning to
    Conscious Recollection* 142
engram 18
enteric nervous system 117
entorhinal cortex 119, 144, 164, 174
environmental geometry 57
    in orientation 139–40
epilepsy and memory loss 116–22
episodic memory 121
equipotentiality 18
etak 66–7
Etienne, Ariane 50–2
exploration, hippocampus in 130
    Barnes maze 136–7
    Morris water maze 132–6
    path integration 137–9
    radial arm maze 131–2
    T-maze 130–1

Farrell, Martin 243
finger agnosia 237
forced-sample testing 37
forests, getting lost in 2
frontal lobe 117
functional magnetic imaging 178

Gatty, Harold, *Nature is Your Guide* 85
geometry 56–9
    children's concept of 96–7
gerbils, use of landmarks 44–5
Gerstmann syndrome 237
Gestalt principle of proximity 109
getting lost 4–5, 65
    amnesia 145–9
    children 93
Global Deterioration Scale 223
global remapping 155
goal cells 175

goal-approach cells 165
GPS systems 67
grid cells 195–7
gyri 117

Hampson, Robert 166
Hampton Court maze 11–13
Hasselmo, Michael 174
head direction cells 191–5
    Alzheimer's disease 231–3
    and homing behaviour 216–18
    orientation
        landmarks 200–3, 208–11
        new environments 205–11
        olfactory and tactile cues 193–4
        path integration 203–5, 208–11
    and spatial behaviour 212–16
head direction/grid cell circuit 197–200
heading disorientation 240, 241–3
Hebb, Donald 47
Hebbian synaptic plasticity 173
Hebb's Rule 47
Hermer, Linda 102
hippocampus 115–51
    basic circuit 121
    as cognitive map 125–9
    cortical inputs 120
    lesions of 144–5, 153
        amnesia 145–9
        path integration 149–50
    place cells *see* place cells
    role in alternation 130–1
    role in exploration 130
        Barnes maze 136–7
        Morris water maze 132–6
        path integration 137–9
        radial arm maze 131–2
        T-maze 130–1
    role in navigation 180–5
    role in path integration 182
    in taxi drivers 185–8
homing behaviour 6, 66
    and head direction cells 216–18
    path integration 47–54
Hull, Clark L.
    A Behavioral System 27, 28
    Essentials of Behavior 27
    Principles of Behavior 27
humans
    locale space 140–1
    place cells 175–7
Huntington's disease 184
hypothalamus 118
hypothetico-deductive reasoning 6

idiothetic navigation 49
imagination 153
inertial navigation 49

inferior parietal lobule 235, 236
Inhelder, Barbel
  La Representation de l'Espace chez l'Enfant
    (The Child's Conception of Space) 94
  The Child's Concept of Geometry 96
interpeduncular nucleus 207
introspection 10
invisible target 73–5
itak 66

James, William, *Principles of Psychology* 126
Jeffery, Kathryn 167
Jonsson, Erik 5
  Inner Navigation 3, 4

Kandel, Eric, *In Search of Memory* 19, 47
Kant, Immanuel 126
kinaesthetic memory 14, 16–17
Kinnaman, A.J. 14
Knierim, James 158
Korsakoff's syndrome 118
Kraepelin, Emil 222
Kubie, John 128

landmark agnosia 229, 240, 243–6
landmarks 1–2
  head direction cells 200–3
    orientation 208–11
  and place fields 156–9
  use of 43–6
  virtual 81–2
Lashley, Karl Spence, *Brain Mechanisms of*
  Intelligence 17, 19
Lashley's Maze 18–19
lateral intraparietal area 235
lateral mammillary nucleus 197, 198
Lavenex, Pierre, *The Hippocampus Book* 119
leg size, and circling/veering behaviour 69–70
Levi, Primo 5
  If This Is a Man 2
  The Truce 2
limbic system 118
locale space 126
  animals 129–40
  humans 140–1
long distance orientation 83–6
long-term potentiation 47

magnetic sense 83–6
mammillary bodies 199
mammillothalamic tract 199
map-building 181
maps 67, 127
mass action 18
mazes 9
  Barnes maze 46–7, 136–7
  children's navigation of 113
  Dashiell's maze 19–20

Hampton Court 11–13
Lashley's Maze 17–19
Morris water maze 38–43, 132–6
Olton radial arm maze 31–6, 131–2
Small's maze 13–14
solving 11–14
studies of 11–17
T-maze 36–8, 130–1
Watson's maze 14–17
medial entorhinal cortex 197, 198
medial superior temporal area 236
medulla oblongata 118
Mehta effect 173
memory
  declarative 121
  episodic 121
  and imagination 153
  kinaesthetic 14, 16–17
  non-declarative 121
  semantic 142
  spatial working 111–13
  storage of 142
  see also amnesia
midbrain 118
mini-maps 97–8
Mishkin, Mortimer 122
misorientation 92, 251–3
Money test 225, 244
monkeys, anterograde amnesia 122–3
Morris, Richard 38, 143
Morris water maze 38–43
  role of hippocampus 132–6
Morrongiello, Barbara 101
Moscovitch, Moris, multiple trace theory 142
mossy fibres 119
motor instructions 74
Mountcastle, Vernon 235
Muller, Robert 128, 156, 192
multiple trace theory 142–3
Munro, Cameron 93

Nadel, Lynn 125
  Cognitive Map 140, 141
  multiple trace theory 142
Naismith, William W. 1–2, 5, 65, 251
navigation 5–6, 65–92
  hippocampus 180–5
  inertial 49
  parahippocampal gyrus 177–9
neurofibrillary tangles 231–2
neuropil threads 231
New York subway, wayfinding in 66
non-declarative memory 121
non-spatial tasks 144–5
occipital lobe 117

O'Keefe, John 123, 156
  Cognitive Map 140

Olton, David 31
Olton radial arm maze 31–6
orientation
    across environments 205–11
        brain regions involved 207
        path integration 208–11
    environmental geometry 139–40
    long distance 83–6
    spatial *see* spatial orientation
oriented search strategy 66
overshadowing 41

panic 2–3
Papez circuit 119, 199
parahippocampal cortex 119, 144, 199
parahippocampal gyrus 177–9, 236
parahippocampal place area 179
parahippocampus 246
parasubiculum 164
parasympathetic nervous system 116
parietal cortex 233–40
    anatomy 234–5
    damage to 237–40
    physiology 235–7
parietal lobe 117
path finding 67
path following 67
path integration 6, 47–54
    head direction cells 203–5
        orientation 208–11
    hippocampal lesions 149–50
    manipulation of 54–6
    and place fields 159–62
    role of hippocampus 137–9, 182
perforant path 119
peripheral nervous system 116
perirhinal cortex 119, 144
Peterson, Joseph 191
phase precession 174
Piaget, Jean 93–8
    *La Representation de l'Espace chez l'Enfant
        (The Child's Conception of Space)* 94
    The Child's Concept of Geometry 96
piloting 66–7
place cells 123–5, 153–89
    boundary encoding 162–4
    coherence of 158–9
    encoding of destination 167–72
    humans and primates 175–7
    old versus young animals 172–4
    properties of 128
    receptive fields 154–5
    remapping 155–6
    retrospective/prospective firing 167
    theta rhythm 128, 174–5
place fields
    modulation by behaviour 165–7
    and path integration 159–62

visual landmarks controlling 156–9
place learning 23
place-like activity 176–7
pons 118
posterior cortical atrophy 240
posterior parietal cortex 248
postsubiculum 191, 198, 218
presubiculum 191, 236
primates
    anterograde amnesia 122–3
    place cells 175–7
projective space 94–6
psychometric testing 90–1
psychosis 222–3

radial arm maze 31–6
    role of hippocampus 131–2
Ramón y Cajal, Santiago, *Advice for a Young
        Investigator* 186
Ranck, James 165, 191, 192
rate remapping 155
rats
    Barnes maze 46–7
    cognitive maps 27–9
    Dashiell's maze 19–20
    kinaesthetic memory 14, 16–17
    Lashley's maze 17–19
    path integration 47–54
    radial arm maze 31–6
    Small's maze 13–14
    Tolman's maze 20–6
    use of landmarks 45–6
    water maze 38–43
    Watson's maze 14–17
real world spatial orientation 62–3, 90–1
Redish, David, *Beyond the
        Cognitive Map* 144
reductionism 9
remapping 155–6
    global 155
    partial 155
    rate 155
response learning 23
retrograde amnesia 116
retrosplenial cortex 197, 242
reverse illusions of orientation 3
Rey-Osterrieth figure 178
Rolls, Edmund 176
route following 66

Samuelson, Robert 31
Schaffer collaterals 119
semantic memory 142
sense of direction 4, 17–20, 86–7
    children 98–100
    loss of 178
    manipulation of 54–6
    neural basis 191–219

shape 59–62
  of environment 102–7
Sharp, Patricia 160, 163
signs 67
simulator sickness 81
Skinner, B.F. 21
Small, Willard 11
Snow, Gordon 3
somatic nervous system 116
space
  absolute 125–6
  allocentric 6, 88
  life-span representation of 254
  locale 126, 127
  taxon 126, 127
spatial agnosia 239
spatial cognition 11–14
  Barnes maze 46–7
  children 93–114
  contemporary studies 31–63
  homing by path integration 47–54
  landmark use in open field 43–6
  Morris water maze 38–43
  Olton radial arm maze 31–6
  parietal cortex 233–40
  shape 59–62
  T-maze 36–8
spatial learning 20–6
  geometry 56–9
spatial orientation 4
  Alzheimer's disease 223–4
  head direction cells 212–16
  real world 62–3, 90–1
  requirements for 5
spatial view neurons 176
spatial working memory, children 111–13
Spelke, Elizabeth 102
Squire, Larry 123, 141
Standardised Road-Map Test of
    Direction Sense 225
sulci 117
sun, navigation by 1–2
Swanson, Larry, Brain Architecture 118
sympathetic nervous system 116
synaptic plasticity 173

T-maze 36–8
  role of hippocampus 130–1
target approximation 67
target location, estimation of 75–6
Taube, Jeffrey 192, 212
taxi drivers 181–2
  hippocampus in 185–8
taxon space 126, 127

taxonomy 66–7
telencephalon 118
temporal lobe 117
thalamus 118
  anterior dorsal 197, 198, 216
  lateral dorsal 197
The Forgetting: A Portrait of Alzheimer's 224
theta rhythm 128, 174–5
  phase precession 174
  and spatial learning 174
thigmotaxis 44, 134
Titchener, Edward 10
Tolman, Edward Chase 9
  spatial learning 20–6
Tolstoy, Leo, The Snow Storm 5
topographical disorientation 4, 240–9
topological space 94
transentorhinal region 231, 233
triangle completion tasks 76–82
  animals 79
  blind people 70–2
  in virtual space 80–1
triangulation 76

veering 67–73
vicarious trial and error 28, 172
virtual space
  landmarks in 81–2
  simulator sickness 81
  triangle completion 80–1

walking in circles 67–73
water maze 38–43
Watson, John 10, 14–17
Watson's maze 14–17
wayfinding 66–7
  aided 67
  Alzheimer's disease patients 224–31
  children 107–11
  circling and veering 67–73
  directed 67
  distance estimation 73–5
  estimate of target location 75–6
  invisible target 73–5
  unaided 67
  undirected 67
Weschler Adult Intelligence Test 90
Whishaw, Ian 52
Wood, Emma 168, 217
Wundt, Wilhelm 9–10

Yerkes, Robert 20

Zinyuk, Larissa 38, 208